PHOG

PHOG

The Most Influential Man in Basketball

Scott Morrow Johnson

FOREWORD BY JUDY ALLEN MORRIS

University of Nebraska Press
LINCOLN AND LONDON

Material from the Allen Family Archives and
Forrest C. Allen personal letters used by permission
of Judy Allen Morris and the Allen family.

Library of Congress Cataloging-in-Publication Data
Names: Johnson, Scott Morrow.
Title: Phog: the most influential man in
basketball / Scott Morrow Johnson;
foreword by Judy Allen Morris.
Description: Lincoln: University of
Nebraska Press, 2016. | Includes
bibliographical references and index.
Identifiers: LCCN 2016022204 (print)
LCCN 2016027476 (ebook)
ISBN 9780803285712 (hardback: alkaline paper)
ISBN 9781496217059 (paper: alkaline paper)
ISBN 9780803295391 (epub)
ISBN 9780803295407 (mobi)
ISBN 9780803295414 (pdf)
Subjects: LCSH: Allen, Forrest C., 1885–1974. |
Basketball coaches—United States—Biography.
| BISAC: sports & recreation / Basketball. |
Biography & Autobiography / Sports. | History /
United States / State & Local / Midwest (IA, IL,
IN, KS, MI, MN, MO, ND, NE, OH, SD, WI).
Classification: LCC GV884.A44 J65 2016 (print) |
LCC GV884.A44 (ebook) | DDC796.323092 [B]—dc23
LC record available at https://lccn.loc.gov/2016022204

Set in Lyon by John Klopping.
Designed by N. Putens.

"Apologies for one's work are worthless.
It either justifies itself or it does not."

PHOG ALLEN, 1937

CONTENTS

FOREWORD

Judy Allen Morris

He knew me before I formally knew him. My parents took a brief trip and left me with my grandparents for a week when I was six months old. Evidently, my demeanor was a bit demanding and deafening at bedtime. When writing to my Uncle Frank about me, my grandfather would explain that my distraught grandmother would bring me to him and he would perform magic. His explanation was, "I put her head in my left hand and used my right arm and hand to support her back and gave her a general manipulative treatment along the spine, just stretching intervertebral segments. It was not 10 minutes before she took deep breaths and slept for 3 hours."

Little did I know then that these treatments were the result of a passion that he had since his own childhood. I benefited from the skills he started learning while performing the duties of his mother, who died at a young age, leaving six sons for his father to care for. Always a nutritionist by nature, he planned the meals and included vitamins, natural foods, and some unusual combinations. I'm not sure what horehounds were, but he freely passed them out to my friends—who tried them once and never-more! I was more familiar with his breakfast routine, which I could hear him undertaking when I spent the night. It consisted of raw eggs, milk, ice, and lemon. No, I never felt inclined to partake of it, but maybe it was the inspiration for the character Rocky. His favorite responsibility was to provide ways to heal the injuries, sore muscles, and other ailments of his very athletic brood of brothers.

His name was Dr. Forrest C. Allen, my grandfather, a man whom I adored. Those who knew him well called him Doc. Everyone else knew him by his unique nickname, Phog. Many know about the coach and his influence and successes in basketball. Few know the history of the man and the other life that ran parallel. My grandfather was not a one-dimensional man.

My mom and dad decided to return to Lawrence from Russell, Kansas, where my dad, Milton "Mitt" Allen, had worked in the oilfields and played basketball for the Phillips Petroleum semipro basketball team. Dad had been accepted and enrolled in the university's school of law. We moved into a cottage, half a block from the home where my grandparents raised six children—three girls and three boys. They were all living elsewhere by then but returned frequently with my cousins in tow. It was always great fun to have a gathering of all. The older of the cousins were responsible for naming our grandparents, "Mimi" and "Phoggie." As Phog became more and more noteworthy, I think we all loved the feeling of a very close connection to him by using this term of endearment.

He was a grandchild's dream—the best of storytellers, a master of creating fun, a healer of "ow-ies," a magician who could pull nickels from your ears, a teacher of life skills and good manners.

He had a love of teaching athletics, exemplified by a summer program he initiated through his position as the director of the University of Kansas (KU) physical education department. It was an evening summer playground, open to all children of grade-school age. There were a number of supervised games, lots of equipment for physical development or just fun, dancing activities, and music. The laughter, singing, and participation were a testimony of an evening of good, wholesome fun for parents as well as their children. I was proud to be among them.

At the age of three, when the University of Kansas basketball games were played in the old Hoch Auditorium on campus, the only way to the court from the seats was down long ramps. At the sound of the game-ending horn, my folks would cut me loose and away I went to join my Phoggie on the court. He was always welcoming and patient, allowing me to meet and listen. It was so exciting and fun to behold, especially when players remained on the court. During that 1940 season, I joined my family at Municipal Auditorium in Kansas City to watch the NCAA championship game between Indiana and my Jayhawks that helped launch the NCAA tournament into what it is today. I have a picture of me taken during the game. I am sitting on the railing in the loge seating, using a technique that I have utilized all my life: mouth wide open, yelling at the officials. It's in the genes!

By this age, I truly considered myself the luckiest girl in the world and at the same time felt the pressure of being the special man's granddaughter. The words were never spoken, but I felt that I always had to excel to meet expectations.

One of my most memorable experiences was when I was invited to join both Mimi and Phoggie in the ceremony that would induct him into the Missouri Hall of Fame, along with his longtime friend, Casey Stengel, in 1952. They enjoyed the reunion so very much. I couldn't wait to tell my friends. And then came the trip back to Lawrence. My grandfather was always competing and he never met a speed limit he couldn't beat! I prayed as I lay on the back seat. Never a dull moment with that guy.

The memories are still vivid, even to this day. For me as well as for his players, Phoggie was so much more than just a basketball coach, and I wanted the world to get a true picture of this multifaceted man. When his players went to war, he wrote to them every week. He really cared about his players, about all of his guys. He taught them manners. He taught them about centrifugal force when they were on the train. He just wanted to share everything he could. He was always educating, whether it was health-wise or basketball-wise.

He had a statue in front of the fieldhouse—whatever. That wasn't the essence of the man. I wanted people to understand what a people person he was. He was a deacon of the church; I remember one man who came up to me once and told me, "I never missed church when I knew your grandfather was speaking because I knew I'd be inspired." He had that ability. He was on the draft board, was in politics. He was so involved in life, in the community. Those were all the reasons I thought he was special. That's part of what made him special to me.

About twenty years ago, I was approached by a man named Arthur McClure, a KU graduate who wanted to do a book about my grandfather. Arthur and I became instant buddies. His wife's name was Judy and we had all these things in common; it just clicked. We really hit it off. I, up to that point, had never thought of how important it would be to get Phog's story out there. I didn't know whether there were enough people out there who would remember him.

Arthur did a wonderful job of researching my grandfather's life, and he had put a rough draft together and gotten someone who was interested in publishing it. He was planning to go to a book convention in Las Vegas, and then he was diagnosed with pancreatic cancer and couldn't go. He was gone in two months. It hit him like a huge wave. The book never got made.

There were others who approached me about writing a book, but nothing ever seemed to work out. I kept nosing around for someone who might want to figure it all out and put it together. I really wanted to get something out before I died.

Lo and behold, late in the year 2013, a dear friend from our college days and I met over lunch and I learned that her son was a sportswriter. They came to Lawrence, I met Scott, and the book finally found its author.

In the late 1920s, Phog recruited an Oklahoma phenom named "Skinny" Johnson, who not only became a two-time All-American and a member of the basketball Hall of Fame but lived with my grandparents while doing so. In later years, Phog referred to this young man as the best athlete he ever coached—and that's counting a plethora of great players.

"Skinny" Johnson is the grandfather of this book's author, Scott Morrow Johnson, to whom I owe a huge sense of gratitude for making my dream come true.

ACKNOWLEDGMENTS

First and foremost, I would like to thank Judy Allen Morris for her memories, for her entertaining stories, and for her diligent assistance compiling information about her amazing grandfather. I'm sure Phoggie would be incredibly proud of the time and effort that she has put in over the years to get this book made.

I'd also like to thank the Allen family and former KU players, like Clyde Lovellette, Bill Hougland, Bill Lienhard, and Jerry Waugh, for sharing their stories about Doc Allen.

Thanks also go out to my grandfather, William "Skinny" Johnson, for his ties to the Phog legend and for whatever help he provided from above in bringing Judy and me together. And, of course, I'd like to thank my parents, Fran and Bill, for encouraging me to follow my dreams of being a writer and for all their KU stories that helped inspire me to write this book.

PROLOGUE: FROM NAISMITH TO WILT

It was Allen, perhaps more than any man,

who shaped basketball as it is today.

PHOG ALLEN'S OBITUARY IN THE *KANSAS CITY STAR*

The old man is dying now. His shining light has gone dim. Month by month, week by week, minute by minute, his time is running out.

It's a few weeks before the season opener for the University of Kansas basketball team, which practices a few miles away. While a coach named Ted Owens is preparing his team for a challenging 1972–73 season that will see the Jayhawks try to replace leading scorer Bud Stallworth and his school-record 25.3 points a game, an elderly man is sitting quietly in his house at 831 Louisiana, hidden in the shadows a full generation after coaching his last game. He's alone now, except for a nurse who represents one of his few outlets to the outside world. He's wearing a bright yellow sweater, its hue not that far from the canary handkerchiefs he used to fold up inside the pocket of the beige suit-coats that he wore on game days thirty years earlier. Under the yellow sweater, he wears pajamas. He's wrapped a Turkish blanket around his neck, in much the same way he used to wear towels when he was the one leading KU basketball practices. He's sitting in a chair now, his walker nearby, his legs covered with a blanket to protect them from the chill of a Midwestern winter that seeps through the cracks of his modest house.

A writer representing the *Kansas City Star* magazine has entered his home, hoping to relive the good old days but also curious about what has become of the legendary figure who once stood taller than the Campanile Tower on the University of Kansas campus. Phog Allen reaches out a welcoming hand and shows a surprisingly firm grip. He is about to celebrate his eighty-seventh birthday—if "celebrating" is the proper way to describe this time of one's life. The longtime KU basketball coach chats with the writer for a few minutes, mostly about basketball and the old days. Professional basketball has become a mainstream sport now, even over in nearby Kansas City, where a relocated National Basketball Association franchise just began play. The United States's thirty-six-year run of Olympic domination in the sport came to an end a few weeks earlier. The University of Kentucky basketball coach, a legendary figure whom the old man knows very well, has just been forced into retirement because of a law requiring state workers to retire at the age of seventy. A guy named Endacott has been included in the latest Hall of Fame class. There's plenty of fodder for conversation.

Eventually the old man is asked whether he has any advice for a young basketball coach. His blue eyes flicker, much like a film projector as he stares out into the space of his past. The old man has been largely forgotten by the game he helped to bring to unexpected popularity, and yet decades of memories are still within him, somewhere behind those piercing blue eyes.

And then he speaks in a measured tone, his voice that was once compared to a foghorn now dripping out of him in something just above a whisper.

"There are so few coaches who succeed in proportion to those who fail that I wouldn't advise a young coach to become a coach," the elderly Phog Allen says.

Somewhere, the father of basketball, the man who taught Phog Allen the game, is chuckling inside his grave. James Naismith had given a young man named Forrest Allen similar advice almost seventy years earlier. Some people never learn.

Bill Self is, befitting to his surname, a self-made man. His annual contract of nearly $5 million to coach the University of Kansas basketball team is a product of hard work, dedication to his craft, and a keen eye for the game. He began as an underpaid assistant coach at Kansas and Oklahoma State before working his way up to one of the top jobs in all of college basketball, and by 2014, Self was making more in a month or two than longtime KU coach Forrest "Phog" Allen made over the entirety of his thirty-nine years coaching the Jayhawks.

Self's comparatively high net worth has a lot to do with inflation, but more than anything, his financial rewards have been dictated by the monstrous growth of a multibillion-dollar sport that was created 123 years earlier as a recreational activity meant to be played in warm, cramped gymnasiums on frigid winter afternoons. Coaching, and playing, basketball had become lucrative careers over the years—more so than James Naismith could have ever imagined.

But those who coach rarely get into the profession for the dollars. John Wooden saw coaching as a way to stay in the game when his playing skills had begun to diminish; his first jobs in the profession came while teaching English at high schools in Dayton, Kentucky, and then South Bend, Indiana. Bob Knight started as a junior varsity coach and high school teacher in Cuyahoga Falls, Ohio, before the U.S. Military Academy in West Point, New York, offered him a college coaching job at a modest salary, when Knight was just twenty-four years old. Knight's most famous player there, Mike Krzyzewski, took his first coaching job at West Point as a way to fulfill the requirement of five years of postgraduate military service.

Longtime college basketball coach Roy Williams began his coaching career at Charles D. Owen High School in Swannanoa, North Carolina, where he taught classes, led the varsity basketball and golf teams, served as an assistant on the football team, held the post of athletic director, and sponsored the junior-senior prom—eventually earning him an annual paycheck of $16,000, just above the median U.S. salary in 1978. Williams gladly gave that job up for a huge pay cut—to $2,750 per year—when University of North Carolina basketball coach Dean Smith offered him a job as an assistant coach.

By 2015, the NCAA landscape included more than thirty coaches who were clearing $1 million annually. Wichita State University, fresh off an NCAA tournament win over Self's Jayhawks, rewarded coach Gregg Marshall with a $3-million-a-year deal. But for every Marshall, Krzyzewski, and Self, thousands of men and women at the high school and college levels were struggling just to make ends meet. It's a profession that carries incredible stress, unrelenting hours, and unforgiving job security. The public scrutiny is merciless, which is why Williams likes to quip, "The way I see it, the two easiest jobs in the world are golf course superintendent and being a coach—because everybody knows how to do it better than you do."

So why do it?

"At the very base level," longtime Duke basketball coach Mike Krzyzewski said in 2014, "it's because you love the game and you love to teach, and you love to do it year after year with a new group. It's a pretty exciting life."

When Forrest "Phog" Allen was in college more than a century ago, there were no such things as full-time basketball coaches. The sport was typically played by a club of young players who had a thirst for competition and some free time. Even Allen's first "coaches"—William O'Brien at Independence High School in Missouri, and then James Naismith at the University of Kansas—were little more than facilitators, spending most of their time officiating games and devoting hardly any available minutes to working on fundamentals. Naismith loathed the concept of any man coaching the sport he invented and once tried to talk Phog Allen out of trying to make a career out of it.

But Allen, who never made more than twelve thousand dollars a year during his half century in the game, was never the kind of person to take no for an answer. From his days as a weekend boxer at carnivals to his post-retirement battles with the NCAA, Allen was always fighting for something. Widely recognized as the first full-time basketball coach, Phog exuded passion and a drive for competition that was respected by his players but often misunderstood by outsiders. Allen pushed the "boys" who played for him and occasionally belittled officials, but his sideline demeanor rarely crossed the line.

On one such occasion, Allen was coaching a game against the hated Tigers of the University of Missouri in the late 1940s when his competitive fire blazed beyond control. Missouri was coached by a young upstart who had never previously been a part of the KU rivalry, and things got so heated in the second half of the game that Phog Allen told his opposing coach to "get off the court." The Tigers coach responded by raising a fist and heading toward Allen . . .

The following day, Allen found himself in a hospital bed, preparing to relinquish his coaching duties.

Allen's rise to coaching stardom was overshadowed by his unexpected fall toward obscurity, and over the years even his impact as a basketball pioneer has mostly faded into the shadows. While James Naismith invented the sport, Phog Allen brought it to the masses. His career path rarely took him outside of the one-hundred-mile corridor between Northeastern Kansas and Central Missouri, but Allen's influence spread across the globe and still continues to provide opportunities almost a half century after he took his final breath.

Not just a coach but also a visionary, Allen may well have had a greater impact on the game than men like Naismith, Wooden, and Jordan. His shaping of the sport, and of society as a whole, has not always been appreciated as the years have passed. Part of this had to do with timing, as Allen grew up in the shadow of a man who went on to become a U.S. president and spent his formative years coaching under the eye of the game's inventor. Even his retirement was somewhat overlooked at the time, thanks to the arrival of a basketball player so great that he immediately stole the spotlight in and around Kansas.

But Allen's fade into something like obscurity on the landscape of basketball legends may have more to do with the passage of time than simply with timing.

As basketball legend Bill Walton said when asked in 2015 about the lack of understanding of the Phog Allen era of the game, "all those guys [who witnessed it] are dead."

Those who knew Allen in his heyday would have described him as a man of two faces. He burned plenty of bridges and earned a reputation for being stubbornly opinionated but was also beloved by his players. As longtime friend Knute Rockne once joked, "there are two crazy people in the United States—and Phog Allen is both of them!" The *Sporting News* summed him up by writing, "You just can't be neutral about 'Phog' Allen. You either like him or can't stand him, and that's all right with him as there's nothing neutral about him, either."

Phog Allen served as basketball's bridge from Naismith to Wilt, and he left his fingerprints on just about every major innovation in the sport during the first half of the twentieth century. Those basketball fans who recognize his name know only that Allen was a coaching legend, and it's a badge he would undoubtedly wear with pride. But his legacy should go beyond that.

This is his story.

PHOG

1

Running from Independence

Forrest was on the run. Feet pounding dirt. Sweat glistening off his bare chest on a sweltering Missouri day. It was the dawn of a new century, and Forrest Allen was in love.

The teenager was on his daily run through the town of Independence, Missouri, basking in a routine designed to get his body into shape. Out on these dirt roads of his hometown, Forrest could be alone with his thoughts. Maybe his father was right. Perhaps the cigarettes and the rabble-rousing were sending him down a dead-end street. If Forrest was going to make something of his life, he was going to have to start now.

Maybe the game was the thing that could save him. Basket ball. It had become his first true love, integrating itself into his every thought. And to master the game, Forrest would need to build up the temple of his body. On and on he ran, his heart pounding in the swell of the Missouri heat.

In a sense, Forrest was always running toward something. In front of him was a future only Allen himself could see, pulling him forward with visionary strength. The comforting aroma of elm and cottonwood trees filled the air of Midwestern summer as he ran. The new century swelled with opportunity, and young Forrest was stubbornly beating a path toward greatness.

He ran down Delaware Street, past the Sawyer family mansion on the corner, took a left on Maple Street and on past the First Presbyterian Church. Past the Bank of Independence building and the massive court-house, with its concrete pillars rising up like four adjacent towers. He took another left at the soda fountain where that Truman kid served phosphates on the weekend and a right at the Jackson County jailhouse. He trampled on, down the winding hill toward the southern part of his hometown, his heart pumping and his new shoes kicking up dirt as he jogged the unpaved roads alongside the fields, through the blazing summer heat of eastern Jackson County. On and on he ran, with only his thoughts and the blazing sunlight, alone out in the farmlands at the edge of town.

Beads of perspiration swelled upon his forehead and trickled down the smooth skin of his round face. His chest protruded forward; his fists were balled in a fighter's grip. The sandy hair atop Forrest's head held remarkably firm in place, the well-crafted part on the left side of his scalp gathering sunlight across a sliver of pink skin.

The clacking sound of horse hooves cut through the peaceful silence. As Forrest continued his pace, a man's voice startled him from behind. He slowed and turned to see a horse-drawn buggy pulling up alongside him. Atop the buggy was one of the town's richest residents, a landowner named R. Frank Milton, whose 320-acre plot and beautiful country home were the envy of every man in Independence. Milton slowed his horses to an easy gait. Their clacking hooves whispered to a halt. Forrest paused, his hands on bare hips, and looked up at the man.

"Why are you running?" Milton asked, looking down at the shirtless teenaged boy in the running shorts. "Where are you headed?"

"I'm running to the spring, about five miles from here," Forrest responded breathlessly, "for a drink of water."

Frank Milton scoffed, disgusted by the sight of a boy without a shirt on the roads of Independence. He ordered the horses to reassume their gallop. "You," Milton said scornfully, refusing to look back as he passed the shirtless boy, "are a disgraceful sight."

The horse and buggy paraded off into the distance that lay out in front of him, and Forrest Allen kept on. He couldn't afford to stop. He had to stay in shape. He had to stay ahead of the competition. He wanted to be the best basket baller he could be.

What Forrest probably knew at the time was that he would see Frank Milton again; in a town of six thousand people, it was impossible not to.

What he couldn't have known at the time was that he was about to fall in love again, in love with something other than basket ball. He was going to fall in love with R. Frank Milton's eldest daughter.

The America into which Forrest Clare Allen was born on November 18, 1885, was still battling itself, in conflict with what it was and with what it hoped to be, a full two decades after the conclusion of the civil war. He was a Missourian by birth, born to William and Mary Allen in the northwest part of the Midwestern state, but Allen's bloodlines traced back to a group of Scots-Irishmen known as "Borderers," a defiant band of loyalists who had made land runs from Scotland to Northern Ireland and on to the eastern part of the United States before settling in the American South in the mid-nineteenth century. A fiercely stubborn people whose fighting spirit developed during their century-long rise from peasantry, the Scots-Irish were known for their fearless insolence to authority as well as their tenacious disdain for the status quo.

Allen's grandparents on both sides eventually settled into Virginia, where each of his grandfathers served as Confederate soldiers in the civil war; John Wesley Perry, his grandfather on his mother's side, fought under Gen. Robert E. Lee. In the post–civil war years, many family members continued the generational migration westward from Virginia, to a part of the United States that was caught in its own inner battles.

By the time Allen's father, William, arrived in Missouri in 1871, the Border War between Missouri and neighboring Kansas was ablaze in the heartland, the hatred still simmering from the murderous rampage eight years earlier by a man named William Quantrill and his Missouri gang against a liberal group of Kansas rebels known as the "Jayhawkers." When Quantrill and his men crossed the border to pillage the Kansas town of Lawrence in 1863, killing more than 150 men and boys while setting fire to buildings, they drove a burning stake into the interstate border that would continue to smolder for more than a century.

A nineteen-year-old Virginian named William Allen would ride into Missouri from Virginia's Carroll County eight years later, arriving as one of the thirty original settlers in the town of Jameson, Missouri. He soon began working as town constable and clerk. Eventually, Allen would be recognized as the town's first physician and owner of the only drug store in Jameson. By the time he turned twenty-five years old in 1877, William had impregnated an eighteen-year-old woman named Mary Elexzene Perry and married her. Together, they began a family with the birth of son Homer Perry Allen, in March 1877. Sons Elmer and Harry followed before Forrest came into the world, kicking and screaming like any well-respecting Scots-Irishman, in November 1885. Forrest Clare Allen was born in an unincorporated farm town ten miles east of Jameson called Jamesport. He was the fourth child in a family that would eventually include six boys and would go on to settle down in Independence, Missouri, a community of about six thousand people where the six Allen boys would spend most of their formative years.

Independence was the kind of community where families gathered around a large table for nightly supper before spilling into a summer evening to wrap themselves in the company of a neighbor's porch, which would be lit only by the moon or an occasional gas lamp in a window after sunset. Names and faces brought a comfortable recognition, as it wasn't difficult to notice the out-of-towners who filed in by the dozens for weekend shopping at Independence Square. At the center of town, the square offered a popular soda fountain where teenagers could congregate around malts and phosphate sodas as well as an enormous courthouse, complete with rising stone pillars, which resonantly marked the heart of Independence. Residents looking for a change of scenery could venture east to Kansas City, just a ten-mile trolley ride away, where taverns and shops and the country's second-most busy train stockyards provided entertainment.

Despite its hospitable veneer, Independence was a town also steeped with the stubborn pride of its southern traditions. The Northwest Missouri hamlet featured a part of town known as "Nigger Neck," where most of the "colored" citizens, many of whom had endured slavery earlier in their lives, took up residence. It was a town where Quantrill's men were known to hide out three decades earlier, after runs across the Kansas border to pillage small towns and set fire to homes of the liberal Jayhawkers. By the time the Allen family moved there as the 1880s rolled into the 1890s, the town of Independence still hosted Quantrill reunions for surviving members of the gang's infamous Lawrence Massacre.

While the growing metropolis of Kansas City was considered progressive, Independence was steadfastly stuck in its southern roots. Perhaps these values were what led Forrest Allen off to other places, for despite his loyalty he was never one to settle for the status quo.

William T. Allen, Forrest's father, was a bit of a progressive thinker in his own right. A bookkeeper and salesman who also farmed his own land, William used his entrepreneurial skills in finding creative ways to bring in money. He was known to take his boys—Homer, Elmer, Harry (who went by the nickname Pete), Forrest, Hubert, and Richard—from one county fair to the next, signing them up for boxing matches to help supplement the family savings. Using the pseudonym Pug Allen to remain somewhat anonymous, young Forrest would pull on his gloves—reluctantly at first, though in time he grew to love the sport—and climb into the ring, weekend after weekend. The taste of his own blood came to fuel a competitive fire within him, one that drove Forrest toward something that only sport could provide. He became a quite proficient boxer, and as a basketball coach later in his life, Forrest would use the sport to help develop the hand-eye coordination and footwork of his players. The carnival scene also unearthed a showman side to young Forrest's personality, and his gift for publicity and promotion would be a big part of his career as a coach and flag-bearer for the sport of basketball in years to come.

In Independence, the Allen family lived a Midwestern life of daily chores and constant activity within a budding community where neighbors shared cherry pie and fresh-picked fruit. While Mary Allen, the boys' young mother, kept house, the Allen boys played all sorts of games out back, developing a healthy thirst for competition and the inner passion to win at all costs. Baseball was an early favorite among the Allen boys, who were known to invite neighbors over for spirited games. Before long, young Forrest gained such acumen for baseball that he began serving as an umpire at games played in and around Independence. Forrest Allen quickly became known around town for his big, booming voice while calling balls and strikes. Not overly intimidating in physical stature, young Forrest carried an unexpected volume that soon earned him a nickname on the baseball circuit. The voice was reminiscent of a foghorn, and before long people in and around Independence were calling him "Fog"—although it would be a few years before a young newspaper reporter in Lawrence, Kansas, named Ward "Pinhead" Coble would change up the spelling to give the nickname a little pizzazz.

The boys' father earned his own nickname in those days, thanks in large part to the bevy of athletic endeavors that left him constantly shopping for his kids' footwear. "Shoe" Allen, as Forrest's father William came to be called, was known around town for the grocery store he owned on Market Street. The elder Allen employed young Forrest as a clerk at the Haines-Allen Grocery Company, where Forrest Allen often daydreamed about swinging a bat or catching a football or shooting a free throw. Shoe Allen supported his sons' passion for athletics but didn't believe a career in sports was a worthy endeavor. He was especially cynical about young Forrest's prospects in the working world and sometimes scoffed at the boy's talk about earning a living in athletics. Forrest had spent part of his youth running with a bad crowd and seemed without true direction. William Allen couldn't have seen it at the time, but basketball, known in those years as basket ball, became the driving force that would provide young Forrest with a pathway toward adulthood.

By the turn of the century, the Allen boys had taken to the sport, partly because it required a minimum of five players, meaning the six Allen brothers could field a team of their own—with one sub. The Allen Brothers Basket Ball Team was formed, complete with wool uniforms featuring the letter A and the number signifying each brother's birth order inside a circle on the front; Phog wore the A4 jersey, as the fourth-born. Phog and Pete—four years Phog's elder and wearing jersey A3—towered over their smaller brothers, even the oldest two, Homer (A1) and Elmer (A2). The Allen Brothers would challenge all comers at an old livery barn on the family's property, even taking on college teams if they dared. One brother, Hubert, would brag in later years that the Allen Brothers lost only one game in the five years they played together. Older brother Pete was the tallest and strongest of the Allen boys, and he quickly developed a knack for the game. But it was Forrest who would become the basketball star of the family over time.

At Independence High School, where a sign above the door welcomed students with a Latin phrase that translated to "youth, the hope of the world," Forrest Allen was an unremarkable student who took a liking to a teacher named George Bryant. Mr. Bryant taught his students a sleeping technique that involved reading poetry before bed. Allen became a better sleeper because of it and also learned to appreciate the works of John Keats, John Milton, and Virgil. He fell in love with an Ernest Thayer poem about a burly baseball player from Mudville who wanted one big whack in an important at-bat. The 1888 poem "Casey at the Bat" is about the slugger's inability to deliver a hit when called upon in the clutch. Allen could relate to the idea of an athlete looking for a chance to shine; he was a three-sport star at Independence High, where he played third base in baseball, end in football, and forward in basketball, all for a coach named W. J. O'Brien. Allen kept himself in shape by working summer jobs—he spent one summer in Texas working as a railroad axe man and in a lumber mill—and also by running the streets of his hometown. He was on one such run when Forrest ran into R. Frank Milton, who turned out to be the father of an Independence High classmate named Bessie Milton.

Bessie was two years Forrest's junior, a small girl whom he recognized from church. Forrest didn't know much about her other than the starkness of her charcoal eyes and dark, curly hair, and over time her beauty would cause his heart to flutter. What he didn't know at the time was that Bessie Evalina Milton, like Forrest himself, also had deep Confederate roots, having been part of a family that had retreated from war-torn Virginia in favor of the tranquility of Missouri following the civil war. According to family lore, one cousin was even known to have run with Quantrill's band of rebels back in the day. Bessie's father, Robert Frank Milton, had twenty cents in his pocket when he arrived from Virginia as a teenager. He found work as a farm laborer, making fifteen dollars a month while learning the trade. By the age of twenty-four, he had saved up enough money to purchase a small farm near Wellington, Missouri, where he planted a crop of wheat before returning to Virginia in an effort to woo his high school sweetheart to join him in the Midwest. Elizabeth Myers agreed to accompany Frank Milton on his return trip to Missouri, and her family was so upset that they effectively disowned her; when Elizabeth wrote to her family from Missouri, her letters went without response. She eventually married Frank Milton, whose prodigious wheat fields helped build up a small fortune. Frank and Elizabeth Milton started a family, and by the time Bessie was born, the Miltons were among the wealthiest families in all of Independence. Frank Milton's property on Lee's Summit Road boasted 420 acres of land—the largest acreage in town. Bessie's father was also a very proud man, and he made it known that he did not want his daughter hanging around with a "rascal" like Forrest Allen.

Bessie Milton was a popular student at Independence High School, where her friends included another girl who shared her first name. Bessie Wallace was an athletic classmate who surprised her friends when she began dating an older boy with a serious nature and a thirst for politics, a boy by the name of Harry Truman. While Truman would one day become U.S. president, his future first lady spent a good part of her teen years competing in sports. Basketball was one of Bessie Wallace's favorite sports, and she played on a girls' team that was coached by a classmate named Forrest Allen; it was believed to be his first time coaching basketball at any level. (Harry Truman and Forrest Allen weren't known to be close friends in those years, but Truman would go on to maintain correspondence, on White House stationary, with Forrest's older brother Pete after taking office in 1944.)

Over time, Forrest Allen's heart was swamped by the other Bessie, Bessie Milton, and his pursuit of her was requited in the years that followed. Her wealthy father was so upset that, according to family lore, he once offered his daughter an all-expenses-paid trip around the world if she would promise not to marry Forrest. But Frank Milton's financial incentives were no match for love. In the years that followed, the daughter of the wealthy landowner who had once called Forrest Allen "a disgraceful sight," would grow to love the boy with the strange nickname.

Forrest Allen's other main pursuit during his teenage years was on the basketball court, where he hoped to follow in the footsteps of older brother Pete. The tallest of the Allen boys at just about six feet tall, Harry "Pete" Allen had joined a local team called the Woodsmen and later became a top player for the Kansas City Athletic Club team, which played about ten miles west of the boys' hometown. Pete Allen would go on to become one of the first basketball players at the University of Kansas, and little brother Forrest would on occasion make the sixty-mile trip to Lawrence to be among the handful of people watching the Jayhawks play.

Forrest soon followed his brother's path to the Kansas City Athletic Club, where he would quickly emerge as the best player on his team. He spent countless hours honing his shot at the family home in Independence and soon became known as one of the most dead-eye free-throw shooters in the Kansas City area—an especially important skill in those days because fouls were called for things like turnovers and dribbling violations as well as overly physical play. It was at the KC Athletic Club that Forrest's love for the sport of basketball deepened. He ended up joining a team called the Blue Diamonds and soon became the star forward, designated free-throw shooter, and team manager. Forrest Allen was such an accomplished player that he drew the eye of a spectacled, academic-looking man with a mustache and sandy hair parted in the middle, a man who spent weekends at the KCAC refereeing games.

Forrest knew the man well, for he was not only one of the Athletic Club's most popular referees but also the coach of the University of Kansas basketball team, for which his older brother Pete played.

The man introduced himself to others as Jim, and in time he would approach young Forrest with an offer he couldn't refuse.

2

The "World's Championship"

The doors were open. The cool air was rushing in, the wind howling and hail pelting the sidewalks. The nineteen-year-old, who was both player and promoter, could see some movement through the open doorways that led out to 13th Street, but he didn't have any idea whether there would be nine people or nine hundred when the game was to begin. He'd done all he could to put the game together—to secure the funds, bring in the opponent, and find the venue—and now all that was left was the competition.

But his curiosity was getting the better of him. As the other players warmed up around him, on the cold concrete floor of Convention Hall, he craned his neck to get a view of hallways that led to the entrance doors of the indoor arena. He'd dreamed of this game for months, and now here it was, on display for all to see. Here was his chance to play against the best team in the world. A chance to be a champion. This was his chance to be the hero.

None of it, however, would matter if the fans didn't come out. The last thing he wanted was for this game to be the proverbial tree in the forest. He'd done everything he could to make this game a success, and he couldn't bear the thought of coming up short.

A cool breeze wafted into the arena from an open door. A few fans began trickling in, finding seats around the court. A ball bounced off the edge of the basket and rolled across the cool concrete, toward the center of the court. The time was near. He felt the weight of the moment descend like a dark cloud.

And then he thought of her. He closed his eyes. She was up there somewhere. Was she looking down on him? Would he make her proud?

The autumn of 1904 came rushing at Forrest Allen with the unrelenting force of a cyclone. He was just beginning his senior year at Independence High School, and all of his free time was being filled working at the Haines-Allen Grocery Company on West Maple or playing basketball for the Blue Diamonds or refereeing games at the Kansas City Athletic Club a few miles from his hometown.

The Athletic Club was so fiercely competitive that young Forrest became obsessed with finding out just how good his Kansas City basketball players were. He'd heard about a YMCA team from Buffalo, New York, that was riding an incredible winning streak and beating opponents by margins of 80 or 90 points; the team had once defeated Hobart College with the unimaginable score of 134-0. The Buffalo team was so good that some people in the basketball community believed it to be unbeatable. Allen knew better. No team could be invincible, and nineteen-year-old Forrest Allen—young, healthy, and impervious—believed he had the squad to give the boys from Buffalo quite a challenge.

Ever the dreamer, Forrest began envisioning just such a game. The sport of basketball was still in its early stages and had limited precedent in holding championship events. The Amateur Athletic Union had held its first "national" tournament that year, but travel costs kept the competition to a small number of teams that were exclusively based on the East Coast. And what was supposed to be the recent "debut" of basketball as an Olympic sport failed to include any squads from outside the United States.

Of course, the German YMCA team from Buffalo, New York, had emerged as champions in both the AAU and Olympic tournaments. If Forrest was going to include his Kansas City team in any type of basketball championship, it would surely have to be against the squad from Buffalo.

The seeds of such a game were just being planted when the world came falling down upon Forrest with the weight of flooding waters. On December 4, 1904, Forrest Allen's mother, Mary, a forty-six-year-old homemaker who had spent much of her adult life raising Forrest and his five brothers, passed away suddenly at the family home at 208 North Union Street in Independence. An obituary in the *Jackson Examiner* announced that "Mrs. Mary E. Allen, wife of W. T. Allen, died Saturday morning. . . . Mrs. Allen was born in Shelby County, Mo., in 1858 and had lived in Independence for 17 years." No cause of death was mentioned, and it became lost over the years that followed, as no permanent record remains of how Mary Elexzene Allen's life came to an end. Nor did son Forrest keep any public record of the event or its effect on him. Forrest was nineteen years old at the time, and his world had been dealt a tragic blow that would appear to leave lasting impacts on several facets of his life. He assumed a maternal role in the weeks that followed while tending to two younger brothers who still lived at home. He became somewhat obsessed with health and with the power of healing, and it's conceivable that he also dropped out of school around this time, as although Forrest Allen would later list 1905 as the year he graduated from high school, there is no record of him ever earning a diploma.

Allen was best able to cope with his grief through basketball. Whether it was playing the sport, refereeing contests, or just trying to convert people to the game through word of mouth, Forrest Allen found escape from his sorrow.

He continued to play games at the Kansas City Athletic Club and devised a way to prove that his team was one of the best in the world.

A natural showman who had learned the art of publicity from spending many of his weekends on the carnival circuit, Allen took it upon himself to arrange a series that may well have been one of the first matchups of big-time cross-country opponents in basketball history.

The German YMCA of Buffalo was calling itself the national champion, but Allen thought his team was better and knew of only one way to prove it. And so he wrote a letter. Barely nineteen years old and still without a diploma from Independence High School, Forrest Allen sent a telegram intended to attract the Buffalo YMCA team with a three-game series in

Kansas City that he would bill as the first "World's Championship of Basket Ball." He even offered to pay for all of the visiting team's expenses. His persuasive skills were apparently enough that the Buffalo Germans accepted and agreed to travel halfway across the country just to validate their title. Allen, who had to come up with six hundred dollars to get the Germans to Kansas City, had in many ways consummated his first recruiting coup.

Recruiting would turn into one of Allen's many strengths in his later years as a coach, and it wasn't difficult to see why. Even as a nineteen-year-old tenderfoot, he carried a persona that stood larger than his 5'10" frame. He was just an inch above the average height of a man in the early part of the century but appeared taller, with long limbs, wide shoulders, and a posture that led with the chest, like a man who knew where he was going and how to get there. Forrest Allen had a friendly face that drew in strangers with welcoming eyes—crow's feet eyes that introduced his hard features with soft warmth that provided a smile-like charm even when his mouth remained unmoved. He held his chin high but was always careful to look a man in the eye and remember his name—traits that exuded confidence and earned trust.

He also had an obvious gift for gab, which also came off in his well-scripted writing—as the Buffalo Germans could probably attest. His written word convinced the so-called national champions to travel halfway across the country to face some team from Kansas City, sight unseen. But that was only half the battle in Allen's quest to bring the high-profile "championship" series to the Midwest.

Allen couldn't convince the Kansas City Convention Hall, a massive facility that just five years earlier had hosted the Democratic Convention, to take on the three-game series without some kind of financial compensation up front. So Allen had to rely on friends and local bankers to loan him the money to rent it out. He had to pay for construction crews to cut out holes at either end of the floor, fill them with cement, and erect the structure's first basketball goals.

In order to repay the loans, and finance the expenses of the visiting team from Buffalo, Allen would have to sell tickets—more tickets than had ever been sold for a game of basketball in his part of the country. Allen began shamelessly promoting the "World's Championship" series between his

Athletics of the KC Athletic Club and the Germans of the Buffalo, New York, YMCA. Unabashed, he told the *Kansas City Star*, "Should the Athletics win, the victory will mean the greatest boost amateur athletics ever had in Kansas City." Without a doubt, young Forrest Allen was putting a lot at risk. The kid who would go on to become a staunch critic of gambling throughout his coaching career was in effect putting all of his chips on the table.

His hard work, charisma, and stubborn drive paid off in the end, as he secured three consecutive nights in March to hold a winner-take-all series at Convention Hall. Promoting the series was only the beginning for Forrest Allen, who would also be playing for the home team—an eager squad that carried the weight of a city's pride into the unprecedented series.

Allen's importance to the success of the KCAC Athletics couldn't be overstated. He was playing at a time when one player took all of a team's free throws, and during an era when free throws often accounted for a good majority of the scoring. The way the game had been designed, free throws were awarded for turnovers and other mistakes as well as personal fouls. As designated free-throw shooter, Forrest Allen would have the ball in his hands a lot and could easily shoot his Athletics into, or out of, the series.

By then, as a player, Allen had developed a near-flawless routine at the free-throw line that helped spawn his reputation as one of the top goal-scorers in Kansas City. His delivery started with the hands—in Forrest's estimation, the most important body part in terms of basketball success. He would caress the ball gently between his fingertips, setting his feet the same way every time. Allen would take in a deep breath and not exhale until the ball was released. His two-handed, underhand shots would come off his fingers with the same rhythm every time, his hands finishing above his head with arms extended. With remarkable consistency, Allen's shots went through the basket. He was such a deadeye shooter that Allen could even deliver his underhanded shots from thirty-five feet out with uncanny regularity.

But it was going to take a lot more than deft free-throw shooting to take down the Buffalo YMCA team. The Germans had quite a reputation, winning both the AAU championship and the Olympic competition in 1904. They were larger than life in basketball circles, towering over opponents in a figurative sense if not a literal one. The Kansas City locals seemed quite shocked when, on a Sunday morning the day before the first game, the Buffalo players arrived on a train looking anything but Bunyanesque. As the *Kansas City Times* wrote,

> those who saw the team were surprised at the size of the men. None of them weighed over 160 pounds and the majority are of average height. It was reported that the team was made up of small men, but it was not expected that they were such little fellows.

A crowd of about 1,500 people waded through rain, wind, and hail outside for a chance to watch Allen's Kansas City Athletic Club team and the German YMCA team from Buffalo square off for the first game of the series on March 27, 1905. The concrete floors at Convention Hall were hard and cold while the thirteen players—the Athletics had two subs, while the Germans had just one—warmed up and exchanged pregame pleasantries. The national champions from Buffalo came out with a crafty game plan that took young Allen, his brother Pete, and the Athletics by surprise. In a game refereed by a Buffalo player named Philip Dischinger, the visiting team's lone sub, the Germans poked, grabbed, and tripped their way to an early lead. The physical nature of the game came as a shock to the Allen brothers and their Athletic Club teammates. Years later, in one of the three books written by Allen, he would remember the Buffalo Germans as a "rough-and-ready lot." As Allen wrote,

> all the artistry of swinging an adept hand, clutching an opponent's thumb as he rushed by, giving an opposing player a forward tug in order to pull him over and off his feet at the proper time, cleverly slipping an alien foot sideways to push a competitor's rear foot against his front one while he was running and, thereby, causing him to trip and go headlong, and blocking so cleverly at times that the opposition was confounded and blamed itself for being so awkward and so dull, was theirs. Along with them in their bag of tricks they carried all the questionable early basketball strategy available.

The rough play wasn't all that uncommon in an era when basketball games were often conducted on a court surrounded by chicken wire—thus leading to the term "cagers" to describe those who played the sport. Early

1900s basketball, in the words of a twenty-first-century book called *The Undisputed Guide to Pro Basketball*, "more resembled a mixed-martial arts contest performed by a troupe of midgets than a modern basketball game."

But the Buffalo YMCA team was much more than just a bunch of thugs. Using a quick-strike offense and shooting that the *Kansas City Times* called "the most perfect ever seen here," the Germans jumped out to a 23–21 halftime lead. The two teams continued to trade leads throughout the second half, gathering around the center circle for jump balls after each made a basket, with neither side leading by more than three points. "The Kansas City Athletic club's team never played better," the *Times* reported the next day. "Goals were thrown from all kinds of remarkable angles and the men had remarkable speed." At one point, Dischinger—the Buffalo sub who served as referee—called off a KC Athletic Club basket but didn't explain why, causing anger and confusion as the fast-paced second half wound down to its final ten minutes. Buffalo ended up pulling away for a 40–36 win at the end of a game the *Times* called "the most exciting and best played ever seen in Kansas City." The Allen brothers, Pete and Forrest, scored 13 points apiece to account for all but 10 of the Athletics' 36 points in the loss.

When it was over, several Buffalo players admitted that they'd expected a much easier night. The visiting team was quite surprised to find a team that could actually compete with the national champions.

The buzz of Buffalo's narrow win carried over for the second night of the series, which brought in four thousand fans to find a battered and bruised Athletics team. Pete Allen, Forrest's older brother, entered Convention Hall with a swollen jaw. Forrest was battling a sore back that would be a growing problem for him in the coming years. The Athletics were hobbled, and their proverbial backs were against the wall after losing the first game of a three-game series, so Forrest and his ailing teammates were going to have to find a way to survive another night.

Per the original agreement, game two would be officiated by a local fan from Kansas City. He called the game a lot differently, much to the chagrin of the Germans, and Allen's Kansas City team jumped out to an early 10-point lead. The new official was not nearly as tolerant of the physical tactics of the visiting team, and the Athletics led most of the way, eventually hanging on for a 30–28 win. The victory ended Buffalo's months-long winning streak and set up the deciding third game of the first "World's Championship."

With an unofficial championship on the line, the two teams decided a neutral referee would be in the best interest of everyone involved. Forrest Allen knew just the man for the task, and his credentials were unlike those of anyone else in the sport. The forty-three-year-old man named Jim had attended the first two games of the series and watched with a keen eye. Intelligent, level-headed, and inherently neutral, Jim was just the man to serve as referee for the third and deciding game of the series.

The man agreed to officiate and came out of the stands to join the players on the court for the deciding game of the "World's Championship of Basket Ball." Wearing a wool jersey and a small hat, he took the heavy, leather ball in his hands, waiting to throw it up for the opening tip.

Thousands of eyes watched the man named Jim as game three was about to get underway.

His name was James Naismith.

3

A Man Named Jim

The boys were on their way. He could hear their rowdy voices from above, swaggering around the corner onto State Street and toward the balcony entrance to the gym. With the anguish of an expectant father, James Naismith wrung his hands in anticipation. The game he'd created was about to get a test run, and Naismith didn't really know what to expect. He hadn't even yet come up with a name for the game he'd devised over recent weeks. He couldn't possibly have any idea of what would become of it. All he knew at the time was that his boss had instructed him to come up with an activity for his YMCA class, and James Naismith—"Jim" was the way he introduced himself to strangers—was just hoping not to fail.

He would come to call this a "crucial moment in [his] life," but at the time all Naismith was hoping to do was to develop a solution for the problem in front of him. This group of students was a real challenge; they could be unruly when lacking enthusiasm toward the activity of the day. Generating any level of interest outside of this YMCA building in Springfield, Massachusetts, was the least of Naismith's concerns in a moment that felt significantly less than monumental at the time.

James Naismith stood with a regulation soccer ball between his hands. His palms caressed the brown leather surface, eager to begin. The door flew open, and they entered with unbridled testosterone. Some were full-grown adults, others still navigating through their teen years. They wore vests and button-down shirts, and most sported mustaches. There were eighteen of them in all, streaming in through the doorway that opened onto the balcony above the YMCA gym floor.

Frank Mahan, the wisecracking Carolinian with the Irish eyes, looked down at Naismith from the balcony and mumbled with disinterest, "Huh. Another new game." The others followed, their eyes falling upon Naismith and then over to the two peach baskets he had had attached to the balcony on either side of the gym. He stood beneath them, the leather soccer ball in his hands, as they descended the balcony stairs that led to the gym floor. And so it began.

The roots of baseball are thick with uncertainty, mostly reaching back to a man named Abner Doubleday who may or may not have created the sport. Football's origin is based in the international sport of rugby, which over years evolved into the game we know today.

Basketball's beginnings are much more easily traced to a single man, a single moment. This linear progression is part of what makes the game such a unique pastime in American culture. As Phog Allen would write in a 1937 book about the sport, "[basketball] remains the only major sport that is the invention of one man's brain."

James Naismith, the man sitting in the stands at the Kansas City Convention Hall when Phog Allen and the KC Athletic Club took the court for the first two games of basketball's "World's Championship" in the spring of 1905, was as unlikely a sporting figure as there was. He lacked the coordination, the ego, the foresight, and the charisma required as attributes for greatness in the sports world, and yet an argument could be made that he was the most important person to impact athletics in the twentieth century. (This comes amid the likelihood that Naismith never played the game of basketball in the century—the widely acknowledged belief is that he only played organized basketball on three occasions, and all of those came in the 1890s.)

Naismith had an undeniable, and unprecedented, influence on the sporting world because of the little game that he created in the late nine-teenth century simply by scratching out thirteen original rules on a sheet of paper.

Naismith was hardly the archetype for the role of sports innovator. Orphaned as a nine-year-old boy when both of his parents died from typhoid fever, Naismith went to live with his uncle in a log cabin located in a rural area of Ontario called Almonte. He soon developed the thirst for a career in religion and imagined himself as a minister preaching atop a pulpit. But as Naismith grew into his teenage years, his oratory skills were not among his best attributes; he was a thinker, not a talker.

Naismith was also an average student who was easily distracted. He preferred extracurricular activities to the classroom setting and grew up playing games like hide-and-seek and catch. The pastime that had the biggest influence on his future would be a game called "duck on a rock." That game, which was popular among Canadian children in the nineteenth century, involved two teams attempting to knock a small rock from atop a stump or a larger rock. Players would throw stones toward the small rock in an effort to knock it from its perch, somehow getting the rock past a defender, and Naismith learned over time that it was more effective to lob the stone in an arc rather than to throw it with a baseball-style delivery.

The tossing method became a key element in the game Naismith would create years later, after his plans to study ministry at McGill University in Montreal were abandoned through a series of events that began when two older classmates convinced Naismith to join the rugby team in 1884. Naismith turned to a new pursuit, earning a degree in physical education that would pave the way for his eventual calling.

His decision to become a man of sport rather than a man of the cloth was one Naismith rarely questioned, and yet members of his family never forgave him. Athletics were considered by many to be the devil's tool back in the late part of the nineteenth century, and Naismith's sister was unable to forgive him decades later for pursuing such a secular career rather than a more spiritual profession. As Naismith would later write,

> I asked my only sister if she had ever forgiven me for forsaking the ministry. She shook her head and said, "no, Jim." On the other hand

I received a letter from a former classmate who was moderator of the general assembly in Canada who said, "You with your athletics have done more for the welfare of humanity than any member of our class."

Naismith, who had never even seen the inside of a gymnasium until his college years, earned a bachelor's degree in physical education from McGill in 1887 and was in graduate school when the university's director of physical education passed away. The school offered the job to Naismith. He spent the summer of 1890 touring YMCAs in the United States and ended up in Springfield, Massachusetts, where he accepted a job as a PE instructor at the International YMCA Training School.

Near the end of his first year at the Springfield YMCA Training School in 1891, the thirty-year-old Naismith was presented with the challenge of coming up with a winter indoor activity. He'd been given two weeks to come up with something to keep an overly energetic class of eighteen teenagers busy during the cold months. Naismith, the mild-mannered professorial type who had once dreamed of a life in ministry, was having a difficult time holding the attention of the unruly group of students. YMCA physical education director Luther Gulick Jr. challenged Naismith to come up with a way to keep the boys and men busy while allowing them to burn off energy during the snowy period between football and baseball seasons. Naismith pored over a few ideas before coming up with a game that would be less physical than football, involve more teamwork than baseball, and be designed to feature passing as the main form of advancing the ball. He determined that by having a goal that could not be guarded, the players would have to constantly remain active on defense.

In the din of his office, Naismith scribbled thirteen basic rules that were designed to make a unique game that could be played indoors. The yet-to-be-named activity had been percolating in his mind for months by the time Naismith presented the rules to a YMCA secretary named Miss Lyons a few minutes before an 11:30 a.m. class on December 21, 1891. (Around that same time, a six-year-old boy named Forrest Allen was beginning to hone his physical coordination skills alongside his brothers in Northwest Missouri.) Naismith's game initially involved a leather soccer ball and two boxes, each of which was to be affixed to the wraparound balcony that surrounded the YMCA gym. Naismith asked the YMCA janitor, Pop Stebbins, to fetch two boxes from storage. The janitor demurred.

"I have two old peach baskets down in the storeroom," Mr. Stebbins was said to have told James Naismith on that December day, "if they will do you any good."

The janitor then used a hammer and nails to secure a basket to the balcony on either end of the gym. The balcony just happened to be ten feet high, setting the precedent for the height at which rims would remain for more than a century (despite a well-fought crusade that would be waged by Phog Allen during the second half of his coaching tenure to move it up to twelve feet). Naismith tacked the sheet of paper with the thirteen rules onto a bulletin board.

The eighteen members of Naismith's YMCA class showed up and were split into two teams, with nine players from each side on the thirty-five-by-forty-five-foot court at one time. The object was to advance the ball without carrying it; originally, players could not even dribble the ball, could only advance it by rolling it on the ground, and had to be in a stationary position when they attempted a shot. Most of the thirteen original rules dealt with fouls penalizing players for physical play or for losing the ball out of bounds.

The unofficial debut of basketball resulted in a 1–0 score, with Pop Stebbins, the janitor, having to retrieve the ball with the use of a ladder after the game's only goal. A man named William Chase, a YMCA employee, was credited with the first basket, the only one scored that day, on a shot from about twenty-five feet away. Legend has it that Frank Mahan was so certain the game would catch on that he stole the original list of rules from Naismith—only to return it a few days later when his guilty conscience got the better of him.

Mahan was also the one who suggested a name for the new game. His idea of "Naismith Ball" was shot down by the game's inventor, and so Mahan offered two words that summed up the game most succinctly: "basket ball."

Naismith eventually wrote those two words atop the typed page of the thirteen original rules, and the game was called "basket ball" for about three decades before newspapers began shortening the name to "basket-ball" in the early 1920s.

The first official game in a public venue is recognized as having been played on March 11, 1892, when about two hundred curious fans showed up at an armory in Springfield to see basket ball in person. Nine players from each team were still on the court at a time, and one of them was a Naismith friend named Amos Alonzo Stagg who was attending the YMCA Training School in Springfield. Stagg apparently enjoyed the game but ended up using his brawn in the more physical sport of football, which led him to a Hall of Fame career as a player and coach on the gridiron.

Through the international branches of the YMCA, the game of bas-ketball gained a small groundswell of support in the United States and was taken to countries like France, China, and India before the turn of the century. One of the earliest Springfield players, an exchange student named Genzaburo Ishikawa, brought the game back to his native Japan. Basketball was spreading its wings at a rapid rate.

Through the game he created, James Naismith quickly became well-known in the sporting world, and by 1895 he received an offer to work at the YMCA's largest U.S. branch in Denver, where Naismith would also be able to attend medical school. The thirty-three-year-old Naismith accepted the job, taking his wife and new daughter along for the ride.

The first college basketball game is recognized as having occurred in February 1895, when the Minnesota School of Agriculture & Mining beat Hamline University 9–3 in a game featuring nine players per side. (Some historians point to the January 1896 game between the University of Iowa and the University of Chicago as the first official collegiate game, since it was played with the five-on-five structure that would carry the game through the twentieth century and beyond.) Three years later, in 1898, Naismith was hired as a chapel director and PE instructor at the Univer-sity of Kansas. He became a candidate for the job after the university's chancellor contacted a counterpart at the University of Chicago, looking for someone to run chapel services and teach physical education. The U. of Chicago chancellor contacted Amos Alonzo Stagg, his school's foot-ball coach and Naismith's friend from the Springfield YMCA, and word was passed along about a rare man who could wear both hats. Naismith accepted the job at an annual salary of $1,300. He would also serve as the first basketball coach in KU history, although at the time Naismith held no such official designation. Playing games against YMCA teams and small colleges, like Haskell Institute, Naismith's early Kansas squads were far from juggernauts—and he was more apt to referee a KU game than to provide any strategic input from the bench. He was spending most of his time teaching PE classes and leading chapel services on the KU campus and rarely had time to run practices.

Despite the lukewarm early success the Jayhawks experienced on the court, the sport grew in popularity and became a staple of extracurricular activity at KU. As the *University Weekly* reported in its December 10, 1898, issue, "everyone who is at all interested in athletics is now talking basket ball. . . . It is discussed in the corridors; it is practiced and played in the gymnasium and on the campus. Even the professors have become actively interested in the game and are giving their time of recreation over to this pastime."

Without a sufficient gym, the Kansas basketball team was forced to rent an ice arena in downtown Lawrence for practice sessions. KU's first official game was played in a barn against a YMCA team that included a player named Jesse James Jr., son of a local train robber, who was said to have played "a very ungentlemanly game." The YMCA team also had a player named Pete Allen, whose younger brother Forrest was among the 150 fans in attendance while watching the game from a hayloft. A few years later, in February 1904, Naismith and his Jayhawks team that had come to include Pete Allen got throttled 27-10 at the hands of a Kansas City Athletic Club team led by Pete's nineteen-year-old younger brother.

Forrest Allen—the 5'10" kid with the sandy hair, the round, youthful face, thick lips, deep blue eyes, and broad shoulders—had made quite an impression on James Naismith. He knew the kid had talent and a bucketful of ideas, and Naismith took a liking to him.

But it wasn't until James Naismith came out of the stands to referee a game at Kansas City's Convention Hall on that March day in 1905 that he realized just how special Forrest Allen was.

4

The Hero Arrives

The voices were raining down. The sound circled inside the arena that surrounded him, coming together to form an assault on the eardrums.

Nineteen-year-old Forrest "Phog" Allen stood at the free-throw line and closed his eyes. He could do this. After all he had done just to make this championship game a reality, he was now in position to lead his team to victory. He knew he could do it, but first he had to shut out all the voices. He'd never heard such deafening noise before, had never heard such beautiful chaos. And all because of a simple little game.

A mixture of pride and nerves pumped through his body. He had to block it all out. With his eyes still closed, he could feel the leather against his fingertips, bringing a sensation of calm in the knowledge that he'd done this before. Never in front of this many people, but he had done it before.

When he opened his eyes, Forrest looked at the basketball between his fingers and nothing else. Staring at the ball helped to calm his frayed nerves. He had done this same routine, one hundred consecutive times, every single day. He caressed the leather with his fingertips, spinning the ball to further loosen his anxiety. His right foot was almost touching the free-throw line, his left foot a step behind. He took a deep breath, held the air in his lungs, and bent his knees, crouching slightly to contract the muscles of the thorax.

Slowly, still holding his breath and gripping the ball, Forrest dropped his hands down toward his knees, stopping only when the back of his left hand touched the inside of his left thigh. With a measured, slight squat, he rose and shifted his weight from one foot to the other, then to the balls of both feet, lifting the ball with an underhand release, his whole body in concert, the ball spinning backward toward the basket. He always put just enough English on the ball to make up for the slightest overthrow.

He watched the ball arc toward the basket, noticing now that the crowd had fallen into a quiet hum, just as anxious to watch the path of the ball as was Forrest himself. Spinning in the air, the ball went up and up, then changed its path, down toward the basket twenty feet away. Forrest exhaled.

Convention Hall on 13th and Central was packed to the rafters when the hometown players from the Kansas City Athletic Club and the visiting Buffalo Germans returned to the court for the deciding game of Forrest Allen's "World's Championship of Basket Ball" series on March 29, 1905. They were joined by a PE instructor and chapel director from nearby University of Kansas who was widely regarded as the best referee in the game. James Naismith had watched the first two games of the series from the stands before players from both squads requested his neutrality and officiating skills for game three. He donned a cap and tight wool jersey while holding the bulky, dark leather ball in preparation for the opening tip. The game time had been moved up an hour, to 8 p.m., to accommodate the Buffalo team's train schedule. Another large crowd showed up, pushing attendance over the ten-thousand mark for the three games.

The game of basketball back then was much different from the game being played a century later, with dunks and three-point shots dominating the sport. There weren't even driving layups in those days, as dribbling was nearly impossible with the heavy leather balls, and players had to pass the ball to an established teammate for a set shot. Jump balls were conducted after every made basket. One of the few constants was the free throw, which was originally ruled to count for three points (the same as a field goal in the early years) but had been reduced to just one point in 1895 or '96, a decade or so before Allen's KC Athletic Club team took on the

Germans from Buffalo, New York. Free throws continued to be a crucial part of the game in the ensuing years, as the free-throw line was twenty feet from the basket—five feet farther than it would be at the start of the twenty-first century. The rules also called for one player from each team to serve as designated shooter of all free throws.

And nobody in the Kansas City area shot them with as much deft aplomb as the 5'10" kid from Independence, Missouri, with the catchy nickname. Forrest "Phog" Allen, the wide-shouldered, confident forward who had put the series together, would have to live up to his reputation as a free-throw shooter time and again if his Athletics were to have a chance in game three of the first "World's Championship" of basketball. With his soft-fingered grip and trademark crouch, Allen stood at the line several times in the opening minutes and began his routine. He would pause to take in a breath before tossing his two-handed, underhand flips up toward the basket. Allen's steely blue eyes would follow the path of the ball, every hair on his head carefully parted in place, as he became, shot by shot, a local hero. With Naismith calling a tight game—the sport's gentlemanly inventor held a healthy disdain for physical play—the fouls kept piling up, and Allen spent a good part of the evening standing on the free-throw line.

Allen and his teammates played their best game of the series—if not their lives. The *Kansas City Times* would set the scene the following day, when it reported that Convention Hall was brimming with energy:

> A more enthusiastic, a more excited crowd has seldom assembled in the big hall. The raucous voiced rooter was in his element. Men who have not had their blood stirred to the cheering stage since their college days aided in swelling the tumult, and always the shrill screams of the women could be heard in the chaos of noise. At times, the entire audience seemed to rise to its feet as though moved by a common spring.

The Athletics jumped out to a 10–0 lead, and Buffalo's physical play continued to result in foul calls by Naismith. Forrest stepped up to the free-throw line and delivered, over and over, leading the KC Athletic Club to a 27–10 halftime lead as the local fans cheered his team on. Naismith's non-stop calls frustrated the German YMCA team, so much so that one Buffalo player would later call it "a baby game."

The second half began, and Forrest Allen found himself at the free-throw line again and again, going through his underhand routine, his eyes closed as he felt the surface of the ball, until he was ready to shoot, the air held in his lungs up to the moment when the ball left his steady hands.

In the end, Allen sank 17 free throws as the Athletics breezed to a 45–14 win over the visiting Buffalo Germans, and the talented team from Kansas City Athletic Club had proven its merit as a national power.

Fans spilled from the stands and lifted Forrest and his six teammates onto their shoulders, carrying them around the concrete floor in celebration.

The following day, in the March 30, 1905, edition of the *Kansas City Star* newspaper, a front-page headline proclaimed, "K.C. owns world champions."

Just as important, Forrest Allen more than made up for his financial risk. He would later brag that the series brought in five thousand dollars, not including the six-hundred-dollar reimbursement he had to pay to the Buffalo team to cover its traveling expenses. Allen was lauded for his efforts locally after an unexpectedly large gate of well over 10,000 spectators attended the three games. He was given a hero's welcome and was allowed to keep part of the profits. In the weeks that followed, Allen's efforts would help the Kansas City Athletic Club more than double its membership—from 410 to north of 1,000—and his alterations improved the value of the Convention Hall in that the newly installed baskets provided a novel, more profitable, use for the venue.

Forrest "Phog" Allen had become a local basketball folk hero before his twentieth birthday, and James Naismith knew he could be an important addition to the basketball team at the University of Kansas in Lawrence, about twenty-five miles west of Kansas City. Forrest Allen's older brother had played there under Naismith, but getting the younger Allen to Lawrence was more complicated than it appeared. Harry "Pete" Allen had left the KU basketball program a bit disillusioned after only one season, as payments he'd been promised from a group of local business owners—at a time when such things weren't regulated—dried up. Forrest Allen wasn't sure whether he wanted to follow in his brother's footsteps as a KU basketball player or to stay in his home state and attend the University of Missouri. Lawrence was actually closer to his hometown of Independence than Columbia, Missouri, was, and the University of Missouri was just in the early stages of building a basketball program that was on the verge of making its debut as a varsity sport. But years later, Phog Allen would say that the reason he decided to go to Kansas was mainly in the streets. The ones in Lawrence, he had noticed while visiting to attend older brother Pete's games as a KU football and basketball player, were wider and cleaner than those in Columbia; as Allen would say later in his life, "They hadn't lifted Missouri out of the mud then."

Perhaps motivated by the doubts of a father who never believed he would amount to much, Allen enrolled at KU and began his collegiate experience with designs on one day earning a law degree. (Tuition to law school in those years included a five-dollar matriculation fee and an incidental fee of twenty-five dollars.) The Lawrence into which Forrest Allen arrived in the fall of 1905 was a progressive college town that was blossoming with growth. The Douglas County Courthouse at 1100 Massachusetts Street, with its rising clock tower and Cottonwood limestone exterior, had been completed the previous year. The merchant thoroughfare in downtown Lawrence, having barely escaped the 1903 flooding of the Kaw River, brought out foot traffic and horse-drawn carriages along brick-paved streets that featured an assortment of confectionaries, dressmakers, tobacco dispensaries, and harness outlets. The adjacent South Park included a bandstand, where live music blared on warm summer nights. The KU campus was thriving as well, having recently added a natural history museum known as Dyche Hall.

The University of Kansas had also recently opened its School of Medicine, complete with a faculty of 125 physicians to instruct 162 medical students who were part of the inaugural class. The KU campus sprawled over fifty acres of land, with an overall enrollment of more than 1,200 students.

Allen's arrival on campus created such a stir that the school newspaper in October 1905 proclaimed him "a strong addition to the team. He is one of the world's champions and is said to be the best goal thrower in the world." The KU freshman wore each emblem with pride.

Allen's first foray as a college athlete came on the football field, where he suffered a serious back injury early in KU's 1905 practice season and would never be able to play the sport again. Team doctors tried unsuccessfully to cure his ailing back, and it wasn't until Allen was treated by a therapist using alternative medical practices that he was able to regain any range of motion. The osteopathic method used to cure Allen's back pain piqued a curiosity within him that would, a few years later, lead him toward a new pursuit away from the basketball court and athletics as a whole.

Football injuries were quickly becoming a concern on a national level during that fall, when eighteen deaths resulting from injuries on the gridiron led President Theodore Roosevelt to consider banning the sport altogether. That spawned a meeting of college athletic directors that eventually resulted in the creation of the National Collegiate Athletic Association (NCAA).

Allen's injury, fortunately, was not life-threatening. His back problems effectively ended his football career and opened his mind to a new form of medical therapy, but his time on the basketball court was just about to begin. He spent a few weeks playing on the freshman team alongside a naturally gifted athlete named Tommy Johnson, and eventually the pair became eligible for the varsity basketball team at Kansas.

Allen made his debut as a varsity basketball player on February 8, 1906, when he came off the bench to help lead the Jayhawks to a blowout win over the Wyandotte Athletic Club. He got his first start six days later, scoring 23 points in a 37–17 win over Nebraska. The KU basketball team went on to win a program-best twelve games in 1905–6, ending a six-year streak of losing records in the process. Naismith, whose coaching duties were still extremely limited as he ran the PE department and conducted chapel services, finally had the Jayhawks on the right track—led by Allen, team captain Milton Miller, and Johnson, who was also quite an athlete on the gridiron. Allen closed out his freshman season by scoring 26 points in a 60–13 win over Emporia State. The performance established a record for points scored in a game by a KU player, and nearly ten years would pass before any Jayhawk scored that many points again.

That blowout win over Emporia turned out to be the final game Forrest Allen would play at Kansas. The 1905–6 season was supposed to close out with a contest against a school called Baker University, a college twenty miles south of Lawrence that Allen knew very well. He'd been volunteering as a part-time basketball instructor at the school two nights a week after classes and was undoubtedly looking forward to playing against Baker. But the season finale would end up being called off when Allen came down with a hand injury, leading the two schools to mutually cancel the game.

In his first season as a college basketball player, Forrest "Phog" Allen had established himself as a top scorer and team leader. He developed a tight bond with teammate Tommy Johnson, giving KU a solid nucleus for years to come. As the *Daily Kansan* wrote of Allen after the 1905–6 season, "He is a steady, consistent player who can be depended upon to do all that is possible for the best interests of the team and the university." Allen was so respected by his teammates, and by James Naismith, that he was named captain for the upcoming, 1906–7 season. But he wouldn't be around by the time the campaign began. Another pursuit took Allen down a different path, one that his mentor couldn't understand.

As the oft-told story goes, Naismith called Forrest Allen into his office after the 1905–6 season, chuckling as he held a telegram between his fingers. Baker University, the school twenty miles to the south, in Baldwin City, where Allen had been volunteering to help out on the basketball court, had written Naismith with a strange inquiry. The school was looking for someone to coach the basketball team, and the job would involve a modest salary as well as room and board. The idea made Naismith shake his head, still tittering as he tossed the telegram aside.

Forrest Allen was confused. What in the world was so funny?

"Why, you can't coach basketball," James Naismith famously told Allen on that day. "You just play it."

Allen was taken aback by the statement. Naismith had invented the game of basketball and knew more about the sport than anyone on earth, and yet in that moment, Forrest "Phog" Allen had something to teach *him* about the game.

"You can certainly teach free-throw shooting," said Forrest, a relative expert on the subject. "And you can teach the boys to pass at angles and run in curves."

Naismith, the purest of basketball purists, still wasn't convinced. Basketball was a *recreation*, not a sport, and there was no need for the role of a coach.

But the conversation didn't deter young Forrest Allen, who not only had a different vision but also had an almost desperate need for money. He was just a twenty-year-old sophomore at the University of Kansas, but Forrest "Phog" Allen was about to embark on his first coaching job.

5

The Game Can Be Coached

The mentor was across the way. Twenty-one-year-old Forrest Allen had greeted him warmly—despite his youth, Allen already had a way with people—and now the time had come to do battle.

The 150 or so fans watching from the balcony above couldn't possibly have known the gravity of the moment; decades would pass before the matchup of basketball titans would truly be put into perspective. Those fans seated in the balcony of the gym inside Baker University's Rippey Building were more excited about seeing their little David of a school take on the Goliath of the public university to the north. They were ready to find out just how good this young hotshot of a coach really was.

Forrest Allen tuned them out and focused on the task at hand. Dressed in a dark sweater while crouched down at the center of a circle of players—many of them older than him—Allen barked out a few final instructions before turning his players loose. The gym had very little light, which was to be expected in a town that had yet to be introduced to electricity, and the dark paneling of the wooden backboards attached to the balcony made it nearly impossible for the players to see the new metal basket rims.

Coach Allen placed a four-inch-long whistle between his lips and nodded across the way. James Naismith had a whistle of his own, as well as a laced leather ball. The two coaches made their way to midcourt. Forrest Allen, once the student, watched his mentor toss the ball in the air.

Allen and Naismith were no longer on the same side. On this night, the mentor and his former student were opponents for the first time. The ball was tipped. The game between the Baker University Wildcats and the University of Kansas Jayhawks was under way.

The legendary coaching career of Forrest "Phog" Allen began in the kind of place that made Lawrence, Kansas, seem like a metropolis by comparison. Baldwin City, Kansas, was a desolate prairie town twenty miles south of the University of Kansas campus on a short train ride through farmland and gently stirring wheat fields. With only one intersection and no electricity, Baldwin City had very little to offer a visitor—other than the oldest university in the state of Kansas.

Baker University had been around for forty-eight years by the time Allen arrived in the fall of 1906 to serve as director of athletics and become the school's first official basketball coach. He knew the place well, having refereed basketball games at the school the previous winter, when Allen also helped out as a twice-a-week basketball instructor at Baker while playing for the KU varsity. (In the decades that followed, Allen would officially be credited with the 18-6 record the Baker basketball team posted during that 1905–6 season the year before he was hired.)

The Methodist university was made up of only a hundred or so four-year students in the fall of 1906, and the quiet campus was bursting with the excitement of a new library that was under construction to open the following academic year. The campus was tightly contained, measuring two by three city blocks and surrounded by six hundred acres of university-owned wetlands. The tallest of the handful of buildings on campus was three-story Parmenter Hall, a stone structure topped by a bell tower that wasn't structurally sound enough to actually hold a bell. Nearby Centenary Hall, the only brick building on campus, contained an auditorium large enough to hold chapel services on days when the congregation was too overwhelming to fit inside Castle Hall. Clumps of trees separated the buildings across a hill-less campus that also included a grape arbor and a grounded wooden structure built to hold the bell that had been too heavy to ring inside the tower atop Parmenter Hall.

The student body was a tight-knit group bound by their Methodist beliefs. The school adhered to its own "ten commandments," which mostly spoke of respecting one's professors and concluded with the line: "Thou shalt not covet thy classmate's pony, nor his best girl, nor his old socks, nor his 'gym' shoes."

The gym within Baker University's four-story Rippey Building offered very little light but was large enough to hold free-standing chairs for two hundred fans on the balcony that surrounded the wood-floored basketball court from above. Forrest had not only refereed on the floor but had also played there—as a member of the Allen Brothers Basket Ball Team that had visited Baker in March 1906.

Baker University presented a chance for the twenty-year-old Allen to coach basketball, and he was intent on proving to mentor James Naismith that it could be done. It was the rarest of occupations in those days, something that, as far as anyone could tell, no man had been hired to do exclusively to that point. Allen is recognized by many as the first official full-time coach in basketball history, a designation that is rarely included in the annals of the sport's past. But the job would also cost Allen his playing career at Kansas, where he had broken onto the scene as a star freshman and had already been named team captain for the upcoming season. Baker was offering room and board and a small stipend, enough for Allen to continue his education, and all they asked in return was for him to run basketball practices and help organize the school's fledgling athletic program. He certainly needed the money; because there were no athletic scholarships in those days, he had already used up much of his savings to study law and play basketball at KU. So Allen had accepted the job and fully invested himself in the working world. He soon began coaching simultaneously at Independence High School, his alma mater, while spending his mornings working as a clerk at his father's grocery store. A typical day involved Allen tossing aside his grocer's apron in the early afternoon, heading over to Independence High for late-afternoon practice, then taking a train sixty miles to Baldwin City to run practices at

Baker. Often, he would return home after 10 p.m. This ability to multitask became an integral part of his success as a head coach and basketball flag-bearer in the years that followed.

No one knows what might have become of Allen's career as a player, but what's clear is that he arrived in coaching as a pioneer in the profession. Young, enthusiastic, and a true visionary, Phog Allen was determined to take James Naismith's game and bring it to the masses. He had studied the game under Naismith and had devised ways to make players better at a sport that was still not even two decades old. Twenty-year-old Phog Allen set out to not only teach the game but to *coach* it—just as the job title described. Sometimes that meant showing a player a more efficient way of positioning his hands as he shot the ball. On other occasions, it involved lecturing about the importance of teamwork. How to position oneself defensively. Where to look for the ball coming off the rim. How to prepare oneself between games—whether through cardiovascular exercise, nutritional consciousness, or simply getting enough sleep. Allen himself was at the peak physical condition of his life, and his most effective form of coaching that year came in stripping off his warm-ups and *showing* his young men—many of whom were actually older than him—how to play the game.

Phog's first official Baker team, led by star player Lamar Hoover, won its first thirteen games of the 1906–7 season. He also served as referee for many of the games, a common practice among coaches and managers in those days. The cost was $1.25 for season tickets and a chance to secure one of the free-standing chairs on the balcony overlooking the basketball court inside the Rippey Building.

The unabashed confidence in young Phog Allen had become more like invincibility as his Baker team won game after game after game, leading up to a February 14, 1907, matchup with the Kansas Jayhawks in Baldwin City. In that game, Allen, who by then had turned twenty-one years old, would match wits with his mentor, James Naismith. The student newspaper, the *Baker Orange*, proclaimed two days later, "When the game was called at 7:30 p.m., the Gym was crowded with eager and expectant onlookers." Allen and Naismith both served as referees. Allen's Baker Wildcats rewarded the fans by jumping out to an 18–6 lead, although Naismith punished the fans at the sold-out gym at Rippey Hall by calling a technical foul on the crowd at one point. Allen's Baker Methodists recovered from that and cruised to a 39-24 win. The student had soundly beaten his mild-mannered mentor, and Phog Allen cemented himself as a coach on the rise.

Allen had, in effect, surpassed Naismith in the coaching ranks. The shift in hierarchy had little impact on Naismith, who never considered himself to be a coach anyway. By then in his mid-forties, Naismith was a true gentleman whose lack of competitive fire was becoming a source of tension within the growing KU fan base. Naismith had lost his two top players from the previous year—Allen to the coaching profession, and star athlete Tommy Johnson, who left the team for unknown reasons—and the Jayhawks had, competitively speaking, fallen on hard times.

Allen had no such problems in his first year as head coach, going 14-0 as Baker University's leader. His success as a young coach had a lot to do with his approach to the game, which differed greatly from that of Naismith in that he was driven to succeed at all costs. While Naismith continued to see himself as an educator, Allen was all about winning basketball games. With the right mix of charisma, intimidation, and stubborn ingenuity, Allen was able to get the most out of a Baker University team that was filled with players at or above his age.

Phog Allen's first season as a head coach was an overwhelming success but turned out to be the final one for his coaching mentor. Naismith's Jayhawks went 7-8 in 1906-7, and there were grumblings that perhaps James Naismith had been wearing too many hats. In his eight years at the school, Naismith had not only continued on as KU's chapel director and head of the physical education department but had also become the athletic director. As the *Daily Kansan* wrote after the subpar season, "Dr. James Naismith, the inventor of the game, is so busy with his work as athletic director that he rarely finds time to give the men [on the Kansas basketball team] thorough training."

The KU basketball team's diminishing success at a time when the sport's popularity was blossoming left Naismith feeling like his game was becoming too big for its own good, and so shortly after the 1906-7 season he agreed to step down as head coach so that he could concentrate on his duties as AD and chapel director. The school was in the process of constructing a new gym, and Naismith's ever-expanding duties were only going to become more taxing over the next few months.

The new gym offered a chance for the sport to move to a new level, as evidenced by a November 1907 article in the *Daily Kansan* that announced, "The only thing that stands in the way of a winning team is the lack of a new coach."

The KU basketball program, with one hundred eager players already signed up for a tryout, needed a new face, and the Jayhawks didn't have to go far—twenty miles, as it would be—to find one. Young Phog Allen, with his confident demeanor and steely blue eyes, just twenty-two years old, was tabbed to succeed Naismith despite his youth and lack of a college degree. He continued his duties at Baker University, working part-time at the two schools, and wasn't officially named the KU coach until two days before the 1907–8 season opener. In December of 1907, when Phog Allen could've been a junior at the University of Kansas, he became the first man ever hired to serve primarily as head coach of the KU basketball team, embarking on a coaching journey that began with high expectations. The University of Kansas had recently completed construction on Robinson Gym, a one-hundred-thousand-dollar structure that was considered one of the best facilities in the West and included a third-floor auditorium and basketball court capable of seating three thousand spectators. The three-story limestone structure, its details designed by Naismith, measured 90 feet by 178 feet. It rose up from the ground like a medieval castle, with 1,500 lockers in the basement, a large swimming pool, and two small gymnasiums—one for the men and another for the women. But the architecture of the gym also brought some unique aspects, most notably the on-court pillars and eleven-foot-high ceilings, that caused several schools to refuse to play there. The Jayhawks were also entering their first season in conference play during the 1907–8 year, representing the Missouri Valley Intercollegiate Athletic Association. The stakes were high, and Allen had the kind of confident young swagger that seemed to say, "Bring them on."

Opponents must have thought the young Allen was a team trainer or water boy, for photographs of him as a first-year KU coach show a baby-faced young man who looked closer to fourteen years old than his actual age of twenty-two. A 1907–8 team photograph included a group of players who looked much older than their first-year coach.

On December 13, 1907, just two days after Allen was officially named head coach, fans paid twenty-five cents to see the 1907–8 season opener. Allen and the Jayhawks rewarded them by jumping out to a 31–0 lead on the way to a school-record 66 points. Tommy Johnson, once Allen's teammate at Kansas, returned from the year away to lead the Jayhawks to a 66–22 rout of Ottawa that would serve as victory number one in the Allen era at KU.

But the excitement quickly faded. Ottawa somehow bounced back to beat Kansas six days later—in a game played in a small, dimly lit gym—and Allen's 1907–8 Jayhawks barely got on track before eventually falling into a four-game losing streak that left them with a 3-5 record. The young coach was dealing with adversity for the first time in his fledgling career, and the competitive fire burned within him. Teaching young men how to play basketball was all Forrest "Phog" Allen wanted to do with his life in those years, but winning was becoming just as important an endeavor. He'd have to teach better, to coach *harder*, if he was going to get the most out of this team.

Allen did just that, pushing all the right buttons as KU rattled off twelve straight wins and took thirteen of the next fourteen games to set up a winner-take-all series with Nebraska for the Missouri Valley Intercollegiate Athletic Association title. The Jayhawks and Cornhuskers would decide the conference championship by way of a sweep or, if the two teams were to split, a deciding third game.

Allen's Jayhawks traveled to Lincoln, Nebraska, and edged out the Cornhuskers 28–26 on February 21. The following day, KU beat Nebraska again to clinch the program's first conference title. After the win, the school newspaper reported, "Every Jayhawker methodically executed his assignments in a manner that would credit any university team. There was no individual star—every player turned in excellent games."

Fans of KU basketball had to be feeling good about the program coming off of Allen's first year as head coach. The Jayhawks had posted a school record for wins, going 18-6 and a perfect 6-0 in conference play. Allen's first team had closed out its season by going 15-1 down the stretch and winning seven of eight games on the road to finish out the schedule. The Jayhawker yearbook proclaimed that between two hundred and one thousand fans were showing up for KU basketball games, adding, "For enthusiasm even the most exciting Foot-ball contests could hardly have equaled the rooting and yelling at the spectacular Basket-ball contests this winter."

But Allen wasn't totally invested in KU basketball. As difficult as the venture sounds, Allen was somehow able to continue coaching at Baker University during the 1907–8 season, making the twenty-mile trip via train to serve as head coach of two teams simultaneously, although his Baker team had to find a new home after Rippey Hall burnt down in a fire during the spring of 1907. He also began serving as a volunteer coach at another school in Lawrence called the Haskell Institute. That gig started on December 20, 1907, and balancing the three positions was a difficult prospect even though Allen was able to take a direct train from Lawrence to Baldwin City every afternoon. A typical day involved him running a practice at Baker in the early afternoon, taking a train into Lawrence for a two-hour session at Haskell that began at 5:30, walking a few blocks to lead a Jayhawks session at 8:00, then arriving home at around 10:30, when he would eat dinner alone. Somehow, Allen was able to pull off the feat while compiling a respectable 13-6 record at Baker. One of those wins came against a team called the Allen Brothers Basket Ball Team, and accounts of the matchup recalled Phog Allen playing against the team he coached.

Working at Haskell Institute, a small college two miles southwest of KU, in Lawrence, provided a unique experience for the up-and-coming coach. The school was founded twenty-four years earlier, in 1884, under the guise of offering American Indian students a chance to earn trade degrees in subjects like blacksmithing, tailoring, and farming. In reality, the early years of what was originally called the United States Indian Industrial Training School were more about transitioning Native American youth into mainstream American culture by removing them from reservations. The original school had included twenty-two elementary-aged students, who were discouraged from using their native language and disciplined often in a military-like environment.

The school changed its name in 1887 to Haskell Institute, named after

U.S. representative and Lawrence resident Dudley Haskell. By 1894, thirteen years before Phog Allen's arrival as a basketball coach, the school had a student body of more than six hundred students from almost all of the thirty-eight recognized states in the Union. Over the years, it had begun offering college classes and would become known as Haskell Indian Nations University. By the twenty-first century, school administrators would own up to the institution's questionable beginnings through a plaque greeting visitors to the campus, which offered a frank account of the school's early history.

The Haskell that Allen joined as a volunteer coach in December 1907 seemed to have evolved somewhat from its days as a transition school in that it had become a recognized college by the time he arrived as head basketball coach that fall. The school was a national powerhouse in football, playing a schedule made up of college teams from throughout the Midwest, but Haskell hadn't made many waves on the basketball court. The school's gym, which was actually larger than the one in which the Jayhawks played at KU, included large posts on the playing surface and chicken wire surrounding the court. Allen found a group of players who had been coached to use the posts, the wire, and their hips to their advantage, and one of his priorities was to teach the team about strategy and controlling their overly physical play.

Allen's first Haskell team, whose win total he was never credited with, provided Phog with one of the most memorable trips of his career. He back-loaded the schedule to feature a three-and-a-half-week road trip after the KU season had commenced, and the Indians played twenty-four games in twenty-five nights. They once performed in front of five thousand fans at the Light Guard Armory in Detroit. During that game, the Haskell Indians were so concerned about the officiating that Allen had to take to some unconventional coaching tactics. Allen implored his players to block out the officials, to ignore the calls and let him deal with the refs, but he could tell by the creases in their brows that anger was building.

"Boys, I want you to have confidence in the white man official," Allen told them at last. "He wouldn't steal a ball game even if those S.O.B.'s did steal your land!"

The comment drew laughter from the Haskell players and served its purpose in disarming their frustration. Allen apparently motivated his players enough to win nineteen of the twenty-four games on the tour.

By the summer of 1908, with the basketball seasons of three college teams behind him, a more important pursuit enraptured the young coach. On June 25, 1908, Forrest Clare Allen married Bessie Evalina Milton, his longtime sweetheart from Independence, Missouri. Bessie's father had accepted Phog to the point that the wedding was held on the porch of the Milton family home in Independence. He more than likely had already won over Bessie's mother, setting a personal precedent for Forrest's keen ability to work his way into a mom's heart—a trick he would later use as a recruiter.

With sunny skies and temperatures in the mid-eighties, Forrest Allen and Bessie Milton were wed in front of two hundred guests who were seated in chairs on the lawn of the Milton family's massive acreage. Japanese lanterns lined the aisle, while elder blossoms and wild roses completed the scene. Hubert Allen, Forrest's younger brother, served as his best man.

With his family in order and his coaching career off to a good start, Phog Allen set his sights on the 1908-9 basketball season with renewed focus. The twenty-three-year-old coach had relinquished his duties as head coach at Baker University—Allen was later credited with a three-year record of 45-9 at Baker, including the 18-6 season in 1905-6 that saw him serve as a part-time coach there while playing his only season at KU—meaning he would no longer have to endure the twenty-mile daily commute. But he continued to work at Haskell, where the eager young coach was officially hired as head coach in December 1908—the Indians' twenty-seven wins that season were the only ones credited to Allen's career record—and he soon added another gig when he agreed to return to the Kansas City Athletic Club to coach the basketball team there. The announcement was a big enough deal to make page two of the *Topeka State Journal* in November, but Allen's return to KCAC did not last long.

As the *Daily Kansan* opined in the days leading up to KU's 1908-9 opener, "The Jayhawkers have been handicapped by not having a regular coach to teach them the new points of the game. 'Phog' Allen has been here a few times but his trips have been too scattered to give the team the best results of his coaching." Shortly thereafter, Allen agreed to step down from his KCAC gig and devote most of his time to KU basketball.

But the biggest news Allen received during his second season coaching the Jayhawks came from wife Bessie, who announced she was pregnant with the couple's first child. The news undoubtedly put added bounce in Phog Allen's step, and it may well have motivated him to be an even better basketball coach. If he was going to make a living in coaching, he was going to have to be good enough to support a family—or he was going to have to find a new career path.

His 1908–9 Jayhawks had turned out to be plenty good. After tipping off the season with a December 10 game in Allen's former stomping grounds at Baker University by scrapping out a 4-point win, the Jayhawks really got rolling. Allen's team stormed through eight consecutive in-state opponents to start the season while posting eye-popping scores like 44-16 and 65-15. A 39-9 win over Chilocco Indian School of Oklahoma put the Jayhawks at 9-0 heading into a two-game series with Nebraska in Lawrence.

The first game of that series provided an early glimpse into Allen's ability as a strategist. The young coach used his friend Tommy Johnson, whom he would later recall as "a redheaded, athletic wizard," at the front end of a unique game plan. Heading into the games against Nebraska, Allen noticed that the Cornhuskers were overcommitting on the full-court press and leaving the far end of the floor exposed. Allen instructed Johnson, who also played quarterback on the KU football team, to throw a full-court pass over the Nebraska defense—a tactic that the Jayhawks practiced all week and used to perfection time and again throughout the 48-13 win over the Cornhuskers.

The 1908–9 Jayhawks went on to win their first nineteen games of the season. Washington University of St. Louis ended the streak with a 2-point win in February, and Allen's second season at KU ended with a 25-3 record. After the season, the Jayhawker yearbook proclaimed, "Much credit undoubtedly belongs to Coach Allen for the brilliant record of the season, but he was fortunate in having one of the fastest squads of basketball that has ever gotten together at the University."

Basketball was really beginning to take off in Lawrence, where electric streetcars had recently replaced horse-drawn carriages and the University was beginning its gradual growth on the Midwestern plains.

In just two seasons, Phog Allen had already accumulated forty-three wins—not far behind the fifty-five posted by his predecessor James Naismith in nine seasons at the helm. With a 43-9 record and two conference titles in his first two years as head coach at Kansas, Allen had validated the university's decision to choose him to run its up-and-coming basketball program. The Jayhawks were making a name for themselves on a national level, and Allen had things headed in the right direction. The only thing that could slow him down was a career change.

And that's exactly the path young Phog Allen, twenty-three years old and already on the cusp of becoming a star in the burgeoning world of basketball coaching, decided to take. Despite Allen's immediate success as a pioneer in the coaching profession, basketball would have to wait. He had a bigger pursuit pulling at him in the fall of 1909.

6

Call Him Doc

The high school dropout needed help. The kid who called himself Dutch had a sore left arm and was looking for relief. His arm was supposed to be his ticket to paying for dental school. It was the reason he'd left Central High School in Kansas City, a few classes short of a degree, to become a professional baseball player. Lying on a training table where a medical student named Forrest "Phog" Allen was looking over his sore arm, Dutch explained that he'd been playing with a local pro team called the Kansas City Blues. If his arm didn't get better, Dutch explained, he wasn't going to get many more paychecks. His baseball dream was in jeopardy. He needed Phog to make his arm feel better, or his dreams would be shattered.

His real name was Charles, but soon they would come to calling him Casey. The nickname would begin as K.C., the initials of his hometown, and eventually he would change the spelling to Casey, like the Thayer poem "Casey at the Bat," one of Allen's favorites. "If only Casey could get a whack at that.... For there seemed little chance of Casey's getting to bat."

Allen wanted to make sure this Casey got to bat again. He liked the kid, who was just trying to earn enough money to go to medical school, much like what Forrest himself was doing, while continuing to pursue a baseball career. Beneath the kid's hard exterior, Allen could see a softer side. The kid had also played basketball in high school, and he was pretty good at it. Phog Allen liked anyone who liked basketball. A kid with a love for athletics and a passion for medicine was a person after his own heart. Phog massaged the arm as best he could. He checked the kid's spine.

"Defiance gleamed in Casey's eye. A sneer curled Casey's lip." In the end, of course, Thayer's Casey would strike out. This mighty Casey, too, would one day strike out. He would strike out often; that comes with the job. Charles "Dutch" Stengel, aka Casey, would strike out more than four hundred times during his Hall of Fame career as a Major League Baseball player and manager.

Thanks in part to Phog Allen and his medical touch—they would begin to call him "Doc"—mighty Casey Stengel would get plenty of whacks.

From the time he lost his mother and was forced to help raise two younger brothers in his late teen years, Forrest "Phog" Allen took on a nurturing role that would carry him well into adulthood. A back injury he suffered as a freshman football player at the University of Kansas opened Allen's mind to a form of physical therapy called osteopathy. And his brief career as a basketball coach at KU, Baker University, and the Haskell Institute further piqued his interest in the human body's ability to deal with, and heal from, serious injuries.

As Allen would write in one of his three published books, "The secret of Greek superiority was the Greek body. But there was no secret to this secret: The Greeks invested the whole man with a romantic interest in health for its own sake."

Phog Allen, in addition to his thirst for basketball, held a "romantic interest in health for its own sake." Staying in peak physical shape had become a driving passion, while the effects of conditioning on an athlete's performance piqued his curiosity as a man of sport.

But athletics were not the only thing motivating young Phog Allen in those years, when he also took up his new role as a first-time father. Mary Elizabeth Allen, given the names of both Phog's and Bessie's mothers, was born in April 1909 and gave Allen a new focus in life. Allen—the competitor, the basketball lover, and the father—had a lot of things happening in the summer of 1909, and this complex of forces may well have been the foundation for his change in direction.

After leading the 1908–9 KU basketball team to a school-record twenty-five victories, the twenty-three-year-old Allen stepped away from the coaching profession so that he could study a form of alternative medicine known as osteopathy. Allen had a natural thirst for medical knowledge, but his true reason for changing career paths was that he saw the possibility of meshing sport and osteopathic techniques at some point. By learning to coach and treat his players, Allen could become a coach unlike any other in sport.

The Merriam-Webster online dictionary defines osteopathy as "a system of medical practice based on a theory that diseases are due chiefly to loss of structural integrity which can be restored by manipulation of the parts supplemented by therapeutic measures." Almost like a nineteenth century version of what would later become known as physical therapy, osteopathy blended elements of kinesiology and chiropractic treatment, often relying on spinal adjustments to alleviate pain. A doctor named Andrew Taylor Still, one of the founders of Baker University, is credited with coming up with the word "osteopathy" and with founding a college called the American School of Osteopathy in Kirksville, Missouri, in 1892. A surgeon who later became a Kansas state legislator, Still set out to reform the medical practices of the nineteenth century and came up with a method that used deep tissue healing and electrocurrent therapy to relieve pain in damaged muscles and joints.

Osteopathy provided a quaint pathway into the medical profession that Allen couldn't necessarily have entered through traditional routes. There is no record of Allen receiving a degree at either the high school or college level, so getting into a recognized medical school appeared to be an unlikely option for the twenty-three-year-old basketball coach in the fall of 1909—even though KU had begun offering medical school accreditation four years earlier.

Despite winning forty-three of his fifty-two games as head coach of the Jayhawks (his overall record through the 1908–9 season was 115-23, including his stints at Baker University and Haskell Institute), Allen had decided in 1909 to leave the coaching profession and pursue a career in osteopathy. In the fall of that year, Phog Allen began his first classes at the Central College of Osteopathy in Kansas City, where he would study osteopathic medicine.

Attending classes in the big city was a bit of an adjustment for Allen, who grew up not far from Kansas City and had watched the skyline rise over the years. By 1909, the city had seen the construction of three modern skyscrapers—the Scarritt Building, the Commerce Bank, and the massive, sixteen-story R. A. Long Building—as well as the introduction of electricity. The downtown corridor along Walnut Street was filled with trolleys and horse-drawn carriages as shoppers wandered through a myriad of department stores, carpet shops, and six-story brick buildings. For entertainment, residents could visit the new Kansas City Zoo or venture to the reopened Electric Park, an amusement park in the East Bottoms neighborhood that, during the 1911 calendar year, would bring one million customers through its gates.

Kansas City was a booming, bustling metropolis that may well have seemed like a different planet from Allen's previous college home in Lawrence, Kansas. He left behind a KU basketball team that was coming off a program-best twenty-five-win season and second consecutive Missouri Valley Intercollegiate Athletic Association title in the fall of 1909, and losing its coach at such a young age had to be unsettling for the Jayhawks he left behind. But with star Tommy Johnson returning, along with up-and-comer Verne Long, Kansas basketball had reason for optimism. KU replaced Allen by hiring a man named William Oliver Hamilton, who was coming off of a 12-6 season at William Jewell College in Liberty, Missouri, located about sixty minutes northeast of Lawrence. W. O. Hamilton, as he was known, proved up to the task by winning his first twelve games as head coach at Kansas while leading the 1909–10 Jayhawks to a season record of 18-1.

The game of basketball was going through its own changes in those years, when the introduction of the two-shot foul altered strategies and forced coaches to devise better defensive tactics. The game became less physical in those years, but scoring was still at a premium. With large leather balls that favored passing over dribbling and referees conducting a jump ball after each made basket, the sport was more about patience than athleticism in those years. But the players Allen left behind were certainly good enough—and well versed enough in the game—to continue having success in his absence. With Hamilton running the show, KU basketball was rolling along, and when Phog Allen turned twenty-four years old in November 1909, he had effectively moved on to a life that no longer included the game he loved.

Allen had become a full-fledged student in osteopathy school, where he learned techniques and philosophies that strayed from traditional medical practice. The main difference in the discipline involved hands-on therapy applied to a patient's muscle and joints. Osteopaths could alleviate the pain of a bad back, sore shoulder, or tender ankle through deep-tissue massage and good old-fashioned elbow grease. Allen would come to learn that most leg pain in athletes could be traced to the sacroiliac joint, a part of the pelvis that helps support the spine.

The controversial methods proved effective in certain situations but were often disregarded by traditional medical practitioners, who questioned their long-term effects. Allen enjoyed the practice because it could be performed anywhere at any time—perhaps even in a locker room at halftime of a basketball game. He came to realize that osteopathy and the sport he loved could coexist, and he believed his growing wealth of information on the human body and healing techniques would come in handy if he ever did decide to get back into coaching. Athletic trainers were still uncommon in those years, as the first official guide on treating athletic injuries—*Athletic Training*, a textbook that was later referred to as *The Trainer's Bible*—was still eight years from making its debut, and the National Athletic Trainers Association was decades away from forming. The notion of combining sport and medicine would have therefore been ahead of its time when Allen began taking classes at the Central College of Osteopathy during the 1909–10 academic year.

He had successfully made the transition from young coach to medical student and family man. He continued to practice the osteopathic method, and in 1910 Allen used his training to help a high school baseball star named Charles "Dutch" Stengel get over an arm injury. "Casey" Stengel, as he would come to be known over the years that followed, went on to become a Hall of Fame baseball player and manager who often credited "Doc" Allen with healing his early arm problems.

By his second year of school, Allen had made something of a return to the basketball court as head coach of the Central College of Osteopathy's squad. Allen also spent time officiating games and, in February 1911, made some waves when he refused to referee a KU-Missouri contest. He kept himself healthy through a strict diet based on proteins, fruits, and oatmeal. He was an early opponent of carbohydrates and often said that people "dig their own graves with their teeth." As he once wrote, "One never sees a fat race horse." He encouraged the inclusion of iron in one's diet, suggesting foods like liver, molasses, eggs, peas, beans, and multi-grain cereals. Allen was also known to carry around small glass jugs of milk, taking swigs whenever it was convenient, to provide calcium and vitamin D.

Every morning and night, he would do twelve slow pushups on fingers and toes, fifty heel-to-toe exercises, and six full squats on each leg, with the other leg and both arms extended—daily exercises he would continue well into his sixties. The exercises stemmed from his basketball conditioning and were just as important to building strength in the fingers as they were to developing muscle tone in the arms, chest, and legs. Allen considered the hands to be the key to basketball, and keeping them strong was paramount to a player's success on the court. As Allen would write years later in a letter to his players, "A sprained thumb is a 'dead horse' in basketball. And snappy fingers execute unerring shots with more power and poise than do 'dish-rag' fingers which constantly slop over the ball."

His coaching reputation kept Allen a hot commodity on the basketball market, even while he was off pursuing a career in medicine. His short tenure at KU had left such an impression that schools were still after him to lead their programs. West Point, Washburn College, Westminster College, and William Jewell College all came calling to offer coaching jobs while he was at osteopathy school, but he turned every one of them down.

Allen's second year of osteopathy school brought devastating news: the KU family had lost one of its most successful athletes, and one of Allen's first KU friends, to a sudden tragedy. Tommy Johnson, one of Allen's teammates on the 1907–8 team, who had played under him a year later, lost his life prematurely to a kidney condition on November 24, 1911. Johnson was not only an All-America basketball player but also had the most memorable touchdown in KU football history to that point: a 70-yard run that beat Nebraska in 1909. Less than a year after scoring that touchdown, in the 1910 season opener against Missouri, Johnson got crunched between two defenders and suffered a kidney injury that effectively ended his career on both the gridiron and the basketball court. Complications from the injury eventually led to his death in November 1911, and the impact of that tragedy would still stick with Allen a decade later, when he would lobby for the new football stadium at KU to be named Tommy Johnson Memorial Field; administrators instead would decide to name the facility Memorial Stadium in honor of the 130 KU students who were lost during the four years of World War I.

Allen wrote often of his time with Tommy Johnson, calling him "Kansas' greatest all-around Athlete" and recounting his exploits playing football, basketball, and tennis as well as running hurdles at KU. He once wrote about an episode a few months before Tommy's death, when a KU teammate came to visit Johnson at a hospital and offered condolences about his grave condition.

"Don't feel sorry for me, pal," Tommy was said to have replied. "I've had a swell time. I've lived more in my twenty-two years than a lot of guys do in seventy."

To this, Allen concluded,

Perhaps Tommy was right. Lord Byron died at thirty-six; John Keats at twenty-six; and [Percy] Shelley at thirty. Yet their songs are still winging their way about the world, indestructible and immortal.

Down around old McCook Field [KU's pre–Memorial Field football stadium] on quiet evenings, echoes of Tommy's cleated shoes on the hard football turf may still resound. Tommy Johnson was Kansas' greatest all-around athlete. He took advantage of the time he had. Achievements not years must be Time's answer to people seeking reasons why.

Allen eventually finished his osteopathic studies at the American School of Osteopathy in Kirksville, from which he earned a degree of surgery in osteopathy on June 29, 1912. Because osteopathy was considered an alternative form of medicine, the degree was not a doctorate. This delineation would continue to hound Phog Allen for most of the rest of his life, as players would come to call him Doc and newspapers would often refer to him as Dr. F. C. Allen but fellow members of the faculty would scoff at the titles because of his lack of a PhD.

But the degree would create a new career path, if Allen so desired, and learning how to heal the human body could also come in handy if he ever decided to return to coaching. "A coach who could treat a player's injuries," Allen was known to say, "would have an advantage."

On the court, the KU basketball program kept on winning while Allen had been off pursuing his osteopathy degree. Under W. O. Hamilton, the Jayhawks won their first seven games of the 1910–11 season before cooling off significantly on the way to a 12-6 overall record. Kansas lost its final four games of that season but still won a fourth consecutive conference crown.

Hamilton's Jayhawks went 11-7 the next year, in 1911–12, and won yet another MVIAA title. KU basketball wasn't necessarily thriving—remember, in Allen's final season two years earlier, Kansas went 25-3—but the program was maintaining its supremacy in the conference and was by no means looking to make a change at the top.

And that became significant during the 1912 offseason, when a successful coach who'd been semiretired was suddenly back in the market for a job. Forrest "Phog" Allen, twenty-seven years old and boasting a resume that included an .833 career winning percentage and the two most successful seasons in the short history of KU basketball to that point, was about to get back into coaching after a three-year hiatus.

7

A Teacher among Teachers

The gymnasium was cold. Quiet. Desolate. Something was missing.

The arriving players looked around, seeing nothing but the man known as Doc standing there at center court. He wore a sweatsuit, with a towel wrapped around his neck like a scarf. His hair was combed to one side, not a strand out of place, and he carried a combination of welcoming charm and no-nonsense austerity. His blue eyes seemed to smile around the edges but bore the intensity of a drill sergeant's.

Some of them already knew him. Doc Allen had been at the school a few weeks to that point, he having been hired as the athletic director and coach of the football, basketball, and baseball teams. They'd seen him sauntering around campus, often with a fedora on his head, his chest puffing out inside a flashy suit. But this would be the first time they'd see him in action as a basketball coach.

He told them to form two lines. "Hustle," he said, standing there in the middle of a gym that was empty save for the ten-foot-high baskets on either baseline and the unoccupied seats that surrounded the basketball court.

They did as he said, standing a foot apart from each other while looking around in wonder. That's when it dawned on some of them what was missing. Doc Allen was about to hold his first basketball practice since returning to the profession after three years of osteopathy school, and there wasn't a single ball in sight.

He instructed the players to turn and face each other, then stepped them through a series of motions. Defensive players were on the left; offensive on the right. Put your foot here—not there or there, but here. Foot placement was critical. So was the angle of one's arm and the space between his outstretched hands. If a player was even a fraction of an inch off, he had to do it again. Over and over. Until they all had it right. Then it was time to practice dribbling. And shooting. And passing. All with an imaginary ball. Flick the wrist. Space the fingers just so. Once again, if a single motion was off by so much as a hair, they started over. He showed them the way to throw a hook pass and how to strike the proper defensive pose. This went on for an hour, with one break for them to stretch their fingers and hands. Staying limber was of utmost importance. Finally, one of the players asked Coach Allen when they were going to get an actual ball.

"When you're ready," Phog told them. "And only I will know when you're ready."

The drills went on. Over and over, each detail meticulously rehearsed. At one point, he had the players line up again and face each other. He told them to raise their fists and square off. Like a boxer. Don't forget the feet. The feet are just as important as the hands. He told the players to start trading punches. Don't hit, just throw punches. It's called shadow-boxing. Let's separate the men from the boys.

The Teachers practiced two hours without ever using a ball. When the practice was over, one of the players asked, "Is that it?"

Doc Allen told them there was one more thing. He pulled out a book. It was an autobiography. Written by Helen Keller. He handed it to one of the players and told him to read it and pass it on when he was finished.

As the 1911–12 college basketball season came to an end, the University of Kansas basketball program seemed to be in pretty good hands. W. O. Hamilton had just finished his third season at KU and had a 41-14 record and three consecutive conference titles to show for it. He also held the post of the school's athletic director—known at the time as manager of athletics—while James Naismith continued to serve as KU's director of physical education.

And so if Phog Allen was going to get back into coaching, he was going to have to do it at a new school. Allen had been out of coaching for three years since leading the 1908-9 KU basketball team to a 25-3 record and a second consecutive conference title. His osteopathy degree in hand, Allen was ready to return to coaching basketball.

That opportunity came at a college called Missouri State Normal School, District 2, in Warrensburg, Missouri—a university that would later become known as Warrensburg Teachers College and then Central Missouri State University and then the University of Central Missouri. His wife, Bessie, was an alumna of the school, so Phog Allen knew of it even before he accepted an offer to be athletic director and coach of the basketball, football, and baseball teams at an annual salary of $1,600. As he stared at his first group of basketball players on the Normal School team, the reality was setting in that he wasn't in Kansas anymore. The Teachers, as athletic teams at Warrensburg were called then, were coming off of a 5-8 season on the basketball court and had never played more than fifteen games in a season during the five previous campaigns of Warrensburg basketball. The school had very little basketball history, having experienced just two winning seasons and three head coaches in six years of existence.

The twenty-six-year-old Allen certainly looked the part. He upgraded his wardrobe to feature fedoras and flashy suits, looking dapper while carrying himself with a confident strut. He believed the debonair appearance would rub off on his players, whom he expected to dress well and maintain a clean-cut appearance. The young coach looked like a man in charge, and Allen backed it up by leading the Teachers' football team to a winning record and a conference championship in his first season at the helm.

When the basketball players reported for their first practice, Allen set to work by teaching them the fundamentals. Days passed before he even introduced a basketball to the practice sessions, as Allen had come to find that coaching players the proper techniques before giving them a ball was the most effective way of approaching the kind of expectations he required from his athletes. He preached perfection to each and every player and—more important—Allen demanded error-free execution in the way they worked as a *team*.

Building a cohesive unit took more than just the two-hour sessions on the practice court. Allen, who finally had a coaching gig that would keep him exclusively at one school, set about getting to know each player on a personal level. He needed to find out what made each and every one of them tick and how best to motivate them. No two players took to the same motivational tactics, and when Allen could get them all moving forward as individuals, that's when the proverbial oars in the water would be in tune as one unit.

He was careful to not get *too* close to his players. Allen was only a few years their senior, but he was by no means their contemporary. He was, quite simply, their leader—and Allen took leadership seriously. He kept a stern eye on his players and offered encouragement only when he found it absolutely necessary. Much of his personal correspondence with players came through written letters, many of which had nothing to do with basketball. He would provide written pep talks on everything from schoolwork to interpersonal relationships to family.

Phog "Doc" Allen's first Warrensburg team, with seven eligible players who survived the cut to proudly wear the "N" across the front of their crimson jerseys, got off to a good start by winning five of its first six games. Along the way, the Teachers eked out a narrow victory over Kansas Normal School, with the lone defeat coming by way of a 1-point loss at Missouri. He had loaded up his first season with opponents from his coaching past, with Baker University and Haskell Institute among the teams on the Teachers' 1912–13 schedule and a date with the University of Kansas to close out the season. Baker handed Allen his first dose of humility by hammering Warrensburg 58–35 in the seventh game of the season, serving as a reminder of just how much work was needed. Allen's Teachers played two more games against Baker, winning one of them, and four versus Haskell before Phog hosted his alma mater, KU, in the 1912–13 season finale. W. O. Hamilton and the Jayhawks prevailed 30–24, leaving State Normal School, District 2, with a record of 11-7 at the conclusion of Phog Allen's first season. The Teachers won their first conference title along the way.

The team, and the State Normal School's athletic program, were in good enough shape that Allen earned a significant raise—to two thousand dollars per year—for his efforts.

Around this time, young Phog Allen began tinkering with a theory that scoring baskets could be made easier if a team actually ran set plays. In theory, the team with the ball could be in complete control of the action, beguiling a defense through movement and knowing where each player would be before he got there. Basketball, of course, didn't have huddles and constant breaks in action like the game of football, but Allen believed there was a way to teach his team a few designed plays and then call out from the bench when he wanted his players to run one. His most successful play was one that gave the ball to an open shooter at or near the free-throw line—next to a lay-up, the easiest shot on the court. He started scribbling plays on sheets of paper, often waking up at night in search of a pen when struck by an idea. While he continued to drill his players through constant, laborious work on fundamentals, Allen also began introducing the new plays into his practice sessions, teaching his players how to break down a defense by staying one step ahead. Knowing where your teammate was going to be before he got there, Allen realized, was an immense advantage for ball-handlers in a game based on passing.

But most of his philosophy was built on repetition. "A man's consciousness," he liked to say, "becomes blunted by repetition." Allen would spend countless practice hours teaching his players the defensive stance, even after they believed they'd mastered it. He would illustrate the importance of defensive posture by explaining the difficulty of catching a dog in the backyard because of the way the animal would crouch down, keeping its center of gravity low. Begrudgingly, the players would follow his lead and assume the position, again and again, until it became as comfortable as an old sweater. In less than a year, he had them thinking with one mind, knowing without looking to the bench what Allen wanted from each player in every possible situation.

A much different set of opponents awaited the Teachers in 1913–14, when Allen's unit rolled out to a 15-3 record against an array of schools throughout Kansas and Missouri leading up to the season finale against the University of Kansas. The Jayhawks were coming off of a subpar 1912–13 season that saw their five-year streak of conference titles, started by Allen, come to an end by way of a second-place finish in the MVIAA. But W. O. Hamilton's 1913–14 team, led by Ralph "Lefty" Sproull, ended up getting back on track by going 17-1. That era ended up being part of the apex of Hamilton's tenure with the Jayhawks, who went 16-1 the following year while winning back-to-back conference titles. (Along the way, "Lefty" Sproull would score 40 points in a game to eclipse a KU single-game record that was held by an ex-Jayhawk named Forrest Allen.) Allen's Warrensburg Teachers were making their own noise, thanks in large part to the young coach's innovation of running set plays and his tireless repetition of defensive techniques.

The Jayhawks' February 19, 1914, home date with Warrensburg ended up being one of the most memorable games of the season, if only because of how it started. The Teachers showed up in Lawrence wearing crimson and red uniforms—the same colors as the Jayhawks. The game was nearly cancelled before KU's Hamilton finally relented and sent his players to the locker room to change into their road grays. The Jayhawks made Allen eat a little crow by hammering his Warrensburg team 46–20, ending the Missouri Normal School's season with a 15-4 record.

That would be the final time Phog Allen would face the Kansas Jayhawks as an opposing coach, as the school in Warrensburg would not play KU again until eighteen years later, when Allen was no longer on the Teachers' bench. His record against the school he once attended and had spent two years working for as a young coach included just one victory—over mentor James Naismith—and three losses.

Both the Jayhawks and Teachers were in good hands in the teen years, when the sport was heading into new territory. College basketball was beginning to challenge football and baseball for the attention of American sports fans, much to the chagrin of the game's inventor. Naismith was quietly serving as physical education director at KU but was becoming disenfranchised with the direction his game was taking. In 1914, Naismith wrote, "So much stress is laid today on the winning of games that practically all else is lost sight of, and the fine elements of manliness and true sportsmanship are accorded a second place."

Phog "Doc" Allen may have been as guilty as anyone; winning basketball games had become his unbridled passion. Two years removed from osteopathy school, Allen had become addicted to chasing victories the way many men his age were chasing the almighty dollar. He had the Missouri Normal School, District 2, on path to becoming a small-college powerhouse, but he also had his eye on other opportunities.

After the 1914–15 season, Doc Allen looked into an interesting job opening at Kansas Normal School in Manhattan—the college that would eventually emerge as KU's biggest in-state rival. Allen, who was still coaching and serving as athletic director at Warrensburg, expressed interest in the newly created position of director of athletics at Kansas Normal School in the summer of 1915. But the college passed him over in favor of a man named Zora G. Clevender—and Phog never forgot the slight. Later in his career, Allen would call the failed bid to be hired as AD at the school that became Kansas State "the first time I didn't get a job I applied for . . . . Since then, whenever [Allen's teams would play against] K-State, I try to prove to them that I might have been a success."

It didn't take long after the slight in the summer of 1915 for Allen to get that chance. A few months after being passed over for the job, in January 1916, Allen and his Teachers opened their basketball season with a two-game series with the Kansas Normal School. The college from Warrensburg earned a 1-point win in the first game, then the Kansas Normal School won the next one in what was supposed to be the final game before Missouri Normal School, District 2, was to have moved on in its road trip across the state of Kansas. But the series didn't end there. As the school yearbook recounted,

> with a game each, neither had won the series so a third game was arranged. Doc Allen said he wanted to win or be beaten. That third game was a game of games. First one team would be ahead and then another. The game ended in a tie, 28 all. The extra five minute period was a nerve wracking affair which ended in a tie, 32 all. Another extra period could have ended in a Kansas [Normal School] victory if Culter had made good a free throw. There were but ten seconds to play when the ball left his hand—but it struck the ring, bounced back, [Warrensburg player Foster] Gunn got it, wheeled, and hurled the ball at the goal. It zipped thru the basket at the instant the gun fired for the end of time.

Allen's 1915–16 team won the series, giving Phog a measure of revenge, and the Teachers went on to finish that season with a record of 13-2.

His early Warrensburg teams provided some insight into the kind of coach Allen would become. In a game that was more about strategy than scoring, Allen was constantly looking for ways to put points on the board. His teams were based around the guards, which in that era were literally relied upon to "guard" the ball for most of the game. Allen began toying with the use of on-ball pressure to pick up the tempo in a game that often saw ball-handlers stand around for a full minute before giving it up. The guards were unquestionably the most skilled players on the floor, as most "big" men—at the time, centers were rarely taller than 6'1" or 6'2"—were basically role players whose importance came during the jump ball that followed each made basket.

Allen was keenly aware of how important passing and dribbling ability were at the guard positions, so he constantly worked on the fundamentals to give his players an edge. His dribbling drills typically began from a crouched position, with one knee on the floor like a sprinter at the starting gates before taking off with a low dribble, the ball no more than ten to twelve inches off the floor as the player continued to bend at the waist and knees, protecting the ball. While most coaches preferred the high dribble for speed, Allen believed that the low dribble was more effective because of its ball security—and he perfected this method by introducing charging defenders at practice and teaching a ball-handler to reverse his path. "The dribble presents more opportunities than any other play in basketball," Allen would later write. "A dribbler who cannot recover the ball when an opponent dives for it is worse than no dribbler at all."

He held rigorous practices, continuing to work on fundamentals and taking breaks for shadowboxing, and afterward he circulated the Helen Keller book through his players, without explanation. He was even known to blindfold his players or tie one arm behind their backs at practice on occasion.

During his tenure at Warrensburg, Allen was also spending his time running the athletic department while coaching the Teachers' football team as well. His most memorable moment on the football field came in the fall of 1914, involving a Warrensburg football player named Ray

"Ug" Sermon who had already become a bit of a star on the gridiron. As Phog Allen wrote in a 1937 book, "if no one else could do it, Ug could. He was the neatest bundle of football energy that ever squirmed, twisted, or wriggled its way across a gridiron."

Ug Sermon and the Warrensburg football team were preparing to play a tough Drury College squad when the Teachers' star player decided to stay out too late the night before the game. At 2 a.m., Phog Allen entered Sermon's hotel room to find that he still had not returned from a night on the town, so the coach left him a note saying that Ug need not show up for the game—he'd been kicked off the team. Phog Allen then returned to his hotel suite and talked to his wife, Bessie, who had come along during the road trip. Bessie Allen was a no-nonsense woman whose protective nature as a mother could sometimes be construed as controlling. She had a soft spot for youth and strongly believed in second chances. As Phog's main confidante, Bessie was also the only person who could talk the stubborn man with the Scots-Irish heritage out of making a rash decision. Bessie disagreed with Phog's hastiness in regards to Ug Sermon and suggested that he consult the other members of the team. Phog Allen trusted his wife on all life issues, so he did just that after breakfast the next morning.

Inside a large meeting room, twenty-eight-year-old Phog Allen stood in front of his Warrensburg football players, with Ug Sermon among them, and asked how everyone felt about the situation. A player named Lyle Weeks stood up and made a case for Sermon being allowed to play.

"I admit that he has failed to do the right thing," Weeks said, according to Allen's 1937 account of the incident. "Not one of us is perfect. We have all failed to a certain degree. But the point is, he needs us and we need him. We must stick together!"

The Warrensburg Teachers did stick together, as Doc Allen took Lyle Weeks's advice and allowed the star to play. Ug Sermon repaid them by scoring the only touchdown in a 6–0 upset of mighty Drury. The touchdown stuck with Allen twenty-three years later. He wrote, "This Mercury-footed flyer with the slick pigskin tucked under his arm, defying all laws of gravitation and running at impossible acute angles, lunged, lurched, stiff-armed, pivoted, side-stepped, vaulted, and plunged his way through the vicious tackling of the opposition."

Not only did Allen's written recollection show off his command of the English language, but it also served as a testament to the coach's intense desire to win. This win-at-all-costs attitude, which would serve Phog Allen for decades in his role as a basketball coach, would also set off long-standing rivalries with many opponents throughout the remainder of his coaching career. And it would even come to divide Allen and his mentor, Dr. James Naismith, over time.

Allen certainly had a way of ruffling the feathers of his opponents, and that wasn't always unintentional. One of his first games as a football coach saw Warrensburg beat Kemper Military Academy by a ridiculous score of 127–0, which didn't sit well with the opposing coach. Another coaching rival accused him of poisoning his team's water supply. During his Warrensburg career, Allen became so hated in football-coaching circles that two opposing coaches—Dan Nee of Drury and Harvey McWilliams of the Normal School at Kirksville—accused him of sending spies to their practices and stealing signals during games. Allen countered the charges by filing a defamation lawsuit that requested seventy-five thousand dollars in compensation. The suit would eventually be thrown out and the whole incident called "childish" by the judge and summed up as "professional jealousy among the coaches," but it also resulted in Warrensburg being evicted from the Missouri Intercollegiate Athletic Association.

Another of Allen's Warrensburg athletes was Louis Menze, a contributor on both the basketball court and baseball field who would become one of the first members of the Phog Allen coaching tree. Menze, who was eight years Allen's junior, emerged as a close friend and coaching adversary in the 1930s and '40s, when he coached at Big Six rival Iowa State. Menze would one day count one of Phog Allen's sons among his players.

During his Warrensburg years, Doc Allen was also making waves in sports medicine, a field that wouldn't become acknowledged for another decade. With a degree from the American School of Osteopathy, Allen was proving that his alternative forms of medicine were legitimate. He openly practiced osteopathic techniques on players in the Warrensburg locker room, whether that meant using his fingers to loosen the muscles in a player's foot arch or working the discs of a spine, and he also had a blossoming clinic in town.

It didn't take long before Allen gained a reputation as a skilled healer who could bring quick results. In the fall 1916, a few months after fighting off a nasty case of pneumonia, Doc Allen accepted an invitation from former KU football player Potsy Clark to travel to Champaign, Illinois, where Clark was serving as head coach of the University of Illinois football team. The Illini were struggling with a spate of baffling injuries, and Clark was hoping that Allen could help out. Clark's team captain sprained his ankle so bad that he couldn't even walk the day before a game against Millikin; after a session with Allen, the player was cleared to play. Two offensive linemen were also miraculously cured, as was the ankle of a two-sport star named George Halas; Allen repositioned the joints and got Halas healthy enough to play in a basketball game that night. By the time Allen left town, the *Champaign Daily News* had gotten wind of his healing tactics and proclaimed him a "miracle man."

The University of Illinois hired Phog Allen as an assistant football coach the following year, but the offer was rescinded when the effects of World War I forced the cancelation of the 1917 football season. It marked the second time in two years that Allen had missed out on a job, having been passed over for the AD job at Kansas Normal School in 1915.

World War I was the first of three wars that would involve the United States during Allen's coaching career, and it cast a pall over the second half of his tenure at Warrensburg. Boys from all over the United States were being called into duty, and the rising popularity of athletics took a backseat to a much more significant event that would carry on through the fall of 1918. Basketball was among the few sports that found a spike in popularity during the war years, as the game began to explode on a worldwide level while American troops taught it to fellow soldiers in places like France and Germany.

Allen himself was eligible for duty, having registered for the draft in September 1918, while serving a stint in the Student Army Training Corps (SATC) at Fort Sheridan, Illinois, between the 1917–18 and 1918–19 academic years. He didn't get called to serve and was back living in Warrensburg when the war ended in November 1918.

Through it all, the family of Phog and Bessie Allen continued to expand. The Warrensburg years saw the births of three more Allen children, who joined Mary in a family that grew through the war years while living two blocks south of campus on Union Street. The oldest boy in the family, Forrest Jr., was seven years old by the fall of 1918 and had already taken a special place in his father's heart. Not only did Forrest Jr. carry his father's name, but he was also his first boy. No doubt, Allen had visions of one day coaching Forrest Jr. on a basketball court, where their bond could only deepen. Milton Allen, given his name from his mother Bessie's maiden name, was three years behind Forrest Jr. Daughter Jane joined the family shortly thereafter, giving Phog and Bessie Allen four children as his coaching career prospered at Missouri State Normal School.

Bessie Allen settled into her role of mother and didn't mind staying in her husband's shadow. Living in the town where she'd gone to college, as his coaching career took off she became known less as Bessie and more often as Doc Allen's wife. When she had time, Mrs. Allen would help tutor the players and welcome them over for meals. Phog's players became almost like family—and family was her sole focus in those years.

His osteopathic clinic in Warrensburg was thriving, and Phog Allen was becoming a man about town. His reputation in both sport and medicine had found a home in Warrensburg, Missouri.

After the conclusion of World War I, the Warrensburg basketball team turned in another solid season in 1918–19. The Teachers went 14-6 and had won ten of twelve games down the stretch before dropping the season finale to a team called Schmeizers.

Phog Allen had gone 84-31 in seven years at Missouri State Normal School, District 2, to run up his career total to an astounding 199 victories. He was just thirty-three years old and had his career in front of him by the spring of 1919, but to some people in Warrensburg winning basketball games wasn't enough. Sometimes success could come with a cost, and for Phog Allen, despite his ability to thrive on the basketball court and in the training room, his reputation was about to catch up with him.

The man who had such a promising career in coaching at such a young age was about to be out of work.

8

Once a Jayhawk

The athlete was on the verge of tears. Doc Allen could see the young man through a crack in the office door, but he dared not enter. He could not hear the words being said. Allen resisted the urge to creep closer, to find out what the boy—one of his boys—was doing inside Dr. James Naismith's office in the physical education department at the University of Kansas. Naismith had developed a reputation as a good listener during his time at KU; Phog couldn't dispute that. But this was one of his players, and Allen couldn't stand the thought of being left on the outside. "Esprit de corps, boys!" he had always said, essentially telling his teams it was all for one.

Now, in this moment, Allen felt like an outsider.

Why hadn't the player come to him? What could be so important that the player enlisted the trust of Naismith over that of Allen?

When the session was over, and the door opened, the athlete saw Coach Allen standing on the other side. The player scurried past, leaving Doc Allen and Dr. Naismith alone on either side of the doorway.

"What was that about?" Allen asked, looking into Naismith's office. Dr. James Naismith, with his round spectacles, his worn features and his haggard body, stood from his chair. "If he wanted you to know," Naismith said, "he'd have told you." And then he closed the door.

The second time Phog Allen's career as a basketball coach came to an end was in May of 1919, when the thirty-three-year-old rising star stepped down from his post as head coach at Warrensburg Teachers College. He was out of work, with one eye on an opening at a school he knew very well.

Allen's decision to leave Warrensburg wasn't solely about another opportunity. He would later contend that he'd turned down several offers and a significant pay raise to leave the school, which he did before he had another coaching job in place. The real reason for Doc Allen's decision stemmed from issues surrounding his osteopathy practice. During what would become his final year of coaching the Warrensburg basketball team, there were rumblings about his osteopathic clinic and questions about whether the nontraditional "doctor" was taking away patients from the "real" medical professionals in town. Two of the regents at Warrensburg Teachers College—as Missouri State Normal School had become known during Allen's tenure—were doctors. Their concerns about losing patients to Phog Allen, whose services were both cheaper and more readily available, forced the school to give Allen an ultimatum. If he was going to return to Warrensburg after the 1918-19 season, he would either have to coach basketball or practice osteopathy—he could not do both. Allen decided he would do neither. No one was going to tell him what he could and could not do, and so Allen left the school and began looking in a new direction.

Coincidentally, the University of Kansas was soon looking for a new manager of athletics—a position that later became known as athletic director—after W. O. Hamilton, the man who had replaced Allen as basketball coach in 1909, decided to give up both positions in June 1919 to concentrate on his auto dealership. Hamilton's two losing seasons over the previous four years may have also been a factor, as the KU basketball program had fallen from its perch among the elite teams in the West. KU officials tabbed Baker University athletic director Karl Schlademan to take over as coach of the basketball, track, and freshman football teams, but the school was still looking for a manager of athletics—and Allen was interested in the job.

Hamilton had initially promised the position to former KU football player George "Potsy" Clark, who received a discharge from the army at the conclusion of World War I and was said to have made an agreement to replace Hamilton as manager of athletics while also taking over as the Jayhawks' football coach. Hamilton himself had arranged the hiring of his own replacement, but a scheduled June meeting with Clark in Chicago fell through due to a travel snafu shortly after Clark returned to the United States. In the days that followed, Potsy Clark had some kind of falling out with KU chancellor Frank Strong, resulting in Clark telling the school that he had decided to return to job he once held at the University of Illinois. The Kansas athletic department was suddenly without a leading man and also had less than two months to find a new football coach, leaving the department, in the words of the *Lawrence Journal World,* "simply blown up." Within days, the school announced baseball coach Leon McCarty would take over as football coach, but the school still didn't have a manager of athletics.

After a rushed search, KU's final decision came down to former football coach A. R. "Bert" Kennedy, who had most recently been coaching football at the Haskell Institute, and Allen, who had KU roots and had gone 84-31 over seven seasons at Warrensburg Teachers College. With all of the KU coaching positions filled, Allen was hoping to become manager of athletics while overseeing the department at a school where he had both played and coached basketball more than a decade earlier.

One of the main people making the decision was physical education director James Naismith, who had first discovered Allen as a basketball player and whom Allen considered a confidant. Allen in many ways idolized Naismith, the creator of the game he so loved. But Naismith made it be known that he preferred Kennedy for the job of manager of athletics at Kansas. A difference in philosophy had created a bit of a division between Naismith and his former pupil over the years, and by the time KU's manager of athletics post opened up before the 1919–20 academic year, the pair of future basketball legends had a cordial relationship but greatly differing visions of athletics as a whole.

Naismith had always seen himself as a mind-over-matter type who viewed basketball, the very game he created, as a recreational sport intended to bring out some of the best characteristics in young students. He saw value in the competitive aspect of the game but very little reward in winning a given contest, as evidenced by a quote in Naismith's 1941 autobiography: "Let us all be able to lose gracefully and win courteously." Naismith gave one famous speech decrying the commercialism of sports. Phog Allen, by contrast, was all about winning and the financial effect sports could have on a university. He saw basketball as a rising sport that could bring unprecedented dollars to the University of Kansas, if the athletic department was willing to believe in him and support the game as a money-making endeavor.

Allen had a vision for basketball, one quite different from that of Naismith. He believed in the potential impact of basketball if allowed to mature. Naismith, by contrast, harbored no such aspirations for the game he created. As Allen would later summarize, basketball's inventor was "like the farmer with the grain of corn: He planted it and it grew." *Time* magazine would come to call Naismith "shrewd enough to invent the game of basketball but not shrewd enough to exploit it." Phog Allen would have no such problem. As basketball pioneers went, he was the big-city developer; Naismith was the carpenter who'd built the log cabin by hand and was content to sit on the porch, proudly looking out at the view.

Naismith's true motivation for preferring Kennedy over his former player for the KU athletic manager's job was never publicly disclosed, but Allen did have an important supporter in KU chancellor Frank Strong. A Yale-educated man who had been serving as chancellor at Kansas since 1902, Strong had made a name for himself by bringing in significant funds to KU, eventually resulting in the addition of schools in medicine, journalism, and economics. He may very well have seen financial potential in the hiring of Allen, especially at a time when the school was trying to find ways to add to its coffers, and he pressured the ten-member athletic board to give the former basketball coach the job.

By a vote of 7-2, with one abstaining, Allen was voted in as manager of athletics at the University of Kansas on September 15, 1919. Five days later, Allen's hire was approved by the governor and state board of admission. At a salary of $3,500—about twice what he was making annually at Warrensburg Teachers College—he would oversee the athletic programs throughout the department while devising better ways to use sports as a financial vehicle, driving the growth of the university as a whole.

Allen rejoined a KU that was still reeling from the effects of World War

I, which had concluded a year earlier in the summer of 1918. In the twelve months that had followed the war, the university was still picking up the pieces of financial setbacks and featured a growing student population of around four thousand students that included hundreds of World War I veterans. Men who were old enough to be fully established in the working world were instead beginning their first or second years of college, and the experiences they'd had overseas left the veterans with a vastly different outlook on life than those young men and women who'd been protected by the bubble of innocence on American soil. The war veterans tended to stick together, honoring a "Loyalty First" pact that they'd made in the military while largely disregarding the rules set by the "other" authority figures.

From an athletics standpoint, the University of Kansas that Allen found upon his return was figuring out its own set of issues. The football program was stuck in a pattern of mediocrity exemplified by the fact that it had had three different head coaches in a span of three years, while smaller sports like track and baseball were still trying to forge their ways onto the national map. Basketball was king at KU, but the Jayhawks of the hardwood hadn't finished higher than third in the conference in four seasons and were coming off of a 7-9 campaign. Allen was hoping that new basketball coach Karl Schlademan could take KU basketball to the next level, and he was also looking for ways to give the football and track programs more visibility.

McCarty, the baseball coach, led the KU football team through a modest season that fall, then Schlademan's Jayhawk basketball team beat Emporia State 37-22 in the 1919-20 season opener. That would end up being the only game Schlademan would ever coach, as the twenty-nine-year-old stepped down with the explanation that he would like to concentrate on his duties as a track coach. Phog Allen saw a different motive, one he wouldn't disclose publicly for about a half century. As Allen would hypothesize to the *Kansas City Star* fifty years later, Schlademan's decision was based on being "too scared of these boys coming back from the war." Young, confident, and in the early weeks of his tenure as athletic manager, thirty-four-year-old Phog Allen wasn't scared of anything.

With just two days between the Jayhawks' 1919-20 season opener and a game against Washburn University, Allen didn't have enough time to find another basketball coach in his relatively new job as KU's manager of athletics. And so Phog Allen decided to coach the Kansas basketball team for the night. Donning a tailored suit, he took the court with a team of fourteen players for the second game of the season, an intrastate clash with Washburn. With very little insight into the players and the strengths and weaknesses of the team as a whole, Allen used his entire fourteen-man roster on the way to a 50–40 win, the two hundredth victory of his coaching career. Being back on the court brought an undeniable tingle to the former player and coach, and so Allen stayed on as the KU basketball coach for the next game. And the next. And then the next. And on he went.

Along the way, Phog Allen encountered another disciplinary issue similar to the Ug Sermon incident at Missouri State Normal School, when a KU player named Howard "Scrubby" Laslett had the audacity to take his meal money and go to a picture show, along with teammate John Bunn, before a 1920 Valentine's Day game against Drake. Laslett was just the kind of player who may have driven Schlademan from his post as head basketball coach. "Scrubby" Laslett was fresh off of fighting with the Eighty-Ninth Division in World War I, one of many soldiers who had returned to the KU campus from overseas. Laslett was emblematic of a new generation of war veterans who clung to the military's "Loyalty First" mantra and were therefore unwilling to obey the superiority of anyone outside their circle of soldiers. By missing curfew, Laslett blatantly broke a team rule, and he betrayed Allen's trust by lying about his whereabouts. Allen caught wind of the deception but never confronted the players; he instead stood up before his seven healthy athletes in the minutes before the game against Drake and announced that five of them would be playing the entire game. He called out five of the players' names: "Lonborg! Rody! Bennett! Harms! And Fearing! You are the only five men who will carry they name of Kansas into battle tonight. You have earned that right. There are no substitutes for you." By not naming Laslett and Bunn, Allen had sent a message that they wouldn't be needed on this night. Dutch Lonborg, George Rody, Roy Bennett, Marvin Harms, and a little-used kid named Olin Fearing would be on the court for every second of action on the injury-plagued team.

The undermanned Jayhawks, many of whom were playing through twisted knees and charley horses, rolled out to a big lead and held a comfortable advantage into the fourth quarter when disaster struck. With just three minutes left in the game, one of Allen's five available players had just been whistled for his fourth—and final—foul. Allen was certain that the wrong player had been called for the foul, and he was on his way to the scorer's table to make the necessary correction when the Drake fans began booing and showering him with insults. Allen would later write that he was hoping to call over Drake coach Ossie Solem to include him in the discussion—"feeling that Solem would see my predicament," Allen wrote in a 1937 recollection of that game—but the crowd had gotten so unruly that Phog Allen decided to tuck his tail between his legs and retreat.

He headed back to the KU bench, pointed a begrudging finger toward Laslett, and summoned him to check into the game. The scrappy war veteran tore off his warm-up, ran out onto the floor, and helped close out a Kansas victory.

Several players on that 1919-20 team went on to follow Allen into the coaching profession, with remarkable success. Basketball's first known coach had such an impact on his players that the seeds for an impressive tree of coaches were planted on a team that included Bunn, a fellow senior named A. C. "Dutch" Lonberg, and a rarely used freshman farm boy from Halstead, Kansas, named Rupp. Lonberg and Bunn were key players on that Kansas team, Phog Allen's first upon returning to his alma mater, whereas the Rupp kid was such a nondescript benchwarmer that Phog Allen's own son Forrest Jr., not even ten years old, once leaned over during a game and taped a "Kick Me" sign on Rupp's back without the player noticing.

Lonberg would eventually go on to become one of the nation's finest basketball coaches, winning a national AAU title before leading Northwestern University to the 1931 Helms Foundation national title. Bunn won a 1937 Helms championship while turning Stanford University in California into a national powerhouse. And the benchwarmer named Rupp would surpass both of them in becoming a legendary coach in his own right. Adolph Rupp would eventually win an NCAA-record 876 games at Kentucky during a forty-one-year career that ended in 1972. That threesome, all of whom played for Allen during the 1919-20 season, combined to win 1,494 games as head basketball coaches in the years that followed.

But as a unit, the 1919–20 team could only manage eleven wins during an eighteen-game season in the first year of Allen's return to Kansas. The KU yearbook would sum up the 11-7 season like so: "The Jayhawker record was exceptional, considering local basketball conditions. Kansas teams have had very little coaching in the last few years and the new regime in the athletic department had a bunch of misfit stars from which to run out a machine."

Phog Allen's return to KU fell short of an overwhelming success in his first year back, but he was settling in nicely to his job as manager of athletics. His modest office was on the southwest end of Robinson Gym's second floor, his window looking out from atop Mount Oread at the Wakarusa Valley and the farmlands leading up to Pleasant Grove Hill. On game days, the sounds of dribbling basketballs and squeaking shoes cascaded from the gym a floor above. KU's manager of athletics and acting basketball coach had also begun treating athletes from all around the area, using his osteopathic techniques while fostering his reputation as having the skills to bring about quick healing. He did most of his work on the training table of the KU locker room at Robinson Gym, where athletes from all around the Midwest would come seeking medical advice. His reputation as a healer had grown to the point that football coaches like Knute Rockne, Pop Warner, and Amos Alonzo Stagg came to Allen looking for training tips.

Allen was somehow able to balance it all, and he felt comfortable enough wearing both hats that he decided to stay on as basketball coach beyond the 1919–20 season.

His home life was busy as well, with a family that had now swelled to six children constantly moving inside the comfortable house at 801 Louisiana. The four-bedroom home, with its stucco exterior and massive, framed-in backyard, radiated on a street made up mainly of modest single-level houses. The yard in back included a basketball hoop, where Forrest Jr. would heave balls toward the rim with moderate success while younger brother Milton watched in awe. Another boy, baby Robert, was too young to join the action yet. The boys would throw sand on the dirt-covered "court" surrounding the basket whenever it rained.

Allen was also making an impact in the classroom, where he added a class on coaching to the KU curriculum—the first of its kind in the Midwest.

In the fall of 1920, Phog Allen found himself in another quandary after an agreement with Potsy Clark to coach the football team fell through in the eleventh hour once again, marking the second time in just over a year that Clark had left the athletic department in limbo. With a new chancellor in place at KU, Clark had agreed to return to the school while replacing Leon McCarty as football coach, but the arrival got caught up in red tape. Michigan Agricultural School, which had hired Clark to coach its football team before Allen came calling, refused to let him out of his contract. That meant Clark wouldn't be able to come to Kansas until the following fall. By the time the news got back to Allen, it was too late to begin another coaching search. And so in 1920 Phog Allen added the position of head football coach to his own plate for one season. The school was in the process of coming up with funds for a new football stadium, and Allen's post as both athletic director and head football coach put the onus of the project squarely on his shoulders.

Phog Allen had a limited background in the sport, having played in high school and coached the Teachers football team in Warrensburg, so he knew enough to lead an experienced KU team that averaged only about 165 pounds per man to five victories to start the 1920 season—outscoring opponents 81–3 along the way. In beating Iowa State, Allen used some unconventional methods by relying on a dream to come up with his starting lineup—and to design the key play. The night before the October game, Allen dreamt he was on an airplane with eleven KU football players, all of whom he decided to start in the Iowa State game. His dream went on to feature Harley Little breaking off a long run on a "46" play; Allen then dialed up that play, which involved the right halfback running around left end, and Little scored on an 85-yard scamper on the first snap of the game. The Jayhawks had gotten off to a 5-0 start, and Allen had lived up to his new nickname of "Doc" while helping his own players, and more than a few from the other team, deal with injuries along the way.

But interest in the sport had waned over the years to the point that hardly anyone on campus seemed to notice that the KU football team had started the season so well. When the mighty Oklahoma Sooners hammered KU 21–9 on November 6, the 1920 Jayhawks swallowed a big dose of humility while what support the KU football team had generated came grinding to a halt.

Allen's football team didn't have a whole lot of momentum when the Jayhawks went to Lincoln, Nebraska, to face a powerhouse Nebraska team that had already shut out three of its first six opponents that fall. The Jayhawks were coming off of their first defeat of the season, and interest was waning to the point that the idea of building a new, larger stadium on campus was beginning to seem excessively ambitious. The Cornhuskers jumped out to a 20–0 halftime lead, and jubilant Nebraska fans showered the KU players with insults on their way to the visiting locker room. The most memorable one came from a man who told the scorekeeper to find more chalk because he might run out of it adding up all the Cornhuskers' points by the end of the second half.

As frustrated and downright angry as he had ever been in his coaching career to date, Allen stormed into the locker room practically foaming at the mouth. Before he could get a word out, a KU alumnus threw open the door of the locker room and began tormenting the players with a barrage of four-letter words to describe their pitiful performance. Allen shooed the guy from the halftime scene before giving some pointed comments of his own, and in the end the reenergized Jayhawks rallied to score 20 unanswered points in the second half—resulting in a 20–20 tie with the mighty Cornhuskers.

The excitement generated from that game—even given that it was a tie—was reported to have led to two hundred thousand dollars in donations for a new football facility that would eventually be named Memorial Field. The first football stadium to be built on a college campus west of the Mississippi River, Memorial Field featured enough bleachers behind either sideline to fit twenty-two thousand fans total in the open-ended stadium. Allen would come to call the building of the football stadium "the most delightful and gratifying thing that has come to me in athletics." With its funding raised, Allen had put his stamp on the KU athletic department in less than two years on the job.

Allen had finally asserted himself as the lead player in the Kansas athletic department, and yet the hierarchy of that segment of the university made for some uncomfortable relations. James Naismith remained a key department figure as director of physical education, and the diametrically opposing philosophies of the fellow university employees—along with Allen's transition from Naismith's student and player to his equal colleague—made for a somewhat strained coexistence.

Naismith, having recently spent time overseas as a World War I volunteer while Allen was coaching in Warrensburg, had turned the bulk of his attention toward his physical education students and had little interest in bringing KU basketball to center stage of the national perspective. He had become a confidant to students as well, offering a patient ear and gentleman's trust to anyone who was struggling; at least one such visitor would be an athlete on a team coached by Phog Allen, leading to an uncomfortable run-in at the doorway of Naismith's office. There were some people who believed that Allen became somewhat envious of the relationships Naismith had developed with students, and that only strained the relations between the two basketball pioneers even more.

But mainly the rift between Naismith and Allen had to do with the role of athletics in a university's overall experience. Naismith was against selling tickets to Jayhawks games, which led to one of his biggest disagreements with Phog Allen. Naismith saw the selling of tickets—in 1920, KU basketball games cost thirty-five cents for general admission and fifty cents for reserved seats—as an unveiled way of exploiting student-athletes who were, in Naismith's mind, *students* first. Allen was in favor of selling as many tickets as possible while using the money to help build up the athletic department and the school.

Allen's vision seemed to agree with new school chancellor Ernest Lindley, who replaced Frank Strong in 1920 and four years later would strip Naismith of his title as physical education director. Lindley would give those duties to Allen in 1924, while Naismith would remain on the faculty as a teacher. But Allen did his part to keep Naismith a part of the basketball program, whether that meant inviting him to sit in on team photos or lobbying to get Naismith's name on the NCAA's official book of basketball rules.

As a basketball coach, Phog Allen had developed a strict set of philosophies by the time he began year two of his second stint with the Jayhawks in 1920–21. He had reshaped the game with the use of a set offense and with a defense that primarily used a man-to-man philosophy but also saw some of the earliest incarnations of what came to be known as a zone defense. Allen continued to laboriously drill his players during crisp two-hour practices based in fundamentals. His sessions included lessons on the foot pivot, the techniques of hook and bounce passes, and explanations about the importance on giving each shot a proper arc. Every detail was painstakingly planned out, from the angle a player would take when going after a rebound to the distance from the sideline a player should run down the court: exactly six feet—not five and not seven—to leave enough room so that the player could corral an errant pass. Allen didn't introduce a ball into practices until his players had shown the proper fundamentals and mastered body movement.

Practice, Phog Allen believed, was the only time he was truly in control of a team. If his players developed physical rote through constant repetition, there would be no need for him to do any coaching on game days. In a perfect world, he would do all of his yelling at practice and watch in silence as the players put his lessons to work when it came time for games. "When two teams of equal ability meet," Allen would later write, "the team possessing the better fundamentals usually wins the game." Allen continued to pass around his worn copy of Helen Keller's autobiography, his players obligatorily reading it but many of them not fully comprehending why. Only later would he explain that sense of touch was the most key element to handling a basketball, and Keller's book provided an illuminating explanation of the importance of developing that sense. Deaf and blind, Keller's entire world was at her fingertips, and the acute sense of touch she developed was what he hoped to instill in his players, some of whom he was even known to blindfold on occasion as a teaching tool.

He also liked to run a drill called the "ape man," during which his defensive player would crouch down, wave their arms, and make primate sounds in an effort to throw off the dribbler. While the players were not allowed to speak at practice unless asking a question, Allen gave so much verbal instruction that he often yelled himself hoarse. To remedy his vocal chords, he sucked on horehound candy after every practice and throughout the hours that followed.

Shadow boxing also remained a constant aspect of his practices; years later, he would explain why in print: "Boxing teaches the follow-through more readily than any other sport." Over time, boxing also brought footwork, discipline, and a fighter's mentality that helped shape the toughness of his teams. Allen demanded players take periodic breaks between fundamental drills to stretch the fingers, wrists, ankles, and knees, which Allen considered "the parts of a player's anatomy that are most susceptible to injury." He discouraged drinking water during practice but encouraged gargling to moisten the larynx—a key to keeping players fresh, Allen believed. He also found importance in keeping the larynx warm, which is why Allen could often be seen wearing a Turkish towel around his neck at practices, along with a sweatsuit and gym shoes so he could be ready to jump into the throes of a drill.

The thirty-five-year-old Allen stayed in game shape so that he could most effectively teach his players how to put his techniques into action. "It is said that the eyes are 20 times stronger than the ears," he once wrote, "and a coach who is able to jerk off his warm-ups at will and adequately demonstrate his theories to his players will sell himself to them as an expert in the line of what they want to know." Allen was known to play a feverish game of handball, and at times he would use the sport to discipline his players. Laziness at practice or inattentiveness in meetings was often met with an invitation to meet Phog on the handball court, where forty-five minutes would be enough to send the offending player the intended message. His twice-daily routine of push-ups, finger-to-toe crunches, and one-legged squats continued each morning and night, and Phog Allen took particular pride in the way his body looked shirtless. He was extremely fashion-conscious, with gameday suits becoming more and more dapper throughout the course of a season. Imported tweed suitcoats, usually in grey or beige, were often his preference, and over time fans came to expect his trademark yellow pocket square and red socks.

On game days, he would allow his players to sleep in, and then he would get them together for a large brunch. The Jayhawks would then spend thirty minutes singing and playing around a piano "for the purpose of building team morale." As Allen wrote, "a squad talented in singing and playing rarely suffers from staleness." The coach and players then took a brisk, two-mile walk in whatever weather the day offered; in the Midwestern winters, that often meant snow and cool air that felt like ice on the lungs. After returning to the hotel, Allen liked to have his players sit in front of a fire, with their shoes off and feet close to the heat, because he believed cold feet fostered nervousness. The players would then undergo a midafternoon massage and taping, often administered by Allen himself, before going up to their hotel rooms for some down time, which meant a nap, schoolwork, or simple relaxation before that night's game. Allen was a huge proponent of sleep, and he strongly encouraged his players to use those pregame hours to rest their bodies before battle. He harped on the importance of rest, and later in his career Allen would continually point to the example of a man named Elden Auker, a Major League Baseball pitcher who visited the Jayhawks at their hotel once and spent so much time kibitzing with them that he was too tired to throw strikes in a game he pitched that night. Those two words—"Elden Auker"—became shorthand for players to get off their feet before a game.

The pregame meals were painstakingly set to provide what Allen called "Spizzerinctum"—a self-induced energy that he believed could be increased by the amount of glycogen in one's body. His "boys," as Allen called the players, were given grapefruit, whole-wheat toast, a spoonful of honey, and a cup of hot chocolate before taking the court for pregame shoot-around. Even that was deliberately planned, with Allen forbidding his players to shoot from beyond six to eight feet in warm-ups so that their confidence would be soaring at tip-off.

But Phog Allen's greatest asset was his ability to motivate. He had a gift for gab from an early age and a knack for inspiring the troops. Phog's booming voice demanded attention. His favorite rallying cry was "Esprit de corps!"—loosely translated as "spirit of the team!" He had begun using phrases like "A team that won't be beaten can't be beaten!" He convinced his early KU teams that victory was an obligation—to their teammates, to the school, and to the players that came before them. He demanded silence in the locker room before games, and by the time Allen would stand in front of his "boys," he would have their rapt attention. The formula that developed over time involved Allen writing the names of the five starters on a chalkboard, along with their defensive assignments, before calling each of them out individually and asking, "Are you ready?" He would then take the time to explain in detail why the opponent was beatable and why the Jayhawks would not be beaten.

Paul Endacott, a sophomore on Allen's 1920–21 KU team, once explained Allen's motivational skills as "unusual."

"He would make these talks in the dressing room just before we'd go out," Endacott was quoted as saying in a 1991 book entitled *Kansas Jayhawks: History-Making Basketball*. "Full of fire, I'll tell you. Somebody would say: 'Well, what did he say?' And we'd say, 'Well, what *did* he say?' We didn't remember just what he did say. It could have been anything, but it got us to play."

Over time, Allen's pregame tactics would be compared to some of those used by coaches in other sports. As the *Kansas City Star* would later proclaim, "In this respect, he was to basketball what Knute Rockne was to football."

Much of Allen's effect came from the way he carried himself. There was an intentional distance kept between the coach and his players, who were provided with the expectations and the methods and then required to carry them out on game days. Compliments were not a part of Allen's coaching repertoire, and the bulk of his personal contact with his "boys" still came through written letters. If he sensed a player needed a morale boost, he would put pen to paper and leave a handwritten note in the player's locker. The following day, Allen would say nothing of the letter and be just as hard on the player as the drills went on and on.

His tactics proved worthy on the basketball court, despite a 1920–21 roster that was inexperienced and devoid of much obvious talent. The *Topeka State Journal* was so unimpressed with KU's roster before that campaign began that the newspaper pronounced, "Unless Phog can again accomplish a miracle, Kansas will have rough sledding thru [sic] the basketball season."

Allen answered the bell by leading the Jayhawks to a 6-0 record before the team lost eight of its next ten games on the way to a 10-8 record and fourth-place finish in the Missouri Valley Intercollegiate Athletic

Conference. It would mark one of the few times in Allen's career that his team would start off better than it would finish, as later Phog-coached teams would typically look unspectacular in the early going and peak over the final few weeks of the season. The 1920–21 season would also serve as the low-water mark of Allen's coaching career to date, even though he was pushing the program forward—both as a coach and as head of the school's athletic department.

Allen was also beginning to develop a reputation as an outspoken promoter who wasn't afraid to throw fuel onto a burning rivalry. The University of Missouri often seemed to be his target, from the time he got into a shouting match with Tigers basketball coach W. E. Meanwell in February 1920 to the unkind words he had to say about the Mizzou football team a few months later.

Missouri was a natural target for any KU coach, even one who had spent most of his life living in that state. The Quantrill raid of Lawrence more than a half century earlier was still fresh in the minds of many longtime residents, and the frequent athletic competition between the state's two largest universities kept the fire burning in a less violent, although not always civil, way.

Allen's jumped into the long-standing rivalry with both feet during a February 19, 1920, basketball game that would be described as "rough and tumble" by the *Columbia Evening Missourian* newspaper. Kansas player "Scrubby" Laslett, in the middle of the maelstrom again, got kicked out of the game for his rough play, leading to an argument between Allen and the Missouri coach that almost spilled over. "Phog Allen and Dr. W.E. Meanwell engaged in some personal conversation, each being quite uncomplimentary to the other," the *Evening Columbian* reported the following day. "Their discussions ended without real trouble." The *Kansas City Star* reported that Allen, upset with some unflattering things Meanwell had to say about Laslett, had told the Missouri coach to sit down and stop "acting like a high school coach, a boob."

Whether or not that carried over into the following fall only Allen could have known, but in November 1920, the *Evening Columbian* caught up with Allen before a big football game between the Jayhawks and Tigers and quoted the KU coach as saying, "Of course, we will only use about eleven of our nineteenth string men tomorrow as they will be able to ring up a victory against Missouri. We are much better than Missouri because Missouri is no team at all." Allen added that Kansas would "go through that line like water flows through a garden hose" and challenged the reporter to a wager by saying, "You don't believe it? Well, I'll bet you 55 cents to $900 that what I said will turn out to be the truth."

It turned out that Allen would have lost that bet—gambling and football were never really his thing—as the Jayhawks fell to the Missouri Tigers, 16-7.

Less than three months later, with Missouri on tap for the KU basketball team, Allen said the Jayhawks would "maul" Missou. They didn't, losing back-to-back games by an aggregate score of 74-47 to run Missouri's winning streak against KU to eight consecutive meetings, but it was apparent that the Kansas-Missouri rivalry was boiling in Allen's blood.

Despite the Jayhawks' uninspiring performance on the basketball court during Allen's return in the 1919-20 and 1920-21 seasons, the Missourian-turned-Kansan still found a way to enhance his basketball reputation—thanks in large part to the AAU national tournament that had moved to Kansas City's Convention Hall for the 1921 championships. The spotlight shone bright on Kansas City and its surrounding area, and Allen took advantage of the moment by shaking lots of hands and winning people over with his charismatic smile and basketball know-how. He had a way of putting people at ease with his friendly eyes and had a knack for remembering a man's name, even if months, sometimes years, had passed between interactions.

The AAU, formally known as the Amateur Athletic Union, had emerged as an important platform for the sport of basketball. Formed in the late 1800s to create some kind of uniformity within amateur athletics, the AAU began holding national basketball tournaments as early as 1897 and continued to be the link for amateur teams throughout the country. The rise of college basketball, also an amateur endeavor, led to somewhat of a friendly competition with the AAU by the 1920s.

During the national tournaments in Kansas City, Phog Allen began winning over AAU officials with his charm and opinionated conviction, and soon his name would become familiar in basketball circles all across the country.

It wouldn't take long for the young, outspoken coach with a gift for talking the talk to start walking the walk. After posting two mediocre seasons to restart his career at Kansas, Phog Allen was about to lead the Jayhawks on a storied climb to basketball prominence.

9

Ascent to New Heights

The players were starving. The only food that had been provided had come in the form of dry sandwiches, which the players had gobbled up on the first leg of their Iowa-to-Missouri trip, what felt like a week ago. After that, things had gone awry. Everything had fallen apart. A train malfunction had forced the players to unload in a part of Missouri where none of them had ever ventured. The only silver lining was the restaurant in the distance.

Only when their tired feet brought them to the front door did the coach notice a sign: COLOREDS ONLY. He looked at his players. All of them hungry. None of them "colored."

Phog Allen reached out and opened the door. The patrons turned to find eleven white men and boys, a few of them tall enough that the tops of their heads were not visible through the doorway. They waited outside while their coach made arrangements.

These were the days of strict segregation, at least in this part of Missouri. A group of white college students eating in the same diner as "colored" men, as African Americans were called back then, was simply not an option. But his players were starving. And there was no place else to go.

And so Phog Allen did the only thing he felt he could do. He had the restaurant cleared out so that his players could eat. They barely noticed the men strewn about outside, napkins still tucked into their shirts, as the

KU boys devoured "Ole Missoury" sow-belly, eggs, and lukewarm oatmeal before heading on their way.

The 1921–22 Jayhawks had no way of knowing that they were about to embark on a season that would rank as the best in the history of KU basketball to date and one that, nearly a century later, would still resonate as among the most memorable Kansas seasons of all time. Coming off of a 10-8 campaign that saw KU go 4–8 over its final twelve games, the Jayhawks weren't exactly rolling into the winter of 1921–22 on a high note.

But Phog "Doc" Allen knew his team might be special, and two years on the job had given the returning players a good feel for the thirty-six-year-old coach's system and expectations. Twenty-six players turned out for the team, each of them reporting directly to Allen's office to be surprised by a pop quiz on the rules and fundamentals of the game. They would then be given a rundown of the team expectations and rules, one of which was that no player was to speak at practice unless he was asking a question. None of the players would be cut from the squad, as Allen believed a large team fostered better camaraderie and gave more young men a chance to experience the joy of being part of a team.

Allen had to be most excited about a KU backcourt that included two of the strongest, hardest-working defenders in the conference in juniors Paul Endacott and Charlie Black. Known more for his defense than for his offense, Endacott was a stocky, 5'10" guard who played with such scrappiness that he included hard-shelled kneepads with his uniform. He grew up in KU's backyard, having graduated from Lawrence High School before earning all–Missouri Valley Intercollegiate Athletic Association honors in his first year of eligibility in 1920–21. Endacott and Black gave the 1921–22 Jayhawks a formidable backcourt that thrived on keeping opposing guards from getting into the paint, while 6'4" junior John Wulf provided Allen with his first big man. Wulf's presence served as testament to the growing reputation of Phog Allen, Wulf having come all the way from the southern border of Washington State to play for the Jayhawks because his high school coach had heard unbridled praise for the young University of Kansas coach with the funny name.

One area where Allen knew the 1921–22 Jayhawks were lacking was toughness. In an effort to fix that deficiency, he set up a weeklong prac-tice session in Minneapolis with the University of Minnesota, a physical team that was two years removed from an unbeaten season and Big Ten Conference championship. The two squads matched blows for a week, culminating in a convincing 32–11 Jayhawks win over Minnesota in the 1921–22 season opener. Things were looking up for Jayhawk basketball and its rising star of a coach. Allen's squad eventually rattled off five consecutive wins to open the season, with four of them coming by double-digit margins. Allen used an up-tempo system that moved the ball around—"passing and cutting," he preached, over and over again—and was designed to run opponents off the floor. As author Russell Rice wrote in his 1994 biography on former KU player Adolph Rupp, "You didn't stand around when you played for Allen." Screens were a staple of the movement offense; Allen taught his players the art of the anterior-posterior screen, the lateral screen and the diagonal screen, designed to catch defenders out of position while freezing up a clear path to the basket.

Missouri finally ended the Jayhawks' run with a 35–25 victory, the Tigers' ninth in a row in the Kansas rivalry. The school from Phog Allen's home state still had KU's number. Kansas basketball was on the rise, but it had yet to catch up to Mizzou in the border rivalry.

The loss to the hated Tigers didn't temper any of the bubbling excite-ment heading into a January 30 game against the Kansas City Athletic Club at Convention Hall in Kansas City. Allen's ties to both the KCAC and the arena were only part of the attraction, as the recent AAU tournament played there had solidified Convention Hall's standing as one of the top basketball venues in the country. The Kansas City Athletic Club was also coming off of an AAU national title, which it won in front of ten thousand fans at Convention Hall a few months earlier. In effect, the Jayhawks were being afforded an opportunity to see how they stacked up against the proverbial big boys. The AAU was, in those years, considered the preeminent stage for basketball. Amateur players who had used up their college eligibility would fill the rosters of AAU teams, and matching up with college teams often became like a men-against-boys competition.

A crowd of 4,272 fans showed up to watch Phog Allen's Jayhawks take on the KCAC in what was seen as a pretty rabid rivalry in the era—due in part to the number of former KU players who dotted the KCAC roster over the years. The Jayhawks ended up losing the game 34–32, but KU earned a gate check of one thousand dollars—believed to be the largest take in a college basketball game to date. Allen's progressive visions were beginning to pay off financially for the University of Kansas—with or without the support of Dr. James Naismith.

The back-to-back losses left the Jayhawks staring at a 5-2 record. With seven of its next nine games on the road, all in the month of February, KU was looking at a pivotal stretch that would end up serving as the first great era of Kansas basketball.

The Jayhawks snapped their two-game losing streak with a 41–24 win at Oklahoma behind senior George Rody's 23 points, and the ball kept rolling after that. Iowa State and Kansas State fell victim to KU's wave of momentum, leaving Kansas at 8-2. Oklahoma fell short again on February 11, then Kansas beat Iowa State, Grinnell, and Drake on three consecutive days to set up a pivotal rematch with the hated Missouri Tigers.

The 11-2 Jayhawks had a chance to exact some revenge on their border rivals and could earn a share of the MVIAA Conference title in the process. But beating Missouri was much easier said than done. The Tigers had won nine consecutive meetings in the rivalry, dating back to February 1919, and Missouri was sporting an unblemished season record of 13-0 heading into the game with Allen's Jayhawks on February 21, 1922. But Allen's Jayhawks were on such a roll that one newspaper headline was billing the game as "Battle of [the] Century."

Practices were sharp in the days leading up to the Mizzou game, and one such session brought in a pair of unknown spectators to Robinson Gym. The duo sat conspicuously in the stands while taking notes, only to pique the interest of a twelve-year-old girl named Mary Allen. Phog's oldest child recognized them as former Missouri basketball players and sat down behind them to get a look at their scouting reports. She later turned the information over to her father, who then revised his game plan heading across the border for the game in Columbia.

Allen had to alter his plans again in the minutes leading up to the game, upon hearing that starting forward Armin Woestemeyer had been ruled academically ineligible shortly before tip-off. Rather than throw up his hands in frustration, Allen used the eleventh-hour news to his advantage. He was careful not to let word of the suspension leak out to the Missouri bench, hoping to keep Tigers coach Craig Ruby in the dark until well after tip-off. Allen put Woestemeyer's name in the line of a substitute in the scorebook, which he held during pregame warm-ups so that Ruby could see the names written down. Ruby asked Allen several times whether he had a lineup, but Allen continued to brush him off. He then had Woeste-meyer serve as scorekeeper while wearing his KU warm-ups. The confused Tigers, in an era when a player was only allowed to substitute into a game once, kept one of their top players on the bench so that he would be ready when Woestemeyer checked in. Of course, that never happened.

The strategy paid off. After losing to the rival Tigers by 10 points at home just four weeks earlier, Kansas turned around to beat Missouri 26–16—ending a nine-game losing streak to their interstate rivals. Rody and Endacott outscored the Tigers on their own, with 18 points between them, to lead the Jayhawks to their first win over Missouri since 1919. It also marked the first time a Phog Allen–coached team had beaten the Tigers since 1909 and created a tie atop the Missouri Valley Intercollegiate Athletic Association standings.

Afterward, Allen continued his Missouri-bashing custom when he told reporters, "At the end of the game the Tiger's tongue hung out so far that you couldn't tell whether it was his tongue or his tail."

The Jayhawks went a perfect 10-0 in the month of February and stood at 15-2 overall. Kansas finished off the historic 1921–22 season with a 41–18 victory over Nebraska, the Jayhawks' eleventh win in a row, while Rody's 14.7 points-per-game scoring average led KU to an overall record of 16-2. Missouri had an identical mark of 15-1 in conference games, splitting the MVIAA title. Missouri officials offered to play Kansas in a winner-take-all game as the two teams shared the top spot in the conference, but Allen and the KU chancellor refused the invitation.

There were people in and around Kansas who believed the Jayhawks were playing better than anyone in the country by the end of the 1921–22 season, but there was no way to prove it. The NCAA tournament was not yet in existence—the debut of the Big Dance was still seventeen years away—and that meant that the Jayhawks would not get to play another game, no matter how impressively they had closed out their regular season.

In those days, the only postseason tournament was the National Intercollegiate Basketball Tournament, which was recognized as the first postseason championship in college basketball history but was exclusive to six conferences. The Missouri Valley Intercollegiate Athletic Association was not among them, nor were the Big Ten and the Southwest Conferences. The tournament, which was held in Indianapolis, turned out to be a one-team show as 18-3 Wabash College rolled through three opponents—Illinois Wesleyan, Mercer (Georgia) University, and Kalamazoo (Michigan) College—by an average margin of 26.7 points per victory, an incredible gap in that low-scoring era of basketball.

The Jayhawks could only sit and wonder how they might have matched up with Wabash, which won the national postseason tournament but wasn't officially recognized as a national champion. Not until 1937, a full fifteen years after the 1921–22 Jayhawks had played their last game, did the honors begin to pour in.

The 1921–22 KU team wasn't crowned national champion until years later, when a forty-seven-year-old man named Paul Helms anointed that team as the country's best. Helms, a Syracuse University graduate who had gotten rich on a chain of bakeries all over California, joined up with a sports memorabilia collector named Bill Schroeder in 1936 to form a joint committee designed to recognize unified national champions and give out other awards in college football and basketball. The Helms Athletic Foundation, as it was called, was formed to recognize "official" national champion honors in both sports. By 1937, the foundation started giving out retroactive awards to past teams that its committee deemed worthy of annual championship titles as well.

One of those teams was the 1921–22 KU basketball team. It would go down in the record books as KU's first national championship in basketball. The Helms Foundation also retroactively honored Endacott as an All-American, making him the earliest Kansas player to have received first-team honors.

At least one organization thought the 1921–22 Jayhawks were the nation's best, and in the decades that followed, that season was widely accepted as KU basketball's first national championship year. There had been no celebrations or parades, and society was more infatuated with big bands, silent pictures, and politics than any sporting events in the early 1920s, and yet Phog Allen, in just his third year back at KU, had effectively risen to the top of the basketball world.

Through it all, Allen was using his basketball acumen and medical knowledge in congruence, serving as both coach and trainer. He was one of the first coaches to tape players' ankles, and Allen often spent the majority of the halftime intermission tending to injuries. He also started looking for ways to make the game of basketball better, and at the end of the 1921–22 season, Allen began a movement that would create a new rule that put free throws in the hands of the player who was fouled—in effect, the "designated free-throw shooter" would no longer be a part of the game.

Endacott returned for his senior season in the fall of 1922–23, teaming with backcourt mate Charlie Black to give Kansas as formidable a pair as there was in basketball. The Jayhawks added a sophomore named Tusten "Tus" Ackerman, a 6′3″ forward/center from Endacott's alma mater of Lawrence High School who ended up bearing some of the scoring load lost in Rody's graduation. "Long" John Wulf was back in the middle for Allen's squad.

Having won the final eleven games of the previous season, the Jayhawks rolled into the 1922–23 campaign without any noticeable let-up. A planned five-mile walk in the snow before a season-opening win over Creighton sent the Jayhawks off on their journey, and the conditioning helped KU trample through nine consecutive wins to open the campaign. The pre-season cardio activity came in particularly handy during a January 16, 1923, game at Columbia, Missouri, which nearly ended in a Kansas forfeit.

The Jayhawks were coming off of a three-games-in-three-nights stint in Iowa when their train destined for Columbia broke down nine miles out, in a town called McBaine. After putting the diners of a "colored-only" restaurant through the indignation of clearing out so that the team of eleven white players and coaches could grab a bite to eat, the Jayhawks boarded a picnic van that had been summoned—only to have that mode of transportation break down as well, after just three miles. Hungry, tired, and still sore from the three-game stint, the Jayhawks set out on foot, hoofing it six miles together while singing "The Crimson and the Blue" and "I'm a Jay-Jay-Jayhawk" as they walked. Upon arriving in Columbia, the players reported to their hotel and satiated themselves with porterhouse steak, a baked potato, a half-head of lettuce and cups of cocoa. After a night of rest, the Jayhawks were ready to take on a Missouri Tigers team that was thirsting for revenge after the previous season's streak-snapping loss. The sluggish Jayhawks found enough energy to salvage a 6-6 tie going into halftime but had nothing left in the tank at the break.

The five starters, none of whom had come out of the game in the first half, slumped over in folding chairs, panting in silence as their teammates waved towels over their sweat-soaked heads. They didn't even know whether they had the strength to stand up and take the floor, much less play another half of basketball. It seemed like no time at all had passed when suddenly the referee poked his head in the locker room and told the Jayhawks the second half would be beginning in three minutes.

Exhausted both physically and mentally, the players managed to stand but were as wobbly-kneed as a shot prize fighter. That's when the KU players' self-pity was interrupted by the sound of the Missouri team bursting down the stairs and past the Kansas locker room chanting, "Eat that Rock Chalk Jayhawk up! Eat that Rock Chalk up!"

As Allen would later write, "this was the tie that bound. In the minds of these boys the game took on new meaning. Before it had meant two universities; now it meant two states. The Kansans went on the court again, with jaws set and souls afire."

The rejuvenated Jayhawks came out and matched the Tigers for ten minutes. The score was 8-8, then 10-10. Finally Missouri made a run to pull ahead 16-10 with five minutes left—an almost insurmountable lead in the low-scoring era of the early 1920s.

But KU had one more run in it. Paul Endacott controlled a jump ball and drove for a basket. Charlie Black quickly added another on a drive a minute later, cutting the deficit to 16-14. Endacott grabbed another ball off a tip and drove for the tying score with just three and a half minutes left. Tus Ackerman joined the heroics with the go-ahead score, causing

Missouri to call a timeout. The Jayhawks led by two, then came out of the timeout and got fouled, making the free throw for a 19–16 lead.

Clinging to a three-point lead and holding the ball between two aggressive defenders in the KU backcourt, Kansas guard Charlie Black pulled off a trick that even made Phog Allen flash an I'll-be-darned look of awe. The crafty KU senior set the ball on his hip and stood up straight, calling out to teammate Verne Wilkin as if about to call a timeout. When the two defenders relaxed, Black dribbled between them and into the open court. KU eventually scored to open up a 21–16 lead while capping off an 11–0 run over four minutes of play.

Missouri answered with a basket and a free throw in the final minute, pulling within two points, then KU's Endacott stood outside the circle on a key jump ball with less than a minute remaining. Ackerman tipped the ball in his direction, and Endacott fell on the ball like a fumble in football. A Missouri player tied him up, and another jump ball was called. Endacott fell on the loose ball again. Another jump ball. Over and over again, this continued. "Sixteen times the ball was thrown up," Allen later recounted, and Endacott ended up with the ball every time. (Years later, Endacott would tell author Blair Kerkhoff that the sixteen consecutive jump balls story was "greatly exaggerated" by Allen's retelling, but he did acknowledge the importance of jump balls in the final seconds of that win.) At last the gun went off; the Jayhawks had held on—quite literally—for the 21–19 win.

Afterward, the players had to carry Endacott to the locker room. He slumped over in a chair, where Phog Allen found him unable to catch a breath.

"Upon examination," Allen later wrote, "I found that the intercostal muscles due to overexertion had cramped. He had played himself out."

Allen worked on Endacott for twenty minutes before the star was able to breathe regularly. There was little postgame celebration; no one had much left.

Eight days later, the Jayhawks carried a nineteen-game winning streak into a January 24, 1923, contest against the Kansas City Athletic Club team that was essentially a semipro club made up of former college stars. KU couldn't hit the proverbial broad side of a barn in that game, losing again to the KC Athletic Club, the program's first defeat in almost a full calendar year.

KU bounced back with a 27–21 win at Oklahoma, kicking off a seven-game winning streak that led up to the final game of the season. Missouri came to Lawrence for a winner-take-all game in the season finale, and the matchup generated so much buzz that two thousand fans had to be turned away at the gate.

No one knew it at the time, but Allen had apparently confided in his wife, Bessie, earlier in the season that anything short of an outright conference title would result in him retiring as a basketball coach. His motives weren't entirely known, but Phog Allen told Bessie privately that he was prepared to give up coaching and concentrate on his duties as athletic director and administrator if the Jayhawks didn't win an outright title—and it all came down to that February 28, 1923, game against the hated Missouri Tigers.

Facing a Missouri team that rolled in on a ten-game winning streak, Allen's Jayhawks jumped out to an 8-point lead early in the second half. The Tigers clawed away and scored 8 of the next 10 points to pull within 2 points, at 20–18. A Tus Ackerman free throw and a basket by Waldo Bowman in the final minutes helped Kansas hold off the late charge and win the game 23–20.

The fans that did get inside Robinson Gym were left in a state of stunned disbelief after the win. As the March 1, 1923, edition of the *University Daily Kansan* newspaper reported, "for a moment, everyone sat silent, unable to realize that it was all over—that Kansas had defeated Missouri again, and that K.U. had an all-victorious [unbeaten in conference play] basketball team—the first in the history of the Valley. Suddenly they realized the great climax, and rising to their feet roared forth the 'Crimson and the Blue,' with the hearts full of joy and minds teeming with memory of a great basketball battle and victory."

The 1922–23 Jayhawks had completed a 16-0 run through the Missouri Valley Intercollegiate Athletic Association schedule while winning the school's first outright conference title since 1915. They went 17-1 overall and, unbeknownst to them, probably kept their coach from retiring from the game of basketball.

Phog Allen's team was again among the best in the nation, and both

Endacott and Black were listed with eight others on the consensus All-America team that year. Endacott was widely recognized as the national player of the year, although that award wouldn't become official until the Helms Foundation began its retroactive honors fourteen years later.

The Helms Foundation would also honor Kansas as the 1922–23 national champions, retroactively giving Allen and the Jayhawks titles in back-to-back seasons.

Endacott went on to a five-year playing career with the Phillips Petroleum Company's AAU team, and he would eventually become president of the company. In 1972, almost a half century after leading Kansas to what would later be recognized as back-to-back titles, Paul Endacott was inducted into the Naismith Basketball Hall of Fame.

But losing Endacott and Black to graduation wasn't a program-killer for Phog Allen as the 1923–24 season approached. The veteran coach, who by that time was still not forty years old, had become somewhat of a big shot on the national basketball scene and had no trouble filling the shoes left by outgoing stars. Players from Kansas, and even a few outside the state, were clamoring to play for the man everyone called Doc; Allen's recruiting strategy in those days was simply to stay in the limelight and let the talent come to him. Phog Allen had brought KU to its first golden era of basketball and had an eye on even bigger things.

His next challenge was to bring a higher profile to the KU athletic department as a whole. Kansas football coach John Outland came to him in 1923, two years after the NCAA had held its first national championship in any sport by putting on a track and field meet in Chicago, with an idea about holding a nationally renowned track meet at KU. Allen began planning the early stages of an event called the Kansas Relays. A high-profile track meet could only add to the image of an athletic department that was proving its ability to stay ahead of the pack in terms of fresh ideas. Within the next few years, he would convince a group of internationally known runners from the Tarahumara Indian tribe in Mexico to come to the Relays to compete against Apache and Navajo tribes from the southwestern United States. As a publicity stunt, the Tarahumaras ran barefooted from Kansas City to KU's Memorial Stadium, forty miles away. The following day, they still had enough to blow away the competition at the Kansas Relays.

Like just about everything else Allen touched in those years, the Relays proved to be an overwhelming success. Receipts from the 1923–24 school year showed that more than twelve thousand fans attended the event, with many of them paying $1.50 per ticket, as the Relays brought in receipts of $12,335.50 to the school's budget. Allen convinced sport luminaries such as Knute Rockne and Michigan football coach Fielding Yost to attend the Relays as guest hosts, and he made such an impression on Rockne that they soon became friends and pen pals while jointly admiring one another's coaching skills from afar.

By the early-to mid-1920s, Allen had become the face of the KU athletic department while his longtime mentor, James Naismith, had faded into the background. KU's chancellor Ernest Lindley removed Naismith from his post as director of the school's physical education department in 1924 and replaced him with Allen. Whatever professional animosity continued to brew between the mentor/student pair who had become colleagues was no longer standing in the way of what Allen hoped to do with the KU athletic program. Naismith's opinions no longer mattered.

During his most successful early coaching years, Allen also became an author for the first time by penning *My Basket-Ball Bible*, which came out in 1924. The book, believed to be the first technical guide on basketball mechanics, detailed Allen's early strategies and philosophies, covering everything from on-ball defensive tactics to how to construct a basket. Allen provided some of the earliest tips on how to properly ventilate a gym, how to officiate a game, and how to draw up a schedule. He also gave examples of strength exercises and practice techniques for the sport, complete with a diagram of the weave, and even provided readers with "the correct way to eat an orange."

"Each bite," Allen wrote, "should be masticated fifty times."

A basketball, he added, should be shot one hundred times from the free throw line every day. *My Basket-Ball Bible* would be the first of three books written by Allen, who also spent his free time writing essays for other publications. All of his work would be dictated to wife Bessie; in effect, she had added secretarial duties to a daily schedule that also included tutoring her husband's KU players and keeping the family in order in the two-story, stucco house at 801 Louisiana.

The Allen home was certainly full in those years, with six children ranging in age from fourteen down to two-year-old Eleanor, the last of the Allen bunch. The backyard basketball goal had become a haven for twelve-year-old Forrest Jr., a long-limbed youngster who was developing into quite an athlete, and his nine-year-old brother, Milton. Forrest Jr., with floppy bangs parted down the middle of his long forehead and dark eyes that he'd inherited from his mother, successfully played the part of heroic older brother, with Milton and little Bobby, four years old and always the dutiful tagalong, following his every move.

Phog Allen had a strict rule forbidding his sons from talking basketball at the dinner table, and the typical conversations revolved around school and childhood friends. On Sundays after church, Phog would take the boys down to the basement and teach them to shadowbox, giving them the skills he had learned at a young age. Bessie Allen kept a very close eye on all of her children and seemed to be especially tuned in to where and with whom her kids were spending their time.

On the court, Phog's Jayhawks kept rolling. Kansas lost Endacott to graduation but was able to ride Tus Ackerman to a 16-3 record during the 1923–24 season. It marked the third consecutive MVIAA Conference title for the Jayhawks, who had a 49-6 overall record during that span and had won 81.6 percent of their games (102 of 125) during Phog Allen's two stints as head coach. Just thirty-nine years old, Allen had already amassed 259 career wins—in an era when teams often didn't play even twenty games in a single season.

From 1921 through 1925, Phog Allen held a four-year record of 66-7 with four conference titles—a decade later, the four-year period would also be recognized as featuring two national championships. He'd built a dynasty at his alma mater while proving that basketball, and sports in general, could provide economic benefits to a university. Allen's financial impact on the school in those years was undeniable, despite ongoing struggles by the KU football team, as the Kansas Relays and the growing popularity of KU basketball helped to bring in about twenty-three thousand dollars annually during the mid-1920s. He'd also been the leading player in the two hundred thousand dollars raised for the construction of Memorial Stadium, the KU football field.

And yet the seeds were being planted for a divide between Allen and the academic faculty at KU. His growing popularity was beginning to be met with some animosity and professional jealousy. While players and friends had come to calling him Doc, professors refused to use the nickname or acknowledge any kind of legitimate medical training. There were many in and around KU who were uncomfortable with the notion that the university was becoming known more for its athletics than for academics, and the outspokenness of a sportsman and a "Doc" lacking sufficient credentials made Allen somewhat of an easy target among professors and school administrators.

Through it all, Phog Allen's career as a basketball coach and administrator was thriving. But something that would happen in his personal life would forever change him and make basketball seem like nothing more than a distraction by comparison.

10

A Bitter Winter

The boy was slipping away. Phog Allen had already lost one child, and he'd be damned if he was about to lose another. When his oldest son was stolen away from him in a flash, just fourteen years old and with the whole world in front of him, Phog Allen asked himself what more he could have done—what more he should have done. How could the man they called Doc, a man who had earned a degree in the medical field, have stood by and watched so helplessly while his boy was taken away?

He wasn't going to make that mistake again. His son Milton was not going to slip through his fingers. Phog was going to do something.

"Down to the basement," he told the boy. Phog had run out of patience. He'd tried everything, even military school. He knew the boy was probably finding his own way of coping with the family tragedy. Who knows what goes on inside a teenage kid's head anyway—and now, after something as horrible as this? But the boy's disobedient ways had turned into disregard, to pure and simple rebellion. The boy spent his days smoking and drinking. Fighting. Not unlike a young Phog Allen himself, only the boy wasn't snapping out of it. Basketball wasn't enough to set him straight.

It was time to slap some sense into him. Phog followed the boy downstairs, down to the basement, and dug out two old pairs of boxing gloves. The sport had been a part of him for as far back as Phog could remember.

"Put them on," he said, handing one pair to the boy. Phog put on the other. And there they stood, father and son, eyes blazing. Face to face. Gloves raised.

The late summer of 1925 carried a gilded hope that reflected off the magnificent orange sky of a Kansas sunset. The pre-Depression scene in Lawrence bustled in growth that could be seen and heard all along Massachusetts Street. The New Eldridge Hotel, once the site of William Quantrill's raging fires, was being reconstructed for a second time at an estimated price of one hundred fifty thousand dollars. The Kansas Electric Power Company building and Bowersock Theatre were undergoing remodels. Massachusetts Street was being repaved for the coming school year.

"August, the month of vacations, finds Lawrence in the midst of a building and remodeling project unprecedented in the city," proclaimed the *Lawrence Journal World*.

In June of that year, the newspaper had reported $1.75 million in new business statewide, the third-highest total for any state in the country. Douglas County had received $19,000 from the federal government for roadwork, and the $200,000 construction of Memorial Stadium, KU's new football facility, was in full swing.

By the time the students reported in September, sweltering heat had taken hold of campus; for relief, swarms of students dressed in one-piece wool bathing suits could be seen dipping into Potter Lake at the center of campus. Radio stations were competing for bandwidth after the December 1924 debut of KFKU, the university's first radio station. With years of perspective, one might look back at these pre-Depression times as the end of the innocence.

The KU basketball team had risen out from the shadows of the Midwest and begun to generate some buzz on a national level, thanks in large part to the Jayhawks' brash, young coach. Phog "Doc" Allen was the very picture of his era, with ironed suits and carefully parted hair and his gameday red socks, mowing through life without any hint of mortality. Should his skin be punctured, surely the great Doc Allen would not bleed.

His career and family life were thriving, much like the economy in and around Lawrence, Kansas. By the mid-1920s, Phog and Bessie Allen had a complete family that provided both balance and a sense of grounding. He was not Phog or Doc or the KU basketball coach at the family home at 801 Louisiana, but simply Dad. The only reminder of his basketball ties at home was the basket out back. He spent whatever free time he could find rolling around on the living room floor, engaged in childlike tomfoolery with his two youngest kids, six-year-old Robert and four-year-old Eleanor. His family by 1925 also included a pair of teenagers (sixteen-year-old Mary and fourteen-year-old Forrest Jr.), two preteens (eleven-year-old Milton and nine-year-old Jane), and the two youngins scurrying around to keep up. More than two decades later, in his 1947 book *Phog Allen's Sports Stories*, he would remember his family in those years as "three sons and three daughters—alert, healthy, boisterous and busy—and always eager for vehement debates without obeying any rules or disqualifications." When he wasn't at home, Phog Allen's nonstop work schedule as a basketball coach, administrator, and university professor kept him busy, and he had acquired a full slate of speaking engagements throughout the Midwest, which he would attend by way of train or automobile. His unrelenting spate of obligations left most of the household chores to wife Bessie.

Bessie Allen was the key to Phog's ability to balance his duties, as she kept the children in order. Generations later, Bessie Allen would be described as a no-nonsense, controlling mother whose expectations were high for all six of her children. (By the time her two youngest boys reached high school, she would decide, without much input, who would be going to medical school and who would be the lawyer-in-training; years later, she would write a letter to the future wife of her youngest son, Bob, explaining why she wasn't right for him.) With her dark hair cut short and soft, midnight eyes that could turn cold at the first sign of misbehavior, Bessie Allen was the ruler of the roost. She was a woman small in stature and unassuming in demeanor, the kind of person who could fade into a crowd and was more than happy to stand in the shadows. She helped Phog by typing his notes, tutoring his players, and hosting visiting officials and media members, but her primary duty in life was protecting her six children.

For natural reasons, Phog Allen had developed a particular fondness for his oldest boy over the years. Forrest Jr. not only shared his father's name but also his love for sports. By the age of fourteen, Forrest Allen Jr.

was good enough to have earned a spot on the football team at Lawrence High School. He also played basketball and baseball, just like his father had, and was developing into quite a chip off the old block. There might even come a time, Phog realized, when Forrest Jr. might one day suit up for the Jayhawks and play for Dear Old Dad—a prospect about which Phog Allen had mixed feelings.

As Allen would later write in one of his three published books, "it is always difficult, if not unwise, for a father to attempt to coach his own son."

But the possibility seemed difficult to avoid in an era when young men and women rarely traveled far to attend college. Forrest Jr. and the rest of the Allen children seemed bound to KU and to walking in the huge footsteps of a father who was admired by so many and reviled by a few.

Forrest Jr. and his two younger brothers liked to shoot around on the basket outside the Allen family home, developing the kind of talents that made their father proud while watching from the kitchen window. Forrest Jr. had grown so tall that his two brothers couldn't keep up with him on the dirt basketball court out back, and by the end of the summer of 1925 the daily games withered out. The sweltering heat then yielded to an unexpected cold front—the worst Lawrence had seen in more than a half century.

In the icy autumn days of early October 1925, Forrest Jr. suddenly began feeling ill, and his symptoms quickly worsened. Forrest Sr. initially tended to the malady in the boy's room until a family doctor was brought in to help him days later. The initial diagnosis was typhoid fever, a relatively common disease that, a quarter century earlier, had been the source of 174 deaths per 100,000 people but for which a cure had since been developed. One account given decades later by one of Phog's grandchildren recalled that Forrest Jr. had also begun experiencing excruciating leg cramps to go along with a fever that the boy couldn't seem to shake. According to that account, passed down through generations, Forrest Jr. required round-the-clock observation, and a caregiver was brought in to provide assistance. The caregiver was said to have begun providing massages to the ailing leg at some point, unaware that the source of the pain had been blood clots—which were then dislodged and proceeded to head on a deadly path toward his heart. The fever persisted, leaving Phog and Bessie Allen's firstborn son bedridden for one week, then two. By the final week of October, Forrest

Jr. was still unable to stand or walk. His father and the family doctor, a man named Anderson, were perplexed by his condition.

In the early-morning hours of October 27, Forrest Jr. called out for his father, complaining that he was having trouble breathing. The shriek cut through a quiet house on a still morning. Outside, the wind blew gently in the darkness before dawn, the basketball court behind the Allen home empty on a frozen autumn morning. The *Lawrence Journal World* would later give this account of what happened next:

> Dr. Allen gave him treatment relieving the pain and left the room. A few minutes [later] he called again, as the pain had returned.
>
> Dr. Allen again treated his son, but the condition could not be entirely relieved. Almost before Dr. Allen and Dr. Anderson could realize it, the boy's heart had stopped beating. The heart trouble was a direct result of the typhoid.

At 6:30 a.m. on October 27, 1925, in the throes of the record-setting cold front, Forrest Clare Allen Jr. died at his parents' home on 801 Louisiana. He was just fourteen years old.

The newspaper the following day reported that "his sudden death came as a great shock to his parents and friends," citing typhoid fever as the cause of death. The child's obituary ran over two paragraphs, tucked between an advertisement for a product called Fletcher's Castoria and a short news story about "Jack Frost" forcing an early conclusion to KU's Tuesday afternoon football practice.

No autopsy was ever performed, and the death certificate for Forrest Clare Allen Jr. would list both coagulation of fibrin of the heart and thrombosis, the medical terms for a blood clot that forms inside of a blood vessel, as the causes of death. Typhoid fever was cited as a secondary factor.

On October 29, two days after Forrest Jr.'s death, a small memorial service was led by Dr. Edward Hislop of First Methodist Church at the family home on Louisiana Street. The boy was buried shortly thereafter, under a tombstone that carried the words: "He took life's higher trail of clean, happy, purposeful living."

There is no record of Phog Allen ever speaking publicly about his son's death. Typhoid fever was generally accepted as the cause of death, and

Phog's grandchildren would later admit that even the family never really knew for certain what killed young Forrest Jr., or whether Phog "Doc" Allen had a chance to prevent it.

For many parents stricken by the tragedy of a lost child, the only thing that gives them any strength to carry on is that desperate need for love from their other children. No matter how much a mother or father wants to collapse and succumb to the grief, he or she must press on, step by step, minute by minute, keeping their family together despite the pain. That was probably what Phog Allen did. He kept what was left of his "team" together by moving forward with a stiff upper lip and his chin held high.

In the two published books that Allen wrote over his twenty-two years after Forrest Jr.'s death, the boy's name was rarely mentioned. Even in a thirty-page section titled "Father and Sons" that closed out the 1947 book, *Phog Allen's Sports Stories*, Forrest Sr. wrote of his other two sons but never made reference to Forrest Jr. In the book's prologue, Phog made a passing acknowledgement when he wrote about how his family had changed in the years since his first book had been published in 1924, writing, "Five of our six children were still left to continue growing up." In Allen's 1937 book, *Better Basketball*, which would come out more than a decade after Forrest Jr.'s passing, he would dedicate the work "to the youth of Forrest, Jr., Milton and Robert, and to all youth who travel far and away through many a sport and game."

Despite the sparse mention of Forrest Jr. in the years that followed, the death of Phog Allen's fourteen-year-old son had a profound impact on the legendary coach. There were probably days when he'd look out the kitchen window, half-expecting to see Forrest Jr. dribbling a basketball, only to be struck by the sight of a deserted basketball court in the backyard. Phog was likely to walk past the closed door of his son's bedroom, resisting the urge to look inside. Perhaps the Allen house seemed too cold and large without young Forrest's wondrous energy and smile.

Somehow, Phog Allen was able to carry on. Pushing forward was a much better option than, say, getting one's feet stuck in the sorrow. As Elbert Hubbard, a well-known poet in the late nineteenth and early twentieth centuries, once wrote, "The cure for grief is motion." Allen just kept moving, as he had after his mother's death in 1904, around the time young

Forrest was planning his legendary game against the Buffalo Germans at the Kansas City Convention Hall, and heading into the 1925–26 season he probably felt he would have to do the same.

His first public comments following the tragedy came ten days later, when Allen formally announced the KU basketball schedule but made no mention of his son's death. Jayhawks practices began shortly thereafter, and by the turn of the calendar year, Allen was speaking to reporters about basketball issues while avoiding any mention of his personal life. His biggest concern, he told the *Journal World* newspaper, was the Jayhawks' free-throw shooting heading into the 1925–26 season.

On January 11, less than three months after Forrest Jr.'s death, the Jayhawks opened their season by hosting Washington University of St. Louis. Phog Allen, still stuck in sorrow from an unthinkable tragedy, watched his team lose a season-opening game at home for the first time in his nine seasons as KU's head coach. The 25–18 loss to Washington U. left serious doubts about the direction of the 1925–26 Jayhawks, who responded with wins over Kansas State and Grinnell on back-to-back nights but then lost to Oklahoma to sit at 2-2—Allen's worst record after four games in his career as head coach at KU. The emergence of 6'3" junior center Al Peterson helped turn things around, as the Jayhawks then rattled off fourteen consecutive victories en route to a 16-2 season record and the program's sixth consecutive conference title.

Peterson would lead Kansas to another banner year in 1926–27, when the Jayhawks went 15-2 overall and earned a share of yet another Missouri Valley Intercollegiate Athletic Association title—Allen's seventh in a row.

KU basketball had firmly established itself as a national power, and Phog Allen had the biggest name among college basketball coaches in the country. There were some people in and around Lawrence who believed he had done it at the expense of KU football. By 1927, the outspoken athletic director had already run off two football coaches in a span of three years—Potsy Clark and Frank Cappon, neither of whom appreciated the lack of attention Allen and the athletic department had paid to the football program during their tenures. Fans were getting restless with a football team that had fallen on hard times, and more than one of them wrote letters to the local newspaper asking for Allen to be fired. One infamous letter projected that the way to "get Kansas out of the fog is to get the Phog out of Kansas."

The school did not cave in to the demands, and Allen showed some dedication to the KU football program as he helped guide the renovation of Memorial Stadium in the summer of 1927—a project that would cost $660,000. A trip to the East Coast inspired that project, as Phog Allen returned from a tour of colleges in that part of the country and decided that a horseshoe shape would be best for the football venue.

During those hot months, a scrawny seventeen-year-old boy from Indiana traveled to Kansas in search of a lucrative summer job in the wheat fields—only to find that he had arrived too early in the farming season to find work. He ended up meeting Phog Allen, who hired him to work as a laborer in the expansion of Memorial Stadium. The KU coach found out that the teenager had recently led Martinsville High School to the Indiana state title as a junior and was about to head back to his home state for his senior year. Allen feverishly tried to convince the boy to return to Lawrence as a KU basketball player upon his 1928 graduation, but Phog's recruiting efforts went for naught, as seventeen-year-old John Wooden eventually finished high school and played college basketball at Purdue. Wooden's playing days would pave the way for a legendary coaching career of his own over the next few decades.

In the pre-Depression era of the mid-1920s, Allen continued to push forward. He was steadfastly trying to take the game of basketball to new heights. He took aim at all sorts of rules and was constantly looking for ways to expand basketball's potential as a marketing tool. Allen had helped turn the game into something more like a business, creating a professional wedge between himself and his altruistic mentor, James Naismith. Dr. Naismith may have created the game, but Phog Allen had taken ownership of it, a belief that Phog Allen would continue to carry throughout the remainder of his fifty-year coaching career. Allen despised the thought of outsiders profiting from the game, and the main target of his criticism was gambling. As he said in a 1926 radio interview, "the greatest and most menacing evil in athletics is gambling. It has wrecked every activity where it has sunk its fangs." If Naismith and Allen could agree on one thing, it was that the sport of basketball was best kept from the impurity of outside influences.

Allen was also developing a disdain for how the ever-increasing size of players was beginning to change the game. He began tinkering with the idea of raising the baskets to balance the proverbial scales and generally saw taller players as less talented, simply blessed by their height and rarely able to develop their fundamental skills like dribbling, passing, and shooting.

It was a drum that Allen would continue to beat for most of the rest of his career. He began a crusade that would aim to make the big man a less prominent part of the game. The answer, he maintained for the good part of the next two decades, was to raise the baskets twenty-four inches, up to twelve feet. That would take away the obvious advantage of taller players while speeding up the game in the process. As Allen would surmise, "if we raised the goals, these mezzanine-peeping goons wouldn't be able to score like little children pushing pennies into gum machines."

Phog Allen, a 5'10" ball of dynamite whose own playing career was built on proficient shooting and using the pass and dribble to get defenders out of position, wasn't going to let giants run his favorite sport. He held an affinity for guard play, which he helped to revolutionize from a strictly defensive position to one that could run the offense through slick ball-handling. Allen seemed to sum up his philosophy of how to build a team when he later wrote, "Some of the fastest basketball players I have ever seen, as well as the most dramatic, have been little men." He also knew how important ball-handling was to the sport, noting, "The dribble presents more opportunities than any other play in basketball."

When basketball's Joint Rules Committee put into motion a movement to abolish the dribble from the game of basketball, Allen was obviously opposed. The prospective rule change was brought about by Wisconsin coach W. E. Meanwell, a onetime Allen rival from the University of Missouri, because college players had been taking liberties with the dribbling rules. This required the rulemakers to constantly tweak and revise every offseason. Basketballs were much heavier in those days, with string laces atop one of the spheres of leather surface, and Meanwell believed that getting rid of the dribble would open up the game and make passing a more important aspect.

Never one to sit back and watch, Allen stepped to the forefront of the movement to save the dribble. He voiced his disgust during an address at the 1927 National Education Association meetings, and that speech generated so much buzz that Allen received 160 letters of support from coaches in the coming days and weeks. He decided to get all the coaches from the Missouri Valley Intercollegiate Athletic Association together for an impromptu meeting at the Drake Relays in the spring of 1927. Before long, eight Big Ten coaches agreed to attend the meeting. Other coaches trickled in as well, and soon the group was able to fend off the proposed rule change through sheer power of numbers.

That meeting spawned the creation of the National Association of Basketball Coaches (NABC), an organization that would become a driving force in the changing face of basketball. Allen was named the NABC's first president, and twelve years later the organization would put together the first NCAA men's basketball tournament. With Allen serving as chairman, the NABC would begin to revolutionize the sport over the next decade. The seeds had been planted for Phog Allen to help take the game to heights that James Naismith never could have imagined.

By the late 1920s, the name Forrest "Phog" Allen had become synonymous with basketball, and he had undoubtedly risen to the post of most visible figure at the University of Kansas. But James Naismith was not the only Kansan who was uncomfortable with the increasing role of athletics in the educational environment, and soon Phog Allen pushed himself into the center of another firestorm.

It began when a well-known writer named William Allen White penned a 1927 column deriding the importance of athletics by surmising, "A football or basketball victory only attracts the undesirable students and not those that you particularly care for." Allen was both sharp and quick in defense. He pointed out in a letter to White that athletics could be a pathway to a more educated society, writing, "If a boy is able to compete through his three or four years of college life, he is sure to graduate."

Allen was defiant in his opposition to the notion of athletics taking away from the collegiate experience, and despite his driving passion to win at all costs, Phog did agree with Naismith in the belief that sport could help shape a man. He believed in making winners out of the "boys" who trusted in him as KU basketball players, but even more than that, Phog Allen believed in shaping them into men. Whenever he was asked to name the most successful KU basketball team of all time, Allen was always quick to quip, "I'll tell you in 25 years, when I see how they do in the business world."

Through all of his influence on the game and its steady rise as a mainstream sport, Phog Allen's main focus was still the KU basketball team. Allen brought a seven-year reign of conference titles into the 1927–28 season, and his latest group of undersized scrappers was looking for a scorer to take over for graduated star Al Peterson. The coach was also trying to find a way to survive in a growing game that seemed to just keep getting bigger and bigger. Conference rival Oklahoma had a 6'6" star in Victor Holt, joining Purdue center "Stretch" Murphy as 6'6" All-Americans. Opposing MVIAA teams were finding taller players to move the sport from a guard-dominated game to one geared for big men who could control the tip and dominate the boards, and Allen's growing frustration with the height disparity was apparent whenever his smaller KU team took the floor. His crusade to move the baskets up to twelve feet wasn't generating much support, so Allen's teams were going to have to find other ways to combat bigger opponents.

The Jayhawks' 1927–28 schedule included eighteen games, exclusively against conference foes, and began with KU's three most fierce rivals—Kansas State, Missouri, and Oklahoma—among the first four opponents. All three rivals beat KU as the 1927–28 Jayhawks got off to a 1-3 start. The team never really found the right chemistry, eventually finishing at 9-9 while going 0-6 against Missouri, K-State, and OU. It marked Allen's first time as a head coach failing to finish a season with a winning record, and he set out to find a way to get back on track as the Jayhawks prepared for yet another change: the move from Robinson Gym to the new four-thousand-seat Hoch Auditorium.

Allen believed the new gym could improve recruiting, which would be a good start in his ongoing quest to get KU back to the top while also playing in a new conference called the Big Six. The $350,000 Hoch Auditorium, also to be used for concerts and speaking engagements, did not include a locker room for the home team; the players would dress next door in the facilities at Old Robinson Gym. The team continued to practice at Robinson, using Hoch only on game days. Hoch was an imperfect facility in other ways as well, with dim lighting and faulty sightlines that distracted shooters and created an optical illusion that opposing teams would swear was due to a tilted floor. Decades after its official opening, one of Allen's main rivals would begin referring to Hoch as the "House of Horrors."

How the Jayhawks might turn Hoch Auditorium into a home court advantage was Allen's big conundrum, especially after posting a 9-9 record—his worst as KU's head coach—the previous year. Allen went into the spring of 1928 desperate to find a solution, and he arrived at the strangest of locations.

The answer to the Jayhawks' size problems, Phog Allen presumed, came in the form of a 7'0" Nebraskan who was playing junior-college basketball at Doane College. Harry "High Pocket" Kersenbrock was believed to be the biggest high schooler in the country when the University of Nebraska went out to scout him two years earlier, eventually deciding that he was too uncoordinated to make much of a difference on a college basketball court. Upon receiving a letter from Pop Klein, Kersenbrock's coach at Crete High School, Allen had continued to follow High Pocket's junior-college career and watched him develop into a much-improved big man who could prove to be unguardable in a conference featuring mostly 6'3" and 6'4" post players.

Kersenbrock enrolled at KU in the spring of 1928, and Allen spent practice time putting two bruising football players—Glenn "Zeke" Burton and Harold "Dutch" Houser—on either side of him in an effort to simulate how defenses might try to guard the 7'0" beanpole. Kersenbrock didn't flinch, dominating the beefy defenders while validating Allen's decision to take a chance on him. As Allen would later write, "'High Pocket's elbows were like pistons as they crashed against the heads of the two [defenders]. Burton and Houser would come running out of these scrimmages holding their heads as if cocoanuts [sic] had been dropped on them." The Jayhawks' biggest player would be eligible in the fall of 1928, and Allen couldn't wait to unveil the giant before the rest of the conference.

Kersenbrock returned home to Crete, Nebraska, for the summer, and around dinnertime on June 28, 1928, three days after Phog and Bessie Allen celebrated their twentieth wedding anniversary, Harry "High Pocket" Kersenbrock went canoeing with a friend on the Blue River. At some point the boat capsized, and Kersenbrock went under water. His friend swam safely to shore and called out for Kersenbrock to hold onto the canoe. The 7'0" young man lost his grip and disappeared under the shallow, fast-moving water.

The body of Harold Kersenbrock wasn't found until about an hour later.

Phog Allen received a call from Kersenbrock's sister, Mary, at 2 a.m., delivering the tragic news.

"I could not believe it," Phog Allen would write almost two decades later, in a book entitled *Phog Allen's Sports Stories*. "It seemed that I was having a nightmare from which I couldn't awaken. . . . In that moment all the plans we had for this fine gentle giant of a boy faded dismally in our misery and grief. A bosom friend of our whole family was suddenly gone."

The result was the worst season in the history of KU basketball. The 1928-29 Jayhawks fell to 3-15 and tied for last place in the newly established Big Six Conference. It would mark the low point in Allen's career in terms of win–loss percentage, and the Jayhawks had a long way to go to get back on track.

"Lack of stamina to carry their scoring tactics into the second half was fatal to the Jayhawker basketball team this year," the *Jayhawker* yearbook reported that spring, "and caused them to suffer one of the most disastrous seasons in history."

As Allen would write eighteen years later, "the year of 1929 is still a nightmare to me. It stays alive in memory to remind me that the best laid schemes of men often go awry."

Making matters worse, the Great Depression cast a dark cloud over the entire country that would hover for the next decade. The stock market crash of Black Tuesday hit on October 29, 1929, sending the U.S. government into a catastrophic financial downturn that would siphon the country of both dollars and dignity. It was the darkest of times for the United States, for the Kansas basketball program, and for Phog Allen. And yet there were some who were looking toward sports for relief from the constant flood of despair. Attendance was down at sporting events across the board, but in many ways interest was rising. The importance of athletics, once considered "the devil's work" in American society, was at an all-time high in the late 1920s—as evidenced by the rise of stars like Jack Dempsey, Babe Ruth, and Red Grange in an era when sports were being relied upon to help entertain a grieving nation. Some referred to the twenties as the golden decade of sports, while U.S. president Herbert Hoover, an avid baseball fan, spoke of the importance of sport in that era when he said, "Next to religion, baseball has furnished a greater impact on American life than any other institution." Radio broadcasts of sporting events had become commonplace, and KU basketball debuted on the airwaves in the late 1920s, a significant step for Allen's program.

While most of the country was in economic downturn, Allen found a way to use the athletic program to continually feed the coffers of the university. During his first decade as athletic director, the KU athletic program showed receipts totaling around $1 million. His Relays were responsible for more than $42,000 of university money during the final five academic years of the 1920s, while ticket sales and road allotments from Allen's basketball program had steadily increased through the decade to a total of $18,620.67 for the 1928–29 season.

Phog Allen's own finances, however, were suffering at the time of the Great Depression. By the end of the decade, he was making only about five thousand dollars annually, one of the lowest coaching salaries in the conference. He continued to look for creative ways to add to his annual income. Allen marketed a basketball, a shoe, and a medicine kit, all bearing his well-known name, and in the years that followed he even created a new game, similar to basketball, that was called Goal-Hi. Designed to be played in one's backyard or in a pool, Goal-Hi earned some initial interest from curious sports fans but never really caught on; Allen had proven to be a more capable basketball coach than James Naismith but a vastly inferior inventor of sports. Allen's shoe gained more moderate success but without much staying power. Manufactured by Servus Rubber Co., the shoe sold for three dollars and proclaimed "a certain 'built-in' speed that permits a player to start quickly." Shortly thereafter, Doc Allen also marketed a booklet on sports medicine and treating injuries, complete with a recommendation for footwear—the Phog Allen shoe, of course. He was additionally able to supplement his income by charging twenty-five dollars plus gas mileage for speaking engagements throughout the Midwest. He had become such a featured speaker that the *Daily Kansan* referred to Allen as "a contender for the title of most travelled basketball coach in the world," and by the 1930s he was doing 2,400-mile speaking tours in the offseason.

Allen was finding unique ways to keep the money coming in at a time when most of the nation was struggling just to make ends meet. Allen's mentor, James Naismith, was among the people stuck in a financial freefall. A university-wide pay cut for administrators had left Naismith with a three-thousand-dollar annual salary, down 25 percent from the previous year. Phog Allen's longtime mentor found himself unable to pay his bills, and he was in danger of losing his farm-style house on Stratford Road in Lawrence. This was during a period when Naismith and Allen had been clashing professionally, and yet it was Allen who stepped forward and offered to help out. The former student told his mentor that he would be willing to make payments on the house until Naismith was able to get himself back on track financially. Naismith graciously turned down the offer and decided instead to move into a smaller house, a log cabin on Mississippi Street he had recently built as a second home, but the gesture seemed to transcend some of the disagreements Phog Allen and James Naismith endured with one another during that period of time.

On the basketball court, Phog Allen was still looking for ways to keep up with the ever-growing game of basketball and its recent infatuation with taller players. Allen felt like the predominance of big men was taking the athleticism out of the game, and he continued his quest to get the baskets raised from ten feet to twelve feet, but he was also still trying to keep up with the Joneses by attempting to recruit taller players for his Jayhawks. His attempt to land 7'0" Harry Kersenbrock found a tragic end, and yet Allen pressed on and finally landed another big man in a 6'5" string bean from Oklahoma City who went by the nickname Skinny.

William "Skinny" Johnson lived in the heart of Sooner Country, where fans fervently followed the successful football and basketball programs at the University of Oklahoma, but Allen was able to pull him away through his correspondence with William's mother, Minnie, a Swedish immigrant who was not the first—nor the last—player's mother to fall victim to Phog's charms. On the rare occasion that Allen would actually reach out to recruit a high school star—in those years most players, lured by the program's success, simply showed up on campus hoping for a shot to make the team—he typically appealed to the mother in an effort to sway her son to Lawrence.

Johnson wouldn't be eligible until the fall of 1930, but Allen's Jayhawks weren't waiting around for the new star to carry the load. Coming off of a 3-15 season in 1928–29, which saw KU basketball sink to the bottom of the Big Six standings for the first time, the 1929–30 Jayhawks came in refocused and with a modified game plan that Phog Allen designed to keep his players fresher. Using a slowed pace on offense and a zone defense, the Jayhawks got off to a surprisingly good start. Kansas won its first thirteen games, ending Oklahoma's twenty-nine-game conference winning streak in the process, and eventually finished with an overall record of 14-4. The surprising season breathed new life into the KU basketball program and provided the proverbial light at the end of the tunnel after three and a half years of unexpected darkness both on and off the court. While the Great Depression continued to sink its fangs into the worldwide economy, Allen and the Jayhawks found hope on the basketball court.

What Allen remembered most about that 1928–29 season was a Big Six championship game that featured a quite unorthodox finish. Late in the game, with Kansas clinging to a 1-point lead and trying to stall the clock, Oklahoma star Tom Churchill reached out and punched the ball out of a KU player's hands and into the basket—fifteen feet away. Rules at the time prohibited a player from using his fist to advance the ball—in James Naismith's thirteen original rules of the game, it clearly states, in rule number two, that players may slap or bat the ball but "never with the fist"—and yet no whistle was blown and the basket stood up as the game-winning score, much to the chagrin of Phog Allen.

That loss stuck with Allen, but he had developed a remarkable capacity to move on after defeat. Players over the years that followed could only marvel at how Phog Allen could put all of his emotion into a high-pressure game and then be able to turn it off within minutes of the final gun. The image that most players remembered of Allen in defeat was one of the coach climbing onto a quiet bus, taking a seat in the front row, and loosening his tie before drifting into a peaceful sleep that lasted most of the ride back to campus.

Despite the controversial, season-ending loss to Oklahoma, Allen and the Jayhawks had some momentum heading into the 1930–31 season, and the eligibility of 6'5" big man William "Skinny" Johnson gave the KU basketball team a much-overdue added dimension. Skinny Johnson, who dominated the center jump, would end up leading Kansas to conference titles in each of his three seasons of eligibility, and he would also provide Phog Allen with one of his favorite stories.

Before the 1932 Big Six championship game, once again pitting KU and the Oklahoma Sooners, Allen found out that Skinny Johnson wouldn't be available because of the death of his father, Swan, in Oklahoma City. Johnson was to attend the funeral on the day of the championship game, to be played in Lawrence, four hundred miles north of Oklahoma City, later that night. He was ruled out of the game, and the Jayhawks were ready to move on without their star until Allen received a call from two of Johnson's Phi Delta Theta fraternity brothers the morning of the game. They had arranged for Johnson to take a flight from Oklahoma City to Lawrence, and there appeared to be a chance Skinny might make it for tip-off. The game time was moved back thirty minutes, to 8 p.m., under the guise of accommodating fans who wanted to listen to the start of the Missouri-Kansas State game at 7:30. Phog Allen listened intently during pregame warm-ups for the drone of an airplane flying over Hoch Auditorium. The sound never came, so Allen began preparations for the OU game, believing that Johnson would not be there. It turned out that Johnson's flight had been diverted to an airport five miles away, and he got a ride in a pickup truck the rest of the way before surprising everyone in attendance by running onto the court just before tip-off. Johnson then led the inspired Jayhawks to a 20–6 halftime lead before KU hung on to win the game, and the conference title, 36–27.

But Allen was continuously besieged by tragedy as the twenties roared into the early thirties, having lost an older brother and his father while death also claimed longtime friend Knute Rockne in a March 1931 plane crash. Rockne, a Notre Dame football coach who'd had somewhat of a falling out with Allen over the gate receipts over a KU-Irish basketball series that the two coaches had arranged in the late 1920s, had been visiting his two sons at a Kansas City boarding school before his Kansas City to Los

Angeles flight went down. Rockne was forty-three years old at the time of his tragic death, which rocked the sporting world and undoubtedly left Phog Allen with his own set of swirling emotions.

Having survived a whirlwind of tragedy, beginning with the untimely death of a fourteen-year-old son and the drowning of a big-time recruit, Allen weathered the storm of the Great Depression and felt he had the KU basketball program back on track. But his family life was still out of order following the premature death of his first-born boy. His wife, Bessie, was obviously distraught and unable to find much distraction as she tended to the house where Forrest Jr. had died a few years earlier. Phog was likely overcome by sudden bursts of overwhelming grief as well, although he never shared it publicly. By the early 1930s, Forrest Allen Jr. could have conceivably been playing football, basketball, or both at KU, and not getting an opportunity to coach him must have been a small part of the grief that Phog carried through those years.

His next-oldest son, Milton, who went by the nickname Mitt, was having a particularly difficult time coping with the untimely tragedy and was beginning to stray off track. Mitt Allen was three years younger than Forrest Jr. and seemed to take the death of his older brother harder than anyone. He was eleven years old when young Forrest passed away. In a flash, Mitt became the oldest boy in the family and found himself under a new kind of scrutiny from a father who may or may not have expected him to be just like Forrest Jr. By the time he became a teenager, Mitt had started drinking, smoking, and hanging out with a tough crowd. He often disregarded his father's rules and finally became so unbearable that Bessie and Phog had him shipped off to Culver Academy, a military school in Northern Indiana, for a year during his high school years. When that didn't take, Phog resorted to a more old-school method of tough love, one that took him all the way back to his own teenage years. As the family story goes, Phog Allen once ordered Mitt into the basement to don the boxing gloves for a little one-on-one session with Dad. Phog apparently only needed three punches to put Mitt on the proverbial canvas of the Allen basement floor.

But whatever change in attitude that engendered in Mitt didn't last long. He was soon getting into trouble again, and his father was running out of ways to get him back on track. Phog was hoping that a few years together on the KU basketball team—an opportunity he never got to have with Forrest Jr.—would help father and son get on the same page. Mitt was only sixteen years old when his mother, Bessie, enrolled him in KU's school of engineering. She did her part by personally chauffeuring Mitt to his freshman classes during the fall of 1932. But Mitt, ever the rebel, would simply walk in the front door of the academic building and out the back. In his first year at the University of Kansas, Milton "Mitt" Allen flunked out, much to the embarrassment of his famous father.

This might have been the last straw, but Phog wasn't ready to give up on his son no matter how livid he was at the boy's actions. Phog Allen put out a line to one of his former Warrensburg players, a man named Louis Menze, who was by then coaching at Iowa State University. Phog asked Menze to take his son in and encouraged him to show Mitt some tough love during their time together. Mitt ended up heading 266 miles north to attend school and play basketball for Menze.

The plan worked, as Mitt Allen returned after one year a changed man and eventually emerged as one of the better players on the Kansas teams of the mid-1930s. He had regained his father's trust to the point that Phog allowed him to play what the coach called his "quarterback" position, what later became known as the point guard. But Mitt's return to KU to play for his father wasn't without its tense moments.

There was one incident before a 1936 game against Nebraska when Phog Allen and his oldest living son got into an argument at practice, leading the coach to pull Mitt from the starting lineup for the biggest game of the season. His son had to watch from the bench for most of the first quarter before entering the game and helping the Jayhawks beat Nebraska handily.

Mitt would later tell the story of another afternoon practice at Robinson Gym, on a winter day when the cold air outside seeped into the gym. Mitt had borrowed his father's overcoat the previous night, having gone out on a date. Phog Allen, unbeknownst to son Mitt, had stopped by the locker room on his way to the gym and showed up at practice wearing the coat. Upon seeing his father, Mitt turned white as a sheet, for he remembered at that moment that he'd left a pack of cigarettes in the pocket. Mitt's stomach turned over as he watched his father move his hands into the pockets of the coat and keep them in that position for a long stretch of practice. Phog Allen, the coach and father, said nothing at first. An hour of practice went by without mention before Allen called an abrupt end to the session and sent the players to the locker room. He stopped his son on his way out and said, "Mitt, I had been counting on you this year. But apparently, you don't want to play badly enough."

The cigarettes were never mentioned again.

As Mitt would later write in a letter to his father, "Many times I have recalled this incident, analyzing its effect upon me. I can conscientiously [*sic*] say that if you had dismissed me from the squad at that time, it would have been easier for me. However, the manner in which you handled the situation made me feel all the humility I justly deserved. Your tolerance in this matter further exemplifies your wisdom in dealing with unthinking youth."

There was another incident that saw Mitt Allen lose his patience with a fan who kept heckling his father in a road game. Mitt went into the stands, fists swinging, to defend his old man's honor.

Mitt Allen's senior season came in 1936–37, when the Jayhawks went 15-4, and years later Phog Allen would look back on the experience of coaching his son as one of the highlights of his career. Whatever opportunity he may have lost with the death of his oldest son was replaced in some ways by a chance to find common ground with Mitt, who went on to earn a law degree and became a respected Lawrence attorney.

For Phog Allen, that 1936–37 season came close to being the final one of his legendary career as KU basketball coach. Shortly after the conclusion of the basketball season, Allen was relieved of his duties as athletic director, his inability to field a competitive football team finally catching up with him. The Kansas board of regents voted to strip him of his AD position, and Allen decided that without a doubt he was going to step down as head basketball coach. After nineteen seasons at KU, including one as a young up-and-comer, Phog Allen was finished and on his way to greener pastures. In his 1947 book *Phog Allen Sports Stories*, Allen claimed that he "received an early morning phone call from an executive in a large Midwestern city offering me a salary more than twice my present one." Allen decided to take the job and went downstairs to tell his family.

Sitting at the breakfast table, his youngest son, Bobby, looked at Phog Allen with sadness in his eyes. Bobby Allen, seventeen years old and on the verge of forging his own collegiate path, stared at his father and said, "Dad, Mitt played three years on your teams—and somehow I'd always hoped I'd be able to play under you too, but I guess that won't be possible now, will it?"

That was all Phog needed to hear. He changed his mind and called to turn down the job. He was staying at Kansas. As Phog Allen would write ten years later, in *Sports Stories*, "what father, when his son asked for bread, would give him a stone? It wasn't money, after all." Despite losing his position as KU's athletic director, and the accompanying salary, Phog Allen returned to Kansas and continued on as the university's basketball coach.

As it would happen, Bobby Allen ended up being a key piece to one of his father's best Kansas teams. But before any of that, Phog Allen had some bigger challenges on his plate. Having already started the National Association of Basketball Coaches and turned the University of Kansas into a national powerhouse, Phog Allen was about to take James Naismith's game to even greater heights.

He was about to put the sport of basketball on the largest of international stages.

11

The Day the Game Arrived

The dictator was watching from above. The roar of the crowd surrounded him as the flags from the forty-nine represented countries were raised throughout the arena. The athletes paraded around the one-hundred-thousand-seat stadium, and the man with the thumbprint mustache and the Waffen-SS Panzergrenadier captain's hat looked down upon them, his right arm extended in front of him in salute. The German athletes returned the gesture as they passed.

In this moment, no one could possibly have known just how evil of a monster the dictator was. His atrocities were only just beginning, and the world was still relatively naïve as to his eventual impact on history.

Nor could anyone have understood the significance of these Olympic Games. No one could have known that a black man would outrun and outjump the dictator's Aryan pride on the way to four gold medals, that a rowing team from the University of Washington would create one of the most-read stories of the early twenty-first century, or that the sport of basketball would begin an astronomical rise toward global popularity. No one could have known that names like Owens, Naismith, and, of course, Hitler would be stamped upon the world's consciousness for the rest of the century and beyond.

They were all there, presiding over a set of games that would prove to have as much impact on history as any event in the twentieth century.

And yet there was one man who was not there. The man who helped introduce basketball to the world on the grandest of stages was not in Berlin on that night, when the evil dictator looked down upon the masses. When the 1936 Olympics began, Phog Allen was almost five thousand miles away. And he wasn't happy about it.

By the middle of the 1930s, basketball had made an unexpected rise to become a sport that was about to challenge baseball as America's pastime. James Naismith's silly little game with two peach baskets and thirteen basic rules had become an even bigger sport globally and was helping to create a diversion for Americans still reeling from the Great Depression.

Yet there was one thing basketball had yet to do, and Phog Allen set out to change that.

In 1928, one year after being named president of the National Association of Basketball Coaches, Allen had been given the post of chairman of the Olympic basketball committee. Basketball had yet to become an official Olympic sport—in 1904, the new activity was presented as a demonstration sport in the St. Louis Olympiad but all five teams were from the United States—and Allen was spearheading the movement to introduce it to the games as a full-blown international competition.

He targeted Olympiad X, the 1932 Olympic Games, for inclusion as a demonstration sport. Those games were being held in Los Angeles, giving the United States a bit of a home court advantage in the process. Teams from Canada, Mexico, Japan, and the Philippines were on board for being a part of the 1932 Olympics, along with an American delegation, but the decision-makers opted for football as a demonstration sport, citing their belief that it offered a bigger financial opportunity than basketball could have. A perception existed in those days that basketball was strictly a U.S. sport, but Allen was among the coaches and administrators who knew better. Shortly after the 1932 Games, Allen wrote an article called "The International Growth of Basketball" for the *Athletic Journal*, detailing how big the sport had become overseas. Avery Brundage, who was at the time president of the U.S. Olympic Committee, warned Allen that the sport was not important enough to gain acceptance in the Olympics any time soon and cautioned him about being overly optimistic. Yet the battle did not end there.

Allen's visit to Los Angeles for the 1932 Games, and his article shortly thereafter, had drummed up enough conversation that his focus turned toward Olympiad XI, the 1936 Olympic Games in Berlin, for the debut of international basketball. Adding to the momentum was the June 1932 formation of the International Basketball Federation in Switzerland. FIBA, as the federation was known internationally, helped bring together the European countries as a unified voice to go along with Allen's United States-based campaign. Cofounded by a Springfield College graduate named R. William Jones who was born in Rome and had returned to Europe after college, FIBA added international volume to the cause with the Berlin Games just four years away.

In his 1937 book *Better Basketball*, Allen maintained that another key figure in the discussion was a German exchange student named Fritz Siewecke, who was at the YMCA in Springfield, Massachusetts, shortly after the 1932 Games. According to the book, Siewecke returned to Berlin "in the employment of the Hitler Youth Movement" with a newfound respect for the sport of basketball. "Undoubtedly," Allen wrote in *Better Basketball*, "Herr Siewecke aided in the promotion of basketball for the Berlin Olympic calendar."

Through Allen's six-year efforts and the backing of FIBA, the sport of basketball was officially included as part of the upcoming Olympiad XI. In October 1934, Karl Diem of the Berlin Olympic Committee announced that the sport would make its Olympic debut two years later, in the 1936 Berlin Games. After six years of campaigning, Phog Allen had successfully put the sport of basketball on the Olympic stage.

But his work was far from done. Soon after learning that basketball would be a part of the 1936 Olympics, Allen realized that there was one man in the world who most deserved to be on hand for the historic event. James Naismith, the very creator of the game, would have to be in Berlin—no matter what it took to get him there. Naismith, having had his salary cut and his house foreclosed during the Great Depression, obviously couldn't afford to make the trip on his own finances. The seventy-four-year-old educator's modest teacher's salary, which was available only because state

1. The Allen Brothers Basket Ball Team was willing to take on all comers, even college and professional squads. The team was made up of Forrest "Phog" Allen and his five brothers: (*from left to right*) Harry "Pete" Allen, Phog, Homer, Elmer, Hubert, and Richard. Also pictured is one of Phog's nephews, the first son of oldest brother, Homer. (Photo courtesy of University Archives, Spencer Research Library, University of Kansas Libraries)

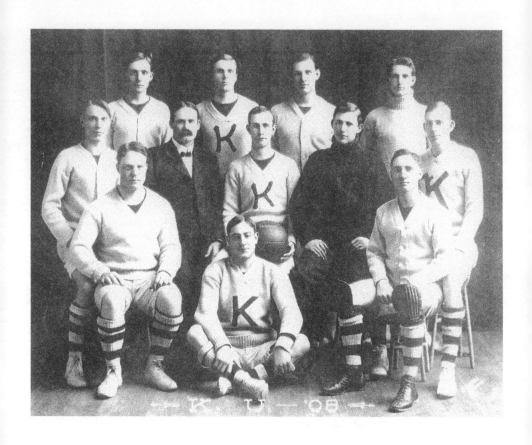

2. Just twenty-two years old and without a high school or college diploma, Phog Allen (*middle row, second from right*) took over for legendary basketball figure James Naismith (*middle row, second from left*) as head coach of the KU basketball team. Allen and Naismith worked together with the Jayhawks in 1907–8 and 1908–9 before the young protégé stepped away from the coaching profession to attend osteopathy school in Kansas City. (Photo courtesy of University Archives, Spencer Research Library, University of Kansas Libraries)

3. Phog Allen seemed to have a love-hate relationship with football for much of his life. Allen, seen here in his University of Kansas letter sweater as a twenty-seven-year-old head football coach at Missouri State Normal School in 1913, was a football player as a KU freshman but suffered a serious back injury in one of the first practices. He went on to coach the sport at the Missouri State Normal School in Warrensburg, where he was so despised by opposing coaches that the Teachers were kicked out of the conference. Allen coached one year of football at KU in 1920 and oversaw the team as athletic director for the years that followed; he was often blamed for the Jayhawks' inability to sustain any football success during the 1920s and 1930s. (Photo courtesy of Arthur F. McClure II Archives and University Museum at the University of Central Missouri)

Missouri Collegiate Champions
1913

4. (*opposite*) Allen always took pride in his attire, as evidenced by the 1913 photo of the coach along with his league-champion basketball team from Missouri State Normal School in Warrensburg. The 1912–13 Teachers were Allen's first team after he took a three-year hiatus to attend osteopathic school. This squad went 11-7 overall and won a conference title, but it couldn't compete with Phog's alma mater, losing 30–24 to the Kansas Jayhawks in the season finale. (Photo courtesy of Arthur F. McClure II Archives and University Museum at the University of Central Missouri)

5. (*above*) Allen, looking dapper in his suit and top hat (*middle, back row*), coached three sports during his Warrensburg years. Baseball helped give Allen his nickname—his foghorn-like voice as an umpire led to the "Phog" moniker—and he went on to use his osteopathic techniques on a young ballplayer named Charles "Casey" Stengel. Allen also coached baseball at Warrensburg State Normal School, a school that employed him until 1919, about the time the university was changing its name to Central Missouri Teachers College. (Photo courtesy of Arthur F. McClure II Archives and University Museum at the University of Central Missouri)

6. Allen's youthful looks, which lasted well into his twenties, led him to often being mistaken for a player. This photo is from his Warrensburg years, when he was a twentysomething coach of football, basketball, and baseball. (Photo courtesy of Arthur F. McClure II Archives and University Museum at the University of Central Missouri)

ATHLETIC COMMITTEE

Dr. Forrest C. Allen, Chairman

Faculty Members

W. W. Parker
Earl Foster
W. E. Morrow

7. This page was taken from the 1919 Warrensburg (MO) State Normal School yearbook, shortly before Allen was chased out of town by influential alumni who didn't take kindly to his medical practice. (Photo courtesy of Arthur F. McClure II Archives and University Museum at the University of Central Missouri)

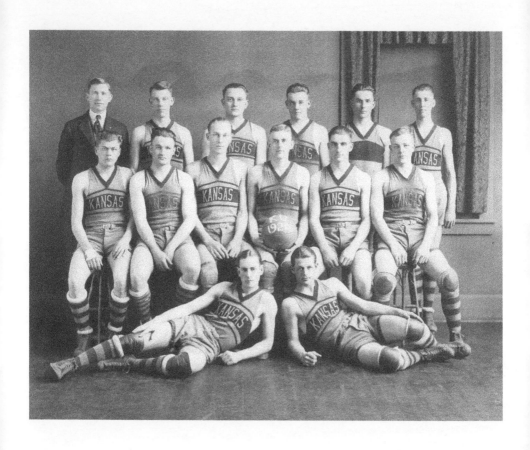

8. The 1920-21 Kansas Jayhawks, in Phog Allen's second year as a coach after his tenure in Warrensburg, went 10-8 but had many of the stars who would end up leading KU to its two Helms Foundation national titles—in 1921-22 and 1922-23. (Photo courtesy of University Archives, Spencer Research Library, University of Kansas Libraries)

9. Paul Endacott is widely regarded as the first great KU basketball player. He was the star of the Jayhawks' championship teams in 1921–22 and 1922–23 and went on to be enshrined in the Naismith Basketball Hall of Fame. Endacott remained so close to Phog Allen over the years that he served as a pall bearer and delivered the eulogy at his former coach's funeral service in 1974. (Photo courtesy of University Archives, Spencer Research Library, University of Kansas Libraries)

10. (*above*) Old Robinson Gym hosted its first game in 1907, when young Phog Allen made his debut as the KU basketball coach. The sport's growth over the years that followed led to the construction of Hoch Auditorium (in 1927) and Allen Fieldhouse (in 1955). During the Hoch years, the Jayhawks continued to use Robinson's lockers and practice courts. The facility also included a modest office in the southwest corner that Allen used while coaching the basketball team and running the Jayhawks' athletic department. (Photo courtesy of University Archives, Spencer Research Library, University of Kansas Libraries)

11. (*opposite*) Though his family life and basketball program went through a lot of turmoil in the mid-1920s, by the time this photo of Allen was taken in 1929 he was back on top. Allen was able to weather the Great Depression on a modest coaching salary, a steady gig as an inspirational speaker, and a series of products bearing his well-known name. (Photo courtesy of University Archives, Spencer Research Library, University of Kansas Libraries)

12. The two most influential men in basketball history, James Naismith (*left*) and Phog Allen, had a complicated relationship that began with a disagreement over whether the game could be coached. Allen took Naismith's creation and turned it into a money-making endeavor, which wasn't necessarily what the game's inventor had intended. Their relationship was somewhat strained through the 1920s before Allen patched things up by getting basketball into the Olympics and coming up with a plan to make sure that his mentor could afford to be in Berlin for the 1936 games. (Photo courtesy of University Archives, Spencer Research Library, University of Kansas Libraries)

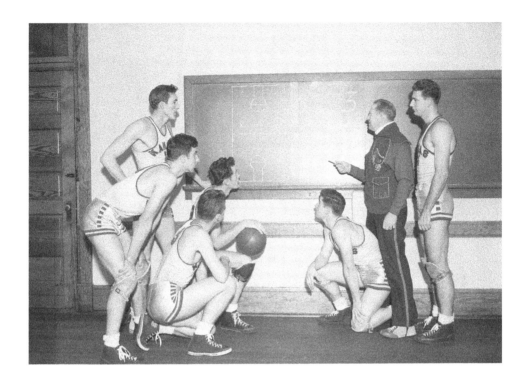

13. (*opposite*) Phog Allen, pictured here with two players in a 1929 portrait, was a very hands-on coach who not only taught his players the finer points of basketball but was also known to tape their feet and ankles as well as attend to their various injuries. When Allen didn't feel like he was getting his point across in practice, he was apt to rip off his warmup and show the players exactly how it was supposed to be done. (Photo courtesy of University Archives, Spencer Research Library, University of Kansas Libraries)

14. (*above*) Allen's typical pregame routine was to write down the names of each KU starter, along with his defensive assignment, before setting down the chalk and looking each player in the eye and asking, "Are you ready?" His effective inspirational methods often led Allen (pictured here in the 1930s) to be called the Knute Rockne of basketball. Allen and Rockne, in fact, developed a pretty close relationship before Notre Dame's legendary football coach was killed in a 1931 plane crash one hundred miles southwest of Lawrence. (Photo courtesy of University Archives, Spencer Research Library, University of Kansas Libraries)

15. Phog Allen took special pride in his physical shape, even in the later years of his coaching career. Allen, shown here in the 1940s, was so vain about his appearance that he was known to take off his shirt at the Lawrence Golf Course and, at times, while trying to make a point in a KU classroom. (Photo courtesy of University Archives, Spencer Research Library, University of Kansas Libraries)

16. Phog Allen's charisma, boisterous opinions, and fiery pregame speeches became his trademark qualities over the years, but those who played for him said his greatest attribute was teaching the game. Allen learned basketball from the man who invented it and took the game to new heights. He's shown here (*center, long sleeves*) coaching the KU basketball team in 1946–47, during a tumultuous season that saw Allen take a medical leave because of a concussion he sustained at a preseason practice. (Photo courtesy of University Archives, Spencer Research Library, University of Kansas Libraries)

17. (*above*) Clyde Lovellette provided Allen with one of his greatest coaching moments when Lovellette led the Jayhawks to the 1951–52 NCAA title. Allen used his gift for gab to talk Lovellette out of a verbal commitment to attend the University of Indiana, and then he rode with Big Clyde to the school's first NCAA tournament championship. (Photo courtesy of University Archives, Spencer Research Library, University of Kansas Libraries)

18. (*opposite*) A rare moment of humility led Phog Allen to target former KU player Dick Harp (*left*) as his first full-time assistant coach in the late 1940s. Harp went on to be the brains behind the Jayhawks' 1952 NCAA title run, and then he took over for Allen when the aging coach was forced into retirement. "It was a great combination," All-American Clyde Lovellette told KU announcer Max Falkenstien in a 1996 interview for Falkenstien's autobiography. "Dick knew basketball, and Doc was the psychologist." (Photo courtesy of University Archives, Spencer Research Library, University of Kansas Libraries)

19. Clyde Lovellette and the Jayhawks returned from Seattle to one of the largest celebrations ever seen in Lawrence. Approximately fifteen thousand fans were lined up to greet the NCAA champion KU basketball team, and when Lovellette asked to put on a fireman's hat, nobody was willing to tell him no. He rode a firetruck down Massachusetts Avenue as the KU students and fans cheered on the school's first NCAA tournament title. (Photo courtesy of University Archives, Spencer Research Library, University of Kansas Libraries)

20. The construction of a new fieldhouse in the 1950s was one of Allen's finest moments. Upon hearing that the school had decided to break a long-standing tradition of not naming a building after a living person by calling it Allen Fieldhouse, the legendary coach said, "In this hour of great recognition of my services to the University of Kansas, I feel very unworthy and deeply grateful." Allen Fieldhouse would go on to become one of the most respected venues in all of sports. (Photo courtesy of University Archives, Spencer Research Library, University of Kansas Libraries)

21. Wilt Chamberlain signed with KU as a wide-eyed, eager high school senior, but his subsequent years in Lawrence would be filled with ups and downs. The racism he discovered upon arriving for his freshman year nearly made Chamberlain retreat to his hometown of Philadelphia, and the unexpected news that he would not get to play for Phog Allen was a difficult pill for the 7'0" young man to swallow. In the end, Chamberlain led Kansas to one NCAA final but left after playing just two seasons for the Jayhawks. His relationship with the school grew so strained over the following years that Chamberlain waited forty years before returning to Lawrence. (Photo courtesy of University Archives, Spencer Research Library, University of Kansas Libraries)

22. During his playing days, Allen was known as one of the top shooters in the country. That was when free throws were shot underhanded and there was no such thing as a set offense. Allen adapted with the times, and he not only taught freshman Clyde Lovellette the art of the hook shot, but he was also instrumental in helping freshman Wilt Chamberlain develop an offensive game before he became eligible to play for the varsity team. Shown here in 1955, when Chamberlain was a freshman, Allen still had a pretty good shot at the age of seventy. (Photo courtesy of University Archives, Spencer Research Library, University of Kansas Libraries)

23. (*opposite*) Coach Phog Allen and 7'0" star Wilt Chamberlain will forever be linked despite their brief time together. How seventy-year-old Allen was able to lure the nation's greatest basketball recruit to Lawrence, Kansas, in the fall of 1955 was a controversy that burned for decades. Allen convinced Chamberlain to play at KU but never got to coach him, thanks to a state law that required government employees to retire at the age of seventy. (Photo courtesy of University Archives, Spencer Research Library, University of Kansas Libraries)

24. (*above*) KU chancellor Frank Murphy (*center*) and Phog Allen were all smiles after the Jayhawks won the 1952 NCAA title, but their relationship hit a sour note when the university's board of regents refused to allow Allen to coach much past his seventieth birthday. Murphy wrote a letter of explanation to the Allen family, but the perceived lack of loyalty from the chancellor left the longtime coach at odds with KU until the day he died. (Photo courtesy of University Archives, Spencer Research Library, University of Kansas Libraries)

25. (*above*) Although his final win total would later be corrected by a basketball historian, Phog Allen (*left*) was originally credited with 746 wins—an NCAA record. Former player Adolph Rupp, a rarely used sub on KU's championship teams in the early 1920s, eventually broke that record while leading the Kentucky basketball program to four national titles. Rupp (*right*) eventually had his record broken by another of Allen's former KU players, North Carolina coach Dean Smith. (Photo courtesy of University Archives, Spencer Research Library, University of Kansas Libraries)

26. (*opposite*) In one of the final photos of Forrest "Phog" Allen, taken in April 1973, the eighty-two-year-old legend poses with former players Adolph Rupp (*standing, left*) and Paul Endacott (*standing, right*). Allen's health was so grave in those months that he was unable to attend a twentieth anniversary reunion of the 1952 NCAA championship team at Allen Fieldhouse. Instead, several former players went to his Lawrence home after the ceremony to pay their respects. Seventeen months later, Allen passed away in that house. (Photo courtesy of University Archives, Spencer Research Library, University of Kansas Libraries)

legislators had waived a law making retirement mandatory at the age of seventy so he could remain on the KU faculty, did not provide Naismith with much savings, and he had never set out to cash in on the sport he created, despite its meteoric rise. Phog Allen would later tell a story of the day in the 1920s when he had presented Naismith with the possibility of profiting off the sport he invented, perhaps by trademarking a Naismith basketball or Naismith goal, and the game's creator just chuckled, telling him, "You bloody beggar, you are always thinking about money."

Phog Allen was doing just that in the early weeks of 1936, when Naismith's former student was trying to come up with a way to get his aging mentor to Berlin. Ever the innovator, Allen went about raising money in the most unconventional way. He began what was known as a "penny campaign," targeting basketball fans in an effort to put together enough cash to send Naismith and his wife, Maude, to Berlin for the Olympic Games. The campaign was to be held during a week in February 1936, with one penny from every ticket sold to college and professional basketball games going to the Naismith Olympic Fund. Rather quickly, high schools and grade schools were also helping to raise money across the country and even in Canada, where Naismith's hometown of Almonte raised $20 at a single high school game. By the end of the week, more than $7,400 had been collected through Allen's "penny campaign"—more than enough to send Naismith and his wife to Berlin, although Maude was unable to make the trip due to a serious health scare.

Allen's gesture touched James Naismith and may well have been the olive branch that served to put to rest all the professional friction that had been simmering between the two over much of the previous two decades. As a thank you to his longtime friend, Naismith presented Allen with a framed, autographed piece of artwork in Naismith's image. The inscription written by Naismith read, "With kindest regards to Dr. F.C. Allen, the father of basketball coaching, from the father of the game, James Naismith."

The artwork remained in Phog Allen's office for the rest of his career, while the nickname bestowed upon him—"the father of basketball coaching"—stuck around as well.

Once Naismith's trip to Berlin was secured, Phog Allen set about getting his own travel plans in order. He had initially expected to be a part of the U.S. team as a coach, but Allen announced before the Olympic Trials tournament that he would only coach the team if his Kansas players represented the United States in Berlin—a possibility only if the Jayhawks were to win the Trials tournament. The tournament began without a strong Long Island University team that was boycotting the Olympics because many of the players were Jewish and protesting the German regime, and KU got off to a good start by beating Utah in the first game of a best-of-three series. But Utah bounced back to win two games in a row and knocked Allen's Jayhawks out of contention for the 1936 Olympics debut. Shortly thereafter, Allen was named the U.S. Olympic Basketball Expedition's director in chief, meaning he would be part of the contingent heading to Berlin but would not be coaching the players.

Part of that contingent would be made up of officials from the Amateur Athletic Union, a longtime Allen ally that he had grown to despise over the years. As the game of college basketball rose, Allen began to believe that the AAU, a competitor that found a way around the amateur rules by giving athletes full-time jobs at corporations that sponsored teams, was exploiting basketball players for its own financial gain. Formed in 1888, the union had become something of a monopoly in terms of funneling basketball players into the postcollege world. The AAU was, in Allen's mind, everything that was wrong with amateur athletics.

Being a part of the Olympic committee, Allen found himself having to work alongside AAU officials and was unable to hide his disdain. He was already spitting mad about the inclusion of AAU teams in the February Olympic Trials, and when Allen got wind of his name possibly being left off of the eighteen-man travel roster, he came unglued.

On May 5, 1936, two months before the U.S. delegation was set to depart for Berlin, Allen announced in a letter to the Olympic committee that he was relinquishing his position as director in chief, citing a lack of ethics by the AAU representatives. Allen claimed that the AAU had misused funds gained at the recent Olympic Trials, a widely popular event held at New York City's Madison Square Garden that was said to have brought in ten thousand dollars. In his May 1936 letter, Allen accused the AAU of using six thousand dollars of that money toward its own administration expenses. "Not a cent," Allen wrote, "was contributed by the A.A.U. to the Olympic basketball fund. The A.A.U. is filled with a group of inert athletic directors who enjoy riding free." Allen's letter also accused the AAU of "deceitful political bartering" and called its members "Olympic oceanic hitch-hikers."

The AAU responded by maintaining that Phog Allen was upset about not being in the original plans for the U.S. delegation that would make the trip to Berlin for the Games. "It looks to me as though Allen saw the hand-writing on the wall," AAU secretary J. Lyman Bingham told the Associated Press in response to Phog's letter. "He planned to hitchhike to Berlin at the expense of the Olympic committee, and, when he saw that there wouldn't be money enough, started knocking and finally quit."

Allen's resignation was the first of many black eyes that the sport of basketball suffered during its 1936 Olympics debut. Naismith's arrival in Berlin was met with surprising news on its own right, as he initially didn't have a pass to attend the event. A New York–based referee named Jim Tobin, claiming that U.S. Olympic chairman Avery Brundage neglected to give Naismith a ticket to the basketball games, got him into the competition. Furthermore, the game was introduced at Olympiad XI as an outdoor sport, played on a surface of salt and sawdust that resembled asphalt in clear weather but turned into a mud-like slush in rain.

Upon arriving in Berlin following an eleven-day cruise from New York, the Americans were informed of several other rule changes that had been approved without their input, among them the abolishment of the three-second violation and a maximum of seven players per squad at each game. There was also initially a rule banning players taller than 6'2" from the 1936 Games, and that would have put the U.S. team—with a pair of 6'8" centers in Joe Fortenberry and Willard Schmidt and a 6'7" forward in UCLA graduate Frank Lubin—in a tough position. The Olympic Committee eventually relented on the height rule, and the U.S. team got around the seven-men-per-team rule by fielding two squads of seven players each that alternated games.

The U.S. team was made up mainly of players from AAU teams in Hol-lywood, California, and McPherson, Kansas—the two teams that emerged from the Olympic Trials, and included just one collegian: 6'4" center Ralph Bishop of the University of Washington. On August 7, 1936, Naismith was given a proper welcome as basketball players from all twenty-one of the participating countries paraded past him. He was subsequently treated to a standing ovation by those in attendance. Naismith addressed the crowd by saying, "When I walked out on a Springfield playground with a ball in my hand and the game in my head, I never thought I'd live to see the day when it would be played in the Olympics."

The United States went on to blow out its first three opponents by an aggregate score of 133–61—not including the 2–0 forfeit the Americans earned in their opener against a team from Spain that was unable to travel because of the Spanish Civil War. The Canadian team rode a strong defense while holding its first three opponents of the medal round to a meager 45 points, eventually advancing to the gold-medal game.

Twenty-one countries were represented in the 1936 Olympic basketball debut, and fate would have it that the gold-medal game would come down to the United States and Canada. After making the four-thousand-plus-mile oversea trek via cruise ship, James Naismith would be watching his native country face his adult home for the first Olympic gold medal in basketball.

The rains came before that August 14, 1936, gold-medal game, leaving the court looking like the tiles surrounding the drain of an outdoor beach shower. U.S. player Sam Balter would later compare the conditions to a water polo contest. "A dribble was not a dribble," he wrote in a 2010 autobiography. "It was a splash."

The Canadians hung tough in the messy game, but in the end they had no answer for the American big men. Fortenberry had a game-high 8 points, matching the total of Team Canada in a 19–8 win. If the seventy-four-year-old Naismith was proud of the gold medals that he personally awarded to each American player on the medal stand, he certainly couldn't have been too boastful about the overall debut of basketball as an Olympic sport.

"We had hoped to display to sports fans of other countries the skills, the science, and the speed of this native American game," wrote Balter, one of the gold medalists from the 1936 title game. "Instead, a comedy of errors and unfortunate circumstances had combined to make a sandlot affair of what should have been the greatest basketball tournament ever."

Despite the inauspicious debut, basketball would remain an Olympic mainstay, and it didn't take long for the sport to become the crowning jewel of the Summer Games. By the latter part of the twentieth century, professional players were representing the United States (a phenomenon that would likely leave James Naismith turning in his grave) and basketball was drawing bigger crowds and higher television ratings than any other Olympic sport (a phenomenon that would likely leave James Naismith beaming with pride). The gold-medal game in 2012 was seen on 12.5 million U.S. televisions. The 2012 Olympics featured the U.S. men earning their fourteenth gold medal in the seventeen Olympiads that Olympic basketball medals had been awarded; the Canadian men's basketball program, meanwhile, would still look back on that 1936 silver as its only medal in the sport.

Phog Allen is widely regarded as the man most responsible for getting basketball into the Olympics, and he made sure that the game's creator was there for the first gold medal game. That turned out to be a blessing for the sport, as Naismith wouldn't be around for the next Olympic Games.

On November 28, 1939, at the age of seventy-nine years old, the man who created the game and taught a young man named Forrest Allen to play it died in Lawrence, Kansas, where he had spent more than half his life. A stroke eventually led to the death of James Naismith, the man who had given basketball its first breath.

Forty-eight years had passed since Naismith's game debuted with a contest featuring eighteen players on a court in Springfield, Massachusetts. By 1939, the year of Naismith's death, an estimated twenty million people worldwide were playing basketball.

On February 28, 1940, three months after James Naismith died, the first college basketball game was televised. Naismith wasn't around to witness that, but he had lived long enough to see the debut of basketball in the Olympics and was still alive when the first NCAA tournament was played in March 1939.

The game he created to distract an unruly class at the Springfield YMCA had certainly come a long way.

12

Stepping Out of the Shadow

The sun was shining. On a December day on the Kansas plains, an afternoon like this was about as common as a mountain range. Phog Allen left his coat in the car and donned a pair of sunglasses. He slicked back his hair and set out across the packed dirt.

The gravestone was not hard to find, despite its modest presentation. The red granite surface laid flat against the ground, light reflecting off the single word—a man's name—across the stone.

Wearing slacks and a collared shirt and tie from a speaking engagement earlier in the day, Phog Allen squatted down and placed the palm of his hand next to the word. NAISMITH. Below that, two smaller names, belonging to James and his wife, Maude. Beneath James Naismith's name in the bottom left corner were two dates, separated by a dash. Phog Allen ran his finger along the dash. Such an incredibly oversimplified way to sum up one man's lifetime, especially this man.

Above where Phog Allen squatted before his mentor's grave, rays of heavenly sun beamed down from the sky. Not even a month had passed since the father of basketball had died, and already his warmth radiated across the flat Kansas skyline.

In the weeks and months and seasons that would come to pass, the single gravestone would be washed over with rain, buried in snow. The memorial would rise up from the ground, just like James Naismith's little game had. In death, Naismith would continue to grow. The honorary site at Memorial Park Cemetery, in the years that followed, would come to include a ten-foot-high monument, bearing the man's likeness in the iconic pose, with basketball in hand. A few feet away, across a dirt path, a Naismith mausoleum would be erected, its massive marble structure covered with flowers and the names of others lost. By the seventy-fifth anniversary of Naismith's death, the gravesite would look more like a shrine than one man's grave.

But not on this day; all of that would come later. As fifty-four-year-old Phog Allen rose from the dirt and looked down at the modest gravestone that was placed flat along the sun-drenched earth just to the left of the cemetery gates, the simplicity was what radiated from the spot; even Naismith's grave had a gentle, understated quality to it.

Phog Allen paid his last respects and turned to walk away. He took a step toward his car, and in that moment his shadow moved from the grass to the gravestone, causing a flash of darkness on the unseasonably sunny day.

The relationship between James Naismith and Forrest "Phog" Allen started out as such a simple one because it was all about a simple game. But as the sport of basketball had grown with Frankensteinian consequences, so had developed the complications. Throughout his adult life, Naismith had seen basketball only as a great game; Allen saw it as something greater.

There was a deep irony in Allen's eulogy of the man who created the game of basketball when he said in 1939, "Dr. Naismith is directly responsible for all the large fieldhouses, the large auditoria and gymnasia where basketball is played today. Before this game was originated there were few large indoor arenas that were used for any indoor sports."

Anyone who knew Naismith and what the man stood for, of course, would be quick to point out that the financial benefits—all those roomy arenas and added dollars—were of little importance to the man who created basketball. Naismith said numerous times late in life that he felt blessed just to have made an impact on so many people.

Naismith's death came nine months after the debut of the NCAA basketball tournament, adding yet another opportunity for outsiders to gain financial rewards off the sport he had created. The National Association of Basketball Coaches that Allen helped to create twelve years earlier was behind the tournament, which would go on to become one of the biggest, and most financially rewarding, events in America by the turn of the twentieth century.

By the time his mentor, James Naismith, passed away in 1939, Allen had not only surpassed him in terms of coaching acumen but had also risen to the top of the basketball landscape. His past decade had seen Allen as a key figure in the 1936 debut of basketball at the Olympic Games as well as the first-ever NCAA tournament in 1939. In between, he found time to write his second book: *Better Basketball*. From his modest office in Robinson Gym, where Allen had posted a sign reading, "It's a Great World to Live in—But You Can't Live in it for Nothing," the veteran coach with the unbroken confidence could look out upon the basketball landscape with visionary pride.

He had, quite simply, outgrown the Naismith shadow. In many ways, Phog Allen was casting quite a shadow of his own—one that not everyone at the University of Kansas was thrilled to watch expand.

In the eyes of some, Allen had become, as a Kansan might say, too big for his britches. His my-way-or-the-highway tactics made for a successful basketball program but also rubbed a lot of his colleagues the wrong way—as evidenced by the KU board of regents' 1937 decision to strip Allen of his post as athletic director.

Allen's handling of the Kansas football program, a subject of controversy for more than a decade, became the source of his demise as AD. During his term as athletic director, Allen went from being deemed by football purists as too meddling to being judged as apathetic. KU football never got off the ground during Allen's eighteen years as athletic director, as his tenure saw almost as many coaching changes (four) as winning seasons (six). Allen's passion as a basketball coach rarely carried over to the department's other sports, and the same could be said for the respect he granted to KU's "other" athletic endeavors.

As author Mike Fisher wrote of Phog in a biography on longtime KU athletic trainer Dean Nesmith, "Allen proved stubborn and independent, a man of genius unable to accept mediocrity from those with whom he worked or coached. Those qualities served him well as a coach and teacher but led him into troubled waters during his administrative duties as athletic director. Phog proved unwilling to master the political prerequisite for an athletic director's survival."

And yet the administration would tolerate him as a basketball coach as long as Allen's Jayhawks kept winning. They did just that, amassing victories like a combine harvesting wheat. Every time Allen donned his gameday suit and trademark red socks, the Jayhawks knew they had a much better chance of winning than of going down in defeat, and his record as head coach provided validation. From 1930 through the end of the 1938–39 season, KU had an incredible win–loss record of 153-37, with seven conference titles to show for it. While the decade-long Great Depression and the 1935 Dust Bowl had siphoned most of the energy out of the country, it couldn't bring down the rising basketball power in Lawrence, Kansas.

In an effort to bring out the best in his teams, Allen had continued using the program's storied history as a motivational ploy, reminding his players that they were carrying KU's past on their shoulders. "Do you want to disgrace KU basketball?" was Allen's favorite rhetorical question to his players. Any let-up in effort would be a letdown to the Jayhawks players that had paved the roads to excellence.

"There is only one group of young men who will run out on the court tonight with 'Kansas' on their jerseys," Allen was known to say before leading his team into battle, "and you have the responsibility of representing all the pride and tradition of the past."

Allen's halftime speeches were both inspirational and unpredictable. On one occasion, he sat down in front of his players and didn't say a single word for the entire ten-minute intermission. On another, he didn't even enter the locker room until seconds before the start of the second half, finally stepping inside to say between gritted teeth, "I don't even want to see you. Get out of here."

As Allen once wrote, "Pregame talks cannot be standardized. A coach must *feel* the spirit of his players just as an artist must feel the color in his painting."

When speaking didn't do the trick, Allen would resort to his old standby of show-don't-tell. Practice sessions often featured the coach, even well into his mid-fifties, stripping off his neck towel and warm-up to demonstrate how to do something correctly. He often surprised players with his ability—most notably during a practice in the 1930s when he was attempting to build the confidence of two struggling Jayhawks. On that occasion, Allen pulled aside players Gordon Gray and Ernie Vanek and gave them a little pep talk, saying, "You're confident. And I want you to *know* when you shoot for the basket it's going in. Like this!" Allen then plucked the ball out of Vanek's hands, whirled and drilled a shot in one motion, leaving the pair slack-jawed.

Another tactic he liked to use was to read letters from "fans" to the players. If a KU supporter was in any way caustic about the play of the team or a particular player, Allen would read the letter aloud in an effort to light a fire.

Through it all, the wins kept piling up. Allen had built on his own NCAA record for career coaching victories, with 481 at the start of the 1939–40 season.

By that time, college basketball had finally come up with a way to officially crown a champion, and Allen was at the forefront of that movement as well. After turning down a chance for his 18-2 Jayhawks to participate in the 1938 National Invitational Tournament due largely to growing wariness of outside promoters making money off the sport, Allen and his NABC coaches' committee led the charge to create a tournament that could keep the profits in the pockets of the schools while recognizing an official national champion. The NCAA tournament would be born the following spring, albeit with an agreement that the NABC would incur any lost revenue.

Allen informed his returning 1938–39 players of this new format through what he called "confidential correspondence" before the first NCAA tournament was official, writing in a summer letter to each of his KU players that the NABC was very close to certifying the first national championship, to be played at the conclusion of the upcoming season. "You can see," Allen wrote, "what a great opportunity you men of the Kansas basketball team will have. . . . This [season] means more to you than to any other group that has ever represented Kansas in basketball."

That 1938–39 Jayhawks would fall short of their collective goal, but the

NCAA tournament went on without them. The Big Dance, as it would come to be known over time, made its official debut in the spring of 1939, with eight conference champions vying for the national title in a traditional bracket format. Oklahoma represented the Big Six after sharing the conference title with Missouri, while third-place KU didn't make the field. Organizers were scrambling in the end to find a venue to host the championship game, and just three weeks before the event Northwestern University offered up its court in Evanston, Illinois. The University of Oregon beat Ohio State 46-33 in the first NCAA championship game, but there was very little interest in the event at the time, and the tournament ended up losing $2,500.

That left the NABC with little choice but to abandon its tournament, enduring the financial loss before relinquishing ownership of the event. Chances were slim that the NCAA tourney would ever be put on again. The financial risks were too great for the NCAA, an organization that was supposed to be about higher learning.

But Allen wouldn't let go of his dream. In typical Phog fashion, he stepped forward with a solution to the problem at hand. Allen suggested that promoters move the 1940 tournament to Kansas City, where he could help market the game in front of a basketball-mad fan base that he knew would be willing to buy tickets. From the time an unknown nineteen-year-old entrepreneur named Forrest Allen had brought in unforeseen cash by convincing the German YMCA team from Buffalo, New York, to come to town, through the annual AAU tournaments that brought in steady money from 1921 through 1934, Kansas City had proved to be a basketball hotbed for national tournaments.

As Allen wrote in an August 1939 letter to Ohio State coach and tournament chairman Howard Olsen, "I have never had charge of any tournament that we have ever lost money on, and I'm not boasting in saying that."

Organizers decided to take Allen's suggestion, and the 1940 NCAA tournament game was set to be played in Kansas City.

The Kansas team that came into that 1939-40 season was recovering from a year that was, by the standards of KU and its fifty-five-year-old coach, a disappointment. The 1938-39 Jayhawks had gone 13-7 overall and finished third in the Big Six Conference. With a returning team that included co-captain Dick Harp, a defensive liability named Howard Engleman who could score in bursts, and a baby-faced guard named Bobby Allen, who had achieved his dream of being able to play for his father, Phog's 1939–40 squad was solid but not overly intimidating. Fans paid $1.25 per game to watch the Jayhawks get off to a surprisingly strong start, winning ten of their first eleven games while prompting their coach to begin calling them the "Pony Express." As Phog Allen liked to explain, "they delivered the mail."

Allen's constant fundamentals work and defensive principles helped give the 1939–40 Jayhawks a chance every time out, but it was his gift for motivation that really hit home with that KU team. He had the Jayhawks fired up for every game, whether that meant pushing the right buttons or having the players slap each other—quite literally—out of a funk. Such was the case at halftime of a February 10, 1940, game at Kansas State. The Jayhawks were trailing at the half, and so Allen had the players line up across from each other and deliver open-handed blows to the face in an effort to light a fire; KU went on to blow out the hated Wildcats in the second half.

Kansas rolled out to one of its best starts in years but was plagued by prolonged scoring droughts. Phog Allen, for all his basketball acumen, couldn't find a way to snap the team out of its shooting slump. After one such game, a KU sophomore approached Allen with a possible solution. His name was Ralph Miller, and his path to KU had been filled with circuitous turns.

Phog Allen first became aware of Miller when his youngest son, Bobby, was playing in a junior high tournament a few years earlier. A lightning-quick kid from Chanute, Kansas, made such an impression on young Bobby Allen that he went home and proclaimed to his father that Ralph Miller was the best player he'd ever seen. Phog Allen began following Miller's career, and by his senior year the Chanute High star was being recruited by seventy colleges across the country. Allen wanted him as badly as any coach but didn't push too hard because he had the understanding that Miller was already KU-bound, mainly due to the fact that Allen had coached both Miller's father and his uncle at Kansas. After one of Bobby Allen's state tournament games with Lawrence High School, Phog stuck around to watch Miller's Chanute team and quickly came to his aid when the star player went down with a hip injury. Doc Allen administered his trademark osteopathic techniques at halftime, and Miller returned to score 26 points over the final two quarters.

But during Miller's senior year of high school, a Stanford University alumnus convinced him to take a look at the Northern California campus, sealing the deal by offering to drive Miller halfway across the country for a visit. Miller enjoyed his trip and even got to meet Stanford star Hank Luisetti, and he made an immediate connection with Cardinal basketball coach John Bunn—a former KU player under Phog Allen. After some late-night pressuring from a group of basketball players, the kid from Chanute, Kansas, announced his intentions to attend Stanford. Only during a return trip to Kansas in Bunn's car did Miller begin to second-guess his decision, which he'd made hastily while surrounded by Stanford players.

The KU athletic department eventually got wind of Miller's cold feet and offered to pay for a train ticket to send him to Chicago, where Phog Allen was doing a speaking engagement. When Miller arrived in the Windy City, Allen gave him his best sales pitch and ended up driving Miller back to Lawrence, using the 550-mile venture to pressure Miller into changing his mind. Miller arrived on the KU campus uncertain of what to do, so he called his father. Harold Miller informed young Ralph that he had better make up his mind quickly, because John Bunn was on his way to Chanute to take him back to Stanford for the summer.

Upon receiving this news, Phog Allen offered to give Miller another ride: back to Chanute to confront Bunn in person. Miller would later write that the meeting that ensued between Allen and Bunn "was not a friendly conversation." Allen reminded Bunn of how he'd given him a job as a KU assistant coach shortly after his 1921 graduation and had paid his salary out of his own pocket because Bunn was desperate for finances. He disclosed that he had gotten Bunn the job at Stanford. Bunn countered that Miller had already given him a commitment. The argument went on and on, getting so heated that Ralph Miller left the room.

When Miller returned about an hour later, his father told him it was time to make a decision. "For the last time," Harold Miller said, "tell these two gentlemen what you are going to do."

Sheepishly, Ralph Miller looked up at John Bunn, then at Phog Allen, then back to Bunn. "I'm sorry, John," he said, "but I have decided to go to Kansas University."

Miller, who was also a quarterback on the KU football team, was the player who approached Phog Allen midway through the 1939–40 season with an idea of how to fix the offense. Miller suggested the coach abandon his three-guard, two-post offense for one that featured one post player, two forwards, and two guards. Allen listened intently before indignantly telling Miller, "Well, Ralph, we're already using the best offense there is."

The 1939–40 Jayhawks stuck with Allen's three-guard system and continued to win games, going 8-2 in the conference to earn a three-way tie for first place. But after a 47–36 humbling at the hands of Oklahoma in the regular-season finale, Phog Allen called the starters together for a team meeting. He announced that the Jayhawks were going to a one-post offense, and then asked Miller what he thought.

"Doc, you know what I think," Miller said.

"Fine, Ralph," Doc Allen told his 6'2" forward, "you're the post man."

The Jayhawks traveled to Wichita for a March 12, 1940, Big Six championship game against an Oklahoma team that had clobbered KU four days earlier, and Phog decided to debut the new offense against the Sooners. Allen also surprised OU by dressing his players in tennis shoes rather than basketball footwear. The floor at the basketball arena in Wichita, where the game was to be played, had hosted a dance the previous evening, and Allen knew from experience that the surface would be slick. He sent team trainer Dean Nesmith out for a few sticks of belt dressing, a grip compound often used in tractors, and the players applied the adhesive to the bottoms of their shoes. With new shoes and a new offense, KU stormed the Sooners to a surprising 45–39 victory—led by Miller's 12 points—to give Kansas the outright Big Six title and earn the Jayhawks their first-ever trip to the infant NCAA tournament.

The NCAA tournament's birth was a huge source of pride for Allen, who would finally get to coach in an event he had helped bring to fruition. His efforts to get basketball into the 1936 Olympic Games were effectively cast aside when Allen wasn't invited to make the trip to Berlin. Then his

1938–39 Jayhawks had fallen short of qualifying for the debut of the NCAA tournament.

At long last, Phog Allen's skills as a coach and a promoter were intersecting, and he had a lot more on the line because the upcoming game would be played in Kansas City.

Four days after beating Oklahoma, KU made its NCAA tourney debut, the first of forty-four appearances in the Big Dance over the fifty-four years that would follow. The first televised game in college basketball had come earlier in the 1939–40 season, in a regular-season tournament held at Madison Square Garden, but in the spring of 1940 NCAA tournament games were still more than a decade away from making their way onto national television. The game of basketball had come a long way but still had a long way to go.

Allen's first NCAA tournament opponent was a familiar one, as the Jayhawks would be squaring off with an Oklahoma A&M team that had recently become an annual nemesis. Coached by thirty-five-year-old prodigy Henry Iba, the Aggies of the Missouri Valley Conference had a way of making things tough on Phog and the Jayhawks. Iba loved to slow the game down and frustrate opponents, and the tactic often left Allen wringing his hands.

When the Jayhawks walked into the arena a few hours before the game, Allen turned to his son Bob, who had once begged him to stay at KU so he could play for his legendary father. "Bob," Doc Allen told him, "here we are."

In their opening game of the NCAA tournament, a subregional in Stillwater, Oklahoma, that would earn the winner a spot in the eight-team field, the Jayhawks used their new-look offense again and jumped out to a 9–3 lead. But a KU technical foul on a botched substitution allowed the Aggies to get back in the game, and the two rivals were tied at halftime (24–24) and again at the end of regulation (40–40) before Dick Harp hit the go-ahead shot on a long, arcing heave in overtime—giving Kansas a 42–40 win. Phog Allen called it "the greatest game I ever saw a Kansas team play," and the fans were so excited that they showed up at Santa Fe Station in Lawrence to welcome the team home later that night.

The win meant KU wouldn't have to travel far again, as the remaining West Regional games were to be played in Kansas City—as was the upcoming national title game. To get there, the Jayhawks would first have to get through a Rice team that featured 6'5" Bob Kinney, the biggest player remaining in the tournament. Allen unleashed one of his famous pregame speeches and used a zone defense to contain Kinney, but the star of that game was KU's Howard Engleman. Having spent most of the season hobbled by a knee injury, Engleman came off the bench to score 21 points in the 50–44 win over the Owls. The victory sent the Jayhawks to the national semifinals, where they would face a tough USC team that had designs on playing for a national title.

Kansas City's Municipal Auditorium, which had been built six years earlier, in 1934, as a replacement for Convention Hall, proved up to the challenge, as a crowd of ten thousand fans validated Allen's hometown confidence by showing up to watch KU face USC in a national semifinal game. Phog Allen walked into the locker room that night and looked his players in the eyes. He paraded back and forth and told them not to be afraid to take chances: "If you have a 'hunch' and think that something will work, try it. Do it. I'll go up or down with you." When the game began, Phog's youngest son, Bob Allen, was struggling through a nightmare of a game that saw him miss every shot he took and get heckled by some of the fans at Municipal Auditorium who shouted, "Give the ball to Junior!" The younger Allen spent a long spell on the bench before returning to action in the final minutes of a close game. The favored USC Trojans held a 40–38 lead with two minutes left when Bob Allen blew past a surprised defender and flipped in a shot to tie the score at 40—drawing a foul in the process.

The scene must have reminded the KU coach of a young Forrest Allen thirty-four years earlier, when he was a fresh-faced up-and-comer with the Kansas City Athletic Club—standing at the free-throw line, ball in hand, game on the line, and fans cheering. The crowds were bigger now, as was the venue, and the way Bobby Allen shot the ball looked nothing like the underhand toss that young Forrest had used to perfection back in the day. The game had certainly come a long way since then. Having a sanctioned national championship tournament was only part of the progress, as basketball rules had changed dramatically—most recently with the introduction of backcourt violations in 1933, the three-second rule that was added in 1935, and the elimination of the center jump after made baskets in 1937. (Phog's crusade for the higher rims, despite his Jayhawks opening the 1934–35 season with a pair of games played on twelve-foot baskets, never gained much following.)

Bob Allen stepped to the charity stripe, cool, calm and collected, and buried his free throw with a one-handed, overhead flick of the wrist for a 41–40 Kansas lead. USC responded with a quick basket at the other end, moving ahead 42–41 with less than a minute left. A story in the *Saturday Evening Post* written a few weeks after the game reported that Bobby's sister Jane, one of Phog's three daughters, fainted when the Trojans scored the go-ahead basket. What happened next, according to the *Saturday Evening Post*, went as follows:

> Then Phog Allen, squirming and thrashing on the Kansas bench, experienced a brain wave. He receives them every once in a while, usually when he is asleep, or when tremendously excited. They come without reason, without logic, but they come, and he follows them without cavil. This time the message was: "Engleman can score!"

Howard Engleman, injured most of the season and a defensive liability when on the floor, had shown a propensity for offense when called upon—as shown by his 21-point effort off the bench one game earlier. With the NCAA semifinal in the balance, Phog had left him on the bench in favor of a better defender. Struck with something like a premonition, Allen summoned Engleman from the bench to check into the game. USC took possession of the ball and attempted to stall out the final seconds, but Bob Allen, playing a "hunch," snuck in out of nowhere and poked the ball away from a Trojans player. Allen dished off to Engleman, who hit the game-winning shot with eighteen seconds left in a 43–42 victory.

As the *Saturday Evening Post* later declared, "it was another miracle in Kansas basketball. Kansas fans should be getting used to them by this time." An emotional Bob Allen celebrating by grabbing his father hand and saying, "Dad, I've paid you back."

"But he might have been thinking," Phog Allen would later write, "'Thanks for giving me my chance to play on one of your teams.'"

Phog Allen's first NCAA tournament appearance resulted in a trip to the finals. KU's home away from home in Kansas City provided the perfect backdrop for the program's first NCAA title game appearance, which would come a mere forty miles from campus—though just across the Missouri border. There, the Jayhawks would play a red-hot Indiana team that was, in many ways, just lucky to be in the tournament. The 1940 Hoosiers, coached by thirty-one-year-old former All-American Branch McCracken, finished second to Purdue in the Big Ten Conference, but the NCAA tournament committee chose Indiana over Purdue as the conference's lone representative because of the Hoosiers' two head-to-head wins over the Boilermakers. Led by a 6'2" center named Marv Huffman, Indiana loved to pick up the pace and went by the nickname Hurryin' Hoosiers. They had rushed through the competition at the East Regional in Indianapolis to set up the March 30, 1940, national title matchup at Kansas City's Municipal Auditorium.

Heading into the game, the Jayhawks knew very little about the Hoosiers. Senior Dick Harp went to the KU library the day of the game and pored through the Chicago newspapers just to learn the Indiana players' names, and a KU alumnus named Stu Chambers wired a ten-page letter to Allen that gave a scouting report on some of the Hoosiers' tendencies. But most of KU's game plan revolved around what Allen's Jayhawks did best: controlling the tempo with good ball handlers, crisp passing, snap decision-making—and defending like their lives depended on it. He also wasn't going to wait to unveil his hottest scorer; on this night, Howard Engleman would replace John Kline as one of the Jayhawks' starting five.

The pressure was on Phog Allen in the hours leading up to tip-off, and not just because his Jayhawks were playing in their first-ever national title game. Allen was also on the hook for making the title game a success— win or lose—because he had convinced the NCAA one year earlier to hold the event in Kansas City. Allen had promised Chairman Howard Olsen that he could turn a profit, and anything short of that would have almost certainly put an end to the NCAA tournament experiment after just two seasons.

In the Municipal Auditorium locker room before tip-off, Allen wrote the names of his starters, alongside those of the Indiana players they would be defending. Chalk in hand, wearing a suit and tie, Allen turned and began reading off the names, looking each starter in the eye as he asked,

"Harp, are you ready?"

"Ebling, are you ready?"

"Miller, are you ready?"

"Allen, are you ready?"

"Engleman, are you ready?"

One by one, the players nodded.

The Jayhawks' trademark defense, perfected under Phog's intensive fundamentals work and rigorous conditioning, was on display in the early going, as it took more than eight minutes for Indiana to make its first field goal. By that time, KU had stormed out to a 10-4 lead and had created a state of near-hysteria among the partisan crowd of ten thousand fans at Kansas City's Municipal Auditorium. The emotion of the moment swarmed over the team, and at least two Jayhawks got so swept up in the moment that they began taking ill-advised shots. At one point, Allen called timeout and berated Miller and Engleman for playing outside of the offense. The timeout seemed to ignite the Indiana players, as Huffman and the Hurryin' Hoosiers turned on a switch that never went off. The big man started hitting shots from the outside, then a reserve named Jay McCreary came off the bench to score a few of his career-high 12 points for the night, leading to a 14-2 run that gave Indiana an 18-12 lead. Allen had no answer for the sudden onslaught, which continued as Indiana outscored Kansas 28-9 over the final twelve minutes of the first half en route to a 32-19 lead at the intermission.

Phog Allen unleashed what was undoubtedly one of his most powerful halftime speeches on that night, on his biggest stage to date. But whatever it was that Phog Allen said or did between halves of the 1940 national championship game against Indiana, it did nothing to slow down the Hurryin' Hoosiers.

Indiana rolled over the Jayhawks 60-42 in a physical game that resulted in 30 fouls, and KU shot just 17 percent from the field, an embarrassing performance in Allen's NCAA championship debut. The Jayhawks "met their Waterloo and with this defeat lost their opportunity to win the National Crown," as Allen would later describe the game in one of his books.

More than a half century later, Harp described the performance to author John Hendel for a book called *Kansas Jayhawks: History-Making Basketball*, saying, "We played pretty well through the tournament and didn't play well then. Maybe we were tired. We played tired. We just didn't play well and got beat badly."

Phog's youngest son, Bob, took the loss particularly hard. Years later, one of Bob Allen's sons would sum up the defeat by saying, "That was probably [Bob Allen's] biggest disappointment in life." And yet the younger Allen would not have traded the experience of getting to play for Phog Allen, his father, for anything.

"It meant everything to him," said Mark Allen, Bob's son and Phog's grandson.

The loss in the championship game would also stick with Phog Allen, but it's likely that he was able to turn the page pretty quickly. Based on Allen's history of being able to brush off a loss, it's not difficult to imagine him climbing onto the team bus after the Indiana game, loosening his tie, and falling into a deep sleep before the driver even pulled away from the curb. Allen's ability to find peace after a tough loss was one of the many personality traits that his players remembered in the years and decades that followed, and yet that 1940 game stuck with Allen for most of his life.

The loss to Indiana was tolerable at the time because, in many ways, the 1940 NCAA tournament was an overwhelming success for the fifty-five-year-old coach. Ticket sales were much better than anyone expected, bringing in $32,228.85 over three nights, and the profits of close to $10,000 showed that the NCAA tournament could indeed be a money-making endeavor. The must-see event that the NCAA tournament would become was still years in the making, and yet that 1940 experience in Kansas City planted the seeds for success.

The day after Indiana beat Kansas in the 1940 NCAA title game, committee chairman Howard Olsen told the *Kansas City Star*, "[Phog] Allen has done a wonderful job this year, and we owe him a vote of thanks. No other person could have accomplished what he did."

Phog Allen, who had begun marketing the championship game all the way back in September of 1939, was being hailed as a hero again but still came away dissatisfied from the experience. Only $750 from those profits went to Indiana and KU, the two schools in the championship game. Allen was so upset at this oversight that he promptly stepped down from the NCAA tournament committee, providing yet another moment of passionate protest from the opinionated Kansas coach with Missouri "Show Me" blood. Since the summer of 1936, in a span of less than four years, Allen had been responsible for the births of two of the biggest events basketball would have to offer—the Olympic basketball games and the NCAA basketball tournament—and had quit his positions on both committees in protest. In some ways, Phog Allen was coming across as bigger than the game itself—something James Naismith had painstakingly avoided doing despite his standing as father of the game.

In the months that followed Naismith's death, Allen had maintained his stature atop the rising mountain of college basketball, and the publication of his second book, *Better Basketball,* served as a guide explaining why—to anyone who would care to endure his expertise. The book, which was published a few months before the printing of Naismith's book *Basketball: Its Origins and Development* (a fact that some people in the Naismith camp perceived as by design and a form of Phog's one-upmanship), highlighted many of his philosophies while including seventy-eight diagrams that unabashedly showed off his basketball acumen. The book broke down every aspect of the sport, from dribbling drills to offensive plays to pregame speeches. He wrote about nutrition and addressing injuries and also gave tips on how to combat player apathy—which he called "the stale athlete." Allen wrote that an apathetic player could be spotted rather easily: "Fatty deposit below the lid is the first to disappear when the player is dissipating or growing stale." His suggestions for dealing with the problem included cutting off practices to allow the players to participate in an impromptu game or to just gather them around in a circle so the team could sing songs together.

The book also featured a section on how to put on a full basketball game presentation, from the dimming of the lights before the national anthem to ideas for halftime entertainment. A showman in coach's clothing, Allen had been one of the first basketball coaches to put on halftime shows—following the idea set by dog breeder and part-time football team owner Walter Lingo in the early 1920s. Allen's ideas included boxing, wrestling, fancy bicycle riding, singing, dancing, tennis, fencing, and "midget basketball"—contrary to the way it sounded, these halftime games would feature kids. Anything but the deafening drone of silence between periods. As Allen wrote, "the modern public deplores dull moments."

Most of Phog Allen's marketing philosophies were ahead of his time, as evidenced by the rise in popularity of Olympic basketball and the NCAA tournament over the second half of the twentieth century. His *Better Basketball* book cautioned, "When competition becomes a business it becomes professional." And yet Phog Allen put few limits on the sport's growth from lug nut to automobile.

Allen's outspoken nature also continued to ruffle feathers around academic circles at KU, where the rising national popularity of a basketball coach who answered to the nickname "Doc" was being met with some hostility. The mere fact that he had never attained a PhD was a sticking point for many administrators while witnessing his rising visibility on and off campus. Like it or not, Phog Allen had become the face of the university.

Despite his charisma and well-spoken soliloquies, Allen was hardly the perfect fit for university public relations. He never met a subject on which he didn't have an opinion, and the KU coach loved the idea of being a foghorn in public forums. His growing popularity and national success only made him more confident in speaking out, and his well-known name made the public more likely to take notice.

"Allen accepted controversy as part of the profession and, in fact, often seemed to seek out and thrive upon conflict," author Mike Fisher wrote in his 1997 biography of longtime KU athletic trainer Dean Nesmith.

In December 1940, Allen began taking aim at the game of football, saying that the sport was losing popularity while declaring, "Football is on the way out." A onetime football coach who had seen the gridiron struggles of KU cost him his job as athletic director in the 1930s, Allen began a gradual distancing from the sport he once loved. Football was too violent, he maintained, and fans were better off watching a gentlemanly sport like basketball in their free time. A few weeks later, in February 1941, Allen took issue with the NCAA's choice of Wisconsin Field House as a site for the upcoming NCAA basketball tournament rather than returning to Kansas City. Allen threatened to boycott the tournament, even though his KU team was coming off of its historic run to the NCAA championship game a year earlier. He pronounced that KU was "not interested in the playoffs sponsored by the N.C.A.A.—an outfit of money grabbers." Shortly thereafter, the Jayhawks turned down an opportunity to face co–Big Seven champion Iowa State in a winner-take-all game that would have determined the conference's representative at the upcoming NCAA tournament. Allen justified the decision by saying his team was "too small and too tired to partake of any post-season play, and besides, I want nothing to do with the NCAA."

A few months after that, Allen would publicly demand an investigation of the University of Oklahoma athletic department, accusing the school of a myriad of transgressions, further inflaming another already heated Big Six rivalry.

Outspoken and ultracompetitive, Phog Allen found time to maintain his success on the court using a tried-and-true method that he had pretty much oiled to perfection. He had begun tinkering with some fast-break aspects to go along with a motion offense of set plays. He allowed his players, a group he assembled based largely on mental makeup, to decide within the flow of the game which method to use based on how many opposing defenders were in position as the ball crossed midcourt. He focused his recruiting efforts on players who had the ability to shine in the classroom as well as the basketball court, believing that a smart player could find ways to win no matter his level of athletic talent. He encouraged his players to hit the books and discouraged them from regarding professional basketball as a postgraduation career option. As Allen liked to say, "when you train your muscles, you have four to nine years; when you train your mind, you have fifty."

And yet the part-time osteopath never lost sight of the importance of physical fitness. He required his players to spend the offseason doing the same physical regimen Allen had endured on a daily basis for most of his entire life, from fingertip pushups to lunges to sit-ups. Anyone who didn't show up for a season in shape, he maintained, would quickly get left behind. As Allen once wrote in a letter to his players, "we have men on the basketball team who will train, and the fellows who will not, or do not, are in for a lonesome existence this year."

Defensively, Allen used what he had begun calling a "Stratified Transitional Man-for-Man Defense With Zone Principle"—a system he described as "impenetrable. The only time the other team can score is when your own team makes a mistake." The defense stemmed from Allen's philosophy of defending odd-man fast breaks, which basically left one man on the ball and another under the basket to force offensive players to shoot over the defenders rather than to get uncontested layups. "An effective defense," he once wrote, "must try to conserve its forces near the basket, by using the principle of the economy of defense." Even in five-on-five half-court sets, Allen came to realize, the system could be effective. With two forwards trapping the ball near midcourt and the other three defenders falling back into a zone, the defense could create turnovers and cut down on scoring in the lane. "A defense must menacingly project its tentacles forward and out," Allen once explained in the book *Better Basketball*. The defense, like many of the concepts that Allen used, was ahead of its time.

Allen's acumen as an X's and O's man was at its career peak. As writer Howard W. Turtle noted in a 1940 feature on Allen in the *Saturday Evening Post*, "Phog has never grown old-fashioned. With each new trend he has changed his tactics, and in many instances has been ahead of the field."

Shortly after celebrating his fifty-fifth birthday in November 1940, Phog Allen was still keeping himself in remarkable physical shape and took such pride in his body that he occasionally golfed without a shirt, even while hobnobbing with some of the most successful doctors and lawyers Lawrence had to offer. "Every man, whether athlete or non-athlete," Allen once wrote, "should have a justifiable pride in his own splendid physique and in the knowledge of being physically fit." He also maintained a steady clientele of osteopathy clients, most of whom he treated on the training table at KU's athletic facility. He continued to tape his players' ankles before games and address their injuries at intermissions and had even begun treating them with a foot-arch roller that he had designed to help loosen up tendons on the soles of players' feet.

He was a picture of health, manic about physical fitness, and a staunch proponent of clean living, all of which made Phog Allen's secret vice almost unfathomable. Through his years of lecturing players and students on the importance of keeping themselves in peak physical condition, Allen was somehow able to maintain a smoking habit that stretched through a good part of his coaching years. Allen was quietly smoking one or two cigarettes per day behind closed doors. One of his players later recalled a time when he walked up on Allen smoking, and the veteran coach carried on a five-minute conversation while holding the smoldering cigarette behind his back, as if pretending it wasn't there. On another occasion, Allen left a lit cigarette on the vinyl seat of his Chrysler, causing a fire that ripped through the vehicle and burned away most of it from the inside out. He showed no sign of shame while posing next to the charred automobile, a large grin on his face, for a newspaper photo that appeared the following day.

Allen guzzled milk at meals and saved the glass jugs for game days, filling them with quarts of water for constant saturation as he coached from the bench. One estimate had him going through six quarts of water per game, as Allen believed that a lubricated pharynx muscle could help calm the nerves. He'd come to wearing eyeglasses in those years and often spent more time tossing barbs at the officials than encouraging his own players. As one of Phog's former players would later say, "Doc didn't praise you a lot; that wasn't his thing."

The reasoning behind Allen's motivational tactics was often unclear, which was by design. He liked to keep players guessing, particularly when it came to their mental focus. In a book called *Tales from the Jayhawks' Hardwood*, KU player Otto Schnellbacher recalled a day when Phog Allen approached him after a particularly good practice. Schnellbacher was expecting to hear rare praise from his coach, but Allen surprised him by telling him, "Otto, you can do three things on this campus. You can play sports, go to school and chase women. You can only do two of them well. Which two do you want to do well?" He then brought up the name of a girl Schnellbacher was known to be dating. Phog knew not only the girl's name but also her phone number, which he presented to Schnellbacher as his way of saying, *Break it off and get back to concentrating on basketball.*

Before, during, and after games, Allen was known for psychological motivation that always kept his "boys" on their toes. His booming voice demanded attention; as former player Bob Dole once wrote in a memoir, "Phog Allen, the venerable coach with the foghorn voice, didn't know how to talk quietly, and probably wouldn't have if he could have." Allen's common mantras included "run their hearts out, then whip them—that's all," "promptness is like godliness," and "*esprit de corps*"—spirit of the team. But he was also known to openly tell his players that he would single them out to press reporters afterward if they diverged from his game plan; if everyone did exactly as he said, he would take full blame for a defeat.

His coaching ways struck a chord with his players, who carried a healthy mix of fear and respect for Allen. As Schnellbacher, who would play for Allen in the 1940s, once said, "he didn't take anything except excellence as a major, but at the same time, you knew when he was chewing you out that he loved you." Allen was always in command, even when it seemed he might be unraveling during a halftime tirade or mid-practice lecture. In his mind he had mastered the sport of basketball and demanded that each of his players do the same.

Allen's competitive fire came out on game days, but he was able to turn it off shortly afterward. Win or lose, he would fraternize with fans on the court at Hoch Auditorium while his players showered in the Robinson Gym locker room next door.

By the dawn of the 1940s, basketball had solidified itself as a sport on the rise in the United States. Professional leagues on the East Coast were thriving, and barnstorming teams like the Harlem Globetrotters were having varied success throughout the country. The game of basketball had made its television debut a month before the KU-Indiana final, on February 28, 1940, in a Madison Square Garden game between the University of Pittsburgh and Fordham University. The championship game between Kansas and Indiana, which was not televised, had brought in ten thousand fans and proven that the NCAA tournament could be a success. Basketball, the Kansas Jayhawks, and Phog Allen were rolling through the early part of the decade, forging a path straight toward stamping their places upon the American sporting lexicon.

But once again, in the winter of 1941, for the second time in Allen's coaching career, basketball would have to take a backseat to something bigger. After Japanese airplanes attacked an unprepared military harbor off the coast of Hawaii, the United States found itself at war again. Even Phog Allen couldn't deny that there were things much more important than winning basketball games.

13

A Greater Calling

The Marine was ready for battle. Twenty-six years old, he had risen to the rank of first lieutenant, had become the kind of young man that made his former coach brim with pride. He had become a leader of men, a passionate defender of his beliefs.

The lieutenant and his fellow Marines in the Third Division approached via tank-like ships called LVTs in the early daylight hours of a warm summer day. The land-and-sea vehicles braved the dangerous reefs and the pounding surf of the north shore waters leading up to the Asan Ridge in Guam. The Marines were ready to roll up onto the beautiful, white-sand beaches in full attack mode on the first day of what would become known as the Battle of Guam.

The first lieutenant's heart pounded with the anticipation of battle as the shimmering orange glow of sunrise reflected off the choppy waters. He was so far from home, so far from the dry heat of North Texas and the year he spent in Oklahoma City. He'd been just a kid then, and so much had happened in the years that followed. He was a man now, had seen things of which he could never speak when—if—he ever made it back to the States. Now, he was something different. He was a different person, if a person at all.

The U.S. troops had already reconnoitered the shores on both the northern and southern strips of Guam, clearing the way for an early-morning arrival two weeks later than originally planned. The lieutenant and his Third Division troops had been awaiting the day with equal parts excitement and dread, and as the LVTs approached there didn't initially appear to be any sign of imminent danger.

But the Japanese military had been waiting, the soldiers tucked behind a concrete wall—a "pillbox"—with only the barrels of their guns exposed. With the suddenness of lightning, they unleashed their artillery and interrupted the silence of dawn with an unrelenting attack. Missiles and falling mortars whistled through the ocean air. Explosions rang out. Smoke billowed into the clear blue sky. When all was said and done, twenty U.S. LVTs had been destroyed. It wasn't yet nine o'clock in the morning.

The lieutenant was among the casualties, his soul given to the international cause of freedom, his body laid to rest in the weeks that would follow. His young life had been cut short by his need to protect the freedom of others.

Lt. Thomas Hunter Jr. had once compared war to a game. Strong, brave, and stricken with the naiveté of youth, the lieutenant would be among the first casualties in an important battle that would carry on for almost three weeks, eventually resulting in the Americans holding off Japan's efforts to take control of Guam.

In the game of sport, there are winners and losers. In war, even the sides that win suffer unspeakable loss. For Doc Allen, the man who once coached him, no lost game could ever come close. Nothing in sport could ever come close to bringing this kind of sorrow.

By the time the United States had been dragged into World War II by the Japanese bombing of Pearl Harbor in December of 1941, the basketball life of Forrest "Phog" Allen had gained legendary status. Fifty-six years old, he had already won 512 games and nineteen conference titles and was largely responsible for basketball being included in the Olympics and for the formation of the NCAA tournament. And yet the thing that brought Allen the most pride in his basketball career came from those players who had gone on to succeed in life.

"I'll tell you in 25 years," he'd said over and over when asked about his best Kansas team, "when I see how they do in the business world."

Many of Allen's "boys" had followed his footsteps into the world of coaching, and with great success. Phog Allen's coaching tree had branched out into the most impressive lineage of coaches college basketball had to offer in the years leading up to World War II. Thirty-nine-year-old Adolph Rupp had already won 162 games, six conference titles, and a Helms Foundation national championship in his ten years at Kentucky. Dutch Lonborg's tenure at Northwestern University included two Big Ten Conference titles and a Helms championship. John Bunn was on a run of three consecutive Pacific Coast South Division titles at Stanford University. And Frosty Cox, a three-year starter for the Jayhawks from 1929 through 1931, was leading a University of Colorado program that had just won the 1940 National Invitational Tournament title. Two years prior to that, in 1938, Phog Allen and his protégés had concurrently owned conference titles in the Big Six, the Pacific Coast South Division, the Southeastern Conference, and the Mountain States Conference.

Phog Allen took pride in turning boys into men, and men into leaders. He loved watching his former players rise into positions of leadership. And in Allen's mind, there were no greater leaders than those in the military. His older brother Pete had gone into the army after leaving the University of Kansas in the early 1900s and risen all the way up to captain. (Although Phog was said to have grown somewhat distant from his brothers after the death of their father, William "Shoe" Allen, in 1937.) Allen was known to make his players stand on long train rides if soldiers were present, offering up their seats even if that meant several hours on their feet during road trips to the East Coast; Phog, of course, would join them in standing. Some of his favorite motivational phrases about "going to battle" and "rallying the troops" were meant in the sincerest form of flattery for a profession that he saw as the highest calling imaginable. The soldier mentality was one Allen encouraged his players to carry into games. "All athletic contests," he liked to say, "are a throwback from the game of war." He hoped his players could learn from the selflessness of soldiers, once writing that the military "demands unyielding sacrifice of self for the good of the whole."

As much as he appreciated the U.S. military, Doc Allen had a job to do as young men from across the nation were being called into duty overseas. As the war raged on, so did KU basketball. While most collegiate sports were canceled during the World War II years, basketball joined football, baseball, and track in providing distractions on U.S. soil.

Ten days after Pearl Harbor, the 1941–42 Jayhawks tipped off with a home game against the University of Denver. The Jayhawks welcomed the return of senior captain Ralph Miller after he missed the entire 1940–41 season with a knee injury. Miller was one of the best two-sport athletes in the Big Six Conference and helped get the 1941–42 Jayhawks off to a 5-0 start, then KU kept things rolling through another tough conference schedule. Allen's boys eventually earned a share of another Big Six title— his eighteenth conference championship as KU's head coach—before knocking off Missouri Valley Conference champion Oklahoma A&M and Allen nemesis Henry Iba in an NCAA district playoff game. That put the Jayhawks in the NCAA tournament for the second time in three seasons, and this time Phog Allen would have to square off with one of his protégés in Colorado coach Frosty Cox. The former KU player had a roster filled with players from the state of Kansas, but the only one of them Phog Allen had tried to make a Jayhawk was a kid from the basketball-rich town of Newton named Leason "Pete" McCloud. Known for a one-handed shot that could be nearly unstoppable, McCloud came into the game with an axe to grind because KU's Allen had offered him a tryout on the team but no scholarship money. The offer had come shortly after Pete McCloud's father passed away, and he didn't have a penny to his name. Having instead accepted a scholarship to play basketball at Colorado, McCloud developed into a star and took revenge on the Jayhawks by scoring 19 points in the 46–44 win in the 1942 NCAA West Regional.

As it turned out, that may have been a blessing in disguise. Ralph Miller was feeling the effects of illness in that game, and very soon afterward he was diagnosed with pleurisy—a condition he apparently developed while swimming at the KU pool. He ended up spending thirty-one days in a hospital but eventually recovered and joined the air force.

As the war continued overseas, Phog Allen adjusted on the court and in the classroom. Physical education had become compulsory for students registered in the selective service, and seemingly overnight the classes swelled from 450 students to 1,800. This spike in classroom size forced Allen to call on several KU football players to help teach his PE classes. Allen also began riding a bicycle to work in those years, as a gas shortage created by World War II left him relying on good old-fashioned manpower to make the two-mile commute to campus.

The ongoing war had a profound effect on Allen in a variety of ways, and not just because many of his top KU players would end up getting called into duty in the coming years. The opinionated, spirited coach with the knack for controversial sound bites began showing the public a more compassionate side as the war carried on. Upon learning in March 1942 that the University of Kansas had established a scholarship in his name, Phog Allen broke down in tears of joy. It marked the first time anyone could remember seeing him shed tears in public. His speech of gratitude was just as emotional and showed out-of-character modesty as Allen offered, "My life has been more than basketball; it has been struggle, sadness, strife and joy. I've been licked so many times, I can't remember them."

Allen was most comfortable when standing in front of his players, whether he was delivering a passionate pregame speech or rallying the "troops" at halftime. On one such occasion early in the 1942–43 season, Allen delivered one of his most memorable halftime speeches, although it had very little to do with basketball.

During halftime of a close game against Fordham at Madison Square Garden, the players gathered around in silence as Allen stood in front of them ready to present a few strategic adjustments. Allen began his speech and looked up to find one of his players with a finger in his nose. The scope of the speech immediately changed, as Allen began speaking on the importance of how to conduct oneself as a man. Winners didn't get caught picking their noses, he preached. His speech unfolded into a talk about winning in business and society, lasting five, then ten minutes, before the intermission ran out and the second half was set to begin.

But the war years took on a more serious tone that had an effect on the entire world, not to mention Lawrence, Kansas. The military pulled away several of Allen's KU athletes. Not long after leading the 1942–43 Jayhawks to a school-record twenty-two wins and a perfect 10-0 record in the Big Six, two stars from that team went off to fight in the war. Otto Schnellbacher, a basketball and football star from Sublette, Kansas, who had become known as "The Double Threat from Sublette," and teammate Charlie Black (no relation to the Charlie Black who played at KU in the 1920s) eventually went overseas to serve their country. Even Ralph Miller spent time in the military, although the knee injury he suffered as a junior kept him from having to leave the country.

Another player who went into action was a two-sport athlete named Thomas "T.P." Hunter. "Teep," as he was known, was a reserve during the KU basketball team's championship-game run in 1940 and a top player on Allen's 1942 baseball team—the only one Phog coached at Kansas— before joining the marines shortly after his 1942 graduation. Allen once described Hunter as a "modest, clean, genteel and resourceful boy, beloved by every classmate and athletic adversary." The 6'3" Texan was a student member of the KU athletic board, one of the most respected athletes on campus and one of Phog's favorites. He had forever endeared himself to Allen when, after the Jayhawks upset USC in the 1940 NCAA semifinals, Hunter confided to the coach that he'd always believed he should have been a starter but that the win over the Trojans confirmed just how good KU's starting five was. Hunter went into duty in 1942 without much fanfare, packing up his things and leaving Kansas for the great unknown.

Through all the changes, Phog Allen kept on winning. Allen had lifted the Jayhawks into one of the nation's finest programs in the early 1920s and rebuilt KU basketball up again through the 1930s, but the apex of his coaching career came during the early 1940s at a time when international conflict overshadowed much of what was happening on the American sports scene. In the comparatively tiny world of basketball, his worth was never as appreciated. A few months after the University of Kansas established a scholarship in his honor, Allen found out in January 1943 that he'd received another award from the Helms Foundation. The fiftieth anniversary of basketball brought a set of honors dedicated to the first half century of the sport, with Phog Allen being named "the greatest basketball coach of all-time." The designation was another feather in the cap of the man whom James Naismith himself had called, seven years earlier, "the father of basketball coaching."

Despite the accolades, Allen couldn't help but to be distracted by the ongoing war. He kept thinking about the boys who were risking their lives overseas, and in 1943 he began serving on the Douglas County Draft Board. Around that same time, Allen started writing and printing a series of newsletters designed as a way of communicating with former KU players serving overseas. The *Jayhawk Rebounds*, as the newsletters were called, served as a forum to keep former Jayhawks serving in the military up to date on the KU community—and vice versa.

One of the eighteen installments of *Jayhawk Rebounds* included a letter that came from Lt. T.P. Hunter, the former baseball pitcher and basketball reserve who had touched Allen so deeply. On New Year's Day 1944, Hunter wrote to Allen detailing a battle in Bougainville, one of the Solomon Islands in the South Pacific, where a Japanese troop had cornered Hunter and his fellow soldiers. Hunter joked that the Japanese soldiers "got me and my boys in a hot box," referring to a schoolyard game played with a baseball and two gloves.

"I have called [war] a game, Doc, and to me that is just about how it seemed," Hunter wrote. "The same is true for most of the boys that return. The bad part of the whole war is these boys who have to give their lives to win. I had some of those [in my marine troop] and for them it must have been more than a game."

That would be the final letter that Allen would receive from Thomas "T.P." Hunter. Less than nine months later, in the September issue of *Jayhawk Rebounds*, Phog Allen wrote,

> Somehow this is the most difficult letter that I have ever attempted to write. Over a dozen times I have begun it and each time I have walked away from my desk because words fail me. I feel such a void. Something has gone from me. Your friend and mine—good, old honest 'Teep', T.P. Hunter (1st Lt. 9th Marines), was killed on Guam, July 21, 1944. And yet this morning he feels closer to me than at any moment that I have known him. Across the miles that span Lawrence and Guam, it

seems so trivial. This thing we call death has brought him closer to me at this very moment than he has been for years. The glories of his life are magnified a hundredfold.

A Chinese philosopher once said, "Life seems so unreal at times that I do not know whether I am living dreams or dreaming life." The life here and the life hereafter seem so much a part of all of us that T.P.'s presence is manifest. He will live forever in our hearts. What more love can a man have that he lay down his life for his friend? He did that. . . .

T.P. Hunter was a great influence for good, whether on or off the athletic field. He was always living vicariously and constructively. Mit [sic] Allen and I were speaking regarding the untimely loss. Mit, always a realist, said spontaneously, "T.P. was perhaps too God-like to live long in this world. . . . It matters not how he [died], I'll bet he took it without a whimper as he took everything that came to him."

The war took its toll on several former Jayhawks, although Hunter was one of the few to lose his life in battle. Howard Engleman, a key figure in the Jayhawks' run to the 1940 NCAA championship game, was burned in a 1945 explosion that killed several comrades overseas. In April of that year, a KU alumnus named Bob Dole was injured in a gunfight in the Apennine Mountains of Italy, taking fire from a German machine gun to his arm and back. Dole, who played basketball under Allen for one season, spent several days, if not weeks, in an Italian hospital before being returned to the United States. Phog Allen visited his hospital bed, a gesture that stuck with Dole throughout his adult life as a politician; he became a U.S. senator before making a run for the U.S. presidency in 1996.

Allen's son, Bob, was also enlisted in the military in those years, at a time when the home of Phog and Bessie Allen was mostly their own. Son Mitt had recently moved nearby, a few houses down, into a small house they purchased on Louisiana Street while he attended law school, and daughter Eleanor spent some time living with her parents while raising a child as a single mother. But mostly, those war years were for Phog and Bessie to spend in their house alone. They got periodic updates from Bob Allen, who eventually returned from the war unharmed.

The war had an obvious effect on Allen's teams as well. KU's 1943–44 and '44–45 seasons weren't up to Phog Allen's typical standards, as the team played on while stars like Charlie Black and Otto Schnellbacher—a two-sport athlete who would go on to play professional basketball and with the New York Giants of the National Football League—were serving their country overseas. The 1943–44 Jayhawks endured a miserable January that saw them lose four times in one six-game stretch, and Allen got so frustrated in one game against Kansas State that he called timeout with four minutes left and told his players that under no circumstances should they run another play. The Jayhawks were trailing 31–17 at the time, and Phog demanded that whoever brought the ball up the court was to take it straight to the hoop—an outlandish strategy in those years that somehow resulted in KU scoring 15 consecutive points to take a 32–31 lead. A controversial call immediately before the Jayhawks' 1-point victory led the K-State fans to tear the jersey off of one of the game officials, and when Phog Allen and his players returned to the team bus shortly thereafter they found four flat tires. The Jayhawks ended up getting stranded in Manhattan, Kansas, for four and a half hours, which served as a pretty apt metaphor for their frustrating season. That 5–5 Big Six campaign was the first time in fifteen years that Kansas had not been above .500 in conference play, and although the Jayhawks showed improvement during a 12–5 season the following year in 1945–46, their second-place finish in the Big Six Conference marked the first time since KU's disastrous three-year run from 1927–28 through 1929–30 that Phog Allen had coached back-to-back years without winning a conference title.

Allen was continuing to make as many headlines off the court as on it. In March 1945, he won a Republican spot in the primary for a city councilman's position, and a few months later he made national headlines by telling a reporter that college football and basketball were being run by gamblers; he added that athletic departments were "sitting in a fool's paradise" by turning a blind eye. He claimed to have direct knowledge of a college game being fixed in New York City and, when further challenged for details, alleged that gamblers had approached at least one participating player before the 1944 national championship game between Utah and Dartmouth at Madison Square Garden. He even confidentially provided to MSG president Ned Irish the name of a player who had been privately expelled from school after meeting with a known gambler. No further investigation was conducted, but Allen continued to assert that a huge gambling scandal would emanate from New York City in the near future. Allen then ticked off another part of the country by naming Lexington, Kentucky, as the epicenter of America's gambling woes and went as far as singling out a Lexington tavern—the Mayfair Bar on East Main Street, just five blocks from the University of Kentucky gym—as the hub of gambling activity. The comments made national news and strained the relationship between Allen and Kentucky coach Adolph Rupp, a former Jayhawk, and the FBI would soon raid the upstairs of the Mayfair—only to find out that Allen was right.

Allen's Jayhawks got things back on track during the 1945–46 season, a campaign they dedicated to fallen war veteran T.P. Hunter by posthumously naming him as the team's honorary captain. With Charlie Black and Otto Schnellbacher returned from the war and accounting for most of the offense, the Jayhawks went 19-1 and turned in a perfect 10-0 record in the conference. When Allen laid out his goals at the beginning of each campaign, winning the conference was at the top of the list. Going unbeaten in conference play was an even bigger feat—what he referred to as an "ever-victorious" season—and his 1945–46 squad became only the fifth Jayhawk team to pull it off.

That set up another NCAA tournament appearance, the Jayhawks' third since the Big Dance's 1939 debut, and it came against a familiar opponent that was emerging as KU's biggest rival of the era. Oklahoma A&M had become a mainstay on KU's schedule, having played the Jayhawks fourteen times in a span of seven seasons even though the two programs were, at that time, in different conferences. The Aggies were coached by forty-one-year-old Henry "Hank" Iba, who had quickly emerged as a capable rival to Phog Allen despite their age difference of nearly twenty years. Iba matched Allen's confidence and basketball knowledge but went about things very differently. Iba carried a cold bench demeanor, his arms folded across his chest at a time when Phog Allen's would probably be flailing in emotional protest.

Even in dealing with other coaches, Iba was often more restrained. He drove Allen crazy with his guarded nature, while Iba once encapsulated

Allen by cracking, "He'll let you know what he thinks." There was an infamous game in which the two hardheaded coaches couldn't agree on a basketball, forcing them to compromise by changing balls at halftime. On another occasion, Iba was so upset about a foul call in a game against the Jayhawks that he refused to sub in for the player who had fouled out, leaving just four players to finish the game.

Not only had Iba risen quickly in the coaching ranks by the end of the 1945–46 season, with a 251-69 record in twelve years at the school that would later become known as Oklahoma State, but his defensive tactics and trademark slowdown offense frustrated Allen like nothing else. His conservative game plan led Allen to come up with a way to force the Aggies to move the ball, and he devised a pretty effective method of combating the constant slowdown tactics of opponents by ordering his KU defenders to rush the ball as it was being held near midcourt.

But this Iba squad wasn't just a bunch of undersized overachievers simply looking to take the air out of the ball. The Aggies boasted one of college basketball's biggest stars in Bob Kurland, a 7'0" senior from outside of St. Louis who had led the Aggies to a national title the previous year. Kurland and DePaul star George Mikan had simultaneously transformed the center position and changed the game of basketball because of their combination of size and shooting ability. He was precisely the kind of player that made Phog Allen want to move the baskets up to twelve feet.

Allen's feelings probably didn't change after Kurland erupted for 28 points in the District 5 NCAA West Regional game against the Jayhawks. The 49–38 loss to Oklahoma A&M knocked the Jayhawks out of the tournament, while Kurland, Iba, and the Aggies eventually went on to win their second-consecutive NCAA title.

The Iba-Allen rivalry would continue through the next decade, the latest of many coaching rivalries during Phog Allen's legendary career, and over time the relationship would evolve into one of mutual respect. Allen's coaching tree was also expanding, although some of his former players had a difficult time making it in the profession early on.

One of those was Ralph Miller, who had spent his injured season in 1941 teaching and coaching at Mount Oread High School in Lawrence to earn credits toward his degree in physical education. The school was a hub for the children of KU professors, and his experience coaching the basketball team was a disaster. As Miller wrote in his 1990 autobiography, "as professors' sons, [the Mount Oread players] tended to be highly intelligent, but not endowed with an abundance of physical talent. I don't recall that we fared very well."

Miller had decided to give up on his coaching career after that season, and he spent three years in the air force following his 1942 graduation from KU, eventually rising all the way up to first lieutenant even though his 1941 knee injury prevented him from being eligible to serve overseas. Upon being discharged in 1945, Miller bounced around the country, living in places like Florida, Texas, and, eventually, the West Coast. He finally settled in Northern California, where Miller managed a playground and swimming pool and also spent some time coaching an AAU team—strictly for fun, as Miller had no intentions of ever returning to the profession.

Only after a longtime friend from Kansas sent him a telegram offering a job at Wichita East High School in 1948 did Miller return to the profession— and that was only because, as Miller wrote in his autobiography, "I had a wife and two children and I was unemployed."

Ralph Miller's career took off from there, resulting in top-three finishes in the state tournament three years in a row before Wichita State University offered him a job coaching its basketball team. In forty years coaching at Wichita State, Iowa, and Oregon State, Miller ended up winning 657 games on the way to being inducted into the basketball Hall of Fame.

Just as Miller's coaching career was about to begin in the mid-1940s, his mentor was falling from grace. The war was over, and the Jayhawks seemed to be headed in the right direction. But Doc Allen, who turned sixty-one years old in November 1946, was about to find himself handing over the coaching duties at the University of Kansas.

14

The Fall of a Legend

The legend was down on the floor. The scrimmage stopped, and the gym fell silent. The players scurried over, standing above him, wondering whether he was dead. His eyes were closed. He wasn't moving. Was he even breathing?

Everything had happened so fast. One second, Phog Allen was standing there, and the next he was laid out on the wooden floor of the court.

These were the moments that would make time stop. The mind can gather so much information in a blip of a second that it becomes overbearing. The flood of stimulus comes so rapidly that nothing emanates from the brain; thought can be frozen by mental paralysis. The brain can be a funny thing that way—amazing thing, really, that it ever works at all. Three pounds of interacting cells, wrapped up into a spongelike organ not much bigger than a man's fist, responsible for learning and comprehending and sensing and creating, for analyzing information and coordinating movement, for communicating and loving and distinguishing the difference between right and wrong. All of this protected by just a single bone, seven millimeters deep, a thin layer of skin and cerebrospinal fluid, separating the most important part of the human body from the chaotic outside world.

No one was saying anything. Seconds passed like hours. There he was, the most visible figure on the University of Kansas campus, the most accomplished coach in the history of college basketball, lying before them—lifeless and limp.

Nobody knew what to do or say. None of them really knew the man, not to his soul. Even those who'd been with him for three or four years—his "boys," as he'd called them—even they didn't really know him. They knew of his insatiable desire to win, his infatuation with Helen Keller, his passion for writing letters. They knew that he was married, though very few of them had actually met his wife. Some of them even knew that he had a secret cigarette habit, though they'd never actually seen him inhaling smoke. What else was there to this man?

He lay on the wooden gym floor, his body motionless. Was it possible that this was the end?

By the time the practices began for the 1946–47 University of Kansas basketball season, Phog Allen and the Jayhawks were on a forward trajectory while the world around them was changing. A year had passed since the end of World War II, Allen family friend Harry Truman had taken over as president, and a professional league known as Basketball Association of America, which would be a precursor to the National Basketball Association, had made its debut back east.

Allen welcomed a new, eager group of players, who reported for practice that fall while several two-sport stars were still playing for the KU football team. On one afternoon in late October, the longtime basketball coach was holding a practice on the first floor court of Robinson Gymnasium, still wearing a shirt and tie, pleated pants, and dress shoes from a speaking engagement in Topeka earlier in the day. He arrived just before practice was to begin and hadn't had time to stop by his upstairs office to change into workout attire.

The session began like any other fall practice, with a large group of players trying to impress Phog enough to earn a spot on the 1946–47 squad. Alongside Allen was former KU player Howard Engleman, who had returned from the war to attend law school. Engleman, still sporting the burn marks from the 1945 destroyer attack that had killed thirty-five of his comrades, was making three hundred dollars per month to coach the freshman team while attending classes toward his law degree. Together, Allen and Engleman were putting the players through a series of scrimmages—more or less a weeding-out session to figure out who had the stuff to play basketball for KU that winter.

At one point, Allen had his head turned when a 6'1", 180-pound player named Ted Bean barreled up the floor, unaware that the legendary coach was in his path. The collision sent Allen, wearing slick-bottomed shoes and a month away from his sixty-first birthday, flying backward. His head slammed onto the hardwood floor.

A silence fell over the gym. The players stopped running and gathered around, using their practice jerseys to wipe the sweat from their faces. To many of them, especially the freshmen, Phog Allen was a legendary figure—more myth than man—and just being in the same room with him was a once-in-a-lifetime dream. And now there he was, lying motionless on the gym floor. The larger-than-life coach stayed like that for several seconds before he started moving his limbs slowly. His eyes opened, and soon enough they helped him into a seated position. His steely blue eyes were filled with confusion, his pupils large and dark. His thinning hair, which in those years he had started to slick back atop his aging scalp, was scattered across his forehead. He was disoriented but quickly shook out of it, ordering the players to get away. They helped him to his feet then stepped aside. Brushing himself off, slicking his hair back into place, Phog Allen looked more embarrassed than hurt.

He told them to get back on the court; practice wasn't over. Engleman knew not to make much of a fuss, and the session continued with Allen watching as if nothing had happened.

Not until Phog Allen got home that night did the headaches set in. He began having dizzy spells. Something was amiss. His wife, Bessie, grew concerned and called their son Bob, who was by then practicing medicine forty miles away in Kansas City. Bob paid a visit and continued to monitor the situation in the days that followed, and when the recurring dizziness and headaches didn't go away he set up an appointment for his father at the University of Kansas hospital in Kansas City.

On November 1, 1946, Phog Allen went in for X-rays and was diagnosed with a concussion. Doctors advised that the sixty-year-old Allen cut back his busy schedule, suggesting that he take a few days off before resuming a less strenuous daily routine.

Anyone who knew Phog Allen would have chuckled at the recommendation, and chances are that the veteran coach did just that. This was the same man who forged his way through a "World's Championship" series in the weeks following his mother's death four decades earlier, who had pressed on after losing his fourteen-year-old son in the 1920s, and who had defied the advice of Avery Brundage by pushing basketball into the Olympics in the '30s. He was the same man who resuscitated the NCAA tournament from certain death by bringing it to Kansas City at the dawn of the 1940s and who had carried the sport of basketball from dimly lit farmhouses to ten-thousand-seat arenas. The one thing Phog Allen had not done during his sixty-plus years on earth was to seek a less strenuous routine—not one day in his entire life.

With a rough schedule on the slate to open KU's 1946–47 season, Allen was taking no chances with the basketball program he had ruled over for most of the twentieth century. He viewed himself as indispensable and certainly wasn't going to let a few headaches get the better of him.

So Allen ignored his doctors and kept pressing on. He was back at practice the next day, all too eager to put the whole incident behind him and continue preparations for another season of KU basketball.

After two-sport stars and World War II veterans Otto Schnellbacher and Ray Evans reported for basketball practice at the end of the football season in early December, the *Lawrence Journal World* proclaimed, "Dr. F.C. 'Phog' Allen, the veteran cage wizard who is starting his twenty-seventh season down the championship trail, isn't ready to admit it but the 1946–47 quintet has all the earmarks of being one of his best."

Phog Allen's concussion seemed to have been forgotten by the time the real practices began. But behind the scenes, there were signals that Allen might be a bit out of sorts. He had such a keen memory that he could meet a man once and still remember his name five years later, and yet in the weeks that followed the head injury Phog began fumbling players' names and practice tactics. He just didn't seem like himself.

The season opened on December 7, and KU got off to its typical start by rattling off four consecutive wins on the way to posting a 5-1 record heading into a December 20 game against nemesis Oklahoma A&M in Kansas City. The Jayhawks dropped that game to fall to 5-2, and in the days that followed Allen began displaying flu-like symptoms. He battled the illness through the post-Christmas Big Seven Holiday Tournament and on into the New Year. The Jayhawks lost a January 2 overtime game against Colorado to fall to 8-4 heading into a pivotal game against the hated Missouri Tigers.

Up to that point, Phog Allen had locked horns with the University of Missouri sixty-seven times, with a 42-25 record to show for it. He had already seen four Tigers coaches come and go during his KU tenure, and he didn't know what to think of Missouri's newest head man, thirty-six-year-old Wilbur "Sparky" Stalcup. The two coaches had no history with one another, Phog Allen still wasn't totally feeling back up to speed from his illness, and the 109th installment of the Border War of college basketball wasn't supposed to have the intensity of some past meetings between KU and Missouri.

And yet in many ways, it turned out to be the fiercest of them all.

To truly understand the Kansas-Missouri rivalry, one needs go all the way back to the nineteenth century, to the time when William Quantrill and a band of Missouri guerillas raided the town of Lawrence, Kansas. The 1861 attack came as a response to the anti-slave Jayhawkers of "Bleeding Kansas" kidnapping the female family members of cross-state rivals known as the Border Ruffians and jailing them in a house that later collapsed from unknown causes. Vowing revenge, Quantrill and his men stormed into Lawrence and went on a rampage in the early morning hours of August 21, 1863. At least 150 people were killed, with 85 widows and 250 fatherless children among the 1,850 people left behind. Several buildings, including the beautiful Eldridge Hotel in the heart of town, burned down in the attack. In addition to giving the University of Kansas a nickname for its athletic teams—KU's first football team in 1890 was known as the Jayhawkers and later shortened to the Jayhawks—the massacre transcended generations and left the border states still worlds apart more than a half century later.

From the time Phog Allen rejoined the KU athletic department in 1919, he had jumped into the KU-Missouri rivalry with both feet. He continually antagonized the rival Tigers with well-chosen words to the press and was unabashed in his dislike of all things Mizzou over the years.

The hatred between Kansas and Missouri was real and deep-rooted, and often the passion could be felt even on the basketball court. KU-Missouri games were rough affairs from the very beginning. During one of the early installments in between Phog Allen's two stints as KU basketball coach, James Naismith was said to have watched the physical play of a Jayhawks-Tigers game and uttered, "Oh, my gracious. They are murdering my game!" A young Allen added fuel to the fire in 1922 when he brashly promised victory over the Tigers and belittled Missouri to the press; after the two teams split their two-game series and tied for the conference crown that season, Allen refused an invitation to settle the score with a winner-take-all game.

By the time the Jayhawks and Tigers took the floor for the January 9, 1947, game at Lawrence, the two schools had already squared off 108 times on the basketball floor—and Allen had been around for most of the meetings. Missouri's coach, Sparky Stalcup, was about to participate in his first. Thirty-six years old and having spent ten years coaching at Maryville Teachers College, Stalcup had led Missouri to a 9-4 record heading into the Tigers' road game at Kansas that January evening.

Allen, still dealing with the headaches and dizziness from the collision about five weeks earlier, was as motivated as anyone. His Jayhawks had a sixteen-year home winning streak against Mizzou, and the thought of losing to the Tigers repulsed him.

His emotions were running high at tip-off, and things really began to unravel as Allen watched a 6-point halftime lead wither away. After a Missouri player was whistled for his fifth foul late in the game, Stalcup began arguing the call with a game official near the Missouri bench. Allen wandered from his spot at the end of the scorer's table to join the conversation, at one time telling Stalcup to "get off the court and stay on the bench." One account of the incident, as written in the *University Missourian*, claimed that Allen bumped Stalcup. The Missouri coach made a fist, raised it in the air, and shouted, "Get the hell back on your side of the court!" Then Stalcup did something even more infuriating when he ended KU's sixteen-game winning streak in the Missouri series by beating Allen and the Jayhawks 39–34.

The coaches would eventually mend their fences, and after an act of sportsmanship by Stalcup during a 1951 rivalry game in which the Missouri coach asked the Tigers' fans to restrain themselves, Phog Allen befriended the Mizzou coach; Allen even had Stalcup speak at a KU sports banquet and later attended his daughter's wedding. But the January 1947 incident served as another black eye in the long-standing rivalry, and it may well have played a factor in Allen's escalating health concerns.

One day after Stalcup and the Tigers beat the Jayhawks in Lawrence, Allen was rushed to Watkins Memorial Hospital at the University of Kansas. Dr. Ralph Canuteson sent him to a Kansas City clinic for further tests and he remained in hospital care while being treated for influenza. Howard Engleman, the freshman coach, took the reins for a varsity game against Oklahoma three days later, on January 13, only to watch KU lose a 9-point halftime lead and fall—the Jayhawks' third defeat in a row. Allen was released from the hospital four days after that, having spent a week under medical care, and upon his release Dr. Edward H. Hashinger strongly recommended a vacation in a warm climate. This time, Allen took the advice to heart. He left his Jayhawks behind and headed west to California.

On January 17, 1947, Engleman officially took over as the Jayhawks' interim coach. Kansas would go 8-5 under Engleman over the final thirteen games of the season, including one memorable victory at Missouri that was played in an empty arena—thanks to a flu epidemic that had hit the Mizzou campus and forced students to stay in their dorm rooms. The 1946–47 Jayhawks finished with a 16-11 record while landing in third place in the Big Six standings.

Allen spent the time away recuperating at his daughter Mary's house in La Jolla, California. The distance gave Allen perspective, and stepping away from a basketball season for the first time in thirty-five years brought him a fresh outlook. He saw himself in a different light and concluded that his coaching tactics weren't as effective as they'd once been. The game had changed over the years, and Allen was realizing that his strategic philosophies were feeling outdated. What he needed was a full-time assistant, a true X's and O's man who could break down opponents and find unique ways to approach the changing game.

It was a rare display of humility from the wildly successful coach with the massive ego, but the time away from KU basketball was just what Allen needed to get refocused. Allen knew exactly the man he should bring aboard.

Dick Harp had been a key member of Allen's 1939-40 KU squad that made a run all the way to the NCAA championship game, and Allen always appreciated his keen basketball mind. Harp had refreshing ideas on how to play defense and was more keyed in to the changing face of basketball. Not nearly as charismatic or experienced as Allen, Harp had youth (he turned twenty-nine in March of 1947) and a fresh perspective going for him.

Allen contacted Harp, who was wrapping up his first season as head basketball coach at William Jewell College in Kansas City, and offered him a job as full-time assistant coach of the KU varsity basketball team—a position that had never previously existed. Harp was flattered by the offer but couldn't see leaving the William Jewell job so soon into his tenure. Allen said he appreciated Harp's loyalty but added that he wasn't giving up. Once recovered from the concussion, he would return for the 1947-48 season without a full-time assistant, but Allen promised that he would be contacting Harp again the following spring.

Allen was good to his word. The 1947-48 Jayhawks, who were by then playing in the expanded Big Seven Conference with new addition Colorado, got hammered in their opener by Emporia State and stumbled to a 9-15 record. He coached without an assistant that year—Engleman had finished law school and moved on to a career as an attorney—and afterward Allen contacted Harp again. The former Jayhawk decided to return to KU as Phog Allen's assistant coach, and Harp soon began handling a lot of the recruiting while playing a key role in game strategy.

Allen's own philosophy after the time away from basketball evolved in the late 1940s, particularly on offense. After spending most of his career preaching about the importance of ball-handling, Allen began shouting to his players, "Damn the dribble. *Pass* the ball!" He continued to beat the drum for twelve-foot baskets but was beginning to lose hope of that change ever being made. The only way to combat the ever-growing basketball player was to find a big man of his own—a prospect that was easier said than done.

Through it all, Allen found time to continue treating athletes, both inside and outside of the KU circle, with his osteopathic techniques. His reputation in the field had expanded over the years, so much so that he'd added a class in athletic training to a teaching schedule that had already included classes called "Coaching Basketball" and "Advanced Coaching Basketball." But he was also adding to his ever-growing list of enemies because of his outspokenness.

When Allen wasn't preaching about the need to raise the baskets and the importance of eliminating gambling from the sport, he was challenging the way the NCAA was governing college basketball. On one occasion, Allen told a group of Notre Dame alumni attending a luncheon in Kansas City that college presidents were "making a sham and a chicanery of college athletics." He also stoked the embers of a simmering rivalry with intrastate adversary Kansas State by accusing the Wildcats of using an ineligible player in the winter of 1947–48. Allen maintained that he had it on good authority that Kansas State's star center, Clarence Brannum, had participated in an AAU tournament in Denver when he should have been attending classes five hundred miles away, in Manhattan, Kansas.

The Kansas State rivalry had become especially fierce in those years, mainly because Wildcats coach Jack Gardner was hell-bent on getting under Allen's skin. Gardner constantly gave reporters fodder by poking fun at Allen, whose standard retort was to condescendingly brush aside the comments by saying, "If the mailman stopped for every dog which barked at him, he would never get the mail delivered." But in these years, Gardner was getting the last laugh—first by ending K-State's ten-year losing streak against the Jayhawks and then by putting together three consecutive wins over Allen's program. Gardner had begun to even the playing field in the state of Kansas, and Phog Allen knew he would have to change his recruiting strategy to keep up. He could no longer rely on KU basketball's history to get the state's top recruits to line up outside his door, begging to play basketball for the Jayhawks. Phog Allen started making more house calls to persuade high school stars to not only stay in the state of Kansas but also to choose Lawrence over Manhattan. He also had new assistant

Dick Harp out on the recruiting trail, meeting face-to-face with top players from all over the state. This had become especially vital in the spring of 1948, when the state's most talented group of recruits in recent memory was about to graduate from high school.

Bill Lienhard was a 6'5" all-state player from Newton, Kansas, a basketball factory where Coach John Ravenscroft taught the one-handed shot in an era when two-handed set shots were the norm. With his one-handed shot, complete with leg kick, Lienhard had become such a deadly marksman that he could score consistently from the top of the key; he was one of the state's best high school shooters in years. Bill Hougland, a smiley 6'4" kid from the farm town of Beloit, Kansas, was a tenacious rebounder and defender. And Bob "Trigger" Kenney was an aggressive guard and the latest in a long line of star basketball players to come from tiny Winfield, Kansas. They were widely considered the top three recruits in the state of Kansas, and Phog Allen wanted each and every one of them in his 1948 recruiting class. Five or ten years earlier, Allen could have sat back and let all three recruits fall into his lap, each one of them begging to play basketball at the University of Kansas. But times had changed; KU basketball wasn't what it used to be. He needed a different recruiting strategy.

On the court, Allen's program continued to struggle. With super-senior Otto Schnellbacher, the twenty-five-year-old World War II veteran, out of eligibility, KU didn't have very high hopes heading into the 1948–49 season. That team, with Dick Harp sitting alongside Phog Allen on game days, ended up going 12-12 overall and again tied for last place in the Big Seven, winning just three conference games. The Jayhawks' two-year conference record of 7-17 marked the worst two-year mark in Phog Allen's thirty-one seasons at the school. KU alumni were growing frustrated, especially when looking at his 10-12 record against rivals Kansas State, Missouri, and Oklahoma over the final three seasons of the decade.

Allen was still considered a legend in the basketball coaching world, but legends seldom last forever. He had set an unsustainable level of excellence during his three-plus decades coaching KU basketball, and his teams were no longer living up to the Phog tradition. He was in his sixties, was relying on his assistant coach more than ever, and was no longer seen as a basketball genius; younger men with fresher ideas were beginning to rise above the aging legend.

As KU player Charlie Hoag later explained to the *Crimson & Blue Handbook*, "while [Allen] was still a great organizer and a great motivator, to me the game was passing him by. He was always trying to do the things [in the late 1940s] that he was doing back in 1930 or 1935."

The headaches and dizziness of his October 1947 concussion had dissipated over the months and years that followed, but there were still signs that he wasn't fully himself. The razor-sharp memory had been replaced by bouts of forgetfulness that Allen mostly cast aside with a quick joke, and he became prone to rambling in and out of stories, often losing his train of thought.

His classroom behavior became questionable on occasion as well. In a memoir written by longtime KU broadcaster Max Falkenstien, Allen was remembered as a bit of an eccentric during that era. Allen had begun using the foot-arch roller that he'd designed to stretch out the bottom of a player's foot in his classes. "It was common for students to be strolling down a hall in Old Robinson Gymnasium during the summer," Falkenstien wrote, "and pass a classroom in which Doc would be standing on a table in front of his class wearing nothing but skivvies."

Demonstrating how to use the roller while not wearing pants seemed to be a somewhat common occurrence for the aging coach. The Falkenstien memoir included a quote from former KU student Bob Timmons: "Demonstrating the use of this device was very important to Doc. As the class went on, more and more clothes came off. I have a good theory why the clothes came off during the lecture. First of all, Doc had a great tan. He used to play golf with his shirt off. Also, Doc was getting along in years, and I think he wanted to show off the fact he was in pretty good shape."

Former KU player Jerry Waugh tells a similar story of an incident a few years later, when Allen was running a coaching clinic at Wichita State University. Allen showed up wearing black socks and boxer shorts, sans his trousers, and explained himself by saying that he'd come straight from a speaking engagement at the Topeka Rotary and had forgotten his change of clothes. "I don't even have a jockstrap on," Allen continued. "But no need to worry, because a dead bird won't fly out of its nest." That got a raucous laugh from the coaches in attendance, but Allen's antics had become a bit unsettling to some.

By most accounts, Allen appeared to be making a slow fall from grace as the 1940s came to an end. His record of 21-27 in the final two seasons of the 1940s was tough for fans to swallow, and his public antics were harder for the school and alumni to take as Allen's Jayhawks slipped toward mediocrity.

"These were tough times for Doc," Falkenstien would write in his autobiography years later. "He focused his attention on the rivalries with Kansas State and Missouri—two teams that were getting the better of the Jayhawks in those years. The KU alumni were not pleased to relinquish bragging rights."

But Allen, who was making six thousand dollars a year to coach the Jayhawks by decade's end, continued to look down from the mountaintop, as if he were still at the peak and unable to accept the possibility that his success might be waning. When he had sent Harp out on the recruiting trail in 1948, Allen told his assistant coach to bring in the state's three top recruits: Lienhard, Hougland and Kenney. When Harp asked how the Jayhawks planned to do that, Allen replied, "Tell them we're about to win a national championship. And that they'll play in the next Olympics." It seemed preposterous at the time, with KU struggling through one of its worst stretches of the Phog Allen era. Harp admitted as much, saying, "You really don't want me to tell them that."

To that, Allen responded, "You're damned right I do."

When he said he was taking Kansas to the 1952 NCAA championship game and the Helsinki Olympics, he meant it; Phog Allen was dead set on getting there, if he could get the right players in place. But it was up to Allen himself to bring in the biggest catch of them all.

For the second time in his career, Phog Allen found himself in desperate need of a big man. His speedy, scrappy, team-first squads of yesteryear simply weren't talented enough to survive in the new age of basketball. If no one was going to buy in to his crusade to move the baskets up from ten to twelve feet, then Allen was just going to have to beat them at their own game. To get back to the top, Allen would need to find a superstar with both size and the talent to match.

Allen's needle-in-a-haystack search sent him to Terre Haute, Indiana, where a Bunyanesque high school star had caught the attention of college basketball coaches from one end of the country to the other. Six-foot-nine Clyde Lovellette was widely considered the best high school center among players in the class of 1948, and Allen spent a considerable amount of time and money trying to lure the Indiana native to Lawrence, even though he'd never seen the big redhead play. Allen's national reputation and gift for gab were keys to his recruiting, but his main tactic involved winning over a player's mother. The pathway to a recruit's signature, Allen believed, was through his mother's heart. A well-timed handwritten letter to Mom could often seal the deal. Such was Phog Allen's angle when he targeted Clyde Lovellette. His pitch to Lovellette's mother involved selling her on "breathing the rarified air" of Mount Oread—a key, Allen claimed, to helping young Clyde deal with his asthma. (He didn't mention that Oread's elevation was only about one thousand feet above sea level—not even three hundred feet higher than Bloomington, Indiana's highest point.) Allen ended up spending more time recruiting Clyde Lovellette than he did on any other high school player he'd seen; he simply had to have him, if the Jayhawks were going to rise back to the top of the basketball perch.

Even after Lovellette spurned offers from dozens and dozens of other schools by deciding he was going to the University of Indiana in nearby Bloomington, Phog Allen kept trying to charm him. He just wouldn't take no for an answer. At one point, Lovellette sent his brother-in-law, Charlie, to St. Louis, where Allen was scheduled to make a speaking engagement, to tell the sixty-three-year-old KU coach face-to-face that Clyde was going to Indiana. Allen wasn't having any of it. He drove his Chrysler New Yorker 170 miles from St. Louis to Terre Haute, and when he pulled onto Lovellette's street the 6'9" high school star ducked into his house to avoid a confrontation with the legendary coach. Phog Allen talked his way into the house and used his well-known persuasive skills to convince the Indiana native to get in his car and join him on a trip to Lawrence, just to see the campus. Lovellette's mother, naturally, gave her blessing.

During the drive, Allen told Lovellette that he was the missing piece to a recruiting class that would win a national championship. He basically guaranteed that if Lovellette went to KU, they would both be on the 1952

U.S. Olympic team—Allen as a coach, and Lovellette as the star player. "We talked and we talked and we talked," Lovellette would later recall. "Phog was a marvelous talker." The sales pitch had Lovellette's attention, and once they arrived in Kansas, the big kid from Indiana fell in love. As he would recall years later of the KU campus in Lawrence, "the tradition, it rains on you out there." He decided to take his size and skill to Lawrence, where Lovellette was about to give Phog Allen his greatest weapon to date.

The man who had convinced the Buffalo Germans to travel halfway across the country for a "World's Champions" game more than four decades earlier, and who had raised enough money—penny by penny—to send James Naismith to Berlin, and who had promised NCAA officials that a national tournament could actually make money, had made another wildly successful sales pitch.

Lovellette joined a freshman class that included fifteen incoming recruits, many of whom were weeded out during their first year at KU. Lienhard, Hougland, and Kenney were among those who survived the cut, having eaten up Harp's national-title promises. They joined Lovellette on a freshman team that gave the KU varsity quite a run in the annual scrimmage. The 6'9" star had been able to dominate high school games without needing to develop much of an offensive game, but Allen knew he would need a George Mikan–like weapon to be just as effective against college competition. So he spent a good part of that 1948–49 season teaching Lovellette the hook shot while the KU varsity team played on without him.

One of the games the varsity team played during that season was in West Lafayette, Indiana, to face Purdue in a game that was held about one hundred miles from the Lovellettes' Terre Haute home. While Big Clyde and the other KU freshmen remained back in Lawrence, Lovellette's mother showed up in West Lafayette to watch the Jayhawks play. Afterward, Phog Allen had the KU varsity players line up to greet her; he instructed each of them to say something kind about her son so that she would know Clyde was in good hands.

In his first year of eligibility, in 1949–50, Lovellette almost single-handedly put the Jayhawks back on the national map. The sophomore big man, using a hook shot that had become unstoppable, led the Big Seven in scoring, at 21.8 points per game, while helping the Jayhawks rally from a 3-5 start to go 14-10 and get back to the top of the Big Seven. KU returned to the NCAA tournament and suffered a 2-point loss to Bradley in the first round, but the unexpected turnaround was enough to earn Phog Allen one of his most prestigious awards.

After the 1949–50 season, Allen was named the NABC coach of the year. Any questions about the decline of The Phog were answered with an emphatic "not finished yet."

While a far cry from Phog Allen's most successful teams, the 1949–50 Jayhawks were an inimitable cast of characters who proved hard to forget. From the wisecracking, flattopped redhead from Terre Haute to point guard Jerry "The Sherriff" Waugh, KU provided plenty of color during an otherwise forgettable season. Waugh's favorite story of that era involved a big man named Gene Peterson with Phi Beta Kappa brains but the kind of speak-before-you-think mouth that kept Phog Allen pulling his hair out. Peterson was among the starters Phog called out before one game, asking his traditional, "Are you ready?" Each of the players that preceded Peterson had looked their coach in the eye and nodded, while Peterson gave the unprecedented response "Well . . . I've kind of got a headache." Before Peterson could finish the sentence, Phog pointed at backup Maurice Martin and shouted, "Maurice, take off your warm-up!"

Waugh also recounted a time following a road defeat when Phog Allen walked onto the team bus, demanded silence, and pulled a sheet of paper from his pocket. He then proceeded to announce, "I'd like to read you my chickenshit list" and promptly rattled off three players' names. Without further explanation, Allen folded up the paper, put it back in his pocket, exited the bus, and took a train back to Lawrence. Only later would the KU players come to discover that the trio to which Allen referred had broken curfew the night before the game.

The 1949–50 Jayhawks also had a pioneer of sorts in Wichita native LaVannes Squires. Three years earlier, in 1947, the University of Indiana had broken an unofficial, quarter-century-old rule that had discouraged major college basketball programs from recruiting black players when the Hoosiers signed a high schooler named Bill Garrett. The Indiana state player of the year, Garrett went on to become a star for the Hoosiers while breaking the color barrier as the Big Ten's first black player.

Allen decided to follow suit in the Big Seven Conference after setting his sights on Squires—a slight, physically unimposing, 6'1" guard/forward at Wichita's East High School. He came from a single-parent family, much like Allen's household had become during his teenage years, and Squires had played for former KU star Ralph Miller at East High—an integrated school that presented an easier transition to a predominantly white university for a 1949 high school graduate from a segregated background than he might otherwise have had. Squires was the first African American to play at KU and the first in the history of the conference that became known in later years as the Big 12.

He became eligible in 1950–51, joining a team that was returning four of its top five scorers—led by the outstanding junior class of Lovellette, Lienhard, Hougland, and Kenney. Phog Allen welcomed his 1950–51 team through typical channels, with a fourteen-page, typed letter that was mailed to each of his players. Allen urged the athletes to show up in peak physical shape and be ready for demanding practices, and he joked that he'd caught sight of Clyde Lovellette over the summer looking "as if he had a watermelon stuffed in his abdomen." The letter also recounted a story of a former University of Missouri player named Ted O'Sullivan, who had once vowed revenge on Allen for ejecting him in a high school game Phog Allen was refereeing in the early 1920s. O'Sullivan enrolled at Missouri with the objective of inflicting revenge on Allen's Jayhawks, but he was never successful as the Tigers lost every meeting with KU in those years. Phog admired the young man's spirit and later hired him to referee games; by the 1940s, they'd become friends, and when O'Sullivan was serving as a military personnel clerk in Fort Leavenworth, he did Allen a favor by adjusting KU player Charlie Black's draft number during World War II. The point of the story, Allen concluded, was that nemeses can often become confidants—Tigers and Sooners and Wildcats may one day be friends. "Remember, 'Upon the fields of friendly strife' are sown the seeds that upon other fields in other years are born the fruits of victory," Allen wrote.

When the players arrived on campus, Allen sat them down for the annual first meeting, which often followed a typical script. He would outline the basics of basketball and remind his players about the expectations of a KU basketball team. At some point, Allen would turn on a reel-to-reel film of a mongoose attacking a cobra from behind. The graphic scene was meant to illustrate the importance of surprise. "Boys, you need to be furtive," he liked to say. "Furtive, like a squirrel."

The 1950–51 Jayhawks opened the season with three convincing wins before heading east to face St. John's at Madison Square Garden in New York City. The Big Apple was already becoming a basketball mecca, with City College of New York coming off of NIT and NCAA titles in back-to-back years and the New York Knickerbockers of the relatively new National Basketball Association rising to prominence. But the truth was that Phog Allen couldn't stand New York. He'd privately referred to New York City basketball as being a bunch of "alley ball players" and ticked off New Yorkers by anointing the city as the epicenter of college basketball's growing gambling problem. A few years earlier, Allen had predicted a "scandal that would stink to high heaven" emanating from the New York City area, and he had never backed down from the comment in the years that followed. Phog was so concerned about his KU players getting contacted by mobsters looking for point-shaving participants that he forbade his "boys" from taking direct calls during their stay in New York City, and he required at least one member of the school's athletic staff to be beside his players at all times.

The Jayhawks were welcomed to the crowded streets of New York by bitter cold weather and were all too relieved to get inside Madison Square Garden, despite its thick air of cigar smoke, for the December 12 game against St. John's. In the first-ever meeting between the two programs, KU took the floor in front of 9,815 fans and engaged in one of the most strange games an Allen team had ever played. There were 65 fouls called in all, but the most incredible statistic came from the number of KU free-throw attempts Phog Allen waved off. Basketball rules in those days allowed for only one free throw on a non-shooting foul, and Allen saw this as a disadvantage to the fouled team. His theory was that a non-shooting foul eliminated the chance for a two-point field goal; it could only result in one possible point on that offensive possession. By waiving the free throw, Allen was presenting his team with an opportunity for two points on a possession rather than being limited to a maximum of one point. He sensed that St. John's was intentionally fouling as a two-for-one strategy from the outset, and so the first ten times a St. John's player was whistled for a foul, Allen waved off the free throw. By the end of the game, he had declined twenty-six free-throw attempts.

Allen was so steadfast in his strategy that he even elected to wave off a free throw with thirty-nine seconds left and the Jayhawks trailing *by one point*. Instead of shooting the free throw for the tie, Allen opted for KU to take the ball out of bounds. The strategy almost backfired when Bill Hougland missed a long shot, but Lovellette tipped it in for the game-winner with twenty seconds left in a contest that the Jayhawks won 52–51.

The win improved KU's season record to 4-0 while the Jayhawks rose to number four in the national rankings. KU then travelled to Lexington, Kentucky, to face a Kentucky team that had won back-to-back NCAA titles in 1947–48 and 1948–49. And the Wildcats were coached by a man whom Phog Allen knew very well.

Adolph Rupp, a forty-nine-year-old KU grad, was a reserve on Allen's first great teams in the early 1920s, and he had since risen up to the top of the coaching profession. With more than four hundred wins and two national titles in his first twenty years as a head coach—all of them at Kentucky—Rupp was considered by many to be the premier coach in college basketball, surpassing his sixty-five-year-old mentor. Rupp had come to calling Allen "the old man" in interviews—an intended joke that Phog didn't necessarily appreciate. That Allen had been involved in getting the FBI to expose a gambling ring five blocks from the University of Kentucky campus a few years earlier only added to the intrigue in a game pitting two basketball powerhouses that had never previously played each other.

A Kentucky record crowd of thirteen thousand fans showed up to see the coaching matchup, as well as a battle between two of the nation's best big men in 6'9" Lovellette and Kentucky 7'0" Bill Spivey. But the game didn't live up to the hype, as Rupp and Spivey turned it into a laugher by halftime. Kentucky's Spivey outscored the Jayhawks by himself in the first half, accounting for 14 points while giving the Wildcats a convincing 28–12 lead. Lovellette had no answer for Spivey on either end of the floor, and in the end Kentucky sent the humbled Jayhawks back to Lawrence by way of a 68–39 dismantling.

Rupp, the student, had gotten the best of Allen, the teacher, in their first head-to-head matchup. The Kentucky coach would go on to win his third national title by the end of the season, surpassing Allen in that category as well, while the 1950–51 Jayhawks would stumble to a 16-8 record and a second-place finish in the Big Seven Conference.

But Allen did earn a victory of sorts in February 1951, when the New York basketball scandal he had seen coming months earlier came to light. Manhattan College, Central College of New York, and Long Island University, three schools in the heart of New York City, were exposed for point-shaving in a three-month stretch that unearthed the seedy side of college basketball. By the following summer of 1952, even Rupp's Kentucky program would be included in the gambling scandal, forcing the Wildcats to cancel their 1952–53 season. (During that investigation, a former Kentucky player named Walt Hirsh testified that Rupp had paid each of his five starters fifty dollars for beating the Jayhawks in 1950–51.)

None of that did much to help the 1950–51 Jayhawks on the court. The 16-8 record was another sign that Phog Allen's legendary rise to the top of college basketball had given way to a steady tumble over the other side of the hill. Younger men like Rupp and Henry Iba were now standing at the top of the mountain, and John Wooden, once the Indiana kid who had helped sling bricks for Phog at KU's Memorial Stadium in the late 1920s, was beginning to make some noise out west at UCLA. The 1952 Olympics were right around the corner, and Allen had four seniors-to-be wondering whether his recruiting promise was just a boisterous cloud of "rarified" hot air.

KU had reason for optimism heading into the 1951–52 season. But nobody could have imagined what was about to happen to Phog Allen and his Jayhawks next.

15

Rising from the Ashes

The old man was out of ideas. His 1951–52 Kansas team had as much potential as any squad in KU history, with a likely All-American in the middle and an experienced supporting cast of players who knew their roles, and yet deficiencies on the defensive end of the floor had Phog "Doc" Allen scratching his head.

These Jayhawks were going to be good, as good as any team Allen had ever coached . . . but were they good enough?

There were certainly people out there who believed that Old Doc had lost his touch, and the emergence of some younger coaches on the national scene had only amplified the noise. On the basketball court, Phog Allen's ego was as big as a sold-out arena crowd, and he wasn't going to let himself get outcoached again.

He'd tapped all his motivational ploys in an effort to get the most out of his team. He'd painstakingly pounded the fundamentals, over and over and over again. None of it was bringing out the best in these Jayhawks. He knew they had more. Doc Allen had made a promise to these seniors that they'd be celebrating a national championship and representing their country at the upcoming Olympics, but without a defensive plan, those goals would surely begin slipping through their fingers.

And so Phog Allen, the winningest coach in college basketball history, did what few legends could bring themselves to do. He asked for help.

Dick Harp, Phog's thirty-three-year-old assistant coach, didn't have anywhere near the wealth of basketball experience. Phog had forgotten more basketball than Dick Harp would ever know. But Harp was younger and more in touch with the new way basketball was being played. Allen called Harp into his office. He led him to the blackboard. He handed Dick Harp the chalk.

The 1951–52 Kansas Jayhawks generated a little buzz heading into the season but were generally regarded as one of several teams who just didn't have enough firepower to unseat the mighty Kentucky Wildcats, winners of three NCAA titles in a span of four years. Losing 68–39 in Lexington the previous winter didn't help KU's cause, especially when considering that up-and-coming UK coach Adolph Rupp had outwitted the Jayhawks' Phog Allen, once his mentor, and was now considered the best basketball coach in the country.

And yet Phog wasn't willingly passing the torch—not without a fight. A rematch between the Jayhawks and top-ranked Kentucky Wildcats was originally on the schedule, offering a chance for redemption, but the game was abruptly canceled amid the ongoing NCAA investigation involving Rupp's program. If Phog Allen and Adolph Rupp were going to square off again, it would have to be in the NCAA tournament at season's end. But first, Allen had to get his Jayhawks there.

One of Allen's best recruiting classes was entering its senior year, with 6'9" All-American Clyde Lovellette leading a team that also included Bill Hougland, "Trigger" Kenney, Bill Lienhard, a heady guard named Dean Kelley, and a bench featuring 6'9" sophomore B. H. Born, Dean Kelley's brother Allen, and LaVannes Squires, the program's first African American player. Oh, and there was also a junior guard named Dean Smith, who served as a role player and would later become a legendary basketball coach in his own right. Smith, who grew up listening to Curt Gowdy call KU games on the radio, had gone to school on academic scholarship and was not considered much of a scoring threat, even by his junior season.

As assistant Dick Harp would later explain in a book about the history of KU basketball, "Dean could play the game and never hurt you. He was an average player. An intensely average player." Dean Smith had spent most of his career at the end of the bench but had gradually ingratiated himself with the coaching staff because of his keen eye for the game. He helped coach both the freshman and junior varsity teams at KU and slowly moved up the varsity bench over the years until Phog Allen had him sitting close enough to add input on game days.

The KU bench also included trainer Dean Nesmith, who had been with the program for fifteen years, as well as team manager Wayne Louderback.

The 1951–52 Jayhawks were unlike any team Allen had coached. They were a business-first group led by a mature senior class and four players—Lovellette, Hougland, Lienhard, and Dean Kelley—who had gotten married during the previous summer. While some of Allen's recent teams had kept him up at night wondering who might step out of line, the 1951–52 squad allowed him to sleep easy. Off the court, they'd gained so much trust that Allen no longer felt the need to conduct bed checks on road trips; on the court, they all knew their roles and bonded well; each player wore red Chuck Taylor shoes. The team had experience, size, and depth, the latter of which would provide to be vital as Lienhard couldn't shake an illness early on and key reserve Charlie Hoag was hobbled by a groin injury that lingered from the football season.

There was plenty of buzz about the team—in Lawrence and beyond—when practices began, and somehow Doc Allen found time to take in one of his most notable patients between workouts in November 1951. A few months after reviving the career of New York Yankees star Johnny Mize by using his osteopathic methods on an ailing shoulder, Allen welcomed Mize's young teammate for a check-up in Lawrence. Mickey Mantle had suffered a knee injury in the World Series, and the New York Yankees' twenty-year-old slugger turned to Allen for help. The session was enough to allow Mantle, who was later diagnosed with a torn anterior cruciate ligament through which he played the rest of his career, to get back on the field. In 1952, he went on to hit .311, finished third in the voting for American League Most Valuable Player, and led the Yankees to another World Series.

When Allen's focus returned to the KU basketball team in the winter of 1951, he was met with remarkable expectations. The preseason national poll had Kansas ranked eighth in the country, but there was plenty of competition from Big Seven Conference rival Kansas State and from Henry Iba's Oklahoma A&M squad, both of which were also included in the preseason top ten. Allen knew his team might be special, provided the Jayhawks improved on a defense that had struggled down the stretch the previous year. He initially tried to hide his confidence from the press, telling reporters that he would pick Kansas State to win the conference. But a couple of weeks later, when the Jayhawks were officially picked to win the Big Seven, Allen admitted, "When you look at it on paper, [the media's] choice isn't hard to explain. We've lost less lettermen than any other team."

The excitement only grew when the Jayhawks blew out their first four opponents of the 1951–52 season and were off to one of the best starts in the Allen era. Even playing without Lienhard and Hoag for a few games couldn't slow down Allen's team. Without much noticeable speed as they plodded around in their red Chuck Taylors, the Jayhawks were a well-oiled machine that ran a motion offense to near perfection, doing their best to get the ball to Lovellette as often as possible.

The only thing that gave Phog Allen much reason for concern was a defense that still wasn't nearly good enough to give the Jayhawks a realistic shot at competing for any type of championship. The "Stratified Transitional Man-for-Man Defense with Zone Principle" wasn't getting it done, and Allen didn't think his players were good enough defenders to thrive in straight-up man-to-man. Allen turned to his right-hand man, Assistant Coach Dick Harp, and challenged him to come up with a defense that could bring out the best in the 1951–52 Jayhawks.

"I don't know what you're going to do, Dick," Allen said, "but do something. You've got to do something."

Harp devised a pressuring, man-to-man defense that featured a unique method of pushing the pace while relying more on team defense than individual athleticism. Harp began by teaching Allen's "boys" to guard the passing lane, an unprecedented strategy in an era when teams were either guarding opposing players man-to-man or dropping into a zone defense. The system emphasized the quickness of KU's top three guards: Trigger Kenney, Dean Kelley, and sixth man Charlie Hoag. The strategy was for one guard to make the ball-handler pick up his dribble as soon as he crossed midcourt and for the other players to cut off the passing lanes. Lovellette's massive frame allowed him to patrol the lane and clean up any open players who were able to slip past the overcommitted defense; this played to Lovellette's strength, as the big man wasn't regarded very highly as a straight-up, man-to-man defender. The system was designed to throw offenses off their rhythm while speeding up the pace of the game and creating turnovers that led to fast-break layups at the other end of the floor. It was an innovative strategy in an era when zone defenses and play-the-man-not-the-ball tactics prevailed.

The defensive shift was a huge success. KU continued piling up the victories, knocking off seventh-ranked Kansas State and Allen nemesis Jack Gardner in overtime before beating Missouri in the championship game of the Big Seven Conference Holiday Tournament in December. A buzzer-beater by Dean Kelley beat Missouri again two weeks later as Allen's Jayhawks ran their winning streak to thirteen games and rose all the way up to number one in the country, ahead of mighty Kentucky after Rupp's Wildcats had suffered an upset loss to St. Louis University.

Phog Allen had finally gotten back on top, although the ascent came with a bit of an asterisk. In some ways, Harp had taken over the reins of the team and was thereby at least equally responsible for the team's unexpected rise to the top of the national polls. Phog's assistant had done most of the coaching at practices that year and was behind most of the gameday adjustments. Allen stepped in when necessary to deliver impassioned speeches, but mostly it had become Harp's show.

However the coaching dynamics shook out, the results were inarguable. The 13-0 start had KU atop the national rankings for the first time since polling began in 1948. But Phog's ego got the better of him. Not long after the Jayhawks rose to number one, Allen stepped back into the forefront and resumed full control of the team. He coached the team leading into a big game at Kansas State, then again against Oklahoma A&M four days later.

KU lost both games. A promising season was suddenly on rocky ground, as a tie atop the Big Seven Conference left the Jayhawks in jeopardy of missing out on the NCAA tournament for the second year in a row and the fourth time in five seasons. Only one team from the conference would get invited to the NCAAs at season's end, so the Jayhawks had just eight games to get straightened out or Allen's team would be left out of the postseason.

One day after the January 30 loss to Oklahoma A&M, Allen called his players into a meeting room at Robinson Gym. He stood in front of the despondent players, most of them probably expecting a tongue-lashing on the heels of a two-game losing streak. Wearing eyeglasses and a solemn look, Phog Allen opened up a book. He began reading poetry, quoting from one of his longtime favorites, "Casey at the Bat," by Ernest Thayer. Soon enough, tears began to well up in his blue eyes as the words poured out of his mouth. He became more and more passionate as he read the verse

Oh, somewhere in this favored land the sun is shining bright;
The band is playing somewhere, and somewhere hearts are light,
And somewhere men are laughing, and somewhere children shout.

He rose a fist into the air, the teardrops streaming down his face. Even when the mighty Casey struck out to conclude the poem, Allen turned the page and kept on reading. He moved on to a poem entitled "Casey's Revenge," written by longtime sportswriter Grantland Rice:

A whack, a crack, and out through the space the leather pellet flew,
A blot against the distant sky, a speck against the blue.
Above the fence in center field in rapid whirling flight
The sphere sailed on—the blot grew dim and then was lost to sight.
Ten thousand hats were thrown in air, ten thousand threw a fit,
But no one ever found the ball that mighty Casey hit.

At that point, the players' eyes began to fill with tears. Their dreams were not dashed; they would get to swing again. They filed out of the classroom and onto the practice court, ready to give their season a happy ending.

The Jayhawks were refocused, and just as important, Allen knew he had to step aside and hand the strategic part of his job back to Dick Harp, his assistant coach.

Kansas bounced back in a big way, easily beating Iowa State and then Oklahoma A&M. The Jayhawks went on to manhandle Kansas State on the way to an eight-game winning streak that closed out the season. The Jayhawks went 24-3 overall and 11-1 in conference play to win an outright Big Seven Conference title—Phog Allen's twenty-second in thirty-three years as head coach. The conference crown sent the Jayhawks back to the NCAA tournament, marking the fifth time Allen would lead KU into the tourney since its birth thirteen years earlier.

By that point in his career, Allen had been to enough NCAA tournaments to know that the key to success was staying in a routine. He'd maintained a pretty strict pregame ritual over the years, from the morning meal to the team walk along the sidewalks that surrounded the team hotel. He kept himself busy in the minutes before a game by taping each player's ankles, a technique that had become somewhat commonplace for coaches following his lead. Allen continued to be a trendsetter on the sports medicine front by making use of the foot-arch roller, which he administered to each of his players before games, and through a medical liniment he created to help ease muscle soreness. These were among the many medical innovations Doc Allen had carried into the 1950s. In the basement of his Lawrence home, he'd been storing a machine capable of sending electronic currents through a player's injured body part in an effort to speed up the healing process. The machine was used by medical professionals overseas but had yet to be approved for use in the United States. In addition, Allen had also been concocting medical "potions" to help his players maintain a steady diet of nutrients, the most important of which were yeast tablets. Phog ingested yeast as a daily snack, believing it fought bacteria, and he soon created a mixture he called Glycolixer, or just Glyck, made up of two yeast tablets with lemonade and dextrose. He was so convinced of its powers that he kept a gallon jar of yeast tablets on top of his refrigerator at home for his adult children and grandchildren to ingest.

Doc Allen gave way to Coach Phog Allen in the moments leading up to KU's opening game of the 1952 NCAA tournament in nearby Kansas City. The "Allenmen," as they were being called back in Lawrence, stormed out onto the floor and built up a 17-point lead over Texas Christian University. But the upstart Horned Frogs made a furious second-half rally before KU barely hung on for a 68–64 win. Next up was St. Louis, the same team that beat mighty Kentucky earlier in the season. The fifth-ranked Billikens were coming off of a 22-7 regular season and were making their first-ever NCAA tournament appearance. Led by a crafty guard named Ray Steiner who had transferred from Missouri and could frustrate opponents with his lightning-quick change of direction and his ability to drive the lane, SLU breezed into the West Region semifinals by beating New Mexico State. The Billikens rolled into Kansas City with an eye on knocking off Allen's Jayhawks. The winner would be heading to Seattle for the national semifinals; the loser would go home.

In a game played at Kansas City's Municipal Auditorium and televised locally on WDAF-TV, the Jayhawks rode a historic night from Lovellette to put St. Louis away early while continuing the sixty-six-year-old Allen's run toward the national semifinals. Lovellette scored a school-record 44 points in the 74–55 win over St. Louis, putting KU one win away from the national title game.

The next stop was Seattle, Washington, where the four remaining teams would battle for an NCAA title. And defending champion Kentucky would not be among them, thanks to a 64–57 upset at the hands of St. John's during the regional finals. KU was two wins away from a national title, a dream that was beginning to look like a reality as the Jayhawks began their trek to the West Coast. The headline across the top of the *Lawrence Journal World* blared, "All of Lawrence looks to Seattle."

Kansas, St. John's, second-ranked Illinois, and tournament dark horse Santa Clara were set to congregate in Seattle for the semifinals of the 1952 NCAA tournament. Phog Allen hated to fly and wasn't too excited about the airplane trip halfway across the country. His frayed nerves were further shaken when weather conditions redirected the flight to Minneapolis. KU's plane eventually got back in the air, and then some severe air turbulence put Allen's anxiety at an all-time high. At one point, Allen opened his eyes to find Lovellette placing a bouquet of artificial flowers around his head. "Relax, Doc," Lovellette said while hovering over the coach in the well-pressed suit. "If we pile in, you're dressed for the funeral." The joke was enough to put Allen at ease as the airplane leveled out and landed safely in Seattle. Wearing an overcoat and fedora, Allen led the Jayhawks off the airplane and into the fog and rain of Seattle, where his four-year-old recruiting promise of a KU national championship would be tested.

The team bus navigated through a Seattle skyline that was modest by comparison to what it would become. The freeway bridge that would connect downtown to the University of Washington campus hundreds of feet above the Montlake Cut had yet to be constructed; the Space Needle was still a decade away from landing in Seattle. As the team bus took Allen and the players to the north part of town, the windshield wipers cranked through the fog and rain. The bus arrived at the team hotel a few hours later than scheduled, welcomed by a giant telegram signed by 1,500 KU fans that had been sent to Seattle.

It turned out that the Jayhawks were the lucky ones, as the weather caused two of the four teams to be rerouted to Portland while delaying their arrivals for the NCAA semifinals and championship game. Eventually, all four teams arrived for the final three games, which would be played on back-to-back nights at the University of Washington's Hec Edmundson Pavilion. It marked the first time in NCAA tournament history that both semifinals and the national title game would be played in the same city—a format that would later come to be known as the Final Four.

The NCAA tournament had by no means become the Godzilla that would roll into the twenty-first century as one of the most popular events in American sports, but by 1952 it had come a long way. The event had surpassed the National Invitational Tournament as the premier postseason tourney in college basketball. The field had expanded from eight to sixteen teams by the early 1950s, and about a dozen national columnists joined the local beat writers from the four schools involved at the tournament's final weekend. A person could count on two hands the number of photographers attending the event.

Despite the marginal attention by twenty-first century standards, interest in the NCAA's championship weekend was at an all-time high. Fans across the country were poring over box scores in newspapers to provide relief from news of the national polio outbreak and the daily anxiety from fear of Communist spies. The National Basketball Association had been around for three years but had yet to find its niche, and so the NCAA tournament provided the biggest stage the sport had to offer in the early part of the decade.

College basketball had found its place in American culture, and even though NCAA championship games were still two years from making their national television debut, the proverbial eyes of the nation were on Seattle and the three final games of the 1951–52 NCAA basketball tournament.

With a roster that included seniors Bill Hougland, Bill Lienhard, Bob Kenney, the Kelley brothers, 6'9" sophomore B. H. Born, low-scoring role player LaVannes Squires, and future coaching legend Dean Smith, the Jayhawks had plenty of solid role players on that 1951–52 team. But it was pretty clear that everything revolved around Clyde Lovellette.

The senior All-American was leading the country in scoring, at 28.4 points per game, and he was the most anticipated player on any of the four teams in Seattle for the NCAA semifinals. Wherever Lovellette went in Seattle the day before the semifinal game against Santa Clara, fans stopped to get their pictures taken alongside the 6'9" redheaded giant with the flattop. Phog Allen had the biggest star in the Final Four, but the big man at the center of KU's title hopes almost got lost in the fog on the way to the big game.

16

Just Like Any Other Game Day

The shining star had disappeared in the night. The early-evening clouds had wilted into the darkness of a Northwest evening, cloaking the waters of the Puget Sound with a thick coat of fog. Their star was out there somewhere.

Clyde Lovellette, 6'9" and 240 pounds, was nowhere to be found when the Kansas Jayhawks turned out the lamps on the bedside tables of their hotel rooms in the evening hours of March 23, 1952, the night before the national semifinal game. One of the nation's biggest and best players had gone out with a fraternity friend to tour the Seattle waterfront earlier in the evening, and he never came back. Daylight had faded, curfew had come and gone, and KU's biggest and brightest star was not among the players tucked safely into their beds. Even Phog Allen had returned to his hotel room, and Lovellette was still unaccounted for.

Much of KU's success during the 1951–52 season had been about teamwork and players knowing their roles, but the simple fact was that teamwork wasn't going to take them anywhere without their star. Especially in the biggest game of the year. The Jayhawks were one win away from the national championship game, just forty-eight hours from achieving the goal Phog Allen had set for them, had practically promised them, and now they were in danger of letting their dreams evaporate into the Pacific Northwest night. Their savior was missing, and time was running out.

188

How could someone that big just . . . disappear? It was akin to walking across the KU campus one day and realizing the 120-foot-high Campanile War Memorial was gone. Without explanation, Big Clyde was out of the picture. The most visible player in college basketball was on the verge of leaving a hole as big as Lake Washington in KU's starting lineup.

The first great basketball coach and perhaps the sport's most influential pioneer, Phog Allen had accomplished a lot by the time the final weekend of the 1952 college basketball season came around—but one thing he had yet to do was win an outright national title. The only two national championships the Jayhawks had earned were retroactive titles handed down by the Helms Foundation more than a decade after the fact, and neither one of those was considered an official championship. His only trip to a national title game had resulted in an 18-point humbling at the hands of Indiana's Hurryin' Hoosiers in 1940. Kentucky's Adolph Rupp (who had once played for Allen) and Oklahoma A&M's Henry Iba had won a total of five of the previous seven national titles and were considered by most to have surpassed the aging KU coach. A rising star named John Wooden was continuing to make a name for himself out west. And with a state edict in place that university employees must retire at the age of seventy, the clock was ticking on the sixty-six-year-old Allen's chances of winning a national championship.

His prospects of breaking through rested largely on the shoulders of a big Indiana kid who had led the Jayhawks into the national semifinals. Clyde Lovellette, 6'9" tall and 240 pounds, with wide shoulders and a jump-hook shot that simply couldn't be stopped, was the first dominant big man Phog Allen had coached. Less than a decade after George Mikan and Bob Kurland had redefined the position, Lovellette was providing the world of college basketball with another unstoppable big man.

His senior season was beginning to look like one for the ages. Lovellette had led the nation in scoring and had carried Kansas to the brink of its first national championship game, and yet when the Jayhawks went to bed the night before the NCAA semifinal game against Santa Clara, he was not with the team. One of Lovellette's fraternity brothers, a young man named Buddy "Fig" Newton, was captain of the Coast Guard Cutter, stationed in the Puget Sound, and had invited the KU star onto his vessel for dinner the night before the Jayhawks' semifinal game against Santa Clara. A thick fog rolled in while Lovellette was eating dinner, and the ship was unable to return to shore until well after curfew. Once on dry land, a panicked Lovellette rushed back to the hotel, entering the hotel lobby around midnight. He fully expected to find Phog Allen waiting in his signature grey sweatsuit, which had by then come to include the name F. C. Allen stitched in blue across his heart, with a towel wrapped around his neck. But the only person there turned out to be a newspaper reporter who glanced up but didn't seem to notice him. Lovellette rushed up to his room, where teammate Charlie Hoag was still awake and relieved to see Big Clyde return—albeit almost two hours past the team's 10 p.m. curfew. Lovellette bade Hoag a good night and climbed into the two beds that had been pushed together end-to-end to accommodate his massive frame, eventually drifting into sleep.

It's hard to imagine that Lovellette's temporary disappearance would have gotten by Phog Allen without any notice, but nothing was ever said about it. The next time Lovellette saw Allen was at a team breakfast the following day, and the coach didn't give him a second look. It's conceivable, although unlikely, that Lovellette may have simply slipped through the cracks. Allen, who had pinned a handwritten sign reading "You can't hang with owls at night if you want to soar with eagles in the day" in the KU locker room earlier in his career, had become so trusting of his 1951–52 team that he didn't even conduct bed checks. Or Allen may well have chosen to ignore the curfew violation for fear of having to punish his best player one win from the NCAA title game.

All Lovellette knew was that things carried on as usual the next day. After breakfast, Allen led the players through a walk across the University of Washington campus, and then he was with them during a team lunch before sending the players to their rooms for an afternoon nap. "It was," Lovellette would recall decades later, "just like any other game day."

After catching up on his sleep that afternoon, Lovellette took the floor against an underdog Santa Clara team that took advantage of a sluggish KU team. The Broncos jumped out to an 8–7 lead before Lovellette woke up and scored 18 first-half points to put the Jayhawks ahead 38–25 at the half. Kansas was leading 59-39 heading into the fourth quarter, and Phog Allen was so confident that things were in hand that he decided to allow Lovellette, his star, to rest up for the title game. Santa Clara responded by cutting the KU lead to 13 points before Lovellette was back on the floor, eventually scoring 33 points as KU rolled to a 74-55 victory in the NCAA semifinal.

The Jayhawks were back in the NCAA title game, twelve years after Allen had led the 1939-40 KU team to a championship matchup with Indiana. This time around, Allen was older and wiser, and he had a much more talented cast of players surrounding him. The 1951-52 Jayhawks had become the tournament favorites, especially with defending champion Kentucky out of the running, and only one more win stood between Allen and his first official national championship. Tenth-ranked St. John's pulled off another upset by beating number two Illinois and its big star, Johnny "Red" Kerr, in the other semifinal, leaving two teams remaining to compete in the 1952 championship game.

Phog Allen awoke the next morning, on March 26, 1952, with the door of opportunity just one more step away. The NCAA tournament he had helped to initiate fourteen years earlier—and had kept alive by moving it to Kansas City for the 1940 title game—was about to crown an official national champion, and Phog's "Allenmen" were among the two teams left to battle for the trophy. After taking a back seat to younger, more successful coaches throughout most of the 1940s, Phog Allen was back in the spotlight as the eyes of college basketball focused on Seattle for the 1952 NCAA championship game.

During his short time in Seattle, Phog Allen had become the darling of the tournament. Reporters and fans were mesmerized by his huge personality and knowledge of the game. He'd had the same effect on thousands of players, opponents, and fans of the game over the years, even though his background as a basketball pioneer had largely been forgotten. In an era when social media was still forty years away, Allen had built a national fan base by answering letters by hand. He even responded to his hate mail, penning replies like, "Assuring you I would not feel comfortable without receiving an occasional love note from you, I am, sincerely, yours." He had won more games than any man in basketball history, yet there were still plenty of doubters out there. As one national magazine pondered in the spring of 1952, "Phog Allen—Windbag or Prophet?"

In the hours leading up to the title game, Allen explained some of his basketball philosophies to a reporter from the *Seattle Times*, talking mostly about the importance of hand-eye coordination. The legendary coach revealed his fascination with Helen Keller, saying that by reading her autobiography his players "learn there the importance of tactile sensation— touch. It's everything in basketball. My boys learn that the feel of the ball in the hand means as much to them as it does to a pitcher. It's those sensitive fingers that give you control." Allen went on to explain the importance of billiards in helping a player to master his touch and control. More than any other sport, basketball relied on a person's hands. And when the ball was in your hands, as it would be for Allen's Jayhawks in just a few hours, the possibilities were endless.

The overcast skies reflected the orange glow of dusk as Allen and the KU basketball team arrived at Hec Edmundson Pavilion, just a few hundred yards from the shore of Lake Washington. The cool air carried the silence of expectation as the players unloaded the team bus and funneled into the bowels of an empty arena.

In the din of the locker room before the game, Allen found an uptight team. Lovellette would later admit that he felt nervous for the first time all season. KU's best player realized how close the Jayhawks were to winning their first outright title and to giving Phog Allen a long-overdue championship-game victory. The four fourth-year seniors on that 1951–52 team would play together for the final time, while the state law prohibiting a state employee from working past his seventieth birthday meant that the sixty-six-year-old Allen was running out of chances as well.

Allen looked each player in the eye, as if attempting to transmit every ounce of his own confidence to them. Each individual player had his own story, a narrative that had brought him to this very moment in time. Clyde Lovellette had overcome his lifelong battle with asthma and the preteen awkwardness of his own body to emerge as the finest college basketball player in the land. Bill Lienhard had recovered from his early-season illness to become the team's most consistent outside shooter, using his one-handed flick and a kick of the leg to hit from all over the court. Dean

Kelley, the only non-senior starter, had sat on the bench for almost his entire sophomore year before becoming a junior starter and a key piece of the title team. Bill Hougland, the small-town kid who had spent much of his teenage life working on a farm, had grown into a tenacious defender and ferocious rebounder who did most of his damage on the boards after squirming between opposing players, thus earning the nickname Wormy. And Bob "Trigger" Kenney, with his aggressive drives to the basket, a snap-quick release, and a nation-leading 83 percent success rate at the free-throw line, had come from the basketball-rich town of Winfield, Kansas, and grown into the role of Lovellette's complementary scorer. Having someone like "Trigger" Kenney on the team brought comfort to a coach who knew all too well the importance of free-throw shooting.

Nearly a half century had passed since young Forrest Allen, nineteen years old and with a world of possibilities in front of him, stepped to the free-throw line at Kansas City Convention Hall, draining shot after shot after underhanded shot to lead the Kansas City Athletic Club to basketball's first "World's Championship." What would that Forrest Allen think if he were sitting in the locker room now in Seattle, the sound of more than eleven thousand fans outside the closed door buzzing in anticipation before the 1952 NCAA championship game? In a sense, the ghost of a younger Phog Allen was inside that locker room, his head full of well-groomed hair, his young cheeks red with eagerness of playing the game he loved, his hands ready to take the ball and hoist it, two-handed, from a crouched, underhand position, toward the rim.

Standing before his team, sixty-six-year-old Phog Allen, with thinning hair, eyeglasses, and a fancy suit, tried to calm his players down by telling them to treat this night like any other night. His typical motivational tactics of getting a team all fired up before a game were gone; on this night, he needed to bring his players back to a more composed state of all-out focus.

"You know what you need to do," Allen told his players before that 1952 NCAA championship game. "We've worked on this. If we play our game, we will be fine."

A crowd of 11,700 fans was on hand by the time the third-place game ended and the Jayhawks and St. John's Redmen took the floor for the 1952 national championship game. A thirty-member band was blasting out harmony behind music stands on one end of the floor, while overhead spotlights cast a glow on the hardwood floor at the center of the arena. The scheduled tip-off of 9:30 p.m. was anything but convenient to fans listening to the game back in Lawrence, where it was 11:30 p.m. Central time. The first televised NCAA title game was still two years away, leaving KU fans glued to their radios in anticipation. The wait was excruciating for Kansas students and fans hoping to secure the first official NCAA title in program history.

When the game finally tipped off, St. John's coach Frank McGuire tried to slow down the pace of the championship contest while asking beefy big man Bob Zawoluk to play a key role in containing Lovellette. Zawoluk, a 6'6" freshman who was able to play because the NCAA had waived its freshman eligibility rule during the Korean War, came out tugging on Lovellette's jersey, poking him and generally getting under the skin of KU's All-America big man. Lovellette tried to keep his head but came off the court during one timeout and told his coach that he was about to knock the guy's block off.

"You are not going to knock anybody's block off until after the game," Phog Allen responded. "And I promise you, you'll get that freedom. It's your last game; you can do anything you want. If you get put in jail, I'll get you out."

Appropriately, Lovellette opened the scoring of the 1952 NCAA championship game with a free throw—underhanded, of course. Kansas controlled the pace early on, thanks to some hot outside shooting while the Redmen focused their defense on Lovellette, but St. John's pulled to within 10–9 midway through the first quarter. Allen chugged from his water bottle and leaned forward in his folding chair, watching as Trigger Kenney, junior-college transfer John Keller, and Lovellette hit shots to pull the Jayhawks out to an 18–13 lead after one quarter. With St. John's continuing to sag its interior defense to account for Lovellette's offensive firepower, the KU guards started hitting open shots from the outside. Bill Lienhard, kicking one leg in the air as he shot with one hand, scored from the corner and added a twenty-footer as the Jayhawks erupted for 23 second-quarter points, opening up a 41–27 halftime lead.

The locker room scene at halftime was much different than it had been an hour earlier, when a group of nervous young men were hoping not to let their coach down. Now, with a 14-point lead in hand, the Jayhawks were a confident bunch of sweaty players who no longer needed their experienced coach to remind them how good they were.

For KU fans, the only scare of the second half came over a ten-minute stretch during which the radio broadcast back in Lawrence got blacked out by technical difficulties. By the time the feed was restored, the Jayhawks had the game well in hand. KU ended up leading the entire way, with the Redmen never getting closer than 11 points after halftime. Lovellette scored 33 points while breaking all sorts of NCAA tournament records on the way to an 80–63 win over the Redmen. The final whistle came around 1:30 a.m. in Lawrence, where the celebration in the streets began.

Afterward, while still standing on the court at the University of Washington, Phog Allen placed the game ball in the national-championship trophy and presented them to his seniors: Lovellette, Bob Kenney, Bill Lienhard, Bill Hougland, and John Keller. In a team photo taken of the Jayhawks moments after the win, Allen was almost laughing, delirious with joy. The crowd showered the coach and players with applause, but there was no cutting down of the nets in those years. The Jayhawks then filed into the locker room and engaged in a restrained celebration that looked more like relief than all-out jubilation. Players hugged and clapped each other's backs while shaking their heads in disbelief. Consistent to their steady, businesslike approach to the season, the KU players didn't pop any champagne bottles or howl in the celebration of victory. They'd done what they'd set out to do; it was as simple as that. Another goal had been achieved.

Only after a few minutes did they notice that someone was missing. Phog Allen stood outside the locker room, either unable to grasp the gravity of the situation or just allowing himself to bask in it for a few minutes. His career had led to this very stage, beginning with a steady ascent up the mountainside of basketball before the aging coach began to lose his footing along the way. Somehow, he had stayed the course and continued to press forward. He was almost two thousand miles from home, in an unfamiliar part of the country, and Phog Allen had finally reached the pinnacle of his career. As the *Topeka Capital-Journal* would report the following day, "for the misty-eyed but happy Phog Allen, it was the climax of a fabulous coaching record that started 42 seasons ago. The 66-year-old 'Mr. Basketball' now has won every honor the game has to offer."

Allen took it all in, and then he opened the door and fell into the swell of postgame celebration.

Back in Lawrence, the party was just beginning. In the wee hours of March 27, 1952, a majority of the seven thousand students enrolled at the University of Kansas spilled out into the streets, with overcoats wrapped around their pajamas, dancing in front of Old Frazier Hall and climbing the Uncle Jimmy Green statue near the center of campus. One student blew on his trumpet, while others set off firecrackers and broke into the school fight song. The celebration leaked out across Jayhawk Blvd., between cars that were lined up from one end of the street to the other, with horns blowing. The celebrating students broke into the Rock Chalk chant: "Raawwwwwwwwk . . . Chawwwwwwwk . . . Jaaaaaaaay-haawwwwk . . . KUUUUUUU." A few fans began burning copies of LOOK *Magazine*, the only known publication that had left Clyde Lovellette off its All-America team that season. At one point, a group of students gathered around the home of KU's dean of students and roused him from bed with the chant "No school tomorrow! No school tomorrow!" The celebration went on for nearly two hours, until well after three in the morning. (The dean did not cave in to the pressure, however, and classes went on the following day.)

It was the kind of celebration that surely would have brought a smile to Phog Allen's face, if not a tear to his sentimental eye, had he been there to see it. For KU fans, there was unadulterated jubilation; for Allen, who joined his players on a three-hour flight from Seattle in the early hours of March 27, the victory also brought an overwhelming sense of relief.

The championship celebration went on without Allen and the Jayhawks, who took a quiet flight from Seattle to Kansas City with trophy in hand. It may well have been the first plane ride Phog Allen ever enjoyed.

Hundreds of local fans were waiting at the Kansas City Airport when the team plane arrived just after 3 a.m. on a cool spring morning. Allen, dressed in an overcoat, addressed them by saying, "You're all wonderful. The team had some tough going. I'm tremendously proud of their sportsmanship." A reporter for the Associated Press would sum up the late-night celebration by writing, "The sometimes bombastic Phog Allen wasn't 'mad at anybody' last night."

About an hour later, the Jayhawks' bus arrived at the Kaw River Bridge to about fifteen thousand fans lined up along Massachusetts Street—many of them carrying noisemakers like cowbells and horns. As the *Lawrence Journal-World* would describe in later years, "you could get off the bus on the south end of the Kaw River bridge and walked on heads all the way up to the Hotel Eldridge [two blocks away], so thick was the adoring mob." The players then got a firetruck escort from the Lawrence Fire Department, and Lovellette donned a fireman's hat in a famous photo that appeared in newspapers shortly thereafter. Another photograph featured KU chancellor Frank Murphy beaming with pride as he held open a newspaper with the words "KU WINS" emblazoned across the front page. Looking over his shoulder is a smiling Phog Allen, wearing a tie and overcoat and appearing to have shed the weight of expectations he had carried for so long.

Doc Allen had finally reached the pinnacle, and it couldn't have come at a better time. His KU teams were national-champion caliber almost every year, and yet his program's inability to take home a national title had become the monkey on Allen's back that he had fervently tried to ignore. Sixty-six years old and just three years removed from wrapping up two of the worst back-to-back seasons in his tenure, Phog was finally on top—and no one could take it away from him. KU had won its first outright national title, and Phog Allen was no longer falling into the shadows of coaches like Rupp and Iba. The 1951–52 season turned out to be the mountaintop of Allen's four-plus decades in coaching.

And yet the campaign wasn't over yet. Not quite.

Phog Allen and his exhausted Jayhawks still had one more tournament to play, and this time a berth in the 1952 Olympics was on the line.

17

Searching for Gold

The Jayhawks were in trouble. The national championship was already in Phog Allen's back pocket, but the promise he'd made four years earlier to his 1948 recruits was not yet fulfilled. The Jayhawks still had to get to the finals of the Olympic Trials if they wanted to achieve their golden dreams, and the LaSalle Explorers were well on their way to bursting the KU bubble.

The weight of having played four elimination games in less than a week seemed to be sucking the life out of Allen's team. The adrenaline of an NCAA title victory had worn off in the five days since KU beat St. John's, and now the Jayhawks were looking like they'd run out of gas. The battle pitting Allen's NCAA champs and the NIT champion Explorers was turning into a one-sided affair, and Ol' Phog was pounding jars of water like a lesser man might attack pints of whisky.

It was bad enough that the Jayhawks were back in New York City, the kind of cesspool where even Mother Teresa might get dragged into the throes of gambling. The game had nearly gotten called off because Phog didn't trust the neutrality of the East-based officiating crew. Even when that fiasco got sorted out, the Jayhawks still felt like they were playing on foreign soil. The fans from nearby Philly were rooting the Explorers toward Olympic glory, and KU's 13-point deficit might as well have been 30 with the way the Jayhawks were playing. Allen's players were exhausted from two weeks of NCAA tournament games and the celebration of their lives, and now it was all coming to a slow, painful death right before Phog's eyes.

Phog Allen ran his fingers through thinning hair and looked up at the scoreboard. He reached for another jug of water. He glanced at Assistant Coach Dick Harp. Then at trainer Dean Nesmith and junior guard Dean Smith, the three of them seated side by side by side on the KU bench. None of them had anything to offer in the way of comfort.

Allen took one last pull off his water, finishing what was left in the glass jug. All of his hopes and dreams were slipping away.

Phog Allen's Olympic dream began a quarter century earlier, when he was a forty-something coach beginning his quest to get the sport of basketball onto the biggest of international stages. He had achieved that goal when basketball was accepted into the 1936 Olympic Games, but a disagreement with officials from the AAU led Allen to quit his post as director of the U.S. team and he never got to make the trip.

By the time the 1952 Olympic year came around, Phog Allen was not only a legend in the coaching profession but also a flag-bearer for the sport—and, after the 1952 NCAA finals, he had become a three-time national champion. But he had still never been to the Olympics, and his '52 Jayhawks were out to change that.

In those years, U.S. basketball didn't simply pick twelve players from the NBA or even take a team of collegiate All-Stars. An Olympic Trials tournament helped select the national team, as well as its coach, and so Allen and the NCAA champion Jayhawks were still going to have to earn their way to Helsinki, Finland, for the '52 games. The format had been altered from earlier Olympics, which had included a Trials tournament made up of NCAA and AAU teams and was basically a winner-take-all system. By 1952, the Trials allowed for the top collegiate team—usually decided in a game between the NCAA champion and the winner of the prestigious National Invitational Tournament—to earn seven spots on the fourteen-man Olympic squad; the other seven roster spots would be spread out among the AAU champs and the remaining collegiate All-Americans.

(AAU players were considered amateurs because they were not directly paid to play basketball, only to work full-time jobs for the companies that owned the teams.)

KU earned a spot in the Olympics Trials by way of its win over St. John's in the NCAA championship game. The Jayhawks went on to beat Springfield Teachers College in a game played in Kansas City in the opening round of the Trials, thereby solidifying a trip to New York City to continue on in the Olympic-qualifying tournament at Madison Square Garden. Traveling to the Big Apple was a double-edged sword for Phog Allen, who was excited about the opportunity but may well have felt like he was going into the jaws of an alligator. He had been warning of the dangers of New York City for a good part of a decade, calling it a hotbed of gambling activity. Just a few months earlier, Allen was the center of national controversy when he said, "It is more than mere chance that the past two major college basketball scandals have broken out of New York." Allen continually railed against the city for its culture of crime and its mob ties, and native New Yorkers didn't appreciate the old man from the Midwestern plains acting like an expert on the subject of their metropolitan mecca.

The aging coach from the prairie certainly had the attention of basketball enthusiasts in the Big Apple. As KU player Charlie Hoag later explained in the *Crimson & Blue Handbook*, "they didn't like Phog Allen back in New York City. But I'll tell you one thing, he drew a crowd. When we landed, the reporters were all there to see Phog Allen."

The media was especially eager to hear from him after Allen initially refused to take part in the Madison Square Garden Trials unless a Midwestern referee was flown in to serve as one of the two game officials. Allen didn't trust a crew of East Coast officials in a game involving Kansas and LaSalle University of nearby Philadelphia, and so he was fully prepared to pull his team out of the tournament if a referee from the Midwest wasn't part of the officiating crew. The U.S. Olympic committee eventually granted his wish, and when the Jayhawks arrived in New York for the Trials, Allen explained his reasoning to an eager gathering of reporters, saying, "We don't have a chance to win with two Eastern officials in Madison Square Garden."

LaSalle, the NIT champion from Philadelphia, had an opinionated coach of its own in Ken Loeffler. The forty-nine-year-old Pennsylvania native was quoted as calling the Jayhawks "hicks" before the tournament, and he reportedly came close to getting into a fistfight with Allen in the hotel lobby a few hours before the opening round. Suffice to say, Phog Allen's emotions were running high heading into the semifinals of the Trials at Madison Square Garden. The March 31 game between KU and LaSalle would determine which college team got to take half the spots on the fourteen-man Olympic roster and would give the winning coach a chance to be on the coaching staff for the U.S. team.

The LaSalle Explorers were led by the country's best freshman in Tom Gola, a 6'6" athletic forward who grew up not far from the school in Philadelphia. Gola was able to play because of the NCAA rule that gave freshmen eligibility at a time when many of the country's college-aged men were serving in the Korean War. Gola had averaged a double-double—15 points and 15 rebounds per game—while leading LaSalle to a 25-7 record and the NIT title.

Gola lived up to all the hype early in the game against KU, when he out-dueled Lovellette in leading the Explorers to a 38–25 lead midway through the second quarter. Allen couldn't believe how poorly his team was playing in a game that would determine the Jayhawks' Olympic fate. A loss would mark the final time this group of KU players would ever be on the court together, while a victory would give at least seven Jayhawks a free trip to the Olympic Games. KU's proverbial back was against the wall, and the Jayhawks needed their star big man to do something about it.

As a consensus All-American, Lovellette was more than likely going to be a member of the U.S. Olympic team no matter what happened at the Trials. Many believed he was the best player in all of college basketball, and the 6'9" star was exactly the kind of player for which smaller international teams would have no answer. Whether it was Allen or somebody else coaching the U.S. team, he was almost certainly going to choose Lovellette to be among the participants already slotted.

But Lovellette did not want to be the only Jayhawk in attendance when the U.S. team headed to Finland in the summer. Three of his fellow KU seniors had come to Kansas under the promise that they'd be Olympians, and now they were one win away from achieving that objective. His coach,

Doc Allen, was in danger of being left out of the games again, sixteen years after the Olympic debut of the sport in Berlin.

In the end, Lovellette delivered, scoring 12 unanswered points in the second quarter to pull the Jayhawks within 5 points at halftime. He unleashed for 15 more points in the fourth quarter, including a layup with 3:25 remaining that gave KU its first lead, at 57–56. Allen's Jayhawks pulled away from there, with Lovellette scoring 40 points for the game in the Jayhawks' 70–65 win.

LaSalle's Loeffler was so hot after the loss that he confronted Lovellette in the hotel lobby the following day, only to get pinned against a wall by the big redhead from Terre Haute. He tried to find Phog Allen but was cut off by Phog's son, Mitt, who had to be separated from the LaSalle coach in a tense postgame scene.

The win had solidified Lovellette's spot on the Olympic roster, along with six other slots for his KU teammates. The only thing left was the Olympic Trials championship, which would determine who would coach the U.S. team in Helsinki. Phog Allen believed he was just the man for the job, and he had the resume to prove it. The only thing missing was a gold medal, and Allen was so close he could almost taste it.

The Jayhawks' opponent for the Trials championship was the Peoria (Illinois) Caterpillars, the champions of the Amateur Athletic Union—another of Allen's nemeses. The Kansas coach had been clashing with the AAU as far back as the 1930s, when he was working hard to get the sport of basketball into the 1936 Olympic Games but had such a difference in philosophy with AAU officials that he eventually resigned from his position as the U.S. team's director of basketball. The AAU had been a big factor in the rise of Allen's career thirty years earlier, when he was an up-and-coming coach glad-handing at the AAU's national tournaments in Kansas City, but since then he had come to loathe the organization for what he perceived as exploitation of players and misuse of funds. The only thing "amateur" about the Amateur Athletic Union, Phog argued, was the way it was run. So beating an AAU team in the Olympic Trials would be the proverbial icing on the cake for a coach who had recently won his first outright NCAA title.

The Peoria Caterpillars were considered the heavy favorites going into the game. The AAU squad was led by NBA draft picks like 6'11" former University of Oklahoma star Marcus Freiberger and former Purdue guard Howie Williams, both of whom had passed on the up-and-coming pro league to play for the corporate-sponsored company team in Peoria. In those days, the NBA was just in its seedling stages. So many of the AAU teams were able to get top college prospects by hiring them to work a full-time job while playing for the company team on the side, thereby maintaining their "amateur" status. The Peoria AAU squad was made up of players in their mid-twenties who were working at Caterpillar, a farm equipment company based in Central Illinois. Allen knew his Jayhawks had a long road to climb heading into the game, and when the Caterpillars stormed out to a 14-point lead in the first half, the crowd of more than six thousand fans at Madison Square Garden grew restless and thirsty for some kind of drama.

At least one fan in attendance turned irate. Phog's son Mitt, sitting next to brother Bob behind the KU bench, heard a fan seated near him grumbling about the mismatch. Mitt turned to confront the guy, who brushed him off by saying that Peoria was on the way to a 25-point win. The act of disrespect upset Mitt to the point that he wagered one hundred dollars that the Jayhawks wouldn't lose by more than 20. (Had he overheard the conversation, Phog probably would have appreciated his son's confidence but would have undoubtedly been disappointed by his gambling.)

Gradually, Phog Allen's team chipped away at the lead until Dean Kelley tied the score 60–60 on a one-handed jumper with fifty-two seconds remaining. Peoria opted to hold the ball for the final shot—there was still no shot clock in those days—and the Jayhawks appeared to be helpless until Lovellette pulled off one of the most unlikely steals of the season. With the 6'11" Freiberger holding the ball as the clock ran down, Lovellette simply reached out with both hands and stripped the ball from his grip. To everyone's shock, Lovellette then pushed the ball to the floor and began dribbling awkwardly toward the basket at the other end of the floor, where he had a path toward an open layup that could have given Phog Allen his long-awaited spot as head coach of the U.S. Olympic team.

As it turned out, the rock-steady Lovellette inexplicably missed the uncontested layup with sixteen seconds left, preserving the 60–60 tie, and the loose ball bounced off the hands of several players before Peoria's Ron Bontemps came up with it and passed to Howie Williams. The twenty-four-year-old former Purdue star heaved an off-balance shot toward the rim with five seconds remaining. The ball arced toward the basket as a hush fell over the crowd and swished through for a 62–60 Caterpillars victory.

For the first time in fifteen games, Allen and his Kansas Jayhawks were forced to endure the bitter taste of defeat. Losing in New York City, and to an AAU team, made the pill even tougher for Allen to swallow.

But for Allen and many of his players, the gold-medal dream was still alive. A thirty-two-year-old man named Warren Womble, who had led the Caterpillars to the Olympic Trials victory, earned the right to serve as head coach of the U.S. Olympic team. Allen, the most experienced and one of the most accomplished coaches in the world of college basketball, was chosen as one of his assistants. The fourteen-man roster included KU's Lovellette, Charlie Hoag, Bill Hoagland, Dean Kelley, Bob Kenney, Bill Lienhard, and John Keller, as well as Peoria's Freiberger, Williams, Frank McCabe, and Dan Pippin to go along with former collegiate All-American Bob Kurland of Oklahoma A&M fame.

The addition of Allen to the Olympic team did not come without controversy. Some officials with the Olympic Committee, upset with how he had clashed with the AAU in the past, initially tried to block him from being a part of the U.S. squad. A national story that appeared in the April 4, 1952, edition of the *Daily Kansan* conjectured that Allen would be left off the team, referring to him as "the osteopathic surgeon whose comments are sharper than any scalpel," but in the end the Olympic Committee accepted his appointment as a U.S. assistant coach.

In July 1952, Phog Allen departed for Helsinki, thus beginning his long-overdue journey to an Olympic Games. The 1952 Olympics brought added anticipation because of the inclusion of a delegation from the Soviet Union for the first time in Olympic history. The Soviets were said to have a solid team that claimed to have won 900 consecutive basketball games and were anointed as a likely contender for an American team that had yet to lose a game in Olympic competition.

Part of the challenge for the U.S. coaching staff was to find a way to blend all the talented players into one cohesive unit in a short amount of time. Another hurdle came from the lack of scouting reports: the American coaches simply didn't know much about the teams they were about to face, especially the mysterious powerhouse from the Soviet Union.

But the biggest obstacle may well have been in the hierarchy of the coaching staff. It's difficult to imagine Phog Allen, sixty-six years old and the winner of 686 career games, including his first official NCAA title a few months earlier, taking a secondary role to anyone—much less a thirty-two-year-old AAU coach from somewhere in Central Illinois. Phog had never been an assistant coach at any level, and the thought of him acquiescing to Warren Womble is a difficult image to muster.

But they made it work. As KU and U.S. Olympic player Bill Lienhard would later say, "[Allen] took kind of a low profile. They consulted before the game on how we would play. . . . Womble was the head coach, and Phog went along with that."

Womble opened the games with a starting lineup that included four players from his Peoria AAU team and former Oklahoma A&M star Bob Kurland—in effect, a group of KU nemeses. The substitution pattern most often saw five KU players check in at a time, replaced by five AAU players at the next substitution. The U.S. team rolled through its first game, leading up to a preliminary-round matchup with the Soviets. The anticipation of that game was so huge that Olympic organizers had to move the venue from a two-thousand-seat tennis center to a stadium twice the size. The Cold War had not yet begun, but it was apparent that the United States and the Soviet Union were the superpowers of the hardwood. That political tensions were beginning to rise in an era when Americans were wary of Communist spies only added to the drama.

Five minutes into the game, Soviet star Otar Korkiia crashed to the court and tripped up Lovellette, who fell and landed on top of him. Korkiia had to be carried off the floor with an injury, and when he returned for the second half with his right hand wrapped up, the Russian star was ineffective. The Americans had already built up a 17-point halftime lead and were well on their way to an 86–58 victory.

Next up was Uruguay's team, which wasn't supposed to provide much of a challenge. Womble benched Lovellette for the game, telling reporters he had Phog Allen's full support, and the United States rolled on to another easy victory without him. Afterward, Womble explained the benching by saying, "Clyde hasn't been playing well, and he hasn't shown the enthusiasm of some of the other boys. . . . I don't know Lovellette too well, but Phog isn't satisfied with the boy's work."

Years later, Lovellette would disclose that Allen was behind the decision—one that initially ticked off Lovellette but that he would grow to understand over time. "I can't really explain why, but I had a tough time getting prepared to play," Lovellette would recall more than a half century later. "If you're not performing, you're a detriment to the team rather than a positive influence. Phog could see that. Instead of leaving me out there, he said: 'Why don't you sit down until you're ready to play?'"

Lovellette eventually got focused, and the 1952 U.S. Olympic team moved on to the medal round, where the Americans ran into their first serious scare in a quarterfinal game against Brazil. A 2-point halftime deficit made Allen and his U.S. team sweat, but the Americans eventually edged Brazil out 57–53 to earn a spot in the semifinals. That set up a game against Argentina, which didn't provide much of a challenge in the semifinal round. The U.S. team breezed through the Argentine squad, and after the Soviet Union held off Uruguay, the rematch was all set: the United States would face the Soviets for the 1952 gold medal.

Phog Allen's confidence was flying high. In a letter dated July 31, 1952, Allen wrote to Lawrence resident Art Weaver of Weaver's Department Store:

> We whipped Argentina today 85 to 76, and play Russia for the championship. We whipped them once and must do it again Sat.
>
> The boys are having fun but there is one place the boys are ready to stand for most any old time now.
>
> Sincerely, Forrest C. Allen "Phog"

The gold-medal game turned out to be more competitive than Allen had expected, as the Soviets weren't in any mood to be "whipped." Learning from its earlier meeting with the United States, the Soviet team enacted a stall tactic in an effort to keep the score low. After ten minutes of play, the

Americans' lead was just 4–3. A late Bill Hougland basket gave the United States a 17–15 advantage at halftime, but the first half was going just as the Soviets had planned. The Americans went into halftime scratching their heads and rubbing their wounds after a physical first half. The Soviet Union's slowdown game had given the Russians hope.

It was Bob Kurland, the former KU rival, who suggested what to do next. His Henry Iba–coached Oklahoma A&M teams had been employing a similar stall technique against the Jayhawks for years, and KU's aggressive half-court trap had solved the question of how to keep an offense from holding the ball and running time off the clock. Kurland offered that opening the second half with five KU players on the floor might break the Soviets' patience. Womble agreed to try it, and Phog Allen had to be beaming inside as he watched five Jayhawks turn the tables on the Soviet team.

The new lineup created several fast-break opportunities, and the American team eventually started hitting shots from the outside while building up a 9-point lead. Womble and Allen then called off the dogs, responding to the Soviets' slowdown tactics with a stall of their own down the stretch. With the United States clinging to a 29–25 lead and five minutes left on the clock, the Americans began holding the ball near midcourt, passing it only when necessary as they watched the seconds and minutes click down. One USSR player grew so frustrated with the Americans' stall tactics that he sat down on the court in a form of protest.

The 36–25 U.S. win was not pretty, but it continued American dominance in the sport created by an adopted Canadian in 1891. And Phog Allen had finally struck gold.

By the time he began his journey back to the United States near the end of the summer in 1952, Phog Allen had won an NCAA record 686 games, twenty-four conference titles, three national championships, and had been part of a gold medal–winning team. Later that fall, he was enshrined in the Missouri Sports Hall of Fame, alongside the high-school baseball star to whom he'd given medical treatment four decades earlier: Charles "Casey" Stengel. And Allen wasn't even close to being finished. He was sixty-six years old, four years away from the mandatory retirement age for state employees, but he was almost certain that the rule would be altered in his case, as it had been for James Naismith.

Despite his age, Phog Allen had as much energy as ever. And he was going to need it, because in the summer of 1952, the University of Kansas had broken ground on a new fieldhouse. The on-campus facility was expected to be the finest in all of college basketball, and it was up to Allen to make sure the team playing inside of it would be worthy of the $2.5 million investment.

18

The Improbable Return

The clock was ticking. Phog Allen was back in Kansas City for one more fleeting chance at glory in the town he once called home. Miraculously in a season filled with miracles, his Jayhawks had rallied to tie the score with just over a minute remaining in the biggest game of the season, and now all Allen could do was stand and watch as the seconds ticked away.

Fifty-nine ... fifty-eight ... fifty-seven ...

The opposing team held the ball near midcourt, waiting for the final shot. In these moments, a basketball coach feels as helpless as ever, unable to do anything but watch futilely from the bench. They're all control freaks, these coaches. Every single one of them—no matter the sport. The only thing worse than losing is losing control of the outcome.

Phog Allen hated leaving a game in the hands of an official, and giving the opponent the final chance at victory was just as maddening. And that was exactly what was happening on this spring evening at the Municipal Auditorium in Kansas City. He was losing control of his own fate.

Fifty ... forty-nine ... forty-eight ...

Surely, Forrest "Phog" Allen would have felt more comfortable if he'd been fifty years younger, standing at the free-throw line, the game in the balance, the ball in his hands. The hands were the key to the game. With strong fingers but a soft touch, the hands were everything in the sport of basketball. The only time a man was truly in control on a basketball court was when the ball was in his hands.

And when it wasn't in his hands?

Forty-three . . . forty-two . . . forty-one . . .

Back in the day, Allen could have simply closed his eyes and blocked it all out, letting his hands do all the work as they gently caressed the leather ball. All the other senses would disappear in those moments. His eyes closed, the sound of an arena turned off, teenage Forrest would have held in his breath and been alone in that moment, in total control.

But now, with the score tied at 68 in the biggest game of the season, the outcome was beyond his reach. The clock was ticking. The opponent was holding the ball, waiting patiently for the final shot.

Thirty-two . . . thirty-one . . . thirty.

Phog Allen watched impatiently as an opposing guard finally made a move for the basket. He drove the lane. Bodies collided. The ball went up. The whistle blew.

The clock showed twenty-seven seconds. A player from the opposing team was headed to the free-throw line. Score tied. Game on the line.

Phog Allen returned from the Olympics in Helsinki with a cleansed reputation. The personality idiosyncrasies and inability to live up to his own standards of success were long forgotten now that Allen had had a hand in an Olympic championship and a national title. The grumblings of a KU faculty that had felt Allen had his own set of rules were being drowned out by the constant claps on the back from others. Allen was as popular a figure as ever on the KU campus, and his national profile continued to expand as well. In basketball circles, he'd become a living legend, the face of his sport and an oft-quoted spokesman for basketball. Interviews and speaking engagements had become almost as much a part of his career as coaching, although he never lost focus on the KU basketball program.

The primary question surrounding the 1952–53 Jayhawks had to do with the biggest star in the program's history—more specifically, how to replace him. Six-foot-nine-inch Clyde Lovellette had been the ninth overall pick in the NBA draft the previous spring but had passed on that opportunity to maintain his amateur status for the Olympics. Big Clyde returned from Helsinki and took a public relations job at Phillips Oil Company in Oklahoma while playing for the Phillips 66ers AAU team. Phog Allen didn't blame Lovellette for continuing his basketball career, even though the longtime coach often discouraged former players from becoming professional athletes. He cringed at the thought of an educated college graduate spending the formative years of his life playing sports for money and often encouraged his players to choose a different profession—using his lawyer son, Mitt, and his doctor son, Bob, as prime examples. As Phog Allen would later say in a speech given at an NCAA convention, "I am not against professional sports, but I would never advise a boy to play professional ball, for the reason that it is too short-lived. If a boy has to go to college four years to learn to be a professional ballplayer, it is a sad commentary on education and the [college degree] he gets."

But more and more players were making careers out of sports, and Lovellette was no different. Allen moved on without him and turned his attention toward the 1952–53 season. His defending national champions had plenty of holes to fill. Six of the seven players who had represented Kansas in the Olympics were gone—even senior-to-be Charlie Hoag was unavailable, due to a serious knee injury he suffered on the football field—and the void Lovellette left was the hardest to fill. The only proven big man the Jayhawks had coming into the 1952–53 season was junior B.H. Born, a 6'9" string bean who averaged just 1.6 points per game as Lovellette's backup in 1951–52.

Born's main role during his sophomore season had been to get Lovellette ready for games. He had spent every practice day banging bodies with the significantly beefier Lovellette and had the bruises to prove it. Lovellette had given Born no respite, not only physically but also mentally. Big Clyde was known to point to a flagpole and crack: "Hey, B.H., you've put on a little weight!" Born was also a lightweight in terms of ability during his early years at KU, and the 1952–53 Jayhawks were going to need him to develop into a decent player if they were going to be any kind of a factor in the Big Seven Conference.

Allen's team couldn't even count on the return of Hoag, a key reserve for the national championship team and star halfback for the football team who was supposed to be a senior starter for the defending champs.

Doc Allen did everything in his osteopathic power to heal Hoag, going as far as bringing him into the basement of his house on Louisiana Ave. to secretly administer electric-shock therapy on the knee using the European machine he had stashed there. But nothing could heal Hoag's torn-up knee.

That left Born, returning starter Dean Kelley, and his younger brother Allen Kelley, along with a controversial transfer from West Point named Gil Reich, to carry the load on a team that had lost almost all the firepower of the national championship unit. Reich, one of only two seniors on the 1952–53 Jayhawks team, had recently enrolled at KU after army officials ruled that he had helped cover up an academic scandal at the military academy, leading to his dismissal from West Point.

A much different KU team from the one that won the 1952 national title came together amid low expectations. The Jayhawks, with just 20 percent of their scoring back from the 1951–52 season, were picked to finish fourth in the Big Seven. Phog Allen had spent most of the offseason reminding reporters that the defending-champion Jayhawks had no chance of repeating. If not for his insatiable will to win at all costs, Phog probably would have written off the 1952–53 campaign as a rebuilding year.

A mediocre 5-3 start left even more questions about KU's ability to get back to the NCAA tournament for the third time in four years. Reich, the West Point castoff, became a key figure filling in for Hoag, but the Jayhawks missed their graduated seniors and took some time to develop chemistry. Born was getting overpowered by shorter, more muscular opponents during that span, but he refused to back down. He fell back on his experience as Lovellette's backup, during which the wide-shouldered redhead would toss him around like a rag doll at practices. On one such occasion, Lovellette threw such a violent elbow that he knocked Born through the swinging doors at Robinson Gym and out into the hallway; Phog told Big Clyde to hit the showers after that outburst. Born knew that if he could battle Lovellette for two years, he could hold up against anyone in the country—and, little by little, his skills began to blossom through the first few games of the 1952–53 season.

The surprising emergence of Born gave the Jayhawks sudden hope. The 6'9" junior, while playing a much different game than Lovellette had the previous year, grew into a go-to scorer who helped carry KU into the

1952–53 conference schedule with some momentum. By the end of the regular season, Born had scored a team-high 16.9 points per game while leading Kansas to a 19-6 record and Phog Allen's twenty-third conference title as coach of the Jayhawks.

Unranked during the preseason, the Jayhawks had risen all the way up to sixth in the country by the time the NCAA tournament began in March. But things looked pretty bleak after an opening-round win over Oklahoma City University, during which stars Born and Reich suffered injuries that left their conditions for the remainder of the tournament in question. After scoring a game-high 20 points in the win over Oklahoma City, Reich came down with a rib injury. Born was in a soft cast after hurting his thumb in the opening-round win. Making the task at hand even more difficult was a second-round opponent Allen knew all too well: Henry Iba's Oklahoma A&M Aggies, a team that had hammered the Jayhawks by 21 points just three weeks earlier.

The rivals traveled to Manhattan, Kansas, home of Kansas State University, for an NCAA tournament game that would give one team a ticket to the national semifinals. Iba's Aggies jumped out to a quick lead and were in control of the game until KU senior Dean Kelly erupted for 10 points in the final two minutes of the third quarter, propelling the Jayhawks to a 61–55 win.

For the second year in a row, Allen was headed to the semifinals of the NCAA tournament. Nobody, not even Allen himself, saw that one coming.

"I've never had as much pride and joy in a team as I've had in this one," Phog Allen said after the Jayhawks had earned their improbable return to the national semifinals. "We haven't got the size, we haven't got the power, but we've got the heart."

Allen may have been feeling a little déjà vu as he prepared for his third NCAA semifinal as a head coach. Not only had his Jayhawks played in what would later be known as the Final Four one year earlier, in Seattle, but the 1952–53 KU team would be heading back to Kansas City to be in a field that included Indiana—the same program that had knocked off Kansas in the 1940 national title game at Kansas City's Municipal Auditorium.

Before Allen could get his rematch with Indiana coach Branch McCracken, the Jayhawks had to figure out a way to knock off fourth-ranked

Washington and its All-America forward, Bob Houbregs. The 6'8" senior had scored 45 points in the Huskies' tournament opener and was leading all scorers heading into the NCAA semifinals.

In an effort to slow down Houbregs, Phog Allen came up with a unique plan that the Jayhawks performed to perfection. The veteran coach told his players to be in a defensive stance waiting for Houbregs just as he crossed the half-court line, whether or not he had the ball, and to fall down as soon as he made contact. The plan resulted in four first-half fouls on Houbregs, who earned his fifth early in the second half. Kansas rolled to a 79–53 victory using what the Associated Press called "a relentless pressing defense that turned the normally poised Westerners [from Washington] into a confused, fumbling lot." After the game, University of Washington coach Tippy Dye said that the Jayhawks "work harder at winning a basketball game than any team I've seen."

Unheralded at the beginning of the season, the 1952–53 Jayhawks had scratched their way into the program's second consecutive national championship game.

Top-ranked Indiana hammered LSU in the other semifinal to set up a rematch of the 1940 national title. For the second time in three national championship appearances, KU would be facing the Hoosiers in Kansas City while Coaches Phog Allen and Branch McCracken matched wits from their respective benches.

The Indiana coach had gotten the better of Allen in the 1940 game, and his Hoosiers were a significant favorite heading into the 1953 final. In the years in between, Phog Allen had driven up into the heart of Hoosier country and talked 1948 high school star Clyde Lovellette out of his commitment to Indiana. McCracken and Allen knew each other well, and there was no love lost heading into the national-title rematch.

Allen and the KU players woke up on the morning of the 1953 NCAA championship game to find out that, for the second year in a row, there was trouble with a Jayhawks big man. B.H. Born, who had not only carried Kansas into the tournament but had also done a pretty good Lovellette impersonation in bringing the Jayhawks all the way to the title game, awoke with a bad cough that he couldn't shake.

But Born showed up ready to play, and Allen led the team through its typical gameday routine before the 1953 national championship game. When it came time to gather in the locker room for a pregame speech on that March night inside Kansas City's Municipal Auditorium, Allen asked longtime team trainer Dean Nesmith to say a few words to the team. Pregame speeches before national championship games had become old hat to the veteran coach, and so Allen gave Nesmith the floor before this one.

In a championship game played in front of 10,500 fans, the Jayhawks and Hoosiers went toe-to-toe from the outset, with Indiana leading by 1 point after one quarter and the score tied at 41 heading into halftime. Allen followed his players into the locker room and was gathering his thoughts when he noticed Born gargling some alum water in an effort to relieve his sore throat. Allen was an advocate of alum water, to which he had introduced Born and many other players over the years, but he did not like the way Born was doing it. The coach grabbed the bottle and demonstrated the proper method of gargling, right there in the Municipal Auditorium locker room at halftime of the national championship game. He made sure his other players were listening as well, going through the demonstration as if he were standing at the front of a lecture hall. There was a proper method to holding your head and a right amount of water to take into your mouth. There was a right way and a wrong way to the actual gargling process, as Allen demonstrated while his sweat-drenched players looked on in shock. Outside the locker room, thousands of fans were anticipating the second half of a national title game that was deadlocked at the break. Seven minutes passed, and halftime was nearly over when assistant coach Dick Harp finally grabbed the chalk and began giving instructions on how the Jayhawks were going to play in the second half.

The game remained close after halftime, going right down to the final minutes. KU's Born, who had spent a good part of the game in foul trouble, was whistled for his fifth foul in the opening seconds of the fourth quarter, with Kansas clinging to a 53–52 lead. In effect, Born had fouled out of the game. But before the 6'9" star could leave the court, Phog Allen went ballistic in front of the KU bench, claiming it was only the fourth foul on Born. Allen went up and down media row, asking each reporter if he'd tallied five fouls on Born. No one had the guts to challenge Phog, and the official scorer changed the statistic book so that Born was allowed to stay in the game. That sent Indiana's McCracken into a fury of his own, as he stormed to the scorer's table to confront Allen and the game officials.

"We are your guests, and you have no right to take advantage of us this way," McCracken said, making reference to the game being played forty miles from the KU campus. "You have no right to rob us."

The point became moot minutes later, with 5:26 remaining in a game the Hoosiers were leading 62–61, when Born was called for a foul again—this time ending his night with 26 points. A 6'3" reserve named Jerry Alberts, who was averaging fewer than 2 points per game, came off the bench as a replacement and the Jayhawks had no answer for 6'10" Indiana star Don Schlundt, who continued to dominate in a game that was neck-and-neck down to the wire.

Indiana held a 68–65 lead with 2:30 remaining when the Hoosiers began to milk the clock, holding the ball in an effort to run as much time off as possible. But after Indiana's Charlie Kraak was whistled for a charging foul with 1:21 remaining and subsequently drew a technical foul for throwing the ball in the air in protest, Allen's Jayhawks had three free throws and a chance to tie the score. KU's Harold Patterson made only one of his two free throws, and then teammate Allen Kelley misfired on the technical-foul shot, leaving Indiana ahead by 2 points, at 68–66.

Kansas retained possession because of the technical foul, and senior Dean Kelley drove in for a score-tying layup with 1:05 remaining to send the pro-Jayhawk crowd at Municipal Auditorium into a frenzied state of anticipation. That tied the score at 68, and the Hoosiers tried to hold for the final shot. Indiana ran the clock down for what was likely to be a chance for Schlundt, who had a game-high 30 points, to attempt the game-winning shot. But Schlundt never got that opportunity. Instead of allowing the Hoosiers to maintain control as the final seconds ticked away, the Jayhawks took the outcome into their own hands. KU's Dean Kelley fouled Bob "Slick" Leonard with twenty-seven seconds remaining, sending the Indiana player to the free-throw line.

Leonard, who would later joke that the pressure led him to feel a warm liquid running down his leg, stepped to the free-throw line with sweat dripping off his forehead and the Kansas City fans screaming in an attempt to throw him off. Leonard dribbled the ball and let go, missing the first shot. The score remained deadlocked at 68 with twenty-seven seconds to go. The pro-Kansas crowd was getting raucous. Leonard stepped up to the line again and heaved his second free throw, which fell through the hoop for a 69–68 Hoosiers lead.

With Born sitting on the bench with five fouls, Phog Allen turned to second-leading scorer Allen Kelley, Dean's brother, to take the last shot. Kansas ran its offense and got Kelley the ball on the wing with five seconds remaining, but he couldn't get an open shot and passed the ball to a wide-open teammate. Jerry Alberts, the little-used reserve who was in the game because of Born's foul trouble, took the pass from Kelley while standing in the corner and heaved up the potential game-winning shot from eighteen feet away as the final seconds ticked off the clock.

Time slowed down as the ball arced through the air, its path on line with the rim as the eleven thousand plus fans took in a collective breath. On a team void of stars heading into the season, Alberts was the least likely of them all to play the part of hero. The 6'3" sophomore had made just 11 field goals during his twenty-six games over two seasons at KU, and he had not taken a single shot in the championship game before hoisting up his off-balance baseline buzzer-beater. Allen, the fiery, control-driven coach, got what he wanted in that his Jayhawks would take the final shot of the 1953 NCAA championship game, but this certainly wasn't the shot—or the man taking it—that Allen would have chosen. A second consecutive national title was on the line, and as Allen watched the ball begin its downward path toward the basket, he took in a breath and felt the taut muscles of his body tighten.

Wearing tortoise-shell glasses and a fancy suit with his trademark pocket square, Allen watched the ball bounce off the rim as the horn sounded. He had lost to Indiana's Branch McCracken in a championship game again. The 69–68 defeat left Allen just short of a second consecutive title, and yet the 1952–53 season may well have marked his finest coaching campaign. He had taken a group of inexperienced bench players, turned them into starters on one of the nation's best teams, and led them all the way to the NCAA title game.

KU's Born would earn the distinction of the tournament's first Most Outstanding Player from a losing team, but that came as little consolation to Allen and the Jayhawks. The heartbreaking 1-point loss left KU playing a constant game of what-if, and fans couldn't help but wonder how the season may have turned out with a healthy Charlie Hoag, or had Allen Kelley taken the final shot, or had B.H. Born still been in the game. In some ways, the 1-point loss to Indiana in the 1953 national championship was harder to take than the 18-point dismantling at the hands of the Hoosiers thirteen years earlier.

And yet it's entirely possible, and well within his character, that Phog Allen would have been able to brush aside the loss rather quickly. His forty-minute bus ride back to Lawrence may have even included a peaceful nap.

The 1953 national title game would also serve as the final game for little-used KU senior Dean Smith. After his freshman year at Kansas, the guard from Emporia, Kansas, had conferred with Phog Allen about going into the coaching profession but "Doc" tried to talk him out of it. Phog told Smith that the medical profession would be a much more sound decision for a college graduate—a conversation similar to the one that James Naismith had had with a young man named Forrest Allen almost five decades earlier.

Despite Phog Allen's suggestion that Dean Smith follow a different career path, coaching was in his blood. Smith joined Phog's coaching staff as an assistant in 1953–54, and that began a long, legendary coaching career for yet another Phog Allen protégé.

When it came time for Phog Allen and his coaching staff to turn their attention forward to the 1953–54 season, they saw light at the end of the tunnel on a team that would return three starters—led by Born. That a new state-of-the-art arena was one year away from completion only added to the excitement for the immediate future of Jayhawk basketball.

But the dreams of Allen making a third consecutive Final Four and rolling into the new fieldhouse on a high note suffered a quick dose of reality as his 1953–54 team lost its first two games of the season. The inside presence of Born and a crafty sophomore from Oklahoma named Dallas Dobbs helped the Jayhawks stay in the hunt for another NCAA tournament berth as KU scratched out a 16-4 record heading into the regular-season finale against Missouri. The same school that had dogged Phog Allen for much of his forty-eight years in coaching was standing between Kansas and a third consecutive NCAA tournament appearance. A win over the Tigers would give Phog Allen an outright Big Seven title and an automatic ticket to the NCAA tourney; a loss would create a tie and put the tournament bid at the mercy of a coin toss.

The Tigers were struggling through another season of mediocrity, which had become common for Missouri basketball in the 1950s. Mizzou was 10-10 overall and 5-6 in the Big Seven Conference, and when the Tigers played KU for the first time earlier that season, the Jayhawks breezed to a 17-point victory. That had marked the eighth consecutive time Kansas had beaten Missouri—a streak that delighted the KU coach with the Missouri birth certificate.

Phog Allen's team looked well on its way to another easy victory during the first half of the March 9 season finale. Missouri clawed away at the deficit to get within 4 points at halftime, trailing 35-31 when the teams went into the break. Allen undoubtedly pounded a fist against his palm while reminding his players that a narrow lead wasn't good enough and that KU basketball was far too proud to let the hated Missouri Tigers think they could compete with the mighty Jayhawks.

Whatever Allen said at halftime of that game did not resonate, as Missouri went out and blew the doors open in the third quarter, outscoring KU 27-15 on the way to taking an 8-point lead. Kansas never got closer than 5 points in the fourth quarter as the Tigers jogged away with a 76-67 victory. Allen called it "the greatest game a Missouri team has played us in 20 years" and was significantly less complimentary of his own team's effort.

"They were as sharp as a razor's edge, freshly honed," he said of the Tigers, "and we were as dull as a worn-out sword with a nicked blade— neither ready nor aggressive."

Missouri's first win over the Jayhawks in eight meetings was a crushing blow to Allen, so much so that he didn't even have interest in taking part in a coin toss with Colorado the following day to determine which school would represent the Big Seven Conference in the NCAA tournament. Allen walked into the office of the Big Seven secretary moments before the coin toss and announced to a small gathering that included Colorado coach H. B. Lee, a few conference officials, and at least one newspaper reporter, "I hope Colorado wins."

On that front, Allen got his wish. The Buffaloes won the coin toss, sending Colorado to the NCAAs for the first time in eight years, while the Jayhawks' season came to an unceremonious end. Allen shrugged at the results of the coin toss, telling reporters, "It'll do [Colorado] good to get into the [tournament]. Now, it wouldn't be anything new to us. Besides, we're in bad shape."

Back in Lawrence, KU basketball fans shed tears. Senior B.H. Born was heartbroken as well, telling the *Journal World*, "We all knew there was an outside chance we'd still go to the NCAA. But we didn't have much hope of winning. For some reason, it hit us all about the same. You've never seen guys as low as we [were] after that Missouri game."

The *Journal World* also ran a column by a writer named Bill Mayer, who criticized Allen for his lack of support for his team at the coin toss. Mayer was covering the team banquet a few days later when Allen unleashed on him, calling the columnist a "pusillanimous, pencil-pushing, purple pissant." Without missing a beat, Mayer asked, "Why purple?" That drew a laugh from everyone within earshot, including Allen, and the tension of the moment eased.

The 1953–54 Jayhawks saw their two-year run of NCAA title games come to an end, but Phog Allen had earned a share of his twenty-fourth conference title in thirty-seven years at KU. He was also sixty-eight years old, two years away from the mandatory retirement age for university employees in the state of Kansas. Time may have been running out on his coaching career, but Allen was about to get some good news. Not only was the state going to allow him to coach past the age of seventy, but he was going to be doing it in an arena that would bear his name.

19

The King Gets His Castle

The hallway was an echo. Deep in the underbelly of the basketball palace that was finally open to the public, the king's shoes tapped along the corridors while he adjusted his tie. The buzz of activity overhead rattled the walls around him. The building was shaking with anticipation.

The game was still forty minutes from tip-off, and yet the energy was already palpable down here, beneath all the action. He was alone in this tunnel, able to take in the peacefulness for a few precious moments before the flood gates would open and the magical night would overwhelm his senses.

Soon enough, he would be standing before his players, looking each one in the eye and seeing more than just the faces of the fifteen men in uniform. In that moment, he would see the faces of so many other boys who had worn the KU cloth. Endacott and Black. Ackerman and Johnson. Mitt and Bobby. Miller and Engleman. Schnellbacher and Evans. Lovellette and Hougland. There had been so many of them over the years, and Phog Allen had loved each and every one like kin. Sometimes he had a strange way of showing it, but turning boys into men was by no means a gentle science.

A lump formed in his throat just thinking about it as the king traipsed along the corridor, his shoe-bottoms clacking through the peacefulness. The emotions were already overcoming him; there was no way the king could lead his men like this.

He basked in his final moment of peace, his shoes echoing along the halls of history. He was at one with the arena down here, soaking in these final seconds before sharing his night with seventeen thousand fans in the wide-open, incredibly spacious arena, before he would get swallowed up in the indoor galaxy that was so vast it made the basketball court tiny by comparison.

The doorway a few steps away seemed to pull him toward the pounding drum of pre-celebration. He could hear now that they were calling his name.

Phog Allen's final steps echoed within the walls of the hallway until he reached out and took hold of the door handle. The anticipation of history propelled him as he pulled the doors open. The energy washed over him like a dust storm.

Brick by brick by brick, Phog Allen had spent the first half of the twentieth century building the game of basketball from its roots as an indoor recreation to a popular American sport to an international pastime, his fingerprints left on every floor of its high-rise structure. Allen had been such a huge part of the game for so long of a time that he had become almost forgotten by his continuous existence, much like a cornerstone concealed by glitzy furniture. His accomplishments didn't seem to mean as much anymore, even to those few remaining people who remembered his early impact on the game.

His molding of the University of Kansas basketball program was similarly obscured by time, and it took a national title and a role in the 1952 Olympics for Allen to remind people of just how important he was and had been. He had earned a new nickname, perhaps the most telling of all, as reporters began referring to Phog Allen as "Mr. Basketball."

By the fall of 1954, Allen's legacy was cemented in history, despite what had been considered a down year by typical KU standards—his 16-4 Jayhawks had missed out on the 1953–54 NCAA tournament after losing a coin toss. His mentor, James Naismith, had been gone for fifteen years but had not been forgotten, as men like Allen had taken his sport to unforeseen heights. The sport of basketball had grown into a foundation of American culture, and the five-year-old National Basketball Association had recently consolidated from seventeen teams to eleven, setting the stage for an organization that would steadily rise over the next decade and become one of the three largest professional leagues in the United States by the end of the twentieth century. The annual NCAA championship game was about to be carried on live national television for the first time—in many ways the unofficial beginning of March Madness.

Phog Allen had undeniably become the most famous of Naismith's former players by climbing the coaching ladder to take his place as the dean of college basketball coaches. Through it all, he was constantly looking for ways to honor his mentor and improve the visibility of Dr. Naismith's name. His latest brainchild was to get Naismith's name on the basketball Hall of Fame, which was still in the planning stages and was five years from inducting its inaugural class.

Allen went on a feverish letter-writing campaign with basketball officials in an effort to honor the longtime KU faculty member on the building that would eventually be erected not far from the Springfield, Massachusetts, YMCA where Naismith had instructed the janitor, Mr. Stebbins, to attach peach baskets to the balcony at either end of the gym.

In one exchange with former KU player John Bunn, who was by then chairman of the Hall of Fame committee, Phog Allen showed off his command of the language, his medical knowledge, and his sense of humor when he wrote, "Your nice letter of February 24 came to me and I assure you that it caused a temporary erythema and a calorific effulgence of the physiognomy, etiologized by one's perceptiveness of the sensorium. . . . In other words, my face is red."

By the time the Naismith Hall of Fame was unveiled five years later, Phog Allen would be bursting with pride. The naming of the institution would serve as another way of keeping the Naismith name alive in the years after his death.

Most of the great men and women to make imprints in their chosen fields are honored posthumously. Eulogies and obituaries and events bearing the names of great leaders come at a time when those being honored are no longer around to hear the praise being lathered upon their legacy. Forrest "Phog" Allen, also known as Mr. Basketball, was one of those rare men who got to attend his own dedication when he became the first person in the history of the University of Kansas to have a building named after him while still alive.

In October 1951, workers from Topeka-based Bennett Construction had broken ground on a new, more modern, $2.5 million arena that was meant to be the envy of college basketball. The structure was designed to host more fans than Kansas State's new Ahearn Field House and to be more state-of-the-art than Missouri's twenty-year-old Brewer Fieldhouse. It was also built to give KU the largest arena in the Midwest. With a proposed seat count of seventeen thousand and rising three stories high, the Jayhawks' new fieldhouse was supposed to bring Kansas basketball into a new era. KU's facility was designed to bring fans closer to the action, at Phog Allen's request, as he believed that the courtside seating in a massive arena could help inspire the home team and distract the visitors—good for at least two or three victories a year, Allen claimed.

The new basketball arena was to be placed upon a field on the southernmost end of KU's main campus, just down the hill from Hoch Auditorium. The facility was, from a planning standpoint, a quarter century in the making; Allen had first floated the idea of a new basketball arena in 1927—just before the Great Depression hit. By the end of 1949, the University of Kansas had secured $750,000 in state money to build a new arena, but it would take another two years for the state legislature to add the other $1.5 million in grant money necessary to get it built.

The rising price of steel during the Korean War put the project on hold for more than a year before planners found a loophole in the federal laws of that era. At a time when the government was offering a significant discount on steel for structures meant to hold weaponry, KU deftly added an armory to its structure just so the school could meet budget. The proposed venue was then presented as an arena for basketball, track, and ROTC training.

The shell of the structure would measure 344 feet by 254 feet, and construction would require 650,000 bricks, 1,624 tons of stone, more than 5,000 Haydite lightweight blocks, 245,000 feet of lumber for the roof, and 4,500 gallons of paint. The final cost of the facility was $2,613,167.

In the fall of 1954, with the school still a few weeks away from opening its new fieldhouse for the latter part of 1954–55 season, KU officials were ready to announce what the structure would be called. The Kansas basketball team was coming off of two NCAA championship game appearances in a span of three years and had already won its first two games of the 1954–55 season when school officials announced before a December 17, 1954, game against Rice that the new arena would be named for the Jayhawks' presiding basketball coach.

Allen Fieldhouse was about to make its debut, along a street that had, a few weeks earlier, been renamed Naismith Drive.

Upon learning that the new fieldhouse would bear his name, Allen told reporters, "In this hour of great recognition of my services to the University of Kansas, I feel very unworthy and deeply grateful. No one can realize my feelings. I am just benumbed and overwhelmed."

The opening of the arena was twice delayed by construction setbacks, eventually forcing the Jayhawks to swap a February 12 home game against Kansas State for a March 1 game at Manhattan. The former game was to be played at Kansas State University, making the March 1 home game against the Wildcats the official opening of Allen Fieldhouse.

After a 4-0 start to the season, the 1954–55 Jayhawks had fallen on hard times leading up to the anticipated opening of the fieldhouse. The graduation of star B.H. Born left KU scrambling for an inside presence, the team had no senior leadership, and the season quickly spiraled out of control. A pair of three-game losing streaks left KU staring at a .500 record heading into the March 1 home game against Kansas State, and the Jayhawks couldn't even find a way to send out Hoch Auditorium on a winning note—losing 66–55 to Nebraska in the final game ever played in that venue.

With the much-anticipated facility in place, the new question surrounding the KU basketball team was how long the man for which Allen Fieldhouse was named would be allowed to coach in it. Phog Allen's seventieth birthday was fast approaching in November 1955, at the start of the following basketball season, and by late January of that year there were still plenty of questions regarding the future of Phog. Kansas state law required government employees, which included those working at a public university, to retire by the age of seventy, meaning Allen's final days as KU basketball coach could very well come in a matter of months—perhaps making 1954–55 his swan song. Almost twenty years earlier, the state had given James Naismith an extension, and there was a motion in place for Phog Allen to receive the same treatment.

Allen was optimistic about his future, especially after meeting with House of Representatives member Karl Brueck on February 2, 1955—nine months before his seventieth birthday. Brueck and Allen came up with a plan that could extend Allen's career as a coach, even if that meant giving up his position as a KU professor. Brueck had collected seventy House of Representatives signatures on a petition proposing that the age seventy rule be waived for Phog Allen. As Brueck told the *Lawrence Journal World*, "there's nothing that says a coach can't stay on the job, or a man can't remain in athletics past 70 years of age."

On February 7, 1955, the Kansas House of Representatives announced that it would adopt a provision that would allow Phog Allen to remain coach beyond his November birthday. The house reformed the mandatory retirement rule to give Allen three more years of coaching, meaning he could have an opportunity to lead the Jayhawks into the late 1950s—what turned out to be a significant moment in KU basketball history because at the time Allen was in the process of recruiting the best high school player of all time.

The news of the legislature's retirement extension capped off a headline-filled 1954–55 season, during which the Jayhawks were struggling on the court but were about to move into their new digs at Allen Fieldhouse. There appeared to be bright things on the horizon for Phog Allen and the KU basketball program. Allen was bursting with pride.

"The action of the Legislature of our great state coupled with my greatest honor in the naming of the Allen Fieldhouse makes me most happy," he said. "My ambition has always been to lead a useful life. This I intend to do always to the utmost of my ability. Any Kansan so recognized would be justly proud."

But Allen still had one more hurdle to clear. While he was assured of finishing the current season and leading the Jayhawks again through the entirety of the 1955-56 campaign the following year, the university's board of regents would have the final say on whether to grant Allen an extension and allow him to keep coaching beyond that. The legislature's provision would officially allow him to coach past his seventieth birthday and right up until the end of the academic year on June 1, 1956, but the following two years were now in the hands of the KU board of regents—and Allen had every reason to believe that he'd have the backing of KU chancellor Frank Murphy and the regents. He had both the energy and the recent run of success to warrant keeping his job. Just nine months away from his seventieth birthday, Allen was as passionate about the game as ever and was already thinking about how to get his program back on track toward another national championship run in the near future.

What was abundantly clear was that the 1954–55 team would not be bringing home any trophies. By the time the opening of Allen Fieldhouse arrived for the March 1 game against rival Kansas State, the Jayhawks were 9-9 and well out of the race for the Big Seven Conference title. Less than two years removed from back-to-back national championship appearances, the KU basketball program already knew it would be missing out on the NCAA tournament for the second consecutive season.

And yet that did little to dampen the celebration for the opening of the new fieldhouse. More than one hundred former KU lettermen showed up for the first game at the venue, a matchup that pitted Allen's struggling Jayhawks against a mediocre K-State team that came into the night with an 11-9 record under second-year coach Tex Winter. A crowd of 17,228 people packed into the arena for the game and a halftime ceremony that would celebrate one of the most influential men in university history.

Phog Allen showed up forty minutes before tip-off, wearing a tweed, pinstripe coat and an expensive tie, and when the fans inside the new fieldhouse first laid eyes on him he was greeted with a rousing ovation. Allen posed for a few photographs and made his way to the KU bench as fans stood and continued to shower him with appreciation. Without any forewarning, Allen walked up to KU assistant Dick Harp and effectively handed over the reins for the evening.

"I don't want to be in a position of asking the boys to do anything special for me," he told Harp. "If they win, I want them to do so for the University. I'll be present but absent at the same time. I'll be in the dressing room before the game and as soon as I can at halftime, after the dedication. But I'm not talking [to the team]. It's up to you, Dick."

As the coaches and players made their way back to the locker room, Allen asked longtime KU trainer Dean Nesmith whether he had any desire to help out Harp with the pregame speech.

"No, Doc," Nesmith replied. "The last time I talked we got beat by Indiana in the NCAA finals [in 1953]. I don't want to louse up anything this evening. It's too important to us all."

Inside the locker room a few minutes later, Allen and Nesmith watched Harp write the names of the starters on the chalkboard, along with their defensive assignments, doing his best to fill Phog's shoes. Harp then turned and faced the 1954–55 Jayhawks with chalk still in hand. He reminded the players how privileged they were to be wearing KU colors, especially on a historic night like this.

"Remember this," he said. "You want to do well tonight for a lot of reasons—for the University, your families, your friends, our followers and even yourselves." Harp's voice began to crack, his words becoming a whisper as he choked back tears and added, "But most of all, we have to win tonight for Doc."

The Jayhawks then ran out and stormed to an 11-point halftime lead over the hated Kansas State Wildcats as Allen watched proudly from a chair to Harp's left. Phog never really felt like his voice was that important on game days—by the time the opposition showed up, his KU teams should be so well-drilled that they could run his system by rote—so watching in silence was easier than one might expect. The tired players jogged off the court at the end of the first half, with Harp and Nesmith trailing, and Phog Allen remained on the court as the lights went down. In the darkness of the stands, no one got up from his or her seat for the customary halftime break. The lit hallways of the concourse remained empty; as the *Lawrence Journal World* newspaper would report the next day, "several thousand 'hot dogs' last night were unsold 'cold dogs' this morning."

A bright light came on above the main court, illuminating the playing surface as several KU students, many of them from other countries, came onto the floor bearing flags to symbolize the international growth of the game. The halftime show was beginning. Students dribbling basketballs and carrying javelins flowed onto the court, along with an ROTC troop going through military drills. When the rhythmic movement stopped, an actor portraying Dr. James Naismith took the court and answered questions as part of a faux interview that took the audience through a choreographed re-creation of the game's beginnings: from the Springfield YMCA gym to the first game played at the university to Forrest Allen as a young Jayhawks player and the infamous "You can't coach basketball" conversation Allen would have with Dr. Naismith. The pageant held the audience captive, and they stayed that way when the lights went down again and the first few notes of a musical march began to play inside the spacious arena. The march, which was called "Mr. Basketball" and had been written by a KU professor named Russell Wiley, was played over the speakers as the group of about one hundred former basketball lettermen quietly began to gather on either side of the court.

Phog Allen sat and watched in silence, his wife, Bessie, at his side. The family's five grown children were in the arena as well, some with children of their own, as a small stage was rolled onto the center of the court. KU chancellor Frank Murphy took the podium first, elaborating on the virtues of the new facility Allen had helped to create. Kansas governor Fred Hall spoke next, followed by a local publisher named Oscar Stauffer, who also served as chairman of the board of regents. Stauffer read a statement, saying, "By unanimous vote, the Regents have named this Fieldhouse in honor of a great Kansan, an outstanding coach and a fine gentleman."

Murphy then took the microphone again, nodding toward Bessie Allen, sitting faithfully by her husband's side, and said, "For just about every special occasion at the University, there has to be a queen, and tonight is no exception. Never has there been a more lovely and attractive regent to grace the campus than tonight's queen, Mrs. Forrest C. Allen."

With these words, Phog Allen felt the tears well up in his eyes. Through all the journeys and battles and heartbreak, through the highs and the lows, on and off the court, Bessie was the one person who was always there for him. A night like this simply wouldn't be complete without her.

Then Phog stepped up to the podium, and the crowd began showering him with applause, rising to their feet in unison as the sixty-nine-year-old coach took in his second standing ovation of the evening. By this point in his legendary career, Allen had won over the masses at the school where he had spent thirty-six of his forty-two years as a basketball coach. The recent back-to-back appearances in NCAA tournament title games had pushed all of the ups and downs of his earlier tenure into the shadows of the past. This night would be about celebrating his legacy and all that Phog Allen had done for the university. Since he had returned to the school as athletic director thirty-six years earlier, KU had grown by leaps and bounds, with nine student-housing facilities and two academic departments being added during his tenure, and Allen had been a huge part of the fundraising over the years. What he had done for the basketball program, and for the athletic department, was only a part of what he'd meant to the university.

When the fans quieted down, Phog Allen addressed them with a joke about how the team's three-game losing streak heading into the K-State game nearly prevented the old coach from making it to the dedication.

"I began to think maybe this is it," he told the crowd. "Now the university can have the dedication of the fieldhouse without breaking the long-standing tradition of no living person having a major university building named after him."

He then spoke of Dr. James Naismith and expressed his gratitude to the man for creating such a wonderful sport: "The game he invented has spread over the entire world and has made clean minds and healthier bodies."

Eloquent, engaging, and filled with humility, Allen was brief in his comments, closing with, "I've been a fortunate coach, and I accept the fieldhouse as a tribute to all the men—past, present and future—of the university."

Allen was then presented with the keys to a new Cadillac, purchased through donations from alumni, before the KU band broke into "Auld Lang Syne" as the man of the hour descended the podium and the stage was taken off the court. A third standing ovation continued as Allen walked off the floor, through the tunnel, and into the Kansas locker room. Harp was just finishing up with some halftime comments as the thirty-five-minute ceremony came to a close, and Allen stood quietly in the shadows before offering his players a soft "go get 'em" to conclude the halftime. The players stood and walked past Allen, out onto the floor, where they continued to control Kansas State on the way to a 77–67 victory to close out the season.

After the victory, a drained Phog Allen told reporters, "They did a marvelous job, a job any coach could be proud of—fieldhouse dedication or not. I'm proud of many things this night, but I'm proudest, I think, of the way my boys came though after losing three in a row."

The 1954–55 Jayhawks would go on to split their final two games and finish the season with an unremarkable record of 11-10, but Phog Allen had reason for optimism in that his young team had gained a year of experience.

At the conclusion of the season, Allen received another honor when he was chosen to speak at the annual NABC luncheon during the weekend of the NCAA title game. Allen made the short jaunt to Kansas City, where he opened his speech by telling a story of a monarch who once offered a prize to the subject who created the greatest and most everlasting statement. The winner, Phog said, was the phrase "This, too, shall pass away."

He also displayed his dry, deadpan humor when he made a crack about dentistry early in the address. "By strengthening ammoniated toothpowder in some brassieres," Allen said, "they have cut down tooth decay to an alarming degree."

That got a good laugh out of the audience, but Allen wasn't there to do a standup routine. He went on to recall the greatest moment of his youth, the day when his Kansas City Athletic Club team beat the Buffalo Germans. Allen recited the names of some of the Germans players, whom he had hosted at a 1942 KU game against St. Bonaventure in Buffalo. Allen went on to devote most of his speech to a variety of subjects that had become points of concern over the years, from the growing popularity of professional sports to the dangers of gambling to the need for administrators to protect the student-athletes from the expanding capitalism of college athletics.

"We are really responsible for the fact that we have gone big time in college athletics," Phog Allen said on that day in March 1955. "We, by our own acts, have professionalized the college player."

The game was certainly changing around him, and Phog Allen saw up close just how different the sport had become when he attended the 1955 NCAA final and watched a 6'9" star named Bill Russell lead the University of San Francisco to its first national title. As Russell used his long arms and long, lean frame to dominate that game, Allen deadpanned, "I'm for the 20-foot baskets."

Finding another Bill Russell would be a next-to-impossible task. But Allen was about to unearth someone who might be even better.

20

The Biggest Fish

The giant was inconsolable. Not once during the entire recruiting process had the 6'11" young man from Philly experienced any kind of racism in this part of the country, and now that he was on his way to the University of Kansas for his freshman year, late at night and just a few miles from the KU campus, he was being turned away at a "white-only" restaurant. Wilt Chamberlain, eighteen years old and black, was livid.

He started screaming and hollering, and the only thing that kept him from tearing the restaurant apart was the presence of his friend Doug, who pushed Wilt away from the doors and back toward his car. Doug had graduated with Chamberlain from Overbrook High School and was accompanying him on his drive to KU, where they would both be freshmen.

Doug was something else as well—he was white. He couldn't possibly understand. They weren't telling Doug he couldn't eat there; they were telling Chamberlain. Only Chamberlain.

This part of the country wasn't supposed to be this way. He'd been assured of it. Phog Allen, Frank Murphy, Dowdal Davis—they'd all promised him that this part of the country wasn't going to be this way. Had Coach Allen deceived him?

Wilt Chamberlain returned to his 1949 Buick, resigned to turning it around. Screw Kansas and its backwater hicks; he was going back to Philadelphia.

Wilt Chamberlain was six feet tall as an awkward ten-year-old kid, and he grew into a lanky, shy teenager with a stutter. He couldn't have stuck out from the crowd more if he'd had a spotlight attached to his forehead, and the big kid was both self-conscious and incredibly gawky for much of his teenage years. But by the time Phog Allen had started recruiting the 6'11" Philadelphia high school basketball star in the mid-1950s, Wilt Chamberlain had become a giant in the sport in more ways than one. He was big in both size and fame, and Wilt the Stilt knew it. Whatever shyness Chamberlain had felt in the ever-growing spotlight was no longer a part of him as he became a national sports star.

Chamberlain grew up in a modest West Philadelphia neighborhood that was made up mostly of Jews and Italians, and in a short time he had risen—literally—into national consciousness because of his unique combination of size and athleticism. Chamberlain had become a Bunyanesque figure who transcended national basketball recruiting in an era when McDonald's All-Americans and five-star basketball camps were still decades away. Everyone knew about The Stilt—a nickname he never liked but came to tolerate.

The stories surrounding Chamberlain's rise were almost as plentiful as his fans, from the 31-points-per-game scoring average he carried through his sophomore year of high school to the three-game stretch during his senior year that saw Chamberlain amass an incredible 242 points. In between, there was a legendary summer game in which the prep star scored 25 points while playing against former KU center B.H. Born—the 6'9" All-American who had been named Most Outstanding Player from the Final Four one year earlier. Born scored just 10 points in the summer matchup, 15 fewer than Chamberlain had, even though the kid from Philly hadn't yet started his senior year *of high school*.

Seeing the giant from West Philadelphia up close had such a huge impact on Born that he realized he might not want to face players that big in the National Basketball Association and instead decided to play at the AAU level. He also made a decision that his alma mater—the University of Kansas—absolutely had to pull out all the stops to get Chamberlain, and he told Phog Allen as much.

Allen, whose first knowledge of Wilton Norman Chamberlain came when KU sports information director Don Pierce showed him a photo-graph of the impressive physical specimen, took Born's advice and sent his son Mitt out east for a closer look. Mitt Allen and a friend named Guy Stanley traveled to the Catskills, where Chamberlain was working as a hotel porter and playing basketball in a prestigious summer league. Upon seeing Wilt up close, Mitt returned to Lawrence with two words of advice for his father: "Get busy."

Getting one of the tallest, and best, high school players in history to make the 1,200-mile trip from the big city of Philadelphia to the comparatively small-town landscape of Lawrence, Kansas, would be no easy task, but Allen had a few factors working in his favor as Chamberlain whittled down his list of schools. The racial gap in the Deep South was so concerning that Chamberlain wasn't going to attend any school in that part of the country. The West Coast wasn't even a consideration for basketball stars back in those days, as John Wooden's UCLA teams were just beginning their rise to prominence. Chamberlain's hometown of Philadelphia had plenty of college basketball history, but the Overbrook High School star was said to be looking for a new city—and places like New York City and New England were also deemed too close to home. Additionally, there was a National Basketball Association territorial draft for college players back then, which meant Chamberlain could be locked into playing for a particular professional team if he decided to play college ball within fifty miles of a big city that had an NBA team.

So Chamberlain's scope narrowed to the Midwest, where schools like Indiana (said to be the early favorite), Illinois, Michigan, Michigan State, Cincinnati, and Northwestern were on his list. There was also the bas-ketball power 1,200 miles away in Lawrence, Kansas, where the program boasted three national titles and a legendary coach who was, at the same time Chamberlain was being recruited, approaching the age of seventy but showing no evidence of slowing down.

Allen also gained a significant advantage after the passing of a momen-tous federal law on May 17, 1954, at the tail end of Chamberlain's junior year of high school. *Brown vs. Board of Education* was based on a class-action lawsuit filed against the Topeka board of education three years earlier, and the 1954 ruling effectively ended segregation in schools. Because the case was rooted in the Jayhawks' backyard, it painted Kansas as a progressive state with very little racial tension—a perception that was only partially true.

KU chancellor Frank Murphy was as eager for the school to land Chamberlain as anyone, and not just because it would give the university a nationally ranked basketball team for the foreseeable future. Murphy was also hoping that a high-profile African American would help break down the racial barriers that still existed in the state, and Chamberlain was just the kind of role model who could start the process. What Jackie Robinson did for baseball, Murphy theorized, perhaps Chamberlain could do for KU and the surrounding area.

In an effort to lure Chamberlain to Lawrence, Allen and Murphy enlisted the help of several local leaders—many of whom were, by careful design, African American. A man named Dowdal Davis, who was editor of an African American newspaper called the *Kansas City Call*, accompanied Allen on a visit to Philadelphia to meet with Chamberlain and his family. Lloyd Kerford, a wealthy quarry owner from Atchison, Kansas, also made the trip, adding another influential African American to Phog Allen's pitch team. Naturally, Allen won over Chamberlain's mother during the visit.

Allen and Chamberlain made for an unlikely pairing, and not just because one was a white man approaching retirement age at a small-town college and the other was a vibrant, young, 6'11" African American teenager from Philly. It was Allen who had, as a rising young basketball coach, written a 1935 essay entitled "Dunking Isn't Basket Ball" and who had later lobbied for the basket to be raised twenty-four inches to a height of twelve feet in an attempt to take the dunk out of the game. "Dunking," Allen once wrote in a 1937 book, "does not display basketball skill—only height advantage."

And yet Allen was doing everything in his power to bring the most dominant dunker in basketball history to Lawrence. When this discrepancy was brought up to Allen during the Chamberlain recruiting process, the KU coach was said to have cracked, "Twelve-foot baskets? What are you talking about? I've developed amnesia."

Having Maurice King, the first KU starter of African American descent, in the starting lineup further painted the Jayhawks as a colorblind program—even though he was only the second African American to ever play basketball at KU. But Allen had precedence in his dealing with black students, and his reputation in race relations had both highs and lows.

As an administrator, Allen was known to have supported the university's unwritten ban on African American athletes in the late 1920s, and when the school was considering a change in the policy a few years later, he encouraged black students to only go out for track because "that didn't require as much body contact as basketball."

Allen's own feelings about race were rarely discussed publicly during his years as a basketball coach, but he did, on occasion, stick up for black students. A story passed down from the 1930s involved Allen in his role as a physical education instructor holding classes at the KU pool. An African American student named Willard Smith, pressed by his roommates to challenge the pool's unwritten "whites only" policy, decided to go for a swim on a day when Allen happened to be teaching swim classes. At least one student got out of the pool when Smith jumped in, and Allen offered some instruction while holding the young man's back in an effort to teach him how to float. Upon realizing that several white students were standing around the pool deck in shock, Allen held out his hands and arms to them and said something to the effect of "Look, none of the black comes off. So get in the pool!"

Allen was also instrumental in the development of an African American student named John McClendon, who arrived on campus in 1935 and was quickly taken under the wing of Dr. James Naismith. McClendon was not on the basketball team but was interested enough in the sport that Allen helped Naismith tutor him on the game during McClendon's years as a physical education major at KU. McClendon went on to become the first African American coach in the history of professional basketball. He also broke down some barriers while at KU, the most notable of which came when McClendon helped to desegregate the public pool.

Like Willard Smith, McClendon challenged the university's white-only policy at the university swimming pool, going as far as to meet with Allen about the issue. Allen initially encouraged McClendon to back down, telling him he would be seen as a troublemaker on campus. But McClendon was able to strike a deal: if Allen opened up the pool to black students for two weeks, and no problems surfaced, the segregation would be lifted for good.

Unbeknownst to Allen, McClendon then told his fellow minority students to stay away from the pool for two weeks. Naturally, no problems emerged, and Allen stuck to his word: he opened the pool to all students. (Upon learning of McClendon's ruse, Phog called him a "smart aleck" but allowed the pool to be available to blacks and whites alike.)

In the decades that followed, McClendon would not remember Allen having too many close friends of color but tried to justify it in an interview with *Kansas Alumni Magazine*, saying, "He was just a product of the system. If he tried to change it, he'd have lost his job." The camaraderie that existed between Allen and the black community by the 1950s was a huge part of the recruitment of Chamberlain, who had grown up in a predominantly white section of Philadelphia and had very little experience with racism.

Phog Allen went into a full-court press in his efforts to land Chamberlain, who could break down some racial barriers, make a mockery of the ten-foot baskets, and single-handedly put the Jayhawks back in contention for NCAA titles. Perhaps the high-profile recruit could also give the aging coach some leverage in his efforts to sway the KU board of regents to waive its retirement rule.

In the end, all the hard work was worth it, as Phog Allen convinced the rising star to play for the Jayhawks. Chamberlain's relationship with the aging KU basketball coach was a big reason for his decision, and Allen's bold recruiting efforts were rewarded with a commitment from the greatest high school player in history.

Upon hearing of Chamberlain's decision to attend KU, Phog Allen wise-cracked, "That's wonderful news. I hope he'll come out for the team."

The oft-chronicled recruiting war for Chamberlain began with two hundred universities and eventually led the 6'11" star to Lawrence. Besides his relationship with Allen, there may have been other enticements as well. Thirty years later, in an interview with the Associated Press, Chamberlain would assert that he was paid four thousand dollars by wealthy KU boosters. In a 2004 biography called *Wilt: Larger Than Life*, Chamberlain's former high school coach intimated that his star player may have received some type of payment for signing with Kansas.

"There were incentives," former Overbrook High School coach Cecil Mosenson was quoted as saying in the 2004 book, which was published well after Allen's death. "I'm not going to say there weren't incentives."

The idea of Chamberlain getting "incentives" had been a hot topic in the late 1950s, after the big kid from Philadelphia had moved on to the NBA, and Phog Allen vehemently denied any illegal recruiting tactics. Even after an NCAA investigation discovered in 1960 that Chamberlain had essentially traded in his 1949 Buick for a new Oldsmobile, with three KU boosters covering the costs, Allen disparaged the credibility of the report and blasted the NCAA and its officials.

Chamberlain's decision to attend KU came under nationwide scrutiny, and even Wilt himself had some early second thoughts. Despite all the work to erase the racial tensions in and around Lawrence, one of Chamberlain's first experiences leading up to his arrival in the fall of 1955 nearly sent him running back to Philadelphia.

Chamberlain and high school teammate Doug Leaman, a white man and marginal player who had been recruited to help lure Wilt the Stilt to KU, had driven all the way from Philadelphia in Chamberlain's '49 Buick when they stopped for dinner at a restaurant just across the Kansas border. In the 2004 biography on Chamberlain, Leaman recounted that the man behind the counter told him, "We don't serve Negroes, but you can sit in the back room."

The incident surprised Chamberlain as much as it infuriated him. The Kansas he'd seen during the recruiting process, which had been carefully choreographed by Phog Allen and KU officials to be without any sign of racism, was nothing like this. Chamberlain was so enraged that he considered going back to Philadelphia but decided instead to drive to Phog Allen's house and bang on his door in the late hours. Allen invited Chamberlain and Leaman into his house and ordered out for hamburgers.

Chamberlain later remembered in his 1973 autobiography,

Well, I found out later why he was so eager to have someone else get the hamburgers for me; even the greasy spoon was segregated, and he knew if I found that out, I'd probably say, "[Expletive] Kansas," and head back to Philadelphia before the first day of classes. It took me a week to realize the whole area around Lawrence, except for one black section of Kansas City, was infested with segregation.

As Chamberlain and Leaman munched on hamburgers that night, Allen talked him off the ledge, assuring Chamberlain that his skin color would never again be an issue in Lawrence. To back up his promise, Allen enlisted the help of his son Milton "Mitt" Allen, a Lawrence attorney who let it be known to every business owner in town that any exclusion based on race would be met with legal action.

According to Chamberlain's biography, Mitt Allen told him, "Look, Wilt, you just go wherever you want. You just sit down in those restaurants and don't leave until they serve you."

It was enough to convince Chamberlain to stick around and honor his commitment to the Jayhawks. In a way, Phog Allen had had to recruit Chamberlain twice: once to attend the University of Kansas, and again to stay there.

As Doug Leaman would later write in a 2006 book, "if it wasn't for coach Allen's fatherly advice, shrewd dealings with a future All-American and his intuitive understanding of racial issues facing the Midwest, Chamberlain would have called it quits. But Wilt respected Phog Allen more than any other coach in the nation, and to his credit, Dippy [Wilt's high school nickname] stayed on."

Chamberlain would remain on Kansas soil, and he would eventually go on to single-handedly change the game of basketball with his unfair combination of size, upper-body strength, and sheer athleticism. He would add two more inches to his already-imposing frame and would go on to become a two-time All-American, Final Four Most Outstanding Player, thirteen-time NBA All-Star, two-time NBA champion, and the most prolific scorer basketball had ever seen.

The only thing that Chamberlain didn't do was play a game for Phog Allen.

The man who spearheaded the effort to land the biggest recruit in the first century of college basketball didn't even get to stick around long enough to coach him. Little did Phog Allen know when Chamberlain arrived on campus in the fall of 1955 that his coaching career was soon to come to a sudden end.

21

Wanting One More Year

The end was near. To Phog Allen, this was what it was like to be stuck on an airplane, hundreds of miles above the ground, your sweaty hands gripping the rails but not really holding on to anything at all. That uncontrolled sense of falling from the sky, that's what scared Allen more than anything in the world, and that's how his career as a basketball coach felt as the 1956 NCAA basketball tournament began without his Kansas Jayhawks.

The talk for so long had been that Mr. Basketball might be coaching his last game, and now that the 1955-56 season finale was in the books, that decision was totally out of his control. He'd gotten assurances from KU chancellor Frank Murphy and landed all-everything recruit Wilt Chamberlain, and now there was nothing for Allen to do but sit and wait.

The wait felt like a freefall from bluer skies.

He had made plenty of allies over the years, but had he made enough? He'd taken the university and the sport to greater heights, but was all that past glory going to buy him another year or two? He had changed, albeit begrudgingly, with the times, whether that meant adjusting his offense, handing over the reins to a more innovative assistant coach, or giving a black student a chance to play KU basketball... but was this really personal progress, or just admission of his own obstinate past?

Allen's stubborn conviction had been the key to the growth of KU's program and, in so many ways, to the sport of basketball, and yet it still continued to be the single thing that kept him from finding even greater heights. Allen had made countless friends over the decades, but his methods had left him with nearly as many enemies—the latest being Harry Henshel of the simpleminded AAU.

As Phog Allen held on and waited for the hopeless feeling of plummeting toward earth to pass, all he could wonder was this:

Had he done enough?

The answer, he soon realized, was simple. Of course, he had done enough, and there was still plenty left to do. He had seen his Kansas basketball program sink to unforeseen depths, he had brought it back to the mountaintop, and now his Jayhawks were sliding down the other side. He knew the run of bad luck was temporary. He could take this program back to the top, and it wouldn't take long to do it. He had two of his top three scorers coming back, along with an incredible freshman class that included the best player in the country, maybe the best player ever. And, besides, he was Phog Allen.

He was the man to do it. The man to bring the program to its rightful spot on the mountaintop. He was as filled with conviction as ever. He was the man. If the KU board of regents would only let him. They were the only ones standing in his way.

Phog Allen called out to Bessie, telling her to bring the typewriter. Be ready for dictation, he said, and call the newspapermen—let them know Mr. Basketball has got something to say.

As daylight faded on another spring day in Lawrence, Phog Allen sat in the darkness of his own future, his career at the mercy of others. The first few practices of the 1955–56 University of Kansas basketball season were upon him, and Allen was being tasked with the nearly impossible feat of staying in the moment.

His seventieth birthday was approaching, the state's retirement law was leaving his future in doubt, and the arrival of the most impressive recruit in school history—if not basketball history—was making it difficult to stay in the moment. And yet Allen somehow found a way to remain focused on the 1955–56 season. All five starters still had eligibility heading into that campaign, including leading scorer Dallas Dobbs. The team also included Kansas City native Maurice King, the second African American to play basketball at Kansas and the first to be a starter for the Jayhawks.

Allen had also brought in one of the finest recruiting classes of his career, although Wilt Chamberlain and the other players from his freshman class would not be eligible because of an NCAA rule forbidding first-year players from competing with the varsity. If this was to be his swan song, as was being widely speculated in and around the state of Kansas, Allen was going to have to find a way to be successful without his biggest and best recruiting coup leading the way.

Phog Allen's seventieth birthday came and went on November 18, 1955, and he was still serving as the team's coach, at a salary of ten thousand dollars per year. The Jayhawks' varsity played an exhibition against the freshman team on that day, and fans were buzzing about a new 7'0" freshman who starred in the game but wouldn't be eligible until the following season. No one was more excited than Phog about the big freshman from Philadelphia who went by the nickname Stilt. Chamberlain lived up to the hype by scoring 42 points and pulling down 29 rebounds while leading the freshmen to an 81–71 win over the varsity. Afterward, an impressed Allen told reporters, "Chamberlain could team with two Phi Beta Kappas and two coeds and give [the varsity team] a battle."

Despite the loss to the freshman team, the KU varsity was looking like a contender when the 1955–56 season officially began. Dobbs, the team's lone senior starter, and King led the team in scoring and got the Jayhawks off to another solid start. The 1955–56 KU team jumped out to a 3-0 record, including a one-point win over a Wichita State team coached by former Jayhawk Ralph Miller. A two-game road trip to Texas resulted in losses to Southern Methodist and Rice, but the conference season saw Kansas get back into position for a return to the NCAA tournament with a 6-2 Big Seven record at the end of January. The Jayhawks were in prime position to challenge rivals Kansas State and Missouri for the conference title.

But the rails began to fall on in February. Dobbs, the team's leading scorer and only senior starter, was ruled academically ineligible. Then a surprising Iowa State team hammered KU in Ames to open the month. Two days later, the hated Missouri Tigers visited Allen Fieldhouse and

handed the Jayhawks their first home defeat of the season, 85-78. After a
1-point loss at Oklahoma on February 17, Kansas was 12-7 overall and 7-5
in the Big Seven—effectively ending KU's run at a conference title and the
automatic NCAA tournament bid that would come with it.

Back-to-back wins over Nebraska and Colorado put the Jayhawks at
14-7 with two games to play. The conference-leading Kansas State Wildcats would visit Allen Fieldhouse for the final home game of the 1955-56
season on March 6. Despite the House of Representatives' February 1955
announcement that Allen would be able to coach beyond the 1955-56 season, there was still enough uncertainty regarding his future that the Kansas
State game was being treated by some as the final home game of Allen's
storied career. His status was in the hands of the KU board of regents,
and the lack of any formal announcement created the impression that
the regents might not be all that excited about bringing Phog Allen back.

Allen himself was indignant about his future. He had no doubt that he
would be back for at least one more season, even though the buzz heading into a March 6, 1956, game against Kansas State was that Phog Allen
might be coaching at Allen Fieldhouse for the final time. Allen walked
into the arena that night to a long ovation from the crowd, and the PA
announcer spent part of the pregame introductions listing off his career
accomplishments. The Jayhawks jumped out to an 8-point halftime lead
but ended up losing 79-68 in front of a sellout crowd.

Allen brushed off postgame questions about the possibility of him never
coaching another game there, saying only of the loss to Kansas State,
"We're not going to cry."

The more pressing issue was that the loss clinched an NCAA tournament
bid for K-State, while the Jayhawks would be sitting out of the postseason
for the third year in a row. Allen used the postgame news conference to
encourage the KU fans to support Kansas State at the upcoming NCAA
regional in Lawrence.

Three days later, with the Jayhawks' final game of the season on tap in
Boulder, Colorado, the *Lawrence Journal World* ran a photograph of Phog
Allen sitting in the stands at Allen Fieldhouse along with the headline
"Retiring Court King and His Palace."

And yet Phog Allen had no plans of retirement. Even after the Jayhawks squandered a 7-point halftime lead to lose to Colorado, Allen was mum on the subject of his future. His Jayhawks had finished the 1955–56 season with a disappointing 14–9 record, and as far as Allen knew he would be back for two more years—per the House of Representatives decision from thirteen months earlier.

In the days that followed the season-ending loss to Colorado, a deep freeze had settled in and cast a quiet pall over the sidewalks of the University of Kansas campus. The Jayhawks' 1955–56 men's basketball season had concluded, and the subject of head coach Forrest "Phog" Allen's future had become little more than a whisper. The local basketball community had turned its attention toward the NCAA tournament that would descend upon Allen Fieldhouse in the third week of March, and after that, KU fans would begin counting down the days until the start of the Wilt Chamberlain era.

With his future in limbo, Phog Allen attended the NCAA tournament games while rooting on rival Kansas State—a school he encouraged local fans to adopt as the "hometown team" for the tourney games. Allen was a true fan of the game who went to NCAA tournaments whenever they were in the area, regardless of whether the Jayhawks had been eliminated. During the 1956 tournament, Allen showed no signs of concern about his uncertain job status. As *Lawrence Journal-World* columnist Bill Mayer wrote of the scene, "Allen was a mighty busy man both nights, what with visits with all his friends, watching the games and talking with newspaper and radio men. The Democrats and Republicans have nothing on Doc in 1956. They're campaigning for office and Doc's bidding to stay another year as K.U. coach past his scheduled June retirement."

Allen's future was in the hands of the KU board of regents, a group that was being led by a car dealership owner named Lester McCoy while Chairman Oscar Stauffer vacationed overseas. Both Stauffer and McCoy were deeply rooted in the Kansas Republican Party, with conservative views that typically leaned toward tradition and following rules to the letter of the law. The regents had until June 30 to decide whether to grant Allen with a provision extending his tenure past the age of seventy, but all indications were that the board intended to make a decision by the end of March in order to accommodate those affected by the ruling.

Allen's understanding was that he would be back for the 1956–57 season, if not beyond, and his belief was grounded by assurances from KU chancellor Frank Murphy, who had plenty of clout with the board of regents. Phog's adult children, years later, would contend that Murphy had given the aging coach an outright promise that he would be back.

But there were those at the university who weren't that comfortable with the prospect of giving Phog Allen special treatment, and not just because several other KU faculty members in recent years had requested extension waivers and been denied. Because of his high-profile position, Allen was continuing to serve as unelected spokesman for the University of Kansas, and the lingering effects of some December 1955 comments he'd made about the Amateur Athletic Union and its director had left a cloud over the university.

Allen held long-standing animosity toward the AAU, going back twenty years to the 1936 Olympics, and he was obviously a proponent of KU athletics. So it had come as no surprise when Allen took issue with the AAU's 1955 decision to suspend former KU distance runner Wes Santee over questionable expenses as an amateur. But Allen seemed to have gone too far during a December 1955 speaking engagement, in which he had classified the AAU as a "mystic hooded order which crucified Wes Santee" and called the organization "a lousy, toady bunch of rats." Most of Allen's ire was aimed at the AAU's director, Colonel Harry D. Henshel, who also served as head of the Olympic basketball committee. Allen had been feuding with Henshel since the AAU director challenged Wilt Chamberlain's amateur status during his freshman year at KU. That had ignited a war of words between Allen and Henshel, and the Santee controversy led Allen to say, "Henshel is a big, fat toad. I wouldn't travel on the same [military] boat with him."

Despite the controversy surrounding him, Phog Allen went about his business as usual in the weeks that followed the conclusion of the Jayhawks' 1955–56 season. As *Time* wrote in the spring of 1956, "After landing the lengthy Wilt 'the Stilt' Chamberlain, recruiting prize of the year, Kansas University's veteran coach, Dr. Forrest C. (Phog) Allen, figured he was a cinch to beat the state board of regents' rule." Allen made very few public comments about the pending board of regents decision, even while attending the NCAA regional in Kansas City in mid-March.

But Allen had never been the type to leave a decision in the hands of others. And so when he called a press conference in late March, people were expecting him to step down gracefully and announce his own retirement before anybody else decided his fate. To see a proud man like Phog Allen stand up in front of a crowded room of reporters and take his future into his own hands seemed to be the most realistic scenario. The press conference would be an easy way for Phog Allen to go out on his own terms.

He walked into the room with a typed sheet of paper in hand, took his place before the reporters and read, "I am enjoying splendid health. And if it should be the will of the people as expressed through the duly constituted governing authorities of the University of Kansas that I continue as basketball coach for another year, it would be the thrill of my life to end a long coaching career with a truly great team."

He went on to call the state law "statutory senility," a phrase he would continue to use over the years. He publicly offered to give up his teaching duties, believing that might amend his status as a government official. Allen was still in good shape, still had a sharp mind, and was just three years removed from his second consecutive appearance in an NCAA tournament championship game. He could easily see himself coaching basketball for years to come but understood that staying at the school through the end of Wilt Chamberlain's tenure might not be a realistic option.

So he made a plea to remain at the school with a provision. "Not for three years," he said, "but for one grand and glorious year."

In effect, Allen was requesting a chance to go out on top. With Chamberlain becoming eligible to add to a team that had three returning starters and a chance to put the KU program back among the nation's elite, whoever coached the 1956–57 Jayhawks was going to have success. Allen believed he was the man to lead the team to another national championship. One year with Wilt was all he requested.

But it's likely that he saw a longer run in the cards. If the state law had been waived, and then Allen and Wilt were able to bring home a national title, it seemed only fitting that the regents would bring him back for a second year, then maybe he could earn another year after that—and on and on. Allen was probably trying to set himself up for more years down the road. Senility be damned; he felt he had a few more good years left.

On March 30, 1956, a few days after Allen's press conference, the Kansas board of regents turned down Allen's request to waive the retirement law. The regents summed up their decision in a brief statement, saying, "This board has nothing but the highest regard for Dr. Allen and his desire to serve . . . however, the benefits resulting from the application of a retirement rule far outweigh its disadvantages and the board unanimously feels that it must be applied to all."

And just like that, the legendary career of Phog Allen was over. Three weeks after leading the Jayhawks into the 1955–56 season finale in Boulder, Colorado, Allen found out that he wouldn't be allowed to coach another game for the KU basketball team.

A coaching career that spanned forty-six seasons, bridging the gap from Naismith to Chamberlain, nurturing the sport from its infancy stages to the million-dollar empire, a tenure that was largely responsible for Olympic basketball and the NCAA tournament, had skidded to a halt. No retirement ceremonies. No standing ovations. Just a decision from a bunch of politicians, and the Phog era was finished.

The man who recruited Wilt Chamberlain would never get to coach him.

"The greatest coaching career in basketball history came to an end today," read the *Lawrence Journal-World*, "as the Kansas Board of Regents unanimously selected Richard F. (Dick) Harp, an assistant since 1949, to succeed the fabulous 70-year-old Dr. Forrest C. (Phog) Allen, 39 years the school's cage chief, as head coach at Kansas University."

Allen was crushed by the decision, feeling betrayed not only by the university but also by its chancellor, Frank Murphy, who had initially given Allen assurances about his job security but had never applied for the promised waiver. Allen turned his back on any explanation from the KU chancellor, who was terse in his public comments on the subject.

"The records made by his basketball teams and . . . the records made subsequently by members of his teams in other business and professional lives are eloquent testimony to his unique abilities in not only building championship teams but also in building first-class citizens," Murphy said after the regents' decision was announced.

Murphy was emotional enough about the decision that he wrote a personal letter to Allen's daughter, Jane Mons, explaining that it would have been unfair to allow the coach to continue at the university beyond his seventieth birthday—mainly because the school had turned down requests from several other faculty members requesting extensions within the previous two years. "Most, if not all of these men, have not wished to retire, and in most instances they have been very capable of carrying on," Murphy wrote. "The same will hold true again this July when six or eight additional first class people will again be retired."

Murphy's letter went on to inform Mons that giving her father special treatment would have augmented resentment at the school and caused faculty members to "feel that in the last analysis the University is more concerned with its athletic fortunes than its academic program."

Murphy's letter concluded, "I am sure you realize that this whole matter has not been an easy one for me. I am a good sports fan, and I love to see successful teams. Come what may, the Allen family will always have a very warm spot in my heart, and I shall always be especially proud of the fact that it was on my recommendation that the greatest building that this campus will ever have will forever bear the name of one of the greatest men that has ever served it—your father."

Phog Allen, the seventy-year-old *ex*-coach, forced into retirement, was reclusive in his goodbye. While he didn't appear to make a conscious effort to avoid the press, his forced retirement was barely addressed in the days and weeks that followed the regents' announcement. Away from the limelight, he undoubtedly went through all the stages of grief, oscillating through denial and anger and sadness as he grappled with the loss of the one identity that brought him the most pride.

In nearly a half century of coaching, Phog Allen had won an NCAA-record 746 games, most of which came while he posted a career record of 590-219 at KU. (At the time, Allen was actually credited with 770 career wins; only after a 1990 study by NCAA statistician Jim Van Valkenburg uncovered a discrepancy in his win total at Baker and Haskell was the official win total corrected.) He had earned three national championships and twenty-six conference titles. He had coached fourteen All-Americans, and by the end of the century eight of his former players would be in the Naismith Basketball Hall of Fame.

He had done a lot in his lifetime, perhaps more than any other man in his sport, and Allen had done it without ever making an annual coaching salary of more than twelve thousand dollars.

After his forced retirement, there would not be any offers from others schools to coach basketball, as several states had similar laws requiring retirement at the age of seventy. The fledgling National Basketball Association was relying on younger coaches with fresh ideas. Allen was still in good health and of a keen mind but didn't draw any interest in a profession made up of younger men.

Within a matter of weeks, Allen's full days of balancing practice schedules, player relations, game plans, media interviews, team dynamics, scouting reports, academic duties, and recruiting had dissolved into a quiet day job at an osteopathy clinic he opened up on Eighth Street in West Lawrence. He had more free time than he knew how to fill.

He put most of his hours into the osteopathy clinic and spending time with his family, but Allen also used his free time to play more golf. He enjoyed the sport but also became frustrated by it, preferring to quote the Woodrow Wilson line "Golf is the ineffectual attempt to put an elusive ball into an obscure hole, with implements ill-adapted to the cause."

Phog Allen also liked to joke about the aging process by saying, "When it takes you longer to recover than it did to get tired, you're getting old."

Neither Phog Allen nor those who loved him were happy with the way things ended at KU. He initially steered clear of the university and refused to attend basketball practices or games in the weeks that followed his forced retirement. He continually referred to the abrupt conclusion to his coaching career as "statutory senility" and privately carried resentment toward the university for the remainder of his life.

"Doc felt as though he had the support of the administration—and then he didn't," former KU player and Dick Harp assistant coach Jerry Waugh said in 2014. "That's what upset him."

Without Phog Allen, the Kansas basketball program moved on, and having Wilt Chamberlain eligible for the 1956–57 season made for a pretty easy transition as Harp took the reins.

The 1956–57 season started in epic fashion, with Chamberlain scoring 52 points and pulling in 31 rebounds—shattering school records in both categories. Phog Allen did not attend the game, opting instead to fulfill a speaking engagement in Bushton, Kansas, where 175 high school students and parents were on hand to hear from the legendary ex-coach. Allen ate dinner at the school and snuck into an administration office to catch some of the KU game on the radio, expressing no surprise when he heard how well Chamberlain was doing in his collegiate debut. The performance left the former coach with equal parts pride and frustration. Allen then took the stage for his speech, during which he told the crowd that he had no plans on attending KU games in the near future but that he would eventually "go only when it's convenient."

Such an occasion came up on December 26, 1956, when Allen was attending a KU–Iowa State game at Municipal Auditorium in the opening round of the Big Seven Holiday tournament. During what was believed to be his first Jayhawks game as a spectator since being forced into retirement, Allen was sitting in the stands when he was approached by a man in a suit who presented him with a court summons. Phog opened the papers and read that he was being sued by Colonel Harry D. Henshel, the AAU director, for thirty-five thousand dollars as part of a libel suit stemming from the comments Allen had made a year earlier, during a speaking engagement in Kansas City. Allen had been quoted as questioning Henshel's military rank while criticizing the AAU's decision to suspend former KU runner Wes Santee. Within the next few weeks, the case would get tied up in legal action.

Meanwhile, Chamberlain and the 1956–57 Jayhawks rolled on without Allen. Kansas beat its first six opponents by double-digit margins and eventually streaked out to twelve consecutive wins to open the season. Kansas basketball was not just the talk of Lawrence but was also becoming the buzz of the sport nationally. The National Basketball Association had found an audience and was beginning to gain some momentum, particularly on the East Coast, but Wilt Chamberlain was already becoming as

well known as professionals like Bob Cousy and Bob Pettit. Chamberlain
had emerged as the face of KU basketball, and he drew such immediate
curiosity that the previous face of the program became blurred over time.
Phog Allen mostly watched the Chamberlain era from afar, preferring
to stay away from the program in an effort to give Harp space. When he
did attend games, Phog sat in the upper concourse, far away from the KU
bench and hoping to remain inconspicuous.

Allen didn't feel his presence was wanted by KU's new coach, and
according to one legend passed down by Phog's son Bob Allen over the
years, on at least one occasion Harp let his feelings be known. Bob Allen
maintained that his father had once shown up at the door of the KU locker
room, only to be told by Harp, "Go away, old man." Whether or not the
incident actually occurred would be difficult to verify in the decades that
followed, and Harp's steadfast loyalty to Phog over the years made the
slight seem hard to imagine. Some people who were with the KU basketball team in those years believe that it was Allen who perpetuated the
schism. But it was clear that Phog Allen no longer felt welcome within
the KU community.

The post-Allen Jayhawks finished Harp's first season as head coach
with a 21-2 record and rolled all the way to the finals of the NCAA tournament, where Chamberlain and company lost one of the most memorable
games in college basketball history—a three-overtime thriller that North
Carolina won 54–53 on a pair of last-second free throws. The game was
televised in the local markets of the participating teams, and it was such
a huge success, from a viewership standpoint, that UNC's Atlantic Coast
Conference soon struck a deal to regularly televise conference games—a
big step in the future of college basketball on television.

Phog Allen's most heralded recruit led the nation in scoring, at 29.6
points per game, in his first season of eligibility. The next year, as a junior,
Chamberlain upped his scoring average to 30.1 points per game but couldn't
get KU into the NCAA tournament. An 18-5 record and second-place finish in the Big Seven Conference weren't good enough for the 1957–58
Jayhawks to reach postseason play. Chamberlain decided to go pro after
that season, and his career at KU was over.

Years later, when looking back on his time at Kansas, Chamberlain would admit only one regret: he didn't get to play for Phog Allen. Chamberlain got along with Harp but never fully accepted him during his time at KU. In later years, he said of the man who replaced Allen, "I don't think [Harp] was the coach for us at that particular time. I think Phog Allen could have done the job for us, and we would have won two or three national championships if he had remained coach."

Allen had a similar regret, saying in the years that followed his forced retirement, "I just wanted one more year. I wanted to coach Wilt Chamberlain with those ten-foot baskets. I was going to make them swallow those baskets."

Phog Allen, an avid sports fan in retirement, continued to follow KU basketball from a distance during his early years of retirement but kept busy with his new osteopathic clinic on 11 East Eighth Street. He opened the clinic shortly after the KU regents declined his waiver request and eventually opened a second clinic in Kansas City, called the Phog Allen Health Center, designed to help businessmen live healthy lives. He mostly stayed in the shadows but soon launched a modest radio and television career that included a fifteen-minute weekly TV program called "The Phog Allen Show," which ran Thursday evenings during the dinner hour. He fervently read newspapers like the *Lawrence Journal World*, *Kansas City Star*, and *New York Times* and was not afraid to pen an editorial letter if he disagreed with something in print. When the *New York Times* ran a 1957 column making fun of Phog's longtime crusade to raise the baskets, Allen responded with a seven-page letter that included the line, "Do not let a few facts spoil a good story."

He also picked another verbal fight with Boston Celtics owner Walter Brown. After Brown became the latest basketball man to question Chamberlain's amateur status at KU, saying he shouldn't be allowed to play in the NBA, Allen went into attack mode, calling Brown "a silk-stocking boy with a fabulous inheritance, [who] wouldn't know what real struggle is." Speaking at a dinner engagement, the slick-tongued Allen added that he felt it was "unfortunate that a wealthy man like Mr. Walter Brown unfairly attacks a Negro boy who has a fine brain and a fine body, and desiring a splendid education, is able to get it through this medium of athletics." Allen concluded by pointing out that Lawrence, Kansas, was founded by

Bostonians, calling them "people who wanted to keep Kansas a free state and abolish slavery. It is ironical that another Boston personality such as Mr. Brown would fetter a fine Negro citizen."

That eventually blew over, but the Harry Henshel lawsuit ended up hanging over his head well into the 1957 calendar year. On March 27, Allen's efforts to obtain a dismissal in the $35,000 U.S. district court suit against him were denied. Allen responded by filing a $225,000 counter-suit against Henshel. (Four decades earlier, as a young, brash, rising head coach at Missouri State Normal School, District 2, in Warrensburg, Allen had responded to a similar lawsuit from an opposing coach in exactly the same way.)

On November 6, 1957, U.S. district court judge R. Joseph Smith signed an order of dismissal in both lawsuits—the original one against Allen and the countersuit against Henshel—and both parties agreed to retract their statements, resulting in the end of the saga.

Two weeks later, a reporter from the *Daily Kansan* caught up with Allen as his seventy-second birthday approached. He was seventeen months removed from his official retirement date, and Allen seemed to be genuinely enjoying his post-coaching life.

"I'm having a picnic. I'm having more fun than I've ever had," Allen told the *Kansan*. He went on to say, "A lot of men got old coaching basketball. I didn't because I always regarded it as recreation. It was just fun, as far as I was concerned."

Allen soon faded into the shadows of the national spotlight but was as busy as ever. His schedule as a motivational speaker included nearly one hundred dates per year by the end of the 1950s.

In 1959, Forrest "Phog" Allen was part of the inaugural class in the Naismith Basketball Hall of Fame—the very one that Allen had helped to name—along with his mentor, Dr. James Naismith. Within the next three decades, they would be joined by eight of his former KU players: John Bunn (in 1964), Adolph Rupp (1969), Paul Endacott (1972), Dutch Lonborg (1973), William "Skinny" Johnson (1977), Dean Smith (1983), Clyde Lovellette (1988), and Ralph Miller (1988). Wilt Chamberlain, whom Allen recruited but never got to coach, was inducted in 1979.

Allen's coaching legacy spoke for itself, but in the years immediately following his retirement his reputation was still somewhat sullied by his moments of outspokenness.

As *New York Times* columnist Arthur Daley had written in 1957, "Phog Allen has been such a provocative, controversial and publicity-conscious character for so long that a great many sports writers instinctively lined themselves on the opposite side whenever the retired basketball coach took a stand on any issue."

This exact process played out in 1960, when an NCAA investigation into his recruitment of Chamberlain and the purchase of the Oldsmobile that The Stilt drove around Lawrence during his three years at KU pushed Phog back into the spotlight. When contacted by the *Topeka Capital Journal*, Allen was quoted as saying that Chamberlain received between fifty and one hundred dollars to do radio interviews while at KU. When the story came out, Allen said that his quotes were misunderstood, adding that the reimbursements were not in violation of NCAA rules. "I referred to these instances merely to point out how great a personality Wilt is," Allen told the *Daily Kansan* in response. "Wilt could go anywhere and attract a great crowd. The point I was making is that he had lots of ways of making money so that he could easily pay for his car. I had no desire to stir up a controversy. I was merely explaining Chamberlain's finances."

But stirring up controversy was an activity that Allen found difficult to avoid. As the Chamberlain investigation dragged on, Allen continued to opine on it from afar. In April 1960, at the age of seventy-four, Allen told the *Daily Kansan*, "If these gum-footed falcons who have been snooping around here the past three years for the NCAA trying to get something on Chamberlain would go somewhere else, they would find a lot more stuff to investigate."

A year after that, Allen called a U.S. senator and demanded an investigation into the funds generated from the annual NCAA tournament. "I know that a year ago the NCAA made over $175,000 from its basketball tournament," he told the Associated Press. "But what has the NCAA been doing with all of its money?"

Later that year, in October 1961, as Allen's seventy-sixth birthday approached, he wrote a letter to the *Topeka Capital Journal* responding to an editorial written about him and his grudges against the AAU and NCAA.

"I am too busy to ever hold a grudge!" he wrote. "And especially against the 'Asinine And Unfair' or the 'Nationally Confused Athletic Absurdity.'"

Phog Allen was loved by many, despised by some, and misunderstood by the masses. He never made any apologies for his coaching career, nor did anyone expect him to. That would not have been Phog.

As *New York Times* columnist Arthur Daley wrote in the year following Allen's forced retirement, "one of basketball's most distinguished personalities for more than three decades has been Dr. Forrest (Phog) Allen of the University of Kansas. No one would be quicker to admit it than Allen himself, a man not noted for extended periods of silence."

Yet in the years that followed his "statutory senility" retirement as KU's longtime basketball coach, he gradually faded into the cellar of silence. The game no longer needed Phog Allen, so old Doc found another arena in which to make a mark.

22

The Sparkle of a Diamond

The clock was ticking. Otherwise, the modest house where Forrest and Bessie Allen had spent their later years was silent and dark. The nurse who had been hired to help take care of the aging legend was off her shift, there were no games on the television, and Phog was lying in bed trying to find sleep. The wheelchair was at his bedside. His grown children and their grown children had lives of their own now; some of them even lived out of state.

Through all of the changes, Phog Allen had stayed put. The university had cast him aside and pushed him away, but he simply hadn't left. The farthest move he had made over the years was from the large, two-story house at 801 Louisiana Street into a smaller cottage, the one he had purchased for his son Mitt's family while his son attended law school, six houses down on the same block. His new residence at 831 Louisiana was easier to maintain, and it was less cumbersome to get around in when his knees had begun to fail him.

As he sat inside the cottage he had come to call home, Phog Allen stared into darkness and listened to the tick of the clock. Whereas he used to live inside the roar of a seventeen-thousand-seat arena that still bore his name, or chat genially with patients at his osteopathic clinic on Eighth Street, Doc had come to spend his hours in virtual silence.

The tick and the tock. Phog Allen was alone.

The University of Kansas campus continued to bustle with youth in the years that followed Phog Allen's "statutory senility" retirement. While fashions transformed from Buddy Holly glasses and button-up sweaters to the shaggy hair and beards of the late sixties and early seventies, and while the KU basketball teams rose and fell, Allen quietly kept going a few blocks northeast of campus.

On the corner of Massachusetts and Eighth Street in West Lawrence, a modest two-story building blended into the landscape without much reason for passersby to grant a second look. The law office on the upper floor belonged to a man named Milton Allen who was one of the top defense attorneys in town and was on his way to becoming county attorney. On the floor below, a pleasant older woman named Bess welcomed visitors with a kind smile and dark eyes while sitting behind a desk inside an immaculate lobby where a few chairs lined the bare walls. There was no indication that the office was the new home of a legendary coach who had left the game of basketball to be tended by others.

Bess Allen would kindly ask a visitor's name and have the patient wait until her husband, Dr. Forrest C. Allen, was ready in the back. At that time, the woman would show the visitor to a pristine, well-kept office with only a single window and a training table at the center of the floor. Doc Allen, with his tortoiseshell glasses and thinning hair, would begin his thirty-minute session by asking the patient to lie on the table, typically face down, the doctor's strong hands searching for pressure points as he set out to relieve the pain. A half hour later, more often than not feeling cured by the healing man's hands, the patient would stand tall and thank him for the relief before paying five or ten dollars to Bess Allen in the lobby on the way out the door.

Over the years, his clients had come to include countless athletes, drawn to Lawrence as word spread of Doc's ability to heal. Casey Stengel, by then a New York Yankees manager who had visited Dr. Allen as a young, rising star, brought Mickey Mantle, Billy Martin, Johnny Mize, and Ted Williams, among others, to Allen for treatment. Allen's 1959 appointment book was packed with nine to ten daily patients, and his popularity as an osteopath was surging such that his docket that year included fifty different names in the first two weeks of January alone.

One of Allen's most controversial patients was a man named Phil Snowden, who came to him in the fall of 1959 because of an ailing back that needed immediate attention. Snowden, who happened to be the starting quarterback at the University of Missouri at the time, was desperate for something to alleviate his pain because he had a big game on Saturday. The game was against the University of Kansas.

Snowden had missed most of the 1959 season due to the upper back injury, but he was so eager to play against KU that the Missouri athletic department reached out to Allen to see whether the coach-turned-osteopath would be willing to give the injury a look.

Doc Allen was happy to help, not necessarily because he still held a grudge against KU but because he never turned away a patient. That his son-in-law, Duane Morris, happened to be the starting quarterback for the Jayhawks didn't matter. Allen treated the ailing Mizzou player for several days, discovering that the source of his discomfort was actually in a part of his shoulder called the rotator cuff, and on Saturday, Snowden led the Tigers to a 13–9 win over Kansas to earn a trip to the Orange Bowl.

Allen's clinic became his focus as he fell into a quiet life spent mostly in the background. He was content to work a modest occupation in a small clinic where he could spend more time with his wife, Bessie, who had lived a good part of her earlier adult years pining for her husband while he was off coaching basketball or giving speeches. After Phog's retirement, the Allens began spending almost all of their time together, except for when Phog was on a speaking tour. His career as a basketball coach seemed to be left in the rearview mirror, as Allen took as much pride in his osteopathic career as he did in coaching, once boasting, "I won more games at the training table than on the sidelines."

Allen's osteopathic work was also ahead of its time in that he was one of the first men who had combined the discipline with athletics. The techniques he used back in his pre-1920s days coaching basketball in Warrensburg, Missouri, represented some of the earliest forms of the occupation that later became known as athletic training, while his post-retirement practice in Lawrence was similar to what would evolve into the late-twentieth century field of physical therapy. In much the same way as he had innovated in the sport of basketball, Allen saw new and revolutionary ways to bring physical healing and athletics together before it became commonplace in American society.

Healing a patient could indeed be as rewarding as coaching a team to victory, even though Doc Allen's new career was devoid of the screaming fans and clicking camera flashes and post-performance interview sessions. Allen had maintained over the years that those things hadn't mattered to him as much as how his "boys" on the KU basketball team turned out as men. Paul Endacott had risen up the ranks of Phillips Petroleum to become president of the international corporation. Ray Evans held a similar position with Traders National Bank in Kansas City, and Otto Schnellbacher played professional baseball, basketball, and football in addition to serving in the military. Howard Engleman became a well-respected lawyer in Salina, Kansas, while several of Allen's "boys" followed in Phog's footsteps by becoming successful coaches. Clyde Lovellette, perhaps Phog Allen's most decorated KU player, followed a modest pro career by becoming a police officer.

The most successful of Allen's former players in the coaching profession was Adolph Rupp, the longtime Kentucky basketball coach who in 1966 broke the NCAA record for coaching victories. The former mark of 770 was held by a man named Phog Allen—although in later years, that total would be refigured to a career win total 746.

Over time, Allen eventually began attending KU basketball games but tried to stay out of the limelight while allowing the program's new coaching staff to operate out of his shadow. The Jayhawks went to the 1957 and 1960 NCAA tournaments, and they were maintaining the success Phog had laid forth in the first half of the century, and he made it a point to watch from a distance.

The only time Allen seemed to overstep his bounds came during a 1964 banquet honoring outgoing coach Dick Harp, the man who had replaced Phog eight years earlier. Harp had a decent run—he won nearly 60 percent of his games and went to two NCAA tournaments—but couldn't have possibly lived up to the level of success Allen left in his wake. Allen was invited to say a few words at Harp's retirement banquet and ended up telling the people in attendance that he had been somewhat disappointed when Harp was named as his replacement over another former

KU player, Ralph Miller. The timing of Allen's comments was curious, and he may well have meant to say that he had hoped Miller had been named as *Harp's* replacement—KU assistant coach and University of Oklahoma alumnus Ted Owens was chosen—but the incident provided evidence that Phog was beginning to show signs of age. He'd had little semblance of a filter as a basketball coach even in his younger years, and as his eightieth birthday approached in the mid-1960s, Allen found himself fumbling to put his thoughts and speech together on several occasions.

Around this time, a former KU player named Don Roberts had begun driving Allen from one speaking engagement to another, as the aging ex-coach had largely lost his ability to operate a car. Allen had also started drifting from his speaking notes from time to time, so Roberts would sit next to Allen on the stage and pull on Phog's trouser leg as a signal for Allen to get back on point. On one such night, at a KU letterman's club luncheon in Ottawa, Kansas, Allen abruptly stopped midway through his speech. He stood behind the podium saying nothing, just staring out at the audience with confusion in his eyes. Roberts jerked on his pant leg but couldn't pull Allen out of his dreamlike state. After a long, uncomfortable silence, Phog told the patient audience, "Fellows, I am very sorry, but I believe that I have given my last speech. I just can't seem to do it anymore." The stunned audience slowly rose from their seats and gave Allen a ceremonial standing ovation.

Allen's closest ties in the post-retirement years remained with his family. His oldest living son, Mitt, once the troublemaker as a rebellious teen, spent his weekdays in the law office right above Phog's osteopathic clinic on Eighth Street. Youngest son Bob Allen had chosen the medical field, due in large part to his older brother Forrest Jr.'s death in the 1920s, and became a surgeon at St. Luke's Hospital in nearby Overland Park. Phog's daughters—Mary, Jane, and Eleanor—had all married and started families of their own. His grandchildren called him Phoggie.

Phoggie's favorite thing in those later years was to sing silly songs to his grandchildren, making up words as he would go. One such activity included a counting game in which Phoggie would plant a child on his knee and count to ten using made-up numbers: "One-a . . . Missouri . . . Zachary . . . Zan . . . Salabo . . . Crackabo . . . Peabody . . . Wiggletale . . .

Dollaway . . . and ten!!!" He entertained his grandchildren by magically pulling coins from behind their ears or by making funny faces that would leave them doubled over in laughter.

The person who remained closest to Allen through it all was still his longtime sweetheart, Bessie. They had celebrated their fiftieth anniversary in 1958, and Bessie Allen, whom the grandchildren all called Mimi, spent most of the 1960s working as a receptionist and office manager at Doc Allen's clinic on Eighth Street. She had been Phog's main support system throughout their adult lives, and by the latter part of the sixties, as the world outside erupted into chaos and assassinations and protest, when skirt hems were rising and women's pants were getting tighter, Bessie Allen quietly took on another role at home. She became her husband's caretaker.

As Phog Allen faded into his late seventies and his health began to wane, he found it harder and harder to get around. He cut back on his hours at the clinic and returned to the speaking circuit on an extremely limited basis. His knees had deteriorated to the point that he could barely stand on his own. While at home, he spent most of his free time sitting in a lounge chair or lying in bed.

Phog Allen's health continued to deteriorate, and he became ill in the spring of 1968, while visiting the West Coast as part of a speaking engagement on alternative medicine. He had to cancel the date but continued with his tour back to the Midwest. In a March 27 letter written at the Ritz Plaza Motor Lodge in Terre Haute, Indiana, en route to a speaking engagement in Indianapolis, Allen wrote Naismith Hall of Fame director Lee Williams to tell him that he was still holding out hope of being able to attend an upcoming enshrinement ceremony for former KU player Adolph Rupp. One week later, on April 3, Bessie Allen wrote a letter to Williams to tell the Hall of Fame official that Phog "came home from Indianapolis quite ill from bronchial influenza. . . . Now he is confined to his bed with antibiotic therapy. He will not be able now to go back to the great dedication [in Springfield, Massachusetts,] as he had so hopefully planned."

Phog battled digestive issues and was no longer able to walk. He was eighty-two years old, confined to his bed and in grave condition. Bessie stayed by his side, as she had done throughout their sixty years of marriage.

Players, sons, daughters, and grandchildren had come and gone over the years, but she'd always been there.

Allen's health slightly improved by July 1968, to the point that he was able to write again. In a July 4 letter to Lee Williams, Phog wrote,

> I am not out of the woods as yet. I have had barium tests of lower bowel, stomach & etc. Also a gall bladder X-ray examanation [*sic*]—no malignancy—but I can't get my pep back—and it's been three months since the start of my asian [*sic*] flu. at least I can write fairly well now if I take long rest. Working a little off and on.

In the days that followed, old age would force Phog Allen into another retirement. He had to give up his career as an osteopath and as a speaker and spent his days confined to a wheelchair inside his home at 831 Louisiana, six doors down from where he'd raised his children. The condition left Phog and Bessie Allen inside their home around the clock, although there were nights when they would host family or friends for supper. On one such night, former player Allen Kelly and his wife were visiting when Phog, sitting in a wheelchair, called out to his wife from the living room to get him something from the kitchen. Bessie ignored him, and he called out again. At this point, Bessie leaned in to Kelly's wife and joked, "I've finally got him where I want him."

While Allen's health faded, he continued to keep tabs on the sport of basketball, which had become a successful venture on television. The NCAA tournament had grown to feature twenty-three teams, and both the 1968 and 1969 fields included three schools coached by Allen's former players: North Carolina and Dean Smith, Wichita State and Ralph Miller, and Rupp's Kentucky Wildcats.

As Rupp's April 1969 Hall of Fame induction ceremony grew closer, Allen wrote Lee Williams one final letter, asking him to pass on his best wishes to Rupp in enshrinement. Phog Allen concluded the letter by writing,

> I can not walk any more. So, Lee, you can bet I won't stray far from home. But I want to greet all of you on that great night with cheers and hurrahs for the future of this great game. Sincerely yours, Forrest C. Allen.

The days passed like years as Phog Allen remained confined to his

Lawrence home, quietly moving from bed to wheelchair to recliner. Phog watched the ever-changing world while sitting in front of the television, where he had begun to spend most of his waking hours.

Soon came another piece of devastating news when Phog and Bessie Allen learned that Mary Allen Hamilton, their first-born child, died in April 1969, three weeks shy of her sixtieth birthday. Hamilton, who was named after Phog's mother, passed away while living halfway across the country in California. Her body would soon be returned to Lawrence, where she would be buried alongside her younger brother, Forrest Jr.

During these difficult months, Phog Allen had come to rely on his wife more than ever. Bessie Evalina Milton Allen had always told her family that her goal was to be "useful to the end," and taking care of her ailing husband had become her life's work. She had taken on the role of his full-time caretaker and stayed by his bedside until he began to gain some of his mobility back. But as the holiday season approached in the winter of 1969, Bessie began to succumb to her own health problems. Eleanor Allen Nelson, the Allens' youngest child, quit her job as a receptionist at the Culver Military Academy in Indiana to help her ailing parents around the house.

On January 4, 1970, Bessie Allen, Phog's longtime wife and best friend, suffered a heart attack and passed away at the age of eighty-two.

Phog Allen was alone. After sixty-one years of marriage, he had no one by his side. The woman whose father had once offered her an around-the-world trip not to marry Phog Allen had been there for all the ups and downs of his adult life. Now she was gone.

He was eighty-four years old, having retired as both a basketball coach and an osteopath. His body was failing, and Allen had lost not only his soul mate but also his caretaker. Now Phog Allen was truly alone.

Eleanor stayed for as long as her finances allowed, but she couldn't afford to be her father's full-time caretaker. Phog Allen's family collectively made the decision to put him in the Indian Creek Nursing Home, thirty-five miles away from his Lawrence home in Overland Park, Kansas. His son, Bob, lived in nearby Kansas City and was able to visit regularly between shifts at the hospital. But Phog was miserable at Indian Creek, so much so that he begged family members to set him free. He hated every minute he spent in the facility, where they took away his freedom and his control. After two weeks, he confided in Bob, telling him, "I've had enough." Phog had that look in his eye, the one that said he wasn't going to take no for an answer. If he was going to die, he was going to do it on his terms, on his home court.

The family relented, allowing Phog Allen to return to his home near campus in Lawrence, where a nurse named Anna Marie Button was hired to watch over him day and night. He lived just two and a half miles from the state of the art basketball facility that bore his name, and yet Phog Allen seemed mostly forgotten by the University of Kansas. He wasn't too eager to keep the relationship alive, either.

Twice the school reached out to Phog to ask him to be a part of important ceremonies at Allen Fieldhouse. In December 1971, with former KU player Adolph Rupp coming to Lawrence for his final appearance as coach at the University of Kentucky—like Allen, Rupp's career would come to an end because of a state law requiring workers to retire at the age of 70—the university asked Phog to be a part of the festivities. He did not show up for the occasion. Two months later, with the school honoring the twentieth anniversary of the 1952 NCAA championship team, Allen was extended another invitation. His health problems had become too grave for him to attend, so he graciously turned down the offer.

But the 1952 players were so eager to catch up with their former coach that they set up a post-ceremony trip to his house. Allen welcomed the group into his home while wearing a KU letter jacket and a lively smile, firmly gripping each of his former players' hands from his seated position in a wheelchair. He wore wood-framed eyeglasses and grinned as if he were thirty years younger, fully enraptured in what turned out to be the final great moment of Phog Allen's life.

His body was breaking down, but Allen's mind was still somewhat keen, albeit more than a bit outdated. By March of 1972, a month after the twentieth anniversary celebration, an Associated Press reporter spotlighted Allen in a feature story, only to find that the questions had to be written on paper because Allen was losing his hearing. Phog answered with his typically blunt rancor, saying things that would have generated front-page headlines earlier in his life—not to mention a generation later. He said basketball could never replace football or baseball as the main

American pastime because "there are not enough players hurt in basketball. Spectators, especially women, like to see people hurt." He added that professional basketball was "reprehensible" because it was taking players out of the college game too early. "Mostly they take advantage of the black boys," Allen continued. "The black boys want to get the money as soon as possible because they have been hungry so long." He later added, "And speaking of black boys, the Negro man is going to take the game away from the white man. They want their place in the sun, and they last longer in a game than the white man."

The racially insensitive comments barely registered as a blip on the radar of American sporting culture at the time, brushed aside as the misguided ramblings of an aging man well past his prime. As inflammatory as Allen's comments seem with perspective, they were largely ignored for one main reason: to the American sports fan, Phog Allen didn't matter anymore.

A few months later, in the fall of 1972, another reporter came by. An ex-KU player and longtime friend of the Allen family named Ted O'Leary, who used to shoot baskets at the Allen home with Forrest Jr., visited Phog's house to do a piece for the *Kansas City Star Magazine*. O'Leary found an elderly man who looked like a shell of the charismatic leader who had been at the front of the KU basketball program for most of the first half of the twentieth century. O'Leary's article described Allen as sitting in a chair with a walker nearby, wearing a Turkish towel around his neck with a yellow sweater over pajamas and a blanket across his lap. "His only slightly-thinning blond hair was smoothed back," O'Leary wrote, "the flesh of his face firm and tinged with pink. Behind glasses his eyes were alert and friendly." Allen's hearing had faded to the point that O'Leary had a difficult time asking him questions, and yet the longtime coach was still able to describe his daily routine and offer some thoughts on the current state of college basketball. O'Leary observed traces of the iconic man who once coached him but also found a calmer man whose opinions carried less outward conviction than they had in previous years. "The Doc Allen of today," O'Leary wrote, "is almost laconic compared with the younger Doc Allen. The intelligence and the quick wittedness are still there but much of the fire is gone."

The article detailed the elderly Allen's daily routine of waking up around

8 a.m., eating a breakfast consisting of oatmeal and two juices—orange and prune—and reading through two local newspapers before lunch. He would take an afternoon nap and drink some buttermilk before watching whatever sports he could find on television in the early evening.

Allen's sense of humor seemed intact, like when he told O'Leary about recently attending the wedding of former Missouri coaching rival Sparky Stalcup's daughter. "Of course Sparky was glad to see me," Allen cracked, "but the rest of those Missourians there looked at me like Jesse James had come back."

Near the end of the session, O'Leary asked Phog Allen whether he had any advice for young men considering the profession of coaching. His answer may well have brought a smirk of irony to the face of James Naismith, had Allen's mentor been alive to read about it.

"There are so few coaches who succeed in proportion to those who fail that I wouldn't advise a young man to become a coach," Allen said. "I'd tell him to become a doctor or a lawyer and do his coaching on the side for fun with a church or YMCA team. The only reason I went into coaching and stayed with it was because I liked it."

That was the last known interview conducted with Forrest Clare "Phog" Allen, whose final two years were lived in the shadows, witnessed only by his nurse, Anna Marie Button, and the occasional visits from family and friends. He spent most days sitting in front of a television set, watching whatever sports he could find while often picking at the hairs on the back of his hand with a small knife—a habit he had developed during his later years.

There were several trips to the hospital throughout the summer of 1974, many of which the Allen family believed would mark the end of Phog's productive life. But the old man rallied each time and convinced his four living children over and over to bring him home when his symptoms lifted.

Inside his modest house, the clock continued ticking. The world outside moved along without him. The KU basketball team was trying to figure out how to follow up on a memorable 1973–74 season that ended with a trip the Final Four, while forty-five-year-old coach Ted Owens wasn't going to have to worry about any state laws ever telling him when he would be forced to retire; by the end of the decade, a federal law would abolish mandatory retirements.

Eventually, Allen's clock ran out. At 3 a.m. on a warm, clear morning on September 16, 1974, Forrest Clare Allen Sr.—known to his former players as Doc and to the rest of the world as Phog—passed away at his Lawrence home. He was eighty-eight years old.

The sun rose a few hours later on a seventy-five-degree day in Lawrence, Kansas, where the 1974–75 KU basketball team was just about to begin its preparations for another season. The final KU game of Phog Allen's lifetime had been an NCAA semifinal loss to Marquette six months earlier, marking the sixth time in school history that the Jayhawks had made it that far in a tournament that Allen's NABC had helped to create thirty-five years earlier.

The obituary that ran in the *Kansas City Star* that week began, "His given name was Forrest Clare Allen. But in the 88 years he stamped his indelible imprint on friend and foe alike he was better known as 'Phog' or 'Doc' . . . or worse. Whatever, Forrest C. Allen reveled in it. Few persons have loved what they did more than Allen. But more important he totally believed in what he did."

The *Star* concluded with the words, "It was Allen, perhaps more than any man, who shaped basketball as it is today."

In the days that followed, the Allen family would receive hundreds, if not thousands, of letters from people offering their condolences. At the next U.S. congressional session, Senator Bob Dole, a former KU player under Allen, spent several minutes speaking on the importance of Phog Allen in American sports.

"He convinced me there was more to life than football and basketball—a large lesson for a young man with expectations like those I entertained before [World War II]—and he helped me realize that there could be other challenges and other rewards in my future," Senator Dole said during the congressional meeting. "I felt an immediate sense of personal loss when I learned of his death Monday. I shall always be in his debt."

The memorial service was held on September 19, a Thursday afternoon gathering at Plymouth Congregational Church. Former KU player Paul Endacott, star of the first national championship teams in the early 1920s, delivered the eulogy.

"Mere words do not have the capacity to rear a fitting memorial for the life and influence of a person so versatile and exceptional as Dr. Forrest C. Allen," Endacott began. "His deeds already have spoken his eulogy."

And yet Endacott was eloquently able to speak to the man's legacy, saying,

> Phog Allen is more than just a legend in the world of sports. He dispersed his talents and boundless energy into many different channels. As with a fine diamond of many facets, no aspect of his life could be dull—each had to sparkle.
>
> Tolerant only of perfection, his many zealous crusades scored notable and long lasting consequences. He often found himself in the role of an innovator—a man ahead of his time. Thus, he frequently had to choose between persistently pursuing goals which his convictions told him were right or surrendering them to opposition which did not possess his same uncanny foresight.

The eulogies that poured out from news agencies throughout the country mostly included Allen's records at KU and profiles of his larger-than-life personality as a basketball coach. *Sports Illustrated* would write that Allen "invented the spectacle of [basketball], literally taking the sport from the cramped gymnasiums of its youth to the far corners of the world."

Kentucky's legendary coach, Adolph Rupp, who had once sat on the Kansas bench and learned from the sport's first full-time coach, told the *Topeka Journal* shortly after Allen's 1974 passing, "Doc will go down in history as the greatest basketball coach of all time."

Allen himself may have written a memorial that encompassed more of his life than just athletics. As Allen had once told a crowd in 1942, thirty-two years before his death, "my life has been more than basketball; it has been struggle, sadness, strife and joy."

The body of Forrest Clare Allen was dressed in his U.S. Olympic team warm-up when he was laid in a casket and placed into the ground at Oak Hill Cemetery in Lawrence, Kansas, not far from a monument honoring the victims of the Quantrill raid more than a century earlier. A large family gravestone, three feet high by six feet wide, bearing the single word ALLEN, stood near a pathway. The grave was surrounded by smaller graves, including four modest stones lying flat on the ground directly in front of the larger one. The graves of Forrest Allen Jr., daughter Mary, wife Bessie, and Phog Allen made a row across the grass. The last in the line would bear the words

Forrest C. "Phog" Allen
Nov. 18, 1885–Sept. 16, 1974
Treasured Husband,
Father,
Friend

The closest tree was a small spruce 50 feet away, meaning Allen's grave would eternally remain in light on sunny days. Even though James Naismith's grave was in the cemetery just across 15th Street, a few hundred yards away, Allen had his own space, had extended himself beyond the Naismith shrine. No matter how much light shimmered from above on a sunny afternoon, there would be no shadows cast upon Phog Allen's grave.

23

Pay Heed, All Who Enter

The coach was lacing up his shoes. The Kansas basketball players would be lacing up theirs a few hours later to take the court at the massive Allen Fieldhouse. The place would be rocking, as it always was, and so these quiet morning hours represented the final moments of peace the coach would have on a typical game day in Lawrence, Kansas.

He stretched and loosened his leg muscles, standing alongside an assistant coach, the athletic director, a couple of golfing buddies, and the dean of the KU law school. They exchanged a few barbs and set out on foot, fleeing the shadow of the fieldhouse and heading up the hill, off through campus. The coach's shoes trampled along the paved sidewalks and out onto 14th Street, cutting through Massachusetts Avenue and on toward 15th, where the group would head east, out along the flatlands near the edge of town, jogging not just for the exercise but also so that the coach could clear his mind. College basketball was not an easy game to master. The sport had gotten so much faster, the players so much bigger. Everyone in the country was looking for an advantage, trying to mainstream their way to a title—but anyone in the game knew there was no such thing as a shortcut to a trophy. The inner dialogue of fast-break outlets and matchup zones and box-and-one defenses was difficult to outrun; coaching basketball had become a 24/7 profession.

They cut off the road, past an eight-foot-high stone structure attached to a gateway, their feet running along pavement and onto a dirt path. Out front, the coach slowed his gait as he ran past the stones, up around the bend. The game strategy and player psychology and defensive adjustments typically left him in these moments, his head clear and his mind sharp. Whatever happened over the next twelve to twenty-four hours, the coach would be able to handle it. Deep down, he knew his job was about more than just winning and losing, even if all the fans cared about was the former. If you're going to coach basketball at Kansas, you're going to win games; anytime you don't, there will be questions.

But none of that mattered in these moments, when the morning jogs helped clear the coach's scrambling mind and freed him of the weight of a fan base that reached far beyond the borders of Kansas. As his slow gait petered out into a brisk walk, and the others passed on by, the coach approached the man he had come to see. Out there in the open, near the three-by-six limestone, he saw the neatly arranged markers along the grass. He knelt before the one closest to the path.

The coach reached out and patted the gravestone.

"Doc," he said, "we need all the help we can get tonight."

With that, Roy Williams, the head basketball coach at the University of Kansas, stood and turned away, his feet picking up pace along the dirt, onto the pavement, out through the stone-draped gates and back onto the streets of Lawrence, where he would catch up to the others. He had a game to win, and now that he had soaked in the inspiration from Phog Allen's grave, Williams could already feel the confidence flowing into his blood.

Without Phog Allen, the Kansas basketball program had carried on. His replacement, Dick Harp, ended up coaching eight seasons at Kansas, with two trips to the NCAA tournament to show for it. He had been succeeded by Ted Owens, who won almost two-thirds of his games over fourteen seasons, including a 1974 trip to the Final Four, before the KU athletic department went looking for another coach to lead the program in 1983. The search led to Chapel Hill, North Carolina, where a former KU player named Dean Smith was having all kinds of success. Smith was one of several former KU players who had kept the Allen legacy alive in his mentor's retirement, with remarkable success in the coaching profession. Smith would eventually be the one to break Rupp's all-time win total, a mark originally held by Phog Allen.

Smith was considered for the KU job in the spring of 1983 at a time when his University of North Carolina program was on top of the basketball world. The Tar Heels had won the 1982 national championship, and Smith boasted some of the most impressive talent in the country— led by a kid named Michael Jordan who would go on to rise to the top of the flourishing National Basketball Association and bring the sport to its apex. While James Naismith and Phog Allen were largely responsible for bringing the sport of basketball from its infancy stages to worldwide acceptance, it was players like Wilt Chamberlain, Magic Johnson, and Jordan who would carry the torch and take the sport to unforeseen, meteoric heights.

The marriage between KU and Dean Smith was so perfect that it never happened, as the North Carolina coach with the unbending loyalty quietly turned down overtures from his alma mater but recommended one of his own former assistants, a young NBA coach named Larry Brown, for the job.

On April 7, 1983, Brown was named head coach of the University of Kansas basketball program, and it didn't take long for him to turn the Jayhawks back into a national-title contender. His coaching staffs included up-and-comers like John Calipari, Alvin Gentry, and a recent Oklahoma State graduate named Bill Self, but Brown's biggest hire may well have been North Carolina high school coach Ed Manning, who brought along his son, Danny, to give the Jayhawks the top recruit in the country in 1984. Danny Manning, the school's most high-profile recruit since Wilt Chamberlain, helped lead KU to the Final Four two years later.

During Manning's senior year at Kansas in 1988, a KU student named Todd Gilmore was sitting in professional practice class, daydreaming about Kansas basketball and the Allen Fieldhouse, when a unique phrase popped into his head. He scribbled nine words at the bottom of his notebook page and later presented them to a friend named Mike Gentemann, who began sketching letters for a banner. With the help of some friends, Gilmore and Gentemann got their hands on ten shower curtains and pinned them together for a thirty-five-foot-long sign. The students received permission from KU's athletic director to hang the sign inside Allen Fieldhouse, which they did in the early-morning hours before a big game against rising national power Duke.

On February 20, 1988, the banner debuted. Fans showed up for the Duke game to find the pinned-together curtains, connected to the rafters with help of a one-hundred-foot rope, bearing the words "Pay Heed, All Who Enter: BEWARE OF *'THE PHOG.'*"

The temporary sign would eventually be replaced by a back-lit replica, permanently adding to the Phog Allen aura at the fieldhouse that bears his name. The sign became a staple of the KU basketball tradition, and Phog Allen's name lived on through another generation of basketball fans.

Within a few weeks of the "Beware of the Phog" sign making its Allen Fieldhouse debut, the Manning-led team, dubbed "Danny and the Miracles," made an improbable run to the program's fourth national title. It marked the second time the Jayhawks ever won an NCAA tournament and the first since Phog Allen had led KU to the 1951–52 title.

A few days after the 1988 NCAA title game, Phog Allen's oldest living son, Milton "Mitt" Allen, passed away.

Larry Brown left for the NBA after that championship season, and new coach Roy Williams, another Dean Smith assistant from North Carolina, kept the Jayhawks near the top of the coaching basketball world without any noticeable drop-off. The "Pay Heed" banner would hang over Roy Williams during every home game, and he maintained a connection with Phog's family during a coaching tenure that would last until 2003. Williams's strong connection with the Allen family was not shared by all members of the KU athletic department in those years. The department continued to capitalize financially on the "Beware of the Phog" slogan, which appeared in products at the KU bookstore, and the Allen family took issue with the name being exploited by a university that had unceremoniously "retired" its legendary coach against his will.

As Phog Allen's descendants grew in number, the school's ticket allotment became an issue as well. Allen's bitterness toward the school that, in his mind, forced him into retirement had been passed down through the generations; the Allen family held a fervent passion for KU basketball over the years but a jaded opinion of the school's administration. One granddaughter, Judy Allen Morris, became so fed up with the KU athletic department that she pulled a family scholarship in Phog Allen's name from that segment of the university and gave it to students in the physical therapy department—to honor her grandfather's osteopathic work over the years.

For the 1997–98 season, the University of Kansas was planning a basketball centennial celebration by bringing together some of the greatest players, moments, and figures in the storied history of KU hoops. In an effort to include the legacy of Phog Allen in the events, the Allen family proposed the idea of erecting a statue of the legendary coach to stand outside the arena. Kansas athletic director Bob Frederick initially told the family that the school didn't want to put a Phog Allen statue on campus, saying the precedent would open the door for countless honorary statues. Years later, Phog Allen's grandchildren would recall Frederick telling them at the time, "If we do it for Phog, we'll have to do it for everybody." Judy Allen Morris responded by telling Frederick that the family was going to get a statue put somewhere in Lawrence and that it would be an embarrassment to the university if the memorial was erected downtown.

The school eventually relented, but only if the Allen family came up with the money through private donations. KU officials refused to pass on names of donors on the athletic department's Williams Fund (in no way related to Roy Williams), which further infuriated the Allens. An alumni group that included several ex-players and the widow of 1920s star Paul Endacott formed a foundation called the Phog Allen Memorial Fund, which raised enough in donations to get the project off the ground.

Three local sculptors submitted statue mock-ups to the Allen family. The first one the family received showed Phog Allen standing next to a fence, with one leg raised, his foot upon the bottom rail and a shock of wheat in his mouth. In the eyes of Phog's family, the statue looked more like a caricature of a Kansan than an honorary memorial. Much to the chagrin of the sculptor and his agent, the family decided to go another direction and went with a KU art professor named Kwan Wu. From his Overland Park studio, Wu designed a much more flattering image of the former Jayhawks coach, complete with the signature Turkish towel wrapped around Allen's throat. The bronze Phog Allen stood proud, with a whistle hanging from his neck and a basketball under one arm. It was the image that the Allen family felt best portrayed the coaching legend.

Wu completed the sculpture in the fall of 1997 and unveiled it at a private showing in Topeka. At a total cost of $175,000, including the man-hours involved in placing the statue on a three-foot-high granite base, the Phog Allen statue was dedicated in December 1997—at a pregame ceremony leading up to a win over Middle Tennessee State. The date marked the ninetieth anniversary of Allen's first game as head coach of the team.

The words beneath Allen's image recount his legendary coaching career and end with the quote about which of his teams was his favorite: "I will have to wait 25 years to see what kind of people they become and their contributions to society." From the ground to the top of Allen's head, the statue stands just about twelve feet high—a height that seems to give an unintentional wink of acknowledgement toward Phog Allen's lifelong battle to raise the baskets.

In addition to having the arena named in his honor, Phog Allen would stand in front of the venue in both spirit and image. Fans entering through the main gate and on into the Allen Fieldhouse would undoubtedly pass his bronze likeness as they descended into the arena where he coached his final game.

Inside the arena, KU basketball continued to thrive under Roy Williams and Bill Self, the onetime KU assistant who left his post at the University of Illinois to take over in 2003. The Jayhawks remained among the top teams in the country year in and year out, while the Allen family watched proudly from a safe distance. There are still some hurt feelings that have transcended the generations, and the family hasn't always been happy with the way the Allen name has been treated over time, but Phog's grandchildren insist that there is no sense of entitlement on their part.

"I don't think we expect anything," grandson Mark Allen said in 2014. "We just expect KU to preserve the legacy of Phog because there wouldn't be a basketball program without him."

Some of Allen's former players understand the frustration of the ex-coach's descendants, and nobody who played for Phog seems to be satisfied with how his coaching career came to a sudden end. But the legacy of the man has mostly remained untainted over the years. Allen's impact on the Kansas program is indisputable, and his legacy is unlikely to be forgotten as long as the fieldhouse and the bronze statue out front are around.

There are those who believe that The Phog is lingering around the KU basketball program in other ways as well.

"Doc Allen is sitting on the backboard," former Jayhawks coach Roy Williams said in 2014, nearly six decades after Phog coached his final game, "swatting some of the other team's shots away."

The fortieth anniversary of Phog Allen's death quietly came and went in September 2014. The University of Kansas campus was just reawakening for another academic year while Bill Self's basketball program was making plans on another run toward the NCAA tournament.

Phog Allen was long gone, but some say that he never really went away.

"He's hovering over that fieldhouse," former KU star Clyde Lovellette said in 2014. "Every time guys come out on the floor, no matter how long Phog's been gone, he's still a really big factor in the winning and losing in that fieldhouse. His presence is felt, every year, on that floor."

Epilogue

SHINING ON

The footprints are in the snow. In the early-morning hours of a winter after-noon in twenty-first-century Lawrence, Kansas, a single pair of footsteps leaves a trail from Naismith Blvd. across the white terrain of a snowfall that descended upon the city overnight. They lead up to the bronze statue of Forrest C. "Phog" Allen, standing twelve feet high above the snow-covered concrete directly in front of the main entrance to Allen Fieldhouse. The footprints die out at the base of the Phog statue, as if the owner of the boots that left them has faded into the darkness.

The college campus just up the hill is about to rise from slumber, shiver-ing with anticipation of another game day of KU basketball. The Jayhawks are in the midst of a typically stellar season, on the way to yet another conference title and a trip to the NCAA tournament—the greatest show in American sports—and in a few hours, the fieldhouse will be rocking with pride while Phog's statue waits outside in the cold and snow.

A gentle breeze blows dust-like snowflakes across the lone set of foot-steps at dawn. The bronze statue stands still in the wind, Phog's head and shoulders flecked with white from the evening snowfall. He stands proudly above the flat land, holding a snow-covered basketball under one arm, his chest sticking out and his back turned to the Allen Fieldhouse as if he's protecting a shrine. There is no one else around; just those mysterious footsteps. From above, these steps are just specks along the white carpet, a trail leading from Naismith Blvd. to the basketball arena fifty yards away.

Within hours, the white snow glimmers in the light, despite the grey sky covered in a blanket of harmless clouds above. The KU faithful begin their descent upon Allen Fieldhouse. They come from fraternity row just up the hill, from Hashinger Hall and the Wagon Wheel and the restaurants and hotels along Massachusetts Street. From East Lawrence and Overland Park and Shawnee Mission and Kansas City. Their cars file in from I-70 and flood the streets surrounding the campus; their foot traffic rustles through the snow. Dressed in blue stocking caps and red winter coats and canary-yellow scarves, they come in packs, their boots kicking up the white blanket of snowflakes as they descend upon Allen Fieldhouse and file past Phog's statue. They squeeze into the doors of the arena and shed their winter wear, arriving at least twenty minutes before tip-off so as not to miss the pregame show. A video presentation will begin overhead, on the eighteen-by-ten-foot, high-definition scoreboard screen, showing a still photo of Wilt Chamberlain, his arms extended toward the screen, followed by a flash-photo playback of KU basketball history. A series of numbers flash by. More than two thousand wins. Fifty-four conference titles. Thirteen Final Fours. Five national championships. Images of Naismith and Allen and Manning. The fans watch in silence, the pride all over their faces.

Outside the arena, the movement peters down to a whisper, finally leaving only the gentle sound of a breeze passing over Phog Allen's statue. Soon enough, the moaning sounds of "Rock Chalk Jayhawk" will seep from inside the arena on an otherwise silent winter evening. The night sky looks down from above to find the stillness outside, upon a snow-covered Midwestern campus that looks something like a ghost town.

Not even those footprints remain now. The trampling footsteps of thousands have washed out the evidence, and all that is left is the silent darkness of another night.

The 2014–15 Kansas Jayhawks bowed out of the NCAA tournament earlier than expected, losing to a rising Wichita State program that was all too happy to knock off the giants from the north, and the basketball world barely stopped to take notice. Bill Self's twelfth KU team, rebuilding after losing a pair of star freshmen who had been selected as two of the top three picks in the June NBA draft, watched as the most exciting bracket tournament in American sports provided millions of hungry fans with another March Madness for the ages. When all was said and done, Mike Krzyzewski's Duke Blue Devils were hoisting the trophy, his fifth national title, in a game that appeared on more than 28.3 million television sets. The advertising numbers exceeded $1 billion in revenue over the sixty-seven-game tournament—more money than the National Football League, the National Basketball Association, or Major League Baseball generated in postseason play. One year earlier, a billionaire named Warren Buffett had offered $1 billion to anyone who could correctly pick all sixty-seven games of the 2014 tournament—no one did—and the phenomenon of bracket-style tournament pools had become such a staple in American culture that the U.S. president annually provided his picks in a popular feature broadcast on ESPN television. The American Gaming Association estimated that 40 million Americans would fill out a bracket, wagering upwards of $9 billion on the NCAA tournament the following year.

Even a visionary like Forrest "Phog" Allen couldn't have seen this coming. The man who once wrote in his 1947 book *Better Basketball* that "dancing should not be permitted on basketball floors" had no idea what would become of college basketball and the tournament commonly known as "The Big Dance." Neither the betting pools nor the over-the-top exposure of college athletes would have brought much satisfaction to Phog if he had still been around to watch the game he loved, but his efforts to bring basketball up from its early roots would likely have left Allen feeling some semblance of pride at what had become of the sport.

As longtime rival-turned-friend Henry Iba once told author Doug Elstun of Allen, "Every move he made, he made with a purpose of trying to better basketball."

While Allen's descendants and the University of Kansas were doing their part to keep Phog's legacy alive, his overall impact on the sport had mostly faded over time. Names like Naismith and Chamberlain were familiar to even the most casual sports fan, and yet Phog Allen—the man who served as the bridge between those two basketball greats and had his fingerprints on just about every basketball innovation over the fifty years that separated them—was known almost exclusively as *just* a longtime coach.

Former KU coach Roy Williams believes that, for whatever reason, Allen's legacy in the sport has simply been blurred by time. He maintains that coaches from a previous generation, those who coached in the sixties, seventies, and eighties, knew what Allen meant to the sport but that his name no longer seems to matter to the current generation.

"Most people right now think Michael Jordan invented the game of basketball," Williams joked. "It's just the generation. Typically, the young people today don't look at the game of basketball like we did before. . . . It's not a slight against what Dr. Allen did. It's just that the game has changed so much."

Williams did his part to keep the name alive during his KU tenure. He maintained a close relationship with the Allen family and posted a keepsake in the KU locker room featuring the cardboard sign Allen had made in the late 1940s, with Phog's handwritten message: "You can't hang with owls at night if you want to soar with eagles in the day."

Roy Williams left the remnant behind when he took over as basketball coach at the University of North Carolina in 2003, and no one seems to know what happened to it. The sign simply got lost over time, much like Phog Allen's legacy. But Williams, due in large part to his time at KU, is among the older generation of coaches who know what kind of paths Allen paved for others.

Williams succinctly describes Allen as a coaching pioneer by saying, "He was—period, the end—the first coach."

Mike Krzyzewski, the longtime Duke University and Team USA basketball coach who by 2015 was considered the dean of basketball coaching, once listed Phog Allen, longtime rival Henry Iba, and KU alumni John McLendon and Adolph Rupp as the "founding fathers" of the coaching profession. In 2014, he said Phog's legacy was still looming large in the sport.

"We're forever grateful that he did get it established as an Olympic sport," Krzyzewski said. "It really shows that he had great vision, in that this was not going to just be a game in the United States but it has the potential to be a global game.

"And he showed that same vision as he developed his program and developed the game during the time he was so influential with the sport."

As of 2014, the one living coach who might have the most insight into Phog's career was the one who had the least to say about it. Dean Smith, his former player and assistant coach before going on to a legendary career at the University of North Carolina, had been stricken with dementia and memory loss in the years leading up to his death in February 2015. Roy Williams is among the so-called second generation of Allen's disciples, who got to hear all about the Phog legacy from above. He served as one of Dean Smith's assistants for eleven years and said the longtime North Carolina coach took a lot from his mentor.

"I heard so much about Doc Allen's practices, about his writing personal letters to his players," Williams said. "He had such a personal touch." Williams added that former Allen player and assistant coach Dick Harp was equally enamored by the Phog legend while working as a UNC assistant with Williams under Dean Smith. "They talked so much about Doc Allen," Williams said in 2014. "He was so revered. It's amazing the pedestal they put him on."

The most extensive description Smith provided of Allen came in the foreword he wrote for Blair Kerkhoff's 1996 book, *Phog Allen: The Father of Basketball Coaching*. "Dr. Allen was a gifted individual," Smith wrote, "who made the most of his gifts to help others in his many, many years of influence."

With each passing generation, those years of influence seemed to fade away as the men Allen coached passed away. Names like Wooden, Abdul-Jabbar, Bird, and Jordan became more synonymous with the game than Forrest "Phog" Allen.

The best explanation as to why Allen's legacy had faded may be contained in a letter written seven decades earlier, penned by a member of the University of Kansas administration. In 1942, when the university had brought Phog Allen to tears by establishing a scholarship in his name, KU law school dean Frederick Moreau wrote a letter that included the line, "When anything becomes tradition, we somehow lose an appreciation of its importance."

Over time, Phog Allen's name had become such a comfortable fabric on the sport of basketball that many people had simply lost appreciation for what he meant to the game.

Bill Hougland has the kind of face that seems eternally caught in a pleasant moment from the past; his smile brightens but never really fades. He's eighty-four years old, and it would be easy to say that his best years are behind him, but the former Kansas Jayhawk basketball player doesn't see life that way. While Hougland may have slowed down and lost a considerable amount of the on-court tenacity that had once led his coach to call him Wormy, he's still living a pretty good life. His idea of a good time lately is to sit back in a chair inside his spacious home on a Lawrence cul-de-sac, his wife Carolee by his side, and talk basketball with his grandchildren. Rarely does the subject of his own playing days come up; Hougland would much rather talk about his grandkids' day at the Bill Self Basketball Camp than anything he did six decades earlier. His memories are mostly eroded by time, his two Olympic gold medals safely tucked away at the Allen Fieldhouse a few miles away.

There was a time when Hougland was constantly on the move. Back in 1952, for example, Hougland flew to Seattle to win an NCAA basketball championship, was in New York City the following weekend to take part in an Olympic Trials tournament, and moved on to Helsinki, Finland, a few weeks after that to compete in his first Olympic Games. He would win a gold medal during his time in Finland, and days later Hougland was on his way back to New York to report for boot camp before heading overseas to serve in the Korean War. The whirlwind continued four years later, in 1956, when Hougland returned to the Olympic Games and became only the second man in the history of the sport to earn two gold medals.

That all seems like a lifetime ago now, as Hougland sits in the den of his Lawrence home, with door closed, and struggles to remember much about the past decade, much less the 1950s. And yet when the subject of his former college coach comes up, Hougland has no trouble reaching out for a memory that remains vivid more than half a century later.

It came during Hougland's tour of duty in Korea, when Phog Allen stopped by the town of Beloit, Kansas, to pay a visit to Hougland's mother and father at work. Hougland goes on to describe a scene of the aging University of Kansas coach, perhaps dressed in a suit from a speaking engagement, his hair thinning and eyeglasses on his face, pulling his Cadillac into the alley behind a hardware store in a small town in Northern

Kansas, parking and discreetly putting out his cigarette. Phog Allen gets out of his car, enters through the back of the hardware store, and pulls up a folding chair. He spends the next half hour visiting with Marion and Grace Hougland. He does this only because he cares about them, and about their son. It's a routine that Phog Allen will continue in McCune and Winfield and Medicine Lodge, throughout the small towns along the Kansas plains.

The scene serves as a testament to how important Allen's "boys" became to him over the years. Even at the peak of his multitasking days of juggling speaking engagements, recruiting visits, and basketball practices, he always found time for the boys-turned-men who once played for him.

"Doc was very, very loyal," Hougland says.

The only time Bill Hougland remembers returning the favor was in Phog Allen's later years, after Hougland came back from the Korean War and had joined Bob Kurland as the only men in history to earn two gold medals in basketball. Hougland was by then working at Koch Industries, a Wichita-based petroleum company that kept him on the road for days on end; Allen was a retired basketball coach and full-time osteopath with a clinic in West Lawrence. Hougland stopped by his former coach's small office on Eighth Street, looking to catch up on old times, when Doc Allen made an offer.

"Get on the table," Phog Allen said. His hair was thinner than Hougland had remembered, but Allen still had a charisma about him that was undeniable. The years had not shaken his confidence nor stripped him of his zest for life.

Hougland followed his coach's order, and just like that, Doc Allen was going to work on his spine. He could feel something amiss, and eventually Bill Hougland would admit to some leg pain. After a few adjustments, the discomfort dissipated. Doc Allen would then inquire about what had become of Hougland's life, and they got to chatting like longtime friends. The subject of basketball barely came up, if at all; Phog Allen was never too interested in the past.

The same can't be said for Phog Allen's former players. Those who played for him all have a favorite Phog story, which they cling to like a family heirloom as the months and years and generations pass by. Jerry "The Sherriff" Waugh has a thousand Phog stories, from the "Chickenshit List" to the dead bird that never leaves its nest, his deadpan delivery drawing a cacophony of laughter upon each telling.

Clyde Lovellette also had plenty of Phog memories, of course, beginning with the time the legendary KU coach drove to Terre Haute, Indiana, to talk him out of his commitment to the Indiana Hoosiers, and running through the Olympic year in 1952. More than six decades later, Lovellette still kicked himself whenever he thought about the missed layup that cost Allen a chance to be head coach of the U.S. team that year. "I screwed up, and I lost the game for Kansas in the final seconds," Lovellette said in 2014, referring to the 1-point loss to the Peoria Caterpillars in the finals of the 1952 Olympic Trials tournament. "I felt really bad it happened that way. All I had to do was give [the ball] to [Bob] Kenney. I took the shot, I missed it, and Phog became assistant coach. I felt terrible."

And yet Phog Allen never mentioned the missed layup to Lovellette. Not once.

From a basketball standpoint, that might be the only regret Lovellette harbored since the day Phog Allen's Oldsmobile pulled into the driveway of his parents' Indiana home all those years ago. Playing for Allen was one of the best things that ever happened to Lovellette, and he wasn't afraid to tell anyone.

During a phone conversation in the early summer of 2014, less than two years before he passed away at the age of eighty-six, Lovellette was remembering his time playing for Allen when his eyes fell upon a photograph of the coach that he'd kept over the years. Lovellette cut off his sentence and began reading the words Allen wrote across the photograph: "To an All-American. See you in 20 years."

Into the phone, Lovellette said, "I don't know why he didn't put my name on it. That was Doc. He was always doing things to make you think."

Phog Allen had a funny way of motivating people. Funny but effective—so much so that his tactics were still working their magic decades after his death. The impact Phog Allen had went well beyond basketball, and that was by design.

Clyde Lovellette, Bill Hougland, and Jerry Waugh were all well into their eighties by the summer of 2014, but to Phog Allen they would always be his "boys." The title brings each one of them his own sense of pride. Doc

Allen may not have ever told his "boys" on the KU basketball team that he loved them, but he let his feelings be known in other ways.

A wise man once told Phog Allen that the game of basketball wasn't meant to be coached. One single man wasn't supposed to have nearly the impact on the sport as a group of young, eager players who knew the meaning of teamwork. Basketball was, from the very start, designed to be about the *team*.

Forrest "Phog" Allen ignored the sage advice passed down by Dr. James Naismith. He created the idea of a basketball coach and set a template for the profession that was still being used decades after he took his final breath. That may be only a small part of his legacy, both on and off the court, but Allen certainly proved Naismith wrong all those years ago.

The game of basketball *can* be coached, after all. Allen was the first to prove it, but tens of thousands have followed in his footsteps.

Coaching basketball was all Phog Allen ever really wanted to do. Helping turn his "boys" into honorable, productive men was something that he felt he *needed* to do. And bringing the sport to the masses, it turned out, was something that he was destined to do.

Independence, Missouri, is a town caught in the traps of history, its twenty-first-century face as nostalgically American as the name implies. One would be hard-pressed to walk a single city block without bumping into a church—sometimes two, even three. There are ninety-one of them in all, representing twenty-three different denominations, all of the structures scattered across a hilltop that overlooks Kansas City in the distance.

The easiest way to get to Independence, aptly enough, is via Truman Road, the thirteen-mile thoroughfare named for the U.S. president and Independence native. Driving from the broken-down parts of Eastern Kansas City to the unsettling stillness of Independence takes one past an assortment of coin-op laundromats, liquor stores, bail bondsmen, and authentic Mexican restaurants; just before the railway bridge near the Independence border, an adult-video store boasts its presence in neon lights.

There is very little evidence of greatness along Truman Road, and the steady rise up a modest hillside into Independence is somewhat majestic by comparison. The Community of Christ Church, its glistening shape rising skyward like a five-story-high unicorn tusk coming out of soft-serve ice cream, announces itself without any attempt at humility. Churches unfold like weeds around the structure, religion coming at a visitor more rapidly than chains of fast-food restaurants.

At the center of town, much of the hamlet's past is still on display on a quiet Saturday morning in the spring, the foot traffic barely a whisper around the massive, 178-year-old courthouse on Liberty and Main. On a sunny day, roads into Independence Square can be backed up by a horse-and-carriage, courtesy of a company that still operates for scenic rides through the historic corridor of town. Many of the shops surrounding it are boarded up, the exceptions including a Bank of America office where four employees pleasantly greet the first customer of the day a few minutes before noon. Not even Wild About Harry, a collectibles shop named for Harry Truman, the most famous Independence resident over the years, has its doors open on a pleasant spring morning. Nor are the ice cream machines pumping next door at Clinton's Soda, where Truman worked as a teenager in the early 1900s.

The city looks a lot like it may have a century earlier, with Queen Anne houses and American Foursquare architecture amidst the 100-year-old buildings scattered throughout the landscape. It's not difficult to imagine exactly how Independence, Missouri, looked 120 years earlier, when Harry S. Truman and a younger neighbor boy named Forrest Clare Allen were just beginning to rise as American icons.

The first thing one asks upon visiting Independence is how a single man rises to greatness from such uninspiring beginnings—let alone two. There are no mountaintops in Independence, a town that rises up modestly with hopeful reverence from the flatlands below. One can see from the hilltop that there are possibilities out there, a world without limits. But getting there is another journey altogether.

This is where Phog Allen's story began. From running the dirt roads in search of a drink of water to the weekend carnival boxing circuit, Forrest C. "Phog" Allen followed his visions and never once gave up on his voyage. He possessed the few traits that separate a man with vision from a true visionary: the wherewithal, the foresight, the confidence, and the stubbornness to turn one man's dream into the reality of millions.

When dusk sets on the town of Independence, and the lights of the historic Truman museum are illuminating through the night, one can almost feel the ache of a small boy, running the dirt paths of his hometown, off toward something greater. Evening bleeds into the dead of night, and silence blankets the town. Lights go out, one by one, through the historic district and the square and the rows of houses constantly interrupted by churches, and darkness sets in. On a cloudless night, the stars above seem to be shining brighter than ever.

NOTES

PROLOGUE

xv   "**It was Allen**": *Kansas City Star*, September 17, 1974.

xvi   "**There are so few coaches**": Theodore M. O'Leary, "A Visit with Phog Allen," *Kansas City Star Magazine*, March 26, 1972.

xviii   "**The way I see it**": Phone interview with Roy Williams, August 25, 2014.

xviii   "**At the very base level**": Taped interview with Mike Krzyzewski, October 17, 2014, Duke Sports Information Department, Duke University.

xix   "**get off the court**": *Columbia Evening Missourian*, February 19, 1920; *Lawrence Journal World*, February 19–20, 1920.

xix   "**all those guys [who witnessed it] are dead**": Author interview with Bill Walton following University of Washington–Arizona basketball game on February 13, 2015.

xx   "**there are two crazy people**": Nino Lo Bello, "Hoop Man of Kansas," *Evanston (IL) Rotarian*, February 1956, 54. In the issue that followed, in April 1956, Allen wrote a letter demanding a correction, writing, "What 'Rock' really said to me was, 'Phog, there are two great athletic games that I don't care for, and basketball is both of them.'"

xx   "**You just can't be neutral**": Nino Lo Bello, "Hoop Man of Kansas," *Rotarian*, February 1956, 54.

1. RUNNING FROM INDEPENDENCE

2   "**a disgraceful sight**": McClure, *Beware of the "Phog,"* 25.

2. THE "WORLD'S CHAMPIONSHIP"

12 "Mrs. Mary E. Allen, wife of": *Jackson County Examiner*, December 6, 1904.

13 "Should the Athletics win": Rains, *Kansas City Star*, March 26, 1905.

14 "those who saw the team": *Kansas City Times*, March 27, 1905.

15 "rough-and-ready lot": Allen, *Better Basketball*, 7.

15 "all the artistry of swinging an adept hand": Allen, *Better Basketball*, 7.

15 "more resembled a mixed-martial arts contest": Shoals and Weinstein, *The Undisputed Guide to Pro Basketball*.

15 "the most perfect ever seen here": *Kansas City Times*, March 29, 1905.

16 "Goals were thrown from all kinds": *Kansas City Times*, March 29, 1905.

16 "the most exciting and best played": *Kansas City Times*, March 29, 1905.

3. A MAN NAMED JIM

18 "crucial moment in [his] life": Rains, *James Naismith*, 44.

19 "Huh. Another new game.": Rains, *James Naismith*, 45.

19 "remains the only major sport that is": Allen, *Better Basketball*, 3.

20 "I asked my only sister if she": Rains, *James Naismith*, xii.

22 "I have two old peach baskets": Webb, *The Basketball Man*, 63.

24 "everyone who is at all interested in athletics": *University Weekly*, University of Kansas, December 10, 1898.

24 "a very ungentlemanly game": Hendel, *Kansas Jayhawks*, 2.

4. THE HERO ARRIVES

27 "A more enthusiastic, a more excited crowd": *Kansas City Times*, March 30, 1905.

27 "a baby game": *Kansas City Times*, March 30, 1905.

28 "K.C. owns world champions": *Kansas City Star*, March 30, 1905.

29 "They hadn't lifted Missouri": Hendel, *Kansas Jayhawks*, 6.

29 "a strong addition to the team": *Daily Kansan*, October 18, 1905.

31 "He is a steady, consistent": Rains, *James Naismith*, 87.

31 "Why, you can't coach basketball" and "You can certainly teach free-throw": Allen, *Coach Phog Allen's Sports Stories*, 174.

5. THE GAME CAN BE COACHED

35 "Thou shalt not covet thy classmate's pony": Baker University catalog, 1905–6.

36 "When the game was called at 7:30 p.m.": *Baker Orange*, February 15, 1907.

37 **"Dr. James Naismith, the inventor of the game"**: *University Daily Kansan*, December 20, 1906.

38 **"The only thing that stands in the way"**: *Daily Kansan*, November 25, 1907.

39 **"Every Jayhawker methodically executed"**: Hendel, *Kansas Jayhawks*, 10–11.

40 **"For enthusiasm even the most exciting Foot-ball contests"**: 1909 *Jayhawker* yearbook.

41 **"Boys, I want you to have confidence"**: Kerkhoff, *Phog Allen*, 26; McClure, *Beware of the "Phog."*

42 **"The Jayhawkers have been handicapped by"**: Elstun, "A Biography of Forrest C. 'Phog' Allen," 11.

43 **"a redheaded, athletic wizard"**: Allen, *Better Basketball*, 89.

43 **"Much credit undoubtedly belongs to Coach Allen"**: 1909 *Jayhawker* yearbook.

6. CALL HIM DOC

45 **"If only Casey could"** and **"Defiance gleamed in Casey's eye"**: Thayer, "Casey At the Bat," *San Francisco Examiner*, June 3, 1888.

46 **"The secret of Greek superiority"**: Allen, *Coach Phog Allen's Sports Stories*, 71.

47 **"a system of medical practice based on"**: Full definition of *osteopathy*, "Osteopathy," Merriam-Webster website, accessed April 2, 2016, http://www.merriam-webster.com/dictionary/osteopathy.

50 **"dig their own graves with their teeth."**: Allen, *Coach Phog Allen's Sports Stories*, 73.

50 **"One never sees a fat race horse."**: Allen, *Coach Phog Allen's Sports Stories*, 72.

50 **"A sprained thumb is a 'dead horse'"**: Letter dated July 26, 1938, from Coach Allen to player Bill Geiger, provided by the Allen family archives.

51 **"Kansas' greatest all-around athlete"**: Allen, *Better Basketball*, 89.

51 **"Don't feel sorry for me, pal"** and **"Perhaps Tommy was right"**: Allen, *Coach Phog Allen's Sports Stories*, 127–28.

52 **"A coach who could treat a player's injuries"**: Krause, *Guardians of the Game*, 6.

7. A TEACHER AMONG TEACHERS

57 **"A man's consciousness"**: Lyle, "Seventy Years and One Thousand Games," *Daily Kansan*, February 19, 1956.

58 **"So much stress is laid today"**: Keith, "The Tradition," *Sports Illustrated*, February 13, 1978, 35–36.

59 **"the first time I didn't get a job I applied for"**: Stallard, *Tales from the Kansas Jayhawks Hardwood*, 9.

59 **"with a game each, neither had won"**: 1905-6 Missouri State Teachers College, District Two, yearbook.

60 **"The dribble presents more opportunities"**: Allen, *Better Basketball*, 115.

61 **"if no one else could do it, Ug could"**: Allen, *Better Basketball*, 439.

61 **"I admit that he has failed"**: Allen, *Better Basketball*, 439-43.

61 **"this Mercury-footed flyer with the slick pigskin"**: Allen, *Better Basketball*, 442-43.

62 **"childish"** and **"professional jealousy"**: *University Missourian of Columbia, Missouri*, January 25, 1915.

63 **"miracle man"**: *Topeka State Journal*, January 9, 1917.

8. ONCE A JAYHAWK

65 **"What was that about?"** and **"If he wanted you to know"**: Webb, *The Basketball Man*, 245.

67 **"simply blown up."**: *Lawrence Journal World*, July 17, 1919.

68 **"Let us all be able"**: Rains, *James Naismith*, 131-32.

68 **"like the farmer with"**: Allen, *Coach Phog Allen's Sports Stories*, 176.

68 **"shrewd enough to invent the game"**: *Time*, February 24, 1936.

69 **"too scared of these boys"**: Hendel, *Kansas Jayhawks*, 20.

70 **"Lonborg! Rody! Bennett!"**: Allen, *Better Basketball*, 444-48.

71 **"feeling that Solem would see"**: Allen, *Better Basketball*, 447.

72 **"The Jayhawker record was exceptional"**: Hendel, *Kansas Jayhawks*, 21.

74 **"the most delightful and gratifying thing"**: Allen, *Better Basketball*, 453-57.

76 **"When two teams of equal ability"**: Allen, *Coach Phog Allen's Sports Stories*, 77.

76 **"ape man"**: Rice, *Adolph Rupp*, 8.

77 **"Boxing teaches the follow-through"**: Allen, *Better Basketball*, 67-68.

77 **"the parts of a player's anatomy"**: Allen, *Better Basketball*, 67.

77 **"It is said that the eyes"**: Allen, *Better Basketball*, 75.

77 **"for the purpose of building"**: Allen, *My Basket-Ball Bible*.

78 **"a squad talented in singing"**: Allen, *Better Basketball*, 74.

78 **"Spizzerinctum"**: Turtle, "Give the Ball to Junior!" *Indianapolis Saturday Evening Post*, December 28, 1940, 41.

78 **"Esprit de corps!"**: Allen, *Better Basketball*, 90.

78 **"A team that won't be beaten"**: Allen, *Coach Phog Allen's Sports Stories*, 77.

79 **"Are you ready?"**: Hendel, *Kansas Jayhawks*, 46.

79 **"unusual"** and **"He would make these talks"**: Hendel, *Kansas Jayhawks*, 22.

79   **"In this respect"**: *Kansas City Times*, "Phog Allen Was a Winner On and Off the Court," *Kansas City Times*, September 23, 1974.

79   **"unless Phog can again accomplish a miracle"**: *Topeka State Journal*, December 9, 1920.

80   **"rough and tumble"** and **"Phog Allen and Dr. W.E. Meanwell"**: *Columbia Evening Missourian*, February 19, 1920.

80   **"acting like a high school coach"**: *Kansas City Star*, February 20, 1920.

81   **"of course we will"** and **"go through that line"**: *Columbia Evening Missourian*, November 25, 1920.

81   **"maul"**: *Columbia Evening Missourian*, February 4, 1921.

9. ASCENT TO NEW HEIGHTS

85   **"You didn't stand around"**: Rice, *Adolph Rupp*, 10.

86   **"Battle of [the] Century."**: *Columbia Evening Missourian*, January 23, 1922.

87   **"At the end of the game"**: Hendel, *Kansas Jayhawks*, 23.

90   **"Eat that Rock Chalk"** and **"this was the tie that bound"**: Allen, *Better Basketball*, 464–69.

91   **"Sixteen times the ball"**: Allen, *Better Basketball*, 468.

91   **"greatly exaggerated"**: Kerkhoff, *Phog Allen*, 74.

91   **"Upon examination"**: Allen, *Better Basketball*, 469.

92   **"for a moment, everyone sat silent"**: *University Daily Kansan*, March 21, 1923.

94   **"the correct way to eat an orange"**: Allen, *My Basket-Ball Bible*.

94   **"Each bite"**: Allen, *Coach Phog Allen's Sports Stories*, 122.

10. A BITTER WINTER

98   **"August, the month of vacations"**: "August Opens to Hum of Industry," *Lawrence Journal World*, August 1, 1925.

99   **"three sons and three daughters"**: Allen, *Coach Phog Allen's Sports Stories*, xi.

100   **"it is always difficult,"**: Allen, *Better Basketball*, 479–80.

101   **"Dr. Allen gave him"**: *Lawrence Journal World*, October 29, 1925.

101   **"his sudden death came"**: *Lawrence Journal World*, October 28, 1925.

101   **"He took life's higher trail"**: Forrest Allen Jr.'s gravestone at Oak Lawn Cemetery in Lawrence, Kansas.

102   **"Five of our six children were still"**: Allen, *Coach Phog Allen's Sports Stories*, xi.

102   **"to the youth of Forrest, Jr.,"**: Allen, *My Basket-Ball Bible*.

104   **"get Kansas out of the fog"**: *Daily Kansan*, December 3, 1936.

104 **"the greatest and most menacing"**: Elstun, "A Biography of Forrest C. 'Phog' Allen," 48.

105 **"if we raised the goals"**: Nelson, *Crimson & Blue Handbook*, 32.

105 **"Some of the fastest basketball players"**: Allen, *Better Basketball*, 77.

105 **"The dribble presents more opportunities"**: Allen, *Better Basketball*, 115.

106 **"A football or basketball victory"**: *Topeka Capital Journal*, 1927.

106 **"If a boy is able to compete"**: Copy of letter provided by Allen family.

107 **"I'll tell you in 25 years"**: This oft-used quote is included on the Phog Allen statue outside of Allen Fieldhouse.

108 **"'High Pocket's' elbows"**: Allen, *Coach Phog Allen's Sports Stories*, 130.

109 **"I could not believe it"**: Allen, *Coach Phog Allen's Sports Stories*, 130.

109 **"Lack of stamina"**: *The Jayhawker* yearbook, spring edition, 1929.

109 **"The year of 1929 is still a nightmare"**: Allen, *Coach Phog Allen's Sports Stories*, 130.

110 **"Next to religion, baseball has furnished"**: "President Herbert Hoover Baseball Related Quotations," Baseball Almanac website, accessed March 6, 2016, http://www.baseball-almanac.com/prz_qhh.shtml.

110 **"a certain 'built-in' speed that"**: On display at Allen Fieldhouse's KU Athletics Hall of Fame in 2014.

111 **"a contender for the title of"**: Elstun. "A Biography of Forrest C. 'Phog' Allen," 48.

112 **"never with the fist"**: Rains, *James Naismith*, 43–44.

116 **"Mitt, I had been"** and **"Many times I have"**: Letter dated February 22, 1942, from Milton Allen to his father in honor of his twenty-fifth anniversary of coaching; Allen recounted the cigarette story in this letter.

116 **"received an early morning phone call"**: Allen, *Coach Phog Allen's Sports Stories*, 196.

117 **"Dad, Mitt played three years"**: Allen, *Coach Phog Allen's Sports Stories*, 196.

117 **"What father, when his son asked"**: Allen, *Coach Phog Allen's Sports Stories*, 196.

11. THE DAY THE GAME ARRIVED

120 **"in the employment of"** and **"Herr Siewecke aided in"**: Allen, *Better Basketball*, 11.

121 **"You bloody beggar"**: Rains, *James Naismith*, 186.

122 **"Not a cent"**: Grundman, "A.A.U.-N.C.A.A. Politics: Forrest C. 'Phog' Allen and America's First Olympic Basketball Team," 118–19.

123 **"It looks to me"**: "A.A.U. Answers Allen's Charges of 'Chiseling," *Chicago Tribune*, May 6, 1936.

124 **"When I walked out on a Springfield playground"**: *New York Times*, August 8, 1936.

124 **"A dribble was not a dribble"**: Balter Kahn, *Sam Balter*.

124 **"We had hoped"**: Balter Kahn, *Sam Balter*.

12. STEPPING OUT OF THE SHADOW

127 **"Dr. Naismith is directly"**: Rains, *James Naismith*, 192.

128 **"Allen proved stubborn and independent"**: Fisher, *Deaner*, 43.

129 **"I don't even want to see you"**: Hendel, *Kansas Jayhawks*, 39.

129 **"Pregame talks cannot be standardized"**: Allen, *Better Basketball*, 94.

130 **"You're confident. And I want you to"**: "Phog Allen Was a Winner On and Off the Court," *Kansas City Times*, September 23, 1974: anecdote told by former KU player Butch Hayes.

130 **"You can see"**: Letter dated July 26, 1938, from Coach Allen to player Bill Geiger, provided by the Allen family archives.

131 **"I have never had charge of any tournament"**: *Kansas City Star*, March 30, 1940.

132 **"they delivered the mail."**: Davis, *100 Things Kansas Fans Should Know & Do Before They Die*.

133 **"For the last time"** and **"I'm sorry, John"**: Withers and Miller, *Spanning the Game*, 12.

134 **"Well, Ralph, we're already"**: Withers and Miller, *Spanning the Game*, 20.

134 **"Doc, you know what I think"** and **"Fine, Ralph"**: Withers and Miller, *Spanning the Game*, 21.

135 **"the greatest game I ever saw"**: *Lawrence Journal World*, March 18, 1940.

136 **"If you have a 'hunch'"**: Allen, *Coach Phog Allen's Sports Stories*, 199.

136 **"Give the ball to Junior!"**: Turtle, "Give the Ball to Junior!" *Indianapolis Saturday Evening Post*, December 28, 1940, 42.

137 **"Then Phog Allen, squirming and"**: Turtle, "Give the Ball to Junior!" *Indianapolis Saturday Evening Post*, December 28, 1940, 23.

137 **"it was another miracle in"**: Turtle, "Give the Ball to Junior!" *Indianapolis Saturday Evening Post*, December 28, 1940, 23.

137 **"Dad, I've paid you back."**: Allen, *Coach Phog Allen's Sports Stories*, 201.

139 **"met their Waterloo"**: Allen, *Coach Phog Allen's Sports Stories*, 33.

140 **"We played pretty well through"**: Hendel, *Kansas Jayhawks*, 43.

140 **"That was probably"** and **"It meant everything to him"**: Interview with Mark Allen, Phog's grandson, in 2014.

140 **"Allen has done a wonderful"**: *Kansas City Star*, March 31, 1940.

141 **"the stale athlete"** and **"Fatty deposits below his lid"**: Allen, *Better Basketball*, 73.

142 "the modern public deplores dull moments.": Allen, *Better Basketball*, 55.

142 "When competition becomes a business": Allen, *Better Basketball*, 7.

142 "Allen accepted controversy as part of the": Fisher, *Deaner*.

142 "Football is on the way out": Nelson, *Crimson & Blue Handbook*, 34.

143 "not interested in the playoffs": "Dr. Allen Turns Heat on N.C.A.A.," *Lawrence Journal World*, March 7, 1941.

143 "too small and too tired": "'Phog' is Jubilant," *Lawrence Journal World*, March 8, 1941.

143 "when you train your muscles": Turtle, "Give the Ball to Junior!" *Indianapolis Saturday Evening Post*, December 28, 1940, 42.

143 "we have men on": Letter dated July 26, 1938, from Coach Allen to player Bill Geiger, provided by the Allen family archives.

144 "impenetrable. The only time" and "An effective defense": Turtle, "Give the Ball to Junior!" *Indianapolis Saturday Evening Post*, December 28, 1940, 41.

144 "A defense must menacingly": Allen, *Better Basketball*, 316.

144 "Phog has never grown old-fashioned": Turtle, "Give the Ball to Junior!" *Indianapolis Saturday Evening Post*, December 28, 1940, 40.

144 "Every man, whether athlete or non-athlete": Allen, *My Basket-Ball Bible*.

145 "Doc didn't praise you a lot": Phone interview with former player Bill Hougland, a member of the 1952 championship team, in 2014.

145 "Otto, you can do three things": Stallard, *Tales from the Jayhawks' Hardwood*, 6–7: story told by Otto Schnellbacher.

145 "Phog Allen, the venerable coach": Dole, *One Soldier's Story*, 61–70.

146 "run their hearts out": Turtle, "Give the Ball to Junior!" *Indianapolis Saturday Evening Post*, December 28, 1940, 41.

146 "promptness is like godliness": Allen, *My Basket-Ball Bible*.

146 "he didn't take anything": Stallard, *Tales from the Jayhawks' Hardwood*, 2.

13. A GREATER CALLING

149 "All athletic contests": Kerkhoff, *Phog Allen*, 135.

149 "demands unyielding sacrifice": Allen, *Coach Phog Allen's Sports Stories*, xiii.

151 "My life has been more than": *Lawrence Journal World*, "A Big Evening for Basketball Coach," March 7, 1942.

153 "I have called [war] a game, Doc": Mayer, "Poignant Jayhawk Memoirs Recall Day Phog Allen Cried," March 13, 2003, kusports.com.

153 **"Somehow this is the most"**: Mayer, "Poignant Jayhawk Memoirs Recall Day Phog Allen Cried," kusports.com.

155 **"sitting in a fool's paradise"**: *Neosho (MO) Daily News*, Associated Press story, December 7, 1945, 1.

157 **"He'll let you know what he thinks."**: Snider, "These Nights Better Forgotten, KU Would Say," *Topeka Capital Journal*, December 20, 1999.

158 **"as professors' sons"**: Withers and Miller, *Spanning the Game*, 16.

158 **"I had a wife and two children"**: Withers and Miller, *Spanning the Game*, 28.

14. THE FALL OF A LEGEND

162 **"Dr. F.C. 'Phog' Allen, the veteran"**: "Jayhawker Cagers Back on the Court," *Lawrence Journal World*, December 5, 1946.

164 **"They are murdering my game!"**: Rains, *James Naismith*, 95.

164 **"get off the court and"**: *Lawrence Journal World*, January 9, 1947.

164 **"Get the hell back on your side"**: *University Columbian*, January 10, 1947.

166 **"Damn the dribble."**: Hendel, *Kansas Jayhawks*, 45.

167 **"making a sham and a chicanery"**: *Florence (SC) Morning News* (and multiple others), May 21, 1948, wire story.

167 **"If the mailman stopped"**: Hendel, *Kansas Jayhawks*, 48.

169 **"while [Allen] was still a great organizer"**: Stallard, *Tales from the Kansas Jayhawks Locker Room*: Charlie Hoag story.

169 **"Demonstrating the use"**: Falkenstien, *Max and the Jayhawks*, 32.

169 **"I don't even have"**: Interview with former player Jerry Waugh, 2014.

170 **"These were tough times for Doc"**: Falkenstien, *A Good Place to Stop*, 27.

170 **"Tell them we're about to win"**: Hendel, *Kansas Jayhawks*, 49.

171 **"breathing the rarified air"**: Falkenstien, *A Good Place to Stop*, 30.

172 **"we talked and we talked"**: Bollig and Vance, *What It Means to Be a Jayhawk*, 50.

172 **"the tradition, it rains on you"**: Interview with Clyde Lovellette, fall 2014.

173 **"Well . . . I've kind of got a headache"**: Interview with Jerry Waugh, spring 2014.

173 **"I'd like to read you"**: Interview with Jerry Waugh, spring 2014.

174 **"as if he had a watermelon"**: Letter dated August 21, 1950, on display at the KU Athletic Hall of Fame at Allen Fieldhouse, in 2014.

174 **"Remember, 'Upon the fields of friendly strife'"**: Letter dated August 21, 1950, on display at the KU Athletic Hall of Fame at Allen Fieldhouse in 2014; the "Upon the fields of friendly strife" quote is attributed to a Major Kohler of the U.S. Military Academy and is used on p. 190   of

Allen's 1947 book, *Better Basketball,* where he mentions that the quote is prominently displayed at the West Point Academy.

175 **"Boys, you need to be furtive"**: Interview with Jerry Waugh, spring 2014.

175 **"alley ball players"**: Stallard, *Tales from the Kansas Jayhawks Locker Room*: Charlie Hoag story.

175 **"scandal that would stink"**: Rosen, *Scandals of '51*, 29.

15. RISING FROM THE ASHES

180 **"Dean could play the game"**: Falkenstien, *A Good Place to Stop*, 34.

181 **"When you look at it on paper"**: Clarkson, "Jays Swing into Final Week of Drills," *Lawrence Journal World*, November 27, 1951.

181 **"I don't know what you're going to do"**: Kerkhoff, *Phog Allen*, 170-71.

183 **"Oh, somewhere in this favored land"**: Thayer, "Casey at the Bat," 1888.

183 **"A whack, a crack"**: Rice, "Casey's Revenge," *Nashville Tennessean*, 1907.

185 **"All of Lawrence looks to Seattle."**: *Lawrence Journal World*, March 24, 1952.

185 **"Relax, Doc"**: Falkenstien, *A Good Place to Stop*, 37.

16. JUST LIKE ANY OTHER GAME DAY

190 **"just like any other game day"**: Phone interview with Clyde Lovellette, fall 2014.

191 **"Assuring you I would not"**: Kerkhoff, *Phog Allen*, xvii.

192 **"Phog Allen—Windbag or Prophet?"**: Burkholder, "Phog Allen—Windbag or Prophet?" *Sport Magazine*, April 1952.

192 **"learn there the importance"**: *Seattle Times*, March 27, 1952.

193 **"You know what you need"**: Phone interview with Clyde Lovellette, fall 2014.

194 **"You are not going to knock anybody's"**: KU archive video of 1952 Kansas Jayhawks season.

195 **In a team photo taken of the Jayhawks**: Courtesy of KU Archives; appeared in numerous newspapers nationwide.

196 **"for the misty-eyed but happy"**: *Topeka Capital-Journal*, March 27, 1952.

196 **"You're all wonderful"**: *New York Times*, March 29, 1952.

197 **"The sometimes bombastic"**: Associated Press story that appeared in several newspapers.

197 **"you could get off the bus"**: *Lawrence Journal-World*, March 28, 1952.

17. SEARCHING FOR GOLD

200 **"It is more than mere chance"**: *Corpus Christi Caller Times*, November 18, 1951, 25.

200 **"they didn't like Phog Allen"**: Nelson, *Crimson & Blue Handbook*.

200 **"We don't have a chance to win"**: *New York Times*, March 31, 1952.

201 **"hicks"** and **came close to getting into a fistfight**: Mayer, "LaSalle, KU Have History," kusports.com, December 11, 2009.

204 **"the osteopathic surgeon"**: *University Daily Kansan*, April 4, 1952, 7.

205 **"[Allen] took kind of a low profile"**: Interview with Bill Lienhard, spring 2014, at Lawrence (KS) Country Club.

206 **"Clyde hasn't been playing well"**: *New York Times*, July 28, 1952.

206 **"I can't really explain why"**: Phone interview with Clyde Lovellette, fall 2014.

206 **"We whipped Argentina"**: Letter on display at the KU Athletic Hall of Fame at Allen Fieldhouse, in 2014.

18. THE IMPROBABLE RETURN

211 **"I am not against"**: *Kansas City (MO) Bulletin*, September 1955: full address of Forrest C. Allen during NABC luncheon.

213 **"I've never had as much pride"**: *Lawrence Journal World*, March 14, 1953.

214 **"a relentless pressing defense that turned"**: *Lubbock Morning Avalanche*, March 18, 1953.

214 **"work harder at winning a basketball game"**: *Seattle Daily Times*, March 18, 1953.

216 **"We are your guests, and you have no right"**: Laskowski and Sutton, *Tales from the Indiana Hoosiers Locker Room*.

219 **"the greatest game a Missouri team"**: *Lawrence Journal World*, March 10, 1954.

219 **"They were as sharp as a razor's edge"**: *Lawrence Journal World*, March 10, 1954.

219 **"I hope Colorado wins."**: *Lawrence Journal World*, March 11, 1954.

220 **"It'll do [Colorado] good to get into"**: *Lawrence Journal World*, March 11, 1954.

220 **"We all knew there was an outside chance"**: *Lawrence Journal World*, March 11, 1954.

220 **a column by a writer named Bill Mayer**: *Lawrence Journal World*, March 11, 1954.

220 **"pusillanimous, pencil-pushing"** and **"Why purple?"**: Falkenstien, *A Good Place to Stop*, 44.

19. THE KING GETS HIS CASTLE

223 **"Your nice letter of"**: Phog Allen correspondence letters provided by the Allen family.

225   "**In this hour of**": Nelson, *Crimson & Blue Handbook*, 37.

226   "**there's nothing that says a coach**": *Lawrence Journal World*, February 3, 1955.

226   "**The action of the Legislature**": *Lawrence Journal World*, February 7, 1955.

227   "**I don't want to be**": *Lawrence Journal World*, March 2, 1955.

228   "**No, Doc**": *Lawrence Journal World*, March 2, 1955.

228   "**Remember this**": *Lawrence Journal World*, March 2, 1955.

228   "**several thousand 'hot dogs'**": *Lawrence Journal World*, March 2, 1955.

229   "**By unanimous vote, the Regents**": *Lawrence Journal World*, March 2, 1955.

229   "**For just about every**": Mayer, "Dedication Game Quite a Sight," *Lawrence Journal World*, February 28, 2005.

230   "**I began to think**" and "**The game he invented**" and "**I've been a fortunate coach**": Mayer, "Dedication Game Quite a Sight," *Lawrence Journal World*, February 28, 2005.

230   "**They did a marvelous job**": *Lawrence Journal World*, March 2, 1955.

231   "**This, too, shall pass away.**" and "**By strengthening ammoniated toothpowder**": *Bulletin*, September 1955: full address of Forrest C. Allen during NABC luncheon.

231   "**We are really responsible**": *Bulletin*, September 1955: full address of Forrest C. Allen during NABC luncheon.

231   "**I'm for the 20-foot baskets.**": *Sports Illustrated*, March 28, 1955.

20. THE BIGGEST FISH

235   "**does not display basketball skill**": Allen, *Better Basketball*, 82.

235   "**Twelve-foot baskets?**": Goudsouzian, "Can Basketball Survive Chamberlain?" 156.

236   "**that didn't require as much**": Newman, *Local Sports Hero*, 48.

236   "**Look, none of the black**": Anderson, "Topekan Jumped in to Right a Racial Wrong," *Topeka Capital-Journal*, February 28, 2001; interview with Mark Allen, Phog's grandson, in 2014.

237   "**smart aleck**": Angevine, "Everybody into the Pool," TheClassical.org, February 8, 2012.

237   "**He was just a product of the system**": Ellsworth, "That's How You Do It," *Kansas Alumni Magazine*, May 12, 2015

237   "**That's wonderful news. I hope**": Cherry, *Wilt*, 38.

238   "**There were incentives**": Cherry, *Wilt*, 38.

239   "**Well, I found out**": Chamberlain and Shaw, *Wilt*, 50.

239   "**Look, Wilt, you just go**": Cherry, *Wilt*, 44.

239 **"if it wasn't for coach Allen's"**: Leaman, *Toilet Tales,* 14.

21. WANTING ONE MORE YEAR

243 **"Chamberlain could team with"**: Armitage, "Center of Attention," accessed August 13, 2014, http://kuhistory.com/articles/
center-of-attention/.

244 **"We're not going to cry"**: *Lawrence Journal World,* March 7, 1956.

244 **"Retiring Court King and His Palace"**: *Lawrence Journal World,* March
9, 1956.

245 **"Allen was a mighty busy man"**: *Lawrence Journal World,* March 19, 1956.

246 **"mystic hooded order"**: "Allen Fires New Blast at AAU Official," *Troy
(NY) Times Record,* April 14, 1965, 24.

246 **"a lousy, toady bunch of rats"**: "Fury from Phog," *Kansas City Star,*
April 3, 1956.

246 **"Henshel is a big, fat toad"**: "Phog Allen Shuns AAU," *Sandusky Regis-
ter,* April 4, 1956.

246 **"After landing the lengthy Wilt 'the Stilt'"**: *Time,* April 9, 1956.

247 **"I am enjoying splendid health"**: "100   Years of Kansas Basketball," *Lawrence Journal World,* February 8, 1998, 11.

247 **"statutory senility"**: Porter, *Basketball,* 9.

247 **"Not for three years"**: "Phog Won More Than Games," *Kansas City
Times,* September 19, 1974.

248 **"This board has nothing"**: *Lawrence Journal World,* March 31, 1956.

248 **"The greatest coaching career"**: *Lawrence Journal World,* March 31, 1956.

248 **"The records made by his"**: *Topeka Capital Journal,* March 15, 1956.

249 **"Most, if not all of these men"**: Letter from KU chancellor Frank Murphy to Jane Mons, obtained from the Allen family.

249 **"feel that in the last analysis"**: Interviews with the Allen family and
former KU players.

249 **"I am sure you realize"**: Letter from KU chancellor Frank Murphy to
Jane Mons, obtained from the Allen family.

250 **"Golf is the ineffectual attempt"**: "Woodrow Wilson Quote," IZQuotes,
accessed March 6, 2016, http://izquotes.com/quote/295248; Wilson
originally said the line as a governor in the 1920s, while Allen later
adopted it in one of his three books.

250 **"When it takes you longer"**: Interview with former KU player Jerry
Waugh in 2014.

250 **"Doc felt as though"**: Interview with former KU player Jerry Waugh in 2014.

251 "go only when it's convenient": Kerkhoff, *Phog Allen*, 195.

253 "I don't think [Harp] was the coach": Cherry, *Wilt*, 69.

253 "I just wanted one more year": Nelson, *Crimson & Blue Handbook*, 50–51.

253 "Do not let a few facts": Letter from Phog Allen to the *New York Times*, provided by the Allen family.

253 "a silk-stocking boy": Goudsouzian, "Can Basketball Survive Chamberlain?"

253 "unfortunate that a wealthy man" and "people who wanted to keep Kansas": *Ottawa Herald*, February 21, 1957.

254 "I'm having a picnic" *Daily Kansan*, November 18, 1957.

255 "Phog Allen has been": Daley, "Blast from the Foghorn Pressing the Button Taking Them in Order without Pain," Sports of the Times, *New York Times*, February 8, 1957.

255 "I referred to these instances": *Topeka Capital Journal*, May 7, 1957.

255 "If these gum-footed falcons": "Phog Urges 'Gum-Footed' NCAA to Quit Snooping," *Daily Kansan*, April 29, 1960.

255 "I know that a year ago": "Phog Allen Sees Need for Kefauver's Help," *Kansas City Times*, May 18, 1961.

256 "I am too busy to ever hold": Hurt, "Capitalizing on Sports," *Topeka Capital Journal*, October 26, 1961.

256 "one of basketball's most": Daley, "Blast from the Foghorn Pressing the Button Taking Them in Order Without Pain," Sports of the Times, *New York Times*, February 8, 1957.

22. THE SPARKLE OF A DIAMOND

259 "I won more games": This quote appears on the Phog Allen statue outside Allen Fieldhouse, among other places.

262 "came home from Indianapolis": Letter from Bessie Allen to Lee Williams, provided by Allen family.

263 "I am not out of the woods": Letter from Phog Allen to Lee Williams, provided by Allen family.

263 "I've finally got him where I want him": "Phog Won More Than Games," *Kansas City Times*, September 19, 1974.

263 "I can not walk any more": Letter from Phog Allen to Lee Williams, provided by Allen family.

266 "there are not enough players hurt" and "Mostly they take advantage of the black boys" and "And speaking of black boys": *Salina Journal*, March 22, 1972, 17.

266 **"His only slightly-thinning blond hair"** and **"The Doc Allen of today"**: O'Leary, "A Visit with Phog Allen," *Kansas City Star Magazine*, March 26, 1972.

267 **"Of course Sparky"**: O'Leary. "A Visit with Phog Allen," *Kansas City Star Magazine*, March 26, 1972.

267 **"There are so few coaches who succeed"**: O'Leary, "A Visit with Phog Allen," *Kansas City Star Magazine*, March 26, 1972.

268 **"His given name"** and **"It was Allen, perhaps"**: *Kansas City Star*, September 17, 1974.

268 **"He convinced me there was more to life"**: Kerkhoff, *Phog Allen*, 134.

268-69 **"Mere words do not"** and **"Phog Allen is more"**: *The Basketball Bulletin*, published by the National Association of Basketball Coaches of the United States, December 1974.

269 **"invented the spectacle"**: *Sports Illustrated*, September 23, 1974.

269 **"Doc will go down in history"**: *Topeka Capital Journal*, September 18, 1974.

269 **"my life has been more than"**: "A Big Evening for Basketball Coach," *Lawrence Journal World*, March 7, 1942.

23. PAY HEED, ALL WHO ENTER

272 **"we need all the help"**: Phone interview with University of North Carolina basketball coach Roy Williams in 2014.

275 **"If we do it for Phog"**: Interviews with Allen grandchildren Judy Allen Morris, Mark Allen, John Allen, and Mick Allen in spring 2014.

277 **"Doc Allen is sitting on the backboard"**: Phone interview with University of North Carolina basketball coach Roy Williams in 2014.

277 **"He's hovering over that fieldhouse"**: Phone interview with former KU star Clyde Lovellette in 2014.

EPILOGUE

281 **"dancing should not be permitted"**: Allen, *Better Basketball*.

281 **"Every move he made"**: Elstun, "A Biography of Forrest C. 'Phog' Allen," 71.

282 **"Most people right now"**: Phone interview with University of North Carolina basketball coach Roy Williams in 2014.

282 **"You can't hang with owls"**: Story relayed through former KU basketball coach Roy Williams.

282 **"He was—period, the end"**: Phone interview with University of North Carolina basketball coach Roy Williams in 2014.

282 **"founding fathers"**: Krause, *Guardians of the Game*, foreword.

282 **"We're forever grateful"**: Phone interview with Duke basketball coach Mike Krzyzewski in 2014.

283 **"I heard so much"**: Phone interview with University of North Carolina basketball coach Roy Williams in 2014.

283 **"Dr. Allen was a gifted"**: Kerkhoff, *Phog Allen*, foreword.

283 **"When anything becomes tradition"**: Hendel, *Kansas Jayhawks*, xiii.

BIBLIOGRAPHY

ARCHIVES AND MANUSCRIPT MATERIALS

Allen Family Archives
Baker University Archives
Baker University Catalogue, 1896
> McClure, Arthur. "Phog Allen, the Man." Unpublished manuscript, 1969.
> Milton family tree, compiled by Ethel Milton
> Forrest C. Allen personal letters
Springfield College Handbook
Texas Tech men's basketball media guide, 2014–15
University of Central Missouri sports information
University of Central Missouri archives
University of Central Missouri men's basketball media guide, 2013–14
University of Central Missouri historian Vivian Richardson
University of Kansas School of Medicine (http://www.kumc.edu
    /school-of-medicine.html)
University of Kansas sports information
University of Kansas, Spencer Library
> *Jayhawker* yearbooks, 1909, 1929, 1952, 1956
USA Basketball (http://www.usab.com/)
William Jewell men's basketball media guide

PUBLISHED WORKS

Allen, Forrest C. *Better Basketball: Technique, Tactics, Tales*. New York: McGraw-Hill, 1937.

——. *Coach Phog Allen's Sports Stories*. Lawrence KS: Allen Press, 1947.

——. "Dunking Isn't Basketball." *Country Gentleman*, February 1935.

——. *My Basket-Ball Bible*. Kansas City KS: Smith-Grieves, 1925.

——. "NABC Address Transcript," *The Bulletin* (National Association of Basketball Coaches), September 1955.

Angevine, Eric. "Everybody into the Pool." TheClassical.org, accessed November 23, 2014, http://theclassical.org/articles/everybody-into-the-pool.

Armitage, Katie H. *Lawrence: Survivors of Quantrill's Raid*. Mount Pleasant SC: Arcadia, 2010.

Balter Kahn, Barbara. *Sam Balter: His Life and Times*. Bloomington IN: iUniverse, 2010.

Barber, Walter Lanier. *Who's Who in American Sports*. Washington DC: National Biographical Society, 1928.

"Basketball Great Phog Allen, 88, Dies in Kansas." *NCAA News*, October 1, 1974, 7.

Berkowitz, Steve. "Kansas Paying Big to Keep Bill Self Employed." *USA Today*, April 3, 2013.

Birdsall & Dean. *History of Daviess County, Missouri*. Kansas City: Birdsall & Dean, 1882.

Bollig, Jeff, and Doug Vance. *What It Means to Be a Jayhawk*. Chicago: Triumph, 2007.

The Bricklayer Mason and Plasterer 15, no. 8 (August 1912).

Brown, Daniel James. *Boys in the Boat*. London: Penguin, 2014.

Burkholder, Ed. "Phog Allen—Windbag or Prophet?" *Sport Magazine*, April 1952.

Chamberlain, Wilt. *A View from Above*. New York: Villard, 1991.

Chamberlain, Wilt, and David Shaw. *Wilt: Just Like Any Other 7-foot Black Man Who Lives Next Door*. New York City: MacMillan, 1973.

Chansky, Art. *The Dean's List*. New York: Grand Central, 2009.

Cherry, Robert. *Wilt: Larger than Life, the Definitive Wilt Chamberlain Biography*. Chicago: Triumph, 2004.

Cockrell, Ewing. *History of Johnson County, Missouri*. Vol. 2. Topeka KS: Historical, 2002.

Creamer, Robert W. *Stengel: Life and Times*. Lincoln: University of Nebraska Press, 1995.

Cunningham, Carson. *American Hoops*. Lincoln: University of Nebraska Press, 2009.

Davis, Ken. *One Hundred Things Kansas Fans Should Know and Do Before They Die*. Chicago: Triumph, 2013.

Davis, Seth. *Wooden*. New York: Times, 2014.

Dole, Bob. *One Soldier's Story: A Memoir*. New York: Harper, 2006.

Douchant, Mike. "March Madness: Growth of the NCAA Tournament." *Sports Illustrated*, March 11, 2003.

Ellsworth, Scott. "That's How You Do It." *Kansas Alumni Magazine*, May 12, 2015.

Elstun, Donald W. Unpublished biography of Forrest C. Allen. Master of Science in Education thesis, University of Kansas, 1967.

ESPN. *Sports Century* (New York: Hyperion, 1999)

——— . *ESPN College Basketball Encyclopedia*. Introduction by Bill Bradley. Bristol CT: ESPN, 2009.

Falkenstien, Max. *A Good Place to Stop*. New York: Power House, 2007.

———. *Max and the Jayhawks: Fifty Years On and Off the Air with KU Sports*. Wichita KS: Wichita Eagle & Beacon, 1996.

Fisher, Mike. *Deaner*. Denver: Lowell, 1997.

Frei, Terry. *March 1939, before the Madness: The Story of the First NCAA Basketball Champions*. Lanham MD: Taylor, 2014.

Fulks, Matt, *Echoes of Kansas Basketball: The Greatest Stories Ever Told*. Chicago: Triumph Books, 2006.

Gilmore, Todd. "History of the 'Beware of the Phog' Banner." RockChalk.com, 1998. Accessed March 7, 2015, http://payheedbanners.com/payheedall whoenterbewareofthephogbannerhistory.html.

Goudsouzian, Aram. "Can Basketball Survive Chamberlain?" *Kansas History Journal* 28, no. 3 (Autumn 2005), http://www.kshs.org/publicat/history /2005autumn_goudsouzian.pdf.

Grigsby, Bill. *Grigs! A Beauuutiful Life*. Champaign IL: Sports Publishing, 2004.

Grundman, Adolph H. "A.A.U.-N.C.A.A. Politics: Forrest C. 'Phog' Allen and America's First Olympic Basketball Team." *OLYMPIKA: The International Journal of Olympic Studies* 5 (1996): 111–26.

——— . *The Golden Age of Amateur Basketball: The AAU Tournament, 1921–1968*. Lincoln NE: Bison Books, 2004.

Hager, Tom. *The Ultimate Book of March Madness*. Fremont CA: MVP Books, 2012.

Hamilton, Whitney. "The House of Horrors." *Daily Kansan*, February 15, 2008.

Hendel, John. *Kansas Jayhawks: History-Making Basketball*. Marceline MO: Walsworth, 1991.

Hersey, Mark D. "Field House of Dreams." Accessed May 8, 2014, http://kuhistory.com/articles/field-house-of-dreams/.

———. "ku's Greatest Team." Accessed May 8, 2014, http://kuhistory.com/articles/kus-greatest-team/.

Hilton, Christopher. *Hitler's Olympics: The 1936 Berlin Games*. Kindle edition. History Press, 2011.

Hiner, Jason. *Mac's Boys: Branch McCracken and the Legendary Hurryin' Hoosiers*. Dallas: Quarry Books, 2006.

Hoffmann, Annette R. "The Buffalo Germans and the 1904 Basketball Tournament in St. Louis." *Journal of Olympic History* 11, no. 3 (September 2003): 19–21.

Hughes, Rich. *Netting Out Basketball 1936: The Remarkable Story of the McPherson Refiners*. Victoria BC: FriesenPress, 2011.

Jayhawk Rebounds. Allen Press, 1944.

Johnson, Kenneth N. *Kansas University Basketball Legends*. History Press, 2013.

Katz, Milton S. *Breaking Through: John B. McClendon, Basketball Legend and Civil Rights Pioneer*. Fayetteville: University of Arkansas Press, 2007.

Keith, Larry. "The Tradition" *Sports Illustrated*, February 13, 1978.

Kerkhoff, Blair. *A Century of Jayhawk Triumphs*. Lanham MD: Taylor Trade, 1997.

———. *Phog Allen: The Father of Basketball Coaching*. Dallas: Masters, 1996.

———. "Phog Allen: Remembered as a Jayhawk but his Greatness Began in Jackson County." *Jackson County Historical Society Journal*, summer 2014.

Krause, James E. *Guardians of the Game*. Olathe KS: Ascend Books, 2008.

Laskowski, John, and Stan Sutton. *Tales from the Indiana Hoosiers Locker Room*. New York: Sports Publishing, 2012 .

Lawrence Journal World. "100 Years of Kansas Basketball." Special section, February 8, 1998.

Leaman, Doug. *Toilet Tales*. West Conshohocken PA: Infinity, 2006.

Leavy, Jane. "Mickey Country." October 5, 2011, http://grantland.com/features/mickey-country/.

Lester, Jim. *Hoop Crazy: College Basketball in the 1950s*. Amazon Digital, 2012.

Lo Bello, Nino. "Hoop Man of Kansas." *Indianapolis Rotarian*, February 1956.

Lyle, Bob. "70 Years and 1,000 Games." *Daily Kansan*, February 19, 1956.

McCool, John H. "Radio Days." Accessed April 3, 2016, http://kuhistory.com/articles/radio-days/.

McCullough, David. *Truman*. New York: Simon & Schuster, 1993.

Meyers, Jack. "Letter from the Publisher." *Sports Illustrated*, February 6, 1978.

Miller, John J. "How Teddy Roosevelt Saved Football." *Wall Street Journal*, April 21, 2011.

Missouri State Teachers College, District 2, 1905–6 yearbook. Accessed at http://digitalcollections.missouristate.edu/cdm4/browse.php ?CISOROOT=/Ozarko.

Naismith, James. Introduction. In *Basketball: Its Origin & Development*, xv. Lincoln NE: Bison Books, 1996.

National Biographical Society. *Who's Who in American Sports*. Washington DC: National Biographical Society, 1928.

Nelson, Eric. *The Crimson and Blue Handbook*. Wichita KS: Wichita Eagle & Beacon, 1993.

"New Game Developed By Noted Basketball Authority." *Athletic Journal* 4 (December 1939).

Newman, Jesse. *Local Sports Hero: The Untold Story of Wesley B. Walker*. Author House, 2009.

"Phog Allen." In *Encyclopedia of College Basketball*. Detroit: Visible Ink, 1994.

Porter, David L. *Basketball: A Biographical Dictionary*. Santa Barbara CA: Greenwood, 2005.

Rains, Rob. *James Naismith: The Man Who Invented Basketball*. Philadelphia: Temple University, 2009.

Rice, Grantland. "Casey's Revenge." *Nashville Tennessean*, June 1907.

Rice, Russell. *Adolph Rupp: Kentucky's Basketball Baron*. Urbana IL: Sagamore, 1994.

Rife, Max L. *Basketball in Its Early Years, 1898–1925*. B.S. thesis, Southwestern College, 1951.

Rosen, Charley. *Scandals of '51: How the Gamblers Almost Killed College Basketball*. New York: Seven Stories, 1999.

Sachare, Alex. *When Seconds Count*. Champaign IL: Sports Pub, 1999.

Schaap, Jeremy. *Triumph: The Untold Story of Jesse Owens and Hitler's Olympics*. Boston: Mariner Books, 2008.

Schlossberg, Dan, ed. *Baseball Almanac*. Chicago: Triumph Books, 2002.

Shoals, Bethlehem, and Jacob Weinstein. *The Undisputed Guide to Pro Basketball*. New York: Bloomsbury USA, 2010.

Smith, Susan, Lyle Niedens, Steve Buckner, and Ted Watts. *Portraits of Excellence: A Heritage of Athletic Achievement at the University of Kansas*. Atlanta: Quality Sports, 1991.

"Sport: Naismith Week." *Time*, February 24, 1936, http://content.time.com/time /magazine/article/0,9171,755860,00.html.

Stallard, Mark. *Tales from the Jayhawks' Hardwood*. Champaign IL: Sports Pub, 2002.

Surdam, David George. *The Rise of the National Basketball Association*. Champaign: University of Illinois Press, 2012.

Swade, Josh. *The Holy Grail of Hoops: One Fan's Quest to Buy the Original Rules of Basketball*. New York: Sports Pub, 2013.

Taylor, Nate. "Kansas Coach Dr. Phog Allen Past Was a Coach at UCM First." *Muleskinnner*, January 3, 2010.

Thayer, Ernest, "Casey at the Bat." *San Francisco Examiner*, June 3, 1888.

Time. "People" column, April 9, 1956.

Turtle, Howard W. "Give the Ball to Junior!" *Saturday Evening Post*, December 28, 1940

Webb, Bernice Larson. *The Basketball Man: James Naismith*. Lawrence: University Press of Kansas, 1971.

Webb, Jim. *Born Fighting: How the Scots-Irish Shaped America*. Danvers MA: Broadway Books, 2005.

Weyand, Alexander M. *The Cavalcade of Basketball*. London, England: MacMillan, 1960.

Wilcox, Pearl, *Jackson County Pioneers*. Independence MO: Jackson County Historical Society, 1975.

Withers, Bud, and Ralph Miller. *Spanning the Game*. Champaign IL: Sports Pub, 1990.

Wolff, Alexander, "The First Cinderella." *Sports Illustrated*, March 22, 2010.

Woodling, Chuck, and John McLendon. *The Kansas Century: 100 Years of Championship Jayhawk Basketball*. Riverside NJ: Andrews McMeel, 1997.

ADDITIONAL NEWSPAPERS CONSULTED

Alton Telegraph, September 18, 1974

Baker Orange, February 16, 1907, and multiple issues in July 1910

Boston Globe, November 1, 1908

Boulder Daily Camera, June 9, 2012

Chicago Tribune, March 28, 2015

Independence Examiner, June 19, 1968

Lexington Intelligencer, February 26, 1910

Omaha Bee, February 4, 1908

San Mateo Times, December 27, 1956

Sandusky (OH) Times, March 4, 1956

Troy (NY) Times Record, March 14, 1965

INDEX